Forest Health

An Integrated Perspective

Forest Health: An Integrated Perspective is the first book to define an ecologically rational, conceptual framework that unifies and integrates the many sub-disciplines that comprise the science of forest health and protection.

This new global approach applies to boreal, temperate, tropical, natural, managed, even-aged, uneven-aged and urban forests, as well as plantations. Readers of the text can use real data sets to assess the sustainability of four forests around the world. Datasets for the case studies are available at www.cambridge.org/9780521766692, and the text provides stepwise instructions for performing the calculations in Microsoft® Excel®. Readers can follow along as the authors perform the same calculations and interpret the results.

Elevating forest health from a fuzzy concept to an ecologically sound paradigm, this is essential reading for undergraduate and graduate students and professionals interested in forest health, protection, entomology, pathology, and ecology.

JOHN D. CASTELLO is Professor and Associate Chair in the Department of Environmental and Forest Biology at the State University of New York College of Environmental Science and Forestry, Syracuse. He has conducted research on the viruses that infect forest and shade trees in the USA, Germany, and New Zealand.

STEPHEN A. TEALE is Associate Professor in the Department of Environmental and Forest Biology at the State University of New York College of Environmental Science and Forestry, Syracuse. His research interests include forest entomology, chemical ecology, pheromones of forest insects, invasive species, and evolution of pheromone communication.

Forest Health

An Integrated Perspective

Edited by

JOHN D. CASTELLO

Professor and Associate Chair, Department of Environmental and
Forest Biology at the State University of New York College of
Environmental Science and Forestry, Syracuse

STEPHEN A. TEALE

Associate Professor, Department of Environmental and
Forest Biology, State University of New York College of Environmental
Science and Forestry, Syracuse

CAMBRIDGE UNIVERSITY PRESS
Cambridge, New York, Melbourne, Madrid, Cape Town,
Singapore, São Paulo, Delhi, Tokyo, Mexico City

Cambridge University Press
The Edinburgh Building, Cambridge CB2 8RU, UK

Published in the United States of America by Cambridge University Press, New York

www.cambridge.org
Information on this title: www.cambridge.org/9780521766692

First published 2011

Printed in the United Kingdom at the University Press, Cambridge

A catalogue record for this publication is available from the British Library

Library of Congress Cataloging-in-Publication Data

Forest health : an integrated perspective / [edited by] John D. Castello, Stephen A. Teale.
     p.   cm.
  ISBN 978-0-521-76669-2 (Hardback) – ISBN 978-0-521-74741-7 (pbk.)
  1. Forest health.   2. Forest ecology.   I. Castello, John D., 1952–   II. Teale, Stephen A.
III. Title.
  SB761.F582 2011
  634.9′6–dc22

                                                              2010040918

ISBN 978-0-521-76669-2 Hardback
ISBN 978-0-521-74741-7 Paperback

Contents

Preface

Would you be able to recognize a healthy forest if you walked through one? We begin our course in "Forest Health" every summer with this question to our students. Of course their answer almost always is no. They are surprised to learn that neither can we! The reason, we explain, is because there is no widely accepted, clear, and concise definition of a "healthy forest." Why not? ... is almost always the next question. Human health is a relatively easy concept. Arguably, it is the absence of disease. But is a healthy forest one without diseased or dead trees? Following about 10 years of unsuccessfully trying to answer these questions from our students, we decided to attempt to develop our own definition.

Fortunately, during the past 10 to 15 years or so, Paul Manion, Professor Emeritus of Forest Pathology at SUNY-ESF, and his students, were developing the baseline mortality concept of sustainability and forest health. The logic of this concept as the foundation for a concise definition of a healthy forest was so compelling that we adopted it for our course, and decided to write this text. So, the essential concepts that form the basis of this book are his, not ours, and we are grateful for, and readily acknowledge, his lucid thinking. Our contribution is the blending of sustainability (i.e., a sustainable diameter distribution) with productivity (i.e., meeting landowner management objectives) to create our two-part definition of a healthy forest. So, Paul, the credit for this book belongs to you and your students, and we hope you are pleased with it. It is to him that we dedicate this book.

The organization of the text is a bit unusual, and may require some explanation. We wanted the text to provide a unique, broad, integrative, and global perspective on forest health because most of our students are biologists not foresters, and they come from many different countries around the world. In addition, we wanted the text to deal with some of the more pressing current health issues facing our global forests. Therefore, Chapters 1, 2, and 3 introduce and explain the main concepts of the book, the mathematics that underlay it, and a few case studies using real datasets for students to assess sustainability. Our students have used these datasets successfully to determine baseline mortality, observed mortality, and sustainability. Chapters 4, 5, 6, and 7 deal with the ecological components of forest health; specifically the biotic components including invasive species, and the abiotic components including Edaptic factors, air pollution, and global climate change. Chapters 8, 9, and 10 address forest health and its human dimension including forest management, the conservation of biological diversity, and the monitoring of forest health. We tried to integrate all these components of forest health into one logical treatise, and our summary of that effort along with a look to the future is presented in the final chapter.

We acknowledge the contributions of many individuals because without them this text would not have been possible. First, we acknowledge our students in forest health and forest pathology whose curiosity and questions provided the spark to undertake this project. Second, we acknowledge the basic concepts of Paul Manion, which form the foundation of the book, and to whom the book is dedicated. Third, we acknowledge Paul Manion, SUNY-ESF for providing the New York State datasets; Rob Allen, Landcare Research, Lincoln, New Zealand for providing the New Zealand mountain beech datasets; D. Jean Lodge, Jill Thompson, Jess Zimmerman, and Nick Brokaw, of the Institute of Tropical Ecosystem Studies, University of Puerto Rico, International Institute of Tropical Forestry, and the USDA Forest Service for the Puerto Rico datasets and for help in transforming the data into usable formats. We also acknowledge financial support from the US National Science Foundation and the Mellon Foundation in support of the Luquillo Long-Term Ecological Research Program; and finally thank John Lundquist, USDA Forest Service, Anchorage, AK, USA for providing the Alaska white spruce dataset. Fourth, we appreciate the thorough reviews of the text provided by Lee Frelich, University of Minnesota; Bill MacDonald, West Virginia University; and Ed Barnard, Florida Division of Forestry. However, any mistakes in fact or in the interpretation of the facts are ours not theirs, and for which we accept full responsibility. Finally, we acknowledge the patience and understanding of our wives Marie Castello and Alison Teale, for putting up with us, and without us, while we labored on this project these past two years.

August 1, 2010

Sadly, within the past week our longtime colleague, friend, and a coauthor of Chapter 8, Professor Emeritus Allan P. Drew passed away. He never saw the finished book, but we are confident that he would have been pleased with it. Thank you, Allan, for your collegiality, friendship, and professionalism over the years, and for your contributions to the book.

March 1, 2011
John D. Castello and Stephen A. Teale

Contributors

R.D. Briggs

State University of New York,
College of Environmental Science & Forestry,
Department of Forest & Natural Resources Management,
Syracuse, NY, USA

J.A. Cale

State University of New York,
College of Environmental Science & Forestry,
Department of Environmental & Forest Biology,
Syracuse, NY, USA

A.E. Camp

School of Forestry & Environmental Studies,
Yale University, New Haven, CT, USA

S.P. Campbell

School of Natural Resources & The Environment,
University of Arizona, Tucson, AZ, USA

P. Cannon

USDA Forest Service, Vallejo, CA, USA

J.D. Castello

State University of New York,
College of Environmental Science & Forestry,
Department of Environmental & Forest Biology, Syracuse, NY, USA

A.P. Drew

State University of New York,
College of Environmental Science & Forestry,

Department of Forest & Natural Resources Management,
Syracuse, NY, USA

M.K. Fierke
State University of New York,
College of Environmental Science & Forestry,
Department of Environmental & Forest Biology,
Syracuse, NY, USA

R.H. Germain
State University of New York,
College of Environmental Science & Forestry,
Department of Forest & Natural Resources Management,
Syracuse, NY, USA

J.P. Gibbs
State University of New York,
College of Environmental Science & Forestry,
Department of Environmental & Forest Biology,
Syracuse, NY, USA

R.W. Hofstetter
Northern Arizona University,
School of Forestry, Flagstaff, Arizona, USA

T.R. Horton
State University of New York,
College of Environmental Science & Forestry,
Department of Environmental & Forest Biology,
Syracuse, NY, USA

D.J. Lodge
USDA Forest Service,
Northern Research Station, Sabana Station,
Luquillo, Puerto Rico, USA

J.E. Lundquist
USDA Forest Service,
Forest Health Protection and Pacific Northwest Research Station,
Anchorage, AK, USA

P.D. Manion
Cazenovia, NY, USA

C.A. Nowak
State University of New York,
College of Environmental Science & Forestry,
Department of Forest & Natural Resources Management,
Syracuse, NY, USA

D.J. Nowak
USDA Forest Service, Northern Research Station,
C/o State University of New York,
College of Environmental Science & Forestry,
Syracuse, NY, USA

D. Parry
State University of New York,
College of Environmental Science & Forestry,
Department of Environmental & Forest Biology,
Syracuse, NY, USA

D.A. Patrick
Paul Smith's College, Paul Smith's NY, USA

B.D. Rubin
Western Ontario University,
Department of Statistical & Actuarial Sciences,
Western Science Centre, London, Ontario, Canada

S.J. Seybold
USDA Forest Service,
Pacific Southwest Research Station, Davis, CA, USA

S.A. Teale
State University of New York,
College of Environmental Science & Forestry,
Department of Environmental & Forest Biology, Syracuse, NY, USA

M.L. Tyrrell
Global Institute of Sustainable Forestry,
Yale School of Forestry & Environmental Studies, New Haven, CT, USA

L. Zhang
State University of New York,
College of Environmental Science & Forestry,
Department of Forest & Natural Resources Management, Syracuse, NY, USA

Section I FOREST HEALTH AND MORTALITY

1

The past as key to the future: a new perspective on forest health

S.A. TEALE AND J.D. CASTELLO

1.1 Introduction

What exactly is forest health? How does one define it? Can it be defined? Is it something real, or is it just another "fuzzy concept?" (More 1996). Would you recognize a healthy forest if you saw one? These are among the questions with which forest ecologists and managers struggle. Many are surprised when they realize that these apparently simple questions do not have simple answers. In spite of the widespread use of the term "forest health," it means very different things to different people. While the notion of a healthy forest has universal appeal, different people have different reasons for needing to know if a given forest is healthy or not. To some, forest health means sustainable timber harvest; to others it means preserving biodiversity or restoring the forest to its condition prior to human disturbance.

1.2 Definitions of forest health

Forest health has been defined from a range of perspectives that can be categorized as either utilitarian or ecological (Kolb *et al.* 1994). Some of the key features of forest health that have been included by various authors include ecosystem "balance," "resilience" to change, plant and animal community "function," and sustainable productivity (Edmonds *et al.* 2000; Raffa *et al.* 2009). Given these diverse perspectives, and the disparate definitions arising from them, it is not surprising that many forest protection professionals find the concept

Forest Health: An Integrated Perspective, ed. John D. Castello and Stephen A. Teale. Published by Cambridge University Press. © Cambridge University Press 2011.

confusing at best, and useless at worst. Is forest health or "ecosystem health" even a valid concept? Ehrenfeld (1992) concluded that it is not. We disagree. The term probably will continue to be used to formulate and to guide societal and landowner management objectives. Thus, a concise and useful definition of forest health is important. The term is used in government mandates regarding forest management goals. In the USA, the Forest Ecosystems and Research Act 1988 mandates surveys to monitor long-term trends in forest health. Furthermore, forest health and its maintenance are now central goals for the desired future condition of US forests (USDA Forest Service 1993a, b, 2003), to some extent replacing sustained commodity output as a management goal. Long-term health monitoring and assessment programs began about 20 years ago, and the data collected have been used to assess trends in forest condition, but how are the data being used to determine if a given forest is healthy or not? And is the approach valid?

From the utilitarian perspective, a forest is healthy if it satisfies management objectives, whatever they might be, and unhealthy if it does not. Consistency with management objectives is central to many such definitions of forest health (Monnig and Byler 1992). However, the utilitarian approach suffers from some obvious and debilitating inadequacies. First, if healthy forests meet management objectives, but creating and maintaining a healthy forest are the management objectives, then we have a case of circular logic where creating a healthy forest depends on the occurrence of a healthy forest. Second, a single forest may be viewed as healthy from one perspective, but unhealthy from another depending upon competing management objectives. This situation is especially problematic where multiple management objectives are mandated, as on most National Forest lands in the USA. The utilitarian approach is most appropriate on forest-lands with unambiguous management objectives, e.g., private industrial forests managed for wood fiber or public wilderness areas managed to preserve biodiversity.

Problems with the utilitarian approach counsel the need for a definition of forest health based upon ecological principles. Such principles have included resilience, the ability of an ecosystem to recover from stress or disturbance; "stability," the ability of an ecosystem to resist change; "ecosystem diversity," "full functionality," and "a balanced ecosystem" to name a few. The problem with this approach is that many of these principles are difficult to define, measure, or apply. What do functionality, resilience, or balanced really mean? These are abstract concepts which may have merit, but they cannot be quantitatively assessed and applied, and certainly not across all forest types for comparative purposes.

The definition of forest health put forth by the Society of American Foresters attempts to bridge both the utilitarian and ecological concepts by defining forest health as the perceived condition of a forest derived from concerns about such factors as its age, structure, composition, function, vigor, presence of unusual levels of insects or disease, and resilience to disturbance – note that perception and interpretation of forest health are influenced by individual and cultural viewpoints, land management objectives, spatial and temporal scales, the relative health of the stands that comprise the forest, and the appearance of the forest at a point in time (Helms 1998).

We must ask ourselves if it is appropriate to apply the term "health" to a population of organisms or even to an entire ecosystem. An unhealthy or dead tree is comparatively easy to recognize. The health of a forest stand or an ecosystem, however, is not because it relates to proper functioning of the ecological processes that regulate that ecosystem, which are not so easily recognized and assessed. In fact, the intensity of effort and the amount of time that is required to adequately assess energy and nutrient flow, trophic level interactions, biodiversity, stability, and resilience to disturbance in an ecosystem is far beyond anything that could be considered practical to a forest manager. Furthermore, the methodologies involved are complex and would potentially vary from case to case yielding non-comparable results. People concerned with forest health (especially entomologists and pathologists) traditionally have focused on tree mortality. However, tree mortality in a forest does not necessarily indicate an unhealthy situation; in fact, some tree mortality is normal, if not essential. In stable populations of organisms, the capacity for reproduction is vastly greater than that which can be supported by the limited resources of the environment (Malthus 1798). Thus, a stable and presumably "healthy" population of trees (i.e., a forest) will have dead and dying trees. While this is readily apparent in a qualitative sense, the manner in which one can quantify acceptable or desirable levels of mortality is less apparent, but is nevertheless both attainable and of critical importance.

1.3 The concept of baseline mortality

Manion and Griffin (2001) viewed a healthy, sustainable, and mature forest ecosystem as one that maintains a stable size-structure relationship by balancing growth with mortality. This concept is based on the **Law of de Liocourt** (1898), which mathematically describes the size structure of forests, and has been applied to the development of a quantitative, ecologically based concept of forest health (Rubin *et al.* 2006). Simply put, it describes the relationship of the density of stems in a forest to their diameter. As a cohort of trees grows, it naturally progresses from many small stems to fewer larger stems. For many, if not most, forests this is represented by a negative exponential

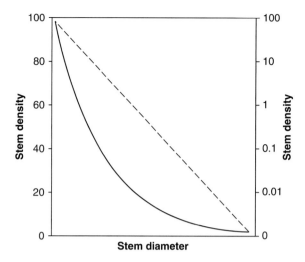

Figure 1.1 The relationship between stem density and stem diameter generally fits the negative exponential function. The line is a curve when plotted on linear axes (–) and straight when plotted on log-linear axes (- - -).

("reverse J") relationship, which when plotted on log-linear axes, becomes a linear relationship (Figure 1.1). It is important to note, however, that at the stand level, other mathematical functions usually describe the diameter distribution better than does the negative exponential (Chapter 2). This is due to high mortality of seedlings and old trees, which causes steep slopes at the tails of the diameter distribution function. If the smallest and largest size classes are omitted from the analysis (as they usually are at a practical level in forestry), then the negative exponential function has excellent predictive ability. Also, when many stands or several tree species are included in the analysis, the aggregate will tend to follow a negative exponential function. Other functions such as the rotated sigmoid, Weibull and modified Weibull generally yield better "fits" to diameter data, but at the cost of non-constant baseline mortality or negative mortality, problems which are avoided by using the negative exponential function, as long as the above caveats are kept in mind.

The slope of this line defines the number of stems of a given size class that must die in order for the population to maintain a stable size structure, i.e., **baseline mortality**. If the mortality of any size class is excessive, then there will be too few stems in the larger size classes as the stand grows, and the size structure will change. If the mortality is too low, then an unstable situation develops as too many trees survive and grow to the next size class and competition among trees intensifies. In the case of sugar maple, *Acer saccharum*, in northern New York State (Figure 1.2), the observed mortality approximates baseline mortality.

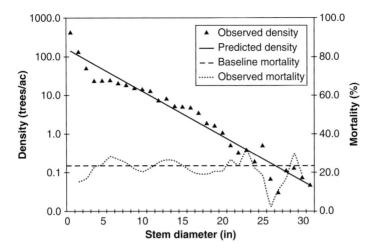

Figure 1.2 Observed and predicted density, baseline mortality, and observed mortality in the sugar maple northern hardwood forest type of northern New York State. The slope of the predicted density is constant and determines the baseline mortality. (From P.D. Manion with permission.)

This indicates that the diameter distribution of sugar maple is stable, or sustainable, in this region. Whether or not the existing structure is desirable is equally as important, but what is deemed desirable depends on the landowner's objectives, and is a separate, but related, issue to be taken up later in this chapter. Using baseline and observed mortalities as measures of sustainability allows one to determine quantitatively if a perceived threat such as a pathogen or insect outbreak is endangering the sustainability of the forest or if it is merely acting as a natural thinning agent. An example of an unstable forest structure is white pine (*Pinus strobus*) in the same region (Figure 1.3). In this case, the observed mortality in the smaller size classes is substantially (two to over three times) greater than baseline mortality. As the forest grows, the deficit of small diameter trees (saplings) becomes a deficit in mid-sized (pole-sized) trees and the diameter distribution at that time will be different than it was initially; thus the structure of this forest is unstable, or unsustainable. At this point, a forest manager may wish to determine the cause of the mortality in the small diameter classes to determine if management action can remedy the problem if the expected change in forest structure is inconsistent with management objectives. This represents a departure from the traditional approach of reacting to apparent forest health threats without first quantifying the severity of the "problem" in the broader context of the growth of the forest.

Our last example, American beech (*Fagus grandifolia*), presents an interesting situation (Figure 1.4 and Chapter 3). The observed mortality in the smaller

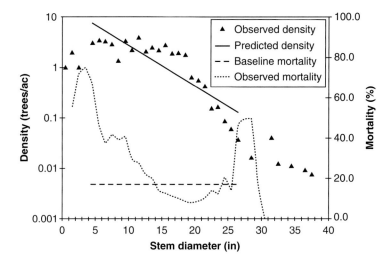

Figure 1.3 Observed and predicted density and mortality of white pine in the forest lands of northern New York State. Excessive mortality in the smaller size classes indicates that the density of the mid-size classes will decline in the future, i.e., the current diameter distribution is unsustainable. (From P.D. Manion with permission.)

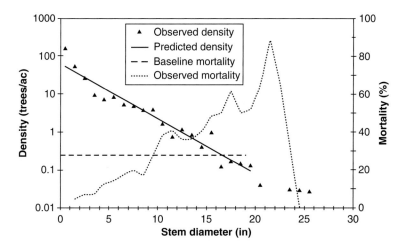

Figure 1.4 Observed and predicted density, mortality, and cutting of American beech in the state forest land in northern New York State. (From P.D. Manion with permission.)

diameter classes is well below baseline mortality, while the observed mortality in the larger diameter classes is substantially higher than baseline mortality. In this case, we can see that the structure of the forest is stable because the surplus of surviving smaller trees is balanced by excessive mortality in the larger size classes. This is due to a non-native, invasive insect and disease complex called beech bark disease (BBD) that has been present in the region for approximately four decades (see Chapter 3). Stands affected by BBD for such long periods are characterized by high mortality of trees over 25 cm diameter at breast height (dbh), and the presence of dense stands of small diameter trees of root sprout and seedling origin. Thus, a long-recognized forest health problem is clearly reflected in a discrepancy between observed mortality and baseline mortality, yet the structure is sustainable.

To label a forest so dramatically altered by an invasive disease healthy would serve no useful purpose, even though the forest has adapted and reached a stable state. Virtually every forest has been disturbed by both natural and/or anthropogenic agents, but the presence of disturbance does not mean that the forest is necessarily unhealthy. The baseline mortality approach gives us an ecologically based method to assess the sustainability of any forest by determining if the mortality caused by any agent of disturbance is causing instability in the system. Yet, many disturbed forested systems have adapted to the disturbance (e.g., elimination of tree species by invasive diseases, introduction of non-native trees) and have reached a stable, sustainable condition. Are these forests forever to be labeled unhealthy because they are not pristine? Or, do we consider them healthy because they are sustainable? The answers to this question will always depend on the perspectives of the individual. A person who places the greatest emphasis on a pristine condition (no human disturbance) may not consider healthy any forest that does not meet that criterion, which excludes from healthy virtually all secondary forests. This would not be a practical definition of forest health for the vast majority of forest landowners and managers. A person who only values resource extraction may consider highly disturbed forests as healthy with little regard to its ecological condition. Similarly, this approach would not have universal appeal. We can solve this dilemma with a two-component definition of forest health. First, a healthy forest must be sustainable with respect to its size structure (i.e., a correspondence between baseline and observed mortality). Second, a healthy forest must meet the landowner's objectives, provided that those objectives do not conflict with sustainability. Management objectives range from ecological (intrinsic) to economic (utilitarian) but these are extremes of a continuous spectrum, not discrete categories. For example, managing a forest for wildlife may have both ecological and utilitarian value. Whether the animals are to be hunted or photographed, or merely seen, the management of the forest is essentially the same. Each component of forest health thus has two possibilities resulting in four combinations (Table 1.1). We propose that forests meeting the landowner's management objectives, whatever they may be, are "productive" forests. Forests that do not are non-productive. In order to be truly productive in the long term, forests must be ecologically **sustainable**.

Table 1.1 *Healthy forests are both productive and sustainable. A sustainable forest is one in which there is a close correspondence between observed mortality and baseline mortality. A productive forest is one that meets long-term ecological and/or economic management objectives*

Management objectives \ Forest Structure	Sustainable	Unsustainable
Productive	Healthy	Unhealthy
Nonproductive	Unhealthy	Unhealthy

Does this concept of forest health address the breadth of organismal diversity and trophic interactions in the ecosystem? Or, is this a narrow concept that only applies to populations of trees? Single or multi-species populations of trees are generally the **foundation species** (Dayton 1972; Ellison *et al.* 2005) of forested ecosystems, i.e., they are the primary producers that dominate the system in both abundance and influence. It follows, then, that if the population structure of the foundation species of an ecosystem is stable, then populations of the other species in that ecosystem are likely to be stable and to interact with each other in a manner that is typical of that community. The baseline mortality concept of forest health is based on a demographic model (the negative exponential function, see Chapters 2 and 3), which is based on size-class structure. The sustainability of populations of organisms is often assessed using life tables and transition matrix models (Caswell 1989). These approaches enable estimation of future population structure (i.e., stability) based on the reproduction and survival of specific age classes (Harcombe 1987). An alternative approach is the use of size classes rather than age classes, which are often difficult to measure in trees (Werner 1975; Hughes 1984); this has been applied to hardwood forests of northeastern North America (Buchman *et al.* 1983). All of these approaches attempt to include the multitude of interacting biotic and abiotic factors that shape the structure and composition of forests (Figure 1.5).

An advantage of the baseline mortality approach to forest health is that it is not necessary to identify the agent that is reducing the health of the forest (although it may be desirable); one only needs to appropriately assess the trees in the forest to determine if the diameter distribution is sustainable. As new invasive insects and diseases appear, some, such as BBD, may diminish the health of the forest, while others will become innocuous components of the ecosystem. Native insects and diseases have been the concern of forest entomologists and

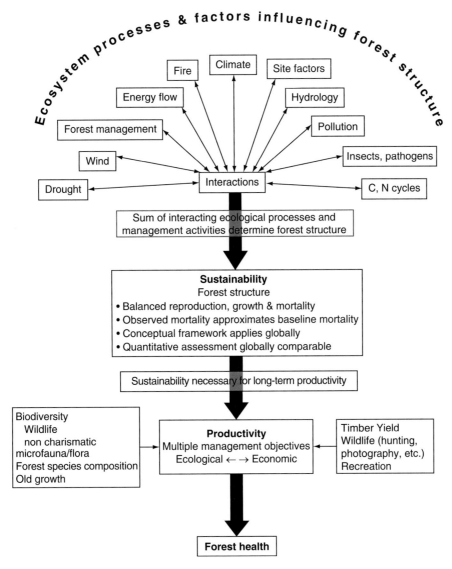

Figure 1.5 Relationships among interacting ecological factors, management, forest structure and sustainability, and productivity.

pathologists for many decades, yet so many of these organisms are essential components of the ecosystem because they are agents of mortality that is essential to maintain stable forest structure. Insect or disease outbreaks are often nothing more than an episode of mortality resulting from an accumulation of insufficient mortality that has produced an unstable forest structure. If the mortality is less than the baseline level, then an agent of mortality will emerge and return the forest to a stable age and size class, and thus health.

If actual mortality is greater than baseline mortality, then the forest cannot sustain its age and size class structure, and is therefore unhealthy.

1.4 Baseline mortality and silviculture

In managed forests under ideal conditions, the principal cause of mortality is the chainsaw. The silvicultural systems employed by foresters have been designed to produce forests that variously fit the negative exponential curve (see Chapter 8). In a managed forest with the sustainable production of wood fiber as a management objective, losses caused by insects and diseases are usually viewed as undesirable. Silvicultural systems are categorized as either even-aged or uneven-aged, yet both types of systems are based on the negative exponential function. Naturally reproducing, uneven-aged stands have a range of tree sizes and ages and generally fit the reverse-J distribution at a single point in time. Even-aged stands do not fit the reverse-J distribution at any one point in time, but generally follow the distribution as they grow and develop. At the landscape level, even-aged forests may be composed of a mosaic of stands of varying age, and at this broader spatial scale may fit the reverse-J distribution even at a single point in time. In both systems, the number of stems must be periodically or continually reduced to allow for subsequent growth. If a forest manager fails to reduce the number of stems in a stand through periodic thinning, eventually another agent will exploit the over-crowded situation and thin the stand naturally. This causes economic loss to the landowner and generates concern over the agent (insect, disease, etc.) that killed the trees, when in reality there was an underlying silvicultural problem. These agents of mortality often are quite imprecise in their thinning measures and cause excessive levels of tree mortality. Insects, diseases, and other disturbances become problematic when they confound management objectives or otherwise alter management plans (Castello *et al.* 1995), or if they induce mortality greater than the baseline for that forest type.

1.5 Biodiversity and forest health

The relationship between biodiversity and forest health is not well understood, but does not appear to be a simple one (see Chapter 9). In general, habitat heterogeneity favors greater biodiversity (Vanbergen *et al.* 2007), suggesting that a mosaic of varying stand structures may be a desirable management strategy. In fact, some of these stand structures may have excessive mortality and could be considered unhealthy from a baseline mortality perspective, but may have higher biodiversity (Kraus 2003, and Chapter 9). In this scenario, forest health almost seems to be at odds with biodiversity, but only at the level of the individual stand. At the landscape level, both forest health and biodiversity can be compatible (Vanbergen *et al.* 2007). If enhanced biodiversity does not necessarily result from the maintenance of sustainability, then perhaps it is most appropriate to view biodiversity as a management objective, rather than as part of an ecological definition of forest health.

1.6 The importance of spatial scale

The concept of a healthy forest also must incorporate the spatial scale. At the scale of the individual tree or small groups of trees of high amenity value (e.g., a homeowner's front yard) no mortality is acceptable, and thus the concept of baseline mortality does not apply because it is based on populations of trees. But it applies equally well to even-aged as well as uneven-aged forests, natural as well as managed forests, plantations as well as virgin forests, and native as well as urban forests. For example, at first blush even-aged stands do not appear to conform to the reverse-J distribution, but they do if considered as a landscape mosaic at a single point in time, or over the lifespan of the stand. Conceptually, the idea of a healthy forest (i.e., baseline mortality) is appropriate at the stand, landscape, and regional levels; however, at levels below the landscape level adequate sampling of the larger diameter classes becomes problematic (Rubin *et al.* 2006). Examples of the landscape level include national forest lands, industrial timber lands, forest preserves, etc., that represent diverse and multiple stands and management objectives.

1.7 Equilibrium vs. non-equilibrium concepts

The baseline mortality approach is an equilibrium model that tells us how the forest will be structured in the future in the absence of environmental change (i.e., non-equilibrium factors). Because the world is "non-equilibrium," a forest may or may not develop as the negative exponential model predicts. However, the baseline mortality approach to assessing forest sustainability enables us to evaluate the impacts of non-equilibrium factors on the size class structure of the forest in a simplified fashion.

1.8 Assumptions for appropriate use of the concept

The use of the baseline mortality approach to assess forest health is dependent upon some important underlying assumptions that must be considered for appropriate use of the method and interpretation of results, and which include the following: (1) The method generally is applicable only at the landscape scale to minimize the influence of individual stand peculiarities. It may, however, be appropriate at the stand level if the stand is fully stocked, and is appropriately sampled (i.e., sample plots are large enough or sufficiently numerous to provide an adequate representation of all diameter/size classes and species of trees in the forest. The plots also should be randomly selected to remove sampling bias). (2) The method used to quantify observed mortality assumes that dead trees remain identifiable to species for about the same time that it takes for the living trees to grow into the next diameter class. Therefore, the decay rate and the growth rate must be taken into account when determining the optimum width of the diameter classes. (3) Observed mortality includes all mortality regardless of cause including cutting, fires, landslides, diseases, and insect pests, etc. (4) The management and disease/pest history of the forest are known, and the silvics and ecology of the species comprising that forest are understood.

1.9 Human activities, forest health, and the outline of the book

All forests are undeniably affected by human activity, and all forest health problems are induced by human activity (though not all human activity causes forest health problems). Some human-impacted forests are sustainable, and some are not. Similarly, some are productive and some are not. Examples of human factors that have caused problems include past land use or harvest practices, fire suppression, overuse of fire, global climate change, pollution, desertification, introduction of invasive species, and recreational activities.

How exactly does one calculate baseline mortality? What are some of the problems that might be encountered when attempting to calculate it? When, where, and under what conditions is its use appropriate? Is it a universally applicable concept? These issues will be addressed in Chapter 2.

If all forest health problems are induced by the activities of man, then what precisely are the roles of the traditional big five disturbance factors (i.e., insects, diseases, fire, drought, and invasive species) in this new concept of forest health? When are these factors problematic, and when are they not? Can we predict when forests are likely to experience health problems, and respond proactively to avert them? How will forests respond to mortality greater or lower than baseline? We provide case studies to illustrate some possibilities in Chapter 3.

Forest health is influenced by many complex and interacting factors. We will examine how biotic agents of mortality including insects and pathogens (Chapter 4) native as well as invasive species (Chapter 5), and abiotic agents such as soils, climate change, and fire (Chapters 6 and 7) interact directly and indirectly to alter forest structure. Invasive species present new and growing challenges to forest management, and their impact on forest health is among the greatest threats to contemporary forested ecosystems.

Assuming that we can recognize an unhealthy forest, or anticipate a potential problem due to mortality levels above or below baseline, what management options are available to the forester and the landowner? We provide examples to illustrate some of the available options in Chapter 8.

Because forests are ecosystems that include many kinds of organisms it is essential to consider the relationship between forest health and biodiversity conservation (Chapter 9).

How are we currently monitoring trends in forest health worldwide? How can we incorporate this new concept into national forest health monitoring programs with the aim of developing a global forest health monitoring network based upon this concept? Such a network would permit a comparison of long-term trends in the health of the world's forests. These questions will be addressed in Chapter 10. Finally, we attempt to integrate the various chapters into one unified concept of forest health in Chapter 11.

References

Buchman, R. G., Pederson, S. P., and Walters, N. R. 1983. A tree survival model with application to species of the Great Lakes region. *Canadian Journal Forest Research* **13**: 601–608.

Castello, J. D., Leopold, D. J., and Smallidge, P. J. 1995. Pathogens, patterns, and processes in forest ecosystems. *BioScience* **45**: 16–24.

Caswell, H. 1989. *Matrix Population Models: Construction, Analysis and Interpretation.* Sinauer Associates, Sunderland, MA.

Dayton, P. K. 1972. Toward an understanding of community resilience and the potential effects of enrichments to the benthos at McMurdo Sound, Antarctica. In: *Proceedings of the Colloquium on Conservation Problems in Antarctica.* Parker B. C. (ed.). Allen Press, Lawrence, KS.

De Liocourt, F. 1898. De l'amenagement des sapinieres. *Bull. Triemestriel Societe Forestiere de Franche-Comte et Belfort, Besancon*: 396–409.

Edmonds, R. L., Agee, J. K., and Gara, R. I. 2000. The concept of forest health. In: *Forest Health and Protection.* McGraw-Hill, Boston, MA.

Ehrenfeld, D. 1992. Ecosystem health and ecological theories. In: *Ecosystem Health.* Costanza, R., Norton, B. G., and Haskell, B. D. (eds.). Island Press, Washington, DC.

Ellison, A. M., Bank, M. S., Clinton, B. D. *et al.* 2005. Loss of foundation species: consequences for the structure and dynamics of forested ecosystems. *Frontiers in Ecology and the Environment* **3**: 479–486.

Harcombe, P. A. 1987. Tree life tables: Simple birth, growth and death data encapsulate life histories and ecological roles. *BioScience* **37**: 557–568.

Helms, J. A. (ed.). 1998. *The Dictionary of Forestry.* The Society of American Foresters, Bethesda, MD.

Hughes, T. P. 1984. Population dynamics based on individual size rather than age: a general mode with a coral reef example. *American Naturalist* **123**: 778–795.

Kolb, T. E., Wagner, M. R., and Covington, W. W. 1994. Concepts of forest health. *Journal Forestry* **92**: 10–15.

Kraus, N. E, 2003. *Relationships between forest health and plant diversity in western New York State forest lands*. MS Thesis SUNY-ESF.

Malthus, T. R. 1798. *An Essay on the Principle of Population*. J. Johnson. London.

Manion, P. D. and Griffin, D. H. 2001. Large landscape scale analysis of tree death in the Adirondack Park, New York. *Forest Science* **47**: 542–549.

Monnig, E. and Byler, J. 1992. Forest health and ecological integrity in the northern Rockies. *USDA Forest Service FPM Rep.* **92**-7.

More, T. A. 1996. Forestry's fuzzy concepts: An examination of ecosystem management. *Journal Forestry* **94**: 19–23.

Raffa, K., Aukema, B., Bentz, B. J. *et al.* 2009. A literal use of "forest health" safeguards against misuse and misapplication. *Journal Forestry* **107**: 276–277.

Rubin, B. D., Manion, P. D., and Faber-Langendoen, D. 2006. Diameter distributions and structural sustainability in forests. *Forest Ecology & Management* **222**: 427–438.

USDA Forest Service, 1993a. Healthy forests for America's future: A strategic plan. *USDA Forest Service MP-1513*.

USDA Forest Service, 1993b. *National Center of Forest Health Management strategic plan. USDA Forest Service*. Morgantown, WV.

USDA Forest Service, 2003. Strategic Plan for Forest Health Protection: 2003–2007. *USDA Forest Service MP-1590*.

Vanbergen, A. J., Watt, A. D., Mitchell, R. *et al.* 2007. Scale-specific correlations between habitat heterogeneity and soil fauna diversity along a landscape structure gradient. *Oecologia* **153**: 713–725.

Werner, P. A. 1975. Predictions of fate from rosette size in teasel (*Dipsacus fullonum*). *Oecologia* **20**: 197–201.

2

Mortality: the essence of a healthy forest

L. ZHANG, B.D. RUBIN, AND P.D. MANION

2.1. Introduction

Chapter 1 explained the importance of diameter distributions to assess sustainability as a component of forest health. In this chapter, we further develop the method and its application, and we explore complimentary statistical tools that have been developed to analyze other aspects of forest condition. The main objective of this chapter is to present the methodology used to calculate baseline mortality, the role of diameter distributions and model fitting in this process, and to review additional conceptual methods to assess aspects of forest health. We make no effort to distinguish among different mortality-inducing agents. We first will look at diameter distributions and how to determine baseline mortality, and then examine other techniques that consider management objectives and spatial scales.

Recently, the importance of determining the causes and consequences of tree mortality at a large spatial scale has been realized (Hansen and Goheen 2000; Holdenrieder *et al.*, 2004). Determining the normal or baseline amount of disease or mortality is an essential part of this effort. If disease or other disturbance is considered an impediment to the optimal use of forest resources, then the ideal disease level is zero. However, if disturbances, pests and diseases are viewed in their full ecological context, then some abundance greater than zero must be considered a "healthy amount of disease" (Manion 2003). We use the term "a healthy amount of disease" to refer to the level of mortality-inducing agents that will induce the needed mortality, regardless of the cause of the mortality.

Forest Health: An Integrated Perspective, ed. John D. Castello and Stephen A. Teale. Published by Cambridge University Press. © Cambridge University Press 2011.

If a certain level of mortality is essential (**baseline mortality**) in a forest, then a corresponding level of mortality-causing agents (biotic and abiotic disease conditions, insects, disturbances, pests, resource shortages, etc.) must be present to maintain a level of mortality that approaches baseline mortality; and it is their cumulative impact that is important. Ideally, to evaluate the effects of a disease (broad sense) on baseline mortality one would have a suitable control area available similar to the area of interest, but where the disease was not observed. Because a controlled study design is nearly always impossible, techniques for estimating baseline mortality necessarily focus on developing suitable estimates based on data from the area of interest itself.

2.2 Forest growth and mortality

In most forests, the density of trees decreases with increasing tree size, but it is important to determine just how much mortality will sustain the structure of a forest and allow smaller trees to replace larger trees so that the future density of trees in every size-class will be the same as the current density. A diameter distribution defines the nature of this relationship, and can be expressed as a histogram of tree density in each of several different tree-size classes, or as a mathematical equation that defines a curve approximating such a histogram. One can use the ratio of trees in successive size classes to estimate the baseline mortality rate per unit of growth that will sustain the current diameter distribution. One must have direct measurements of observed mortality, or measurements of a suitable surrogate variable related to actual mortality rates, to evaluate whether observed mortality differs from baseline.

One method to define explicitly a baseline mortality level is derived by considering diameter distributions. **Diameter distributions** are graphs or mathematical functions that describe the density of trees per unit area as a function of tree diameter. Diameter distributions often are readily calculable at large spatial scales because the necessary data are collected as part of standard forest inventory data collected by many governments (e.g., see Alerich *et al.* 2004 in the USA and, Gillis *et al.* 2005 in Canada and Chapter 10).

The spatial scale at which baseline mortality is defined is of utmost importance. Often disease or mortality problems are studied in places that are pre-selected based on the presence of high levels of mortality or disease. Results of such work say very little about the extent and severity of the problem outside of the study sites, but are sometimes misinterpreted to give a biased picture of the problem. Some phenomena (e.g., outbreaks of some defoliating insects, ice storms) are locally spectacular but have little impact at a large scale (Manion *et al.* 2001; Morin *et al.* 2004). Others are locally subtle or even undetectable (e.g., fire suppression), but are of critical importance at a larger scale (Abrams 1992). Nonetheless, diameter distribution models are used to assess forest structure at stand, forest, and landscape levels.

Given a diameter distribution and a statistical model that fits that distribution, it is possible to calculate the fraction of trees in each class that need to survive (and thus the percentage which must die) in order to maintain the shape of that distribution. The calculation is based on the **q ratio** described by Meyer (1952, also see Chapter 8). For a diameter distribution based on equal-width diameter classes, q is defined as the ratio of the density of trees per hectare in one diameter class to the density of trees in the next larger diameter class. The expected surviving fraction of trees (as trees grow from one diameter class to the next) then is $1/q$ (or the ratio of the density of trees in a diameter class divided by the density in the next smaller class). The baseline mortality then is 1 − the expected surviving fraction, and is expressed in percent mortality per unit of diameter growth (see Figure 3 in Manion and Griffin 2001, or Figure 4.2 in Chapter 4 this volume). The baseline mortality could be converted to annual mortality directly if all the trees grew at exactly the same rate.

Baseline mortality based on diameter distribution slope has been used with two types of available data. In the more data-rich instance, repeat samples are available and the annual death rate and growth rate can be observed. For example, Duchesne *et al.* (2005) monitored sugar maple/beech stands in Quebec, Canada for ten years. From these data, they were able to calculate the average annual growth and death rate for each stand. They used the average growth rate to convert the expected surviving fraction derived from the diameter distribution to an expected yearly survival rate, and compared that to the observed annual survival. Based on this analysis, they were able to show that for small trees the surviving fraction of sugar maple was below the confidence envelope around the expected surviving fraction, whereas, the observed survival rate of beech was greater than expected. This pattern was consistent with other evidence suggesting sugar maple decline (see Chapter 6).

Repeat samples, however, often are not available. In such cases an index related to observed mortality is the only available option. One surrogate variable for baseline mortality/unit growth is the actual count of dead trees (Manion and Griffin 2001). Use of this measurement assumes that tree growth rate and wood decomposition rate is relatively constant across diameter classes (see Chapters 1 and 3). The impact of violating this assumption can be minimized if observed and baseline mortality are averaged over all diameter classes (Manion and Griffin 2001; Manion *et al.* 2001; Munck and Manion 2006). It also requires that the unit of growth is determined so that the average decomposition time is equal to the average time trees take to grow from one size class to the next.

Another alternative is to develop a synthetic index of disease severity. The dwarf mistletoe rating system (Hawksworth 1977), which synthesizes the impact of an important disease into a single number, has been widely implemented and found to be useful in many situations (Mathiasen *et al.* 2008). However, such convenient systems are not available for many diseases or types of forests, especially in cases where tree mortality is spread relatively evenly among several different causes.

A common practice is to assess tree health based on variables such as crown transparency because estimates are easy to generate. More difficult is to ensure that these estimates are reproducible and meaningful (Solberg and Strand 1999). Crown transparency has sometimes been shown to be related to mortality (Dobbertin 2005), and sometimes not (Steinman 2000). An alternative is to develop a system for assessing the probability of short- to medium-term survival of trees based on an integration of different forms of evidence. For example, easily observable crown characteristics that could be included are: crown position, crown dieback, and live crown ratio. Some signs and symptoms of other diseases, such as heartrot, butt rot, and cankers also are relatively easily observed. Tree-marking guides often contain systems to integrate information of these types to gain an overall assessment of a tree's vigor (e.g., see OMNR 2004). Mortality predictions based on one such system are consistent with independent predictions made based on tree growth rates (Hartmann *et al.* 2008). Another system assigns numerical weights for individual defects, and each tree is assigned a liability score based on a summation of its defects (Rubin and Manion 2005, see also Chapter 3). Trees with a cumulative liability score above a certain threshold are considered likely to die before growing into the next diameter class. This system gives results comparable to the observed mortality index.

Fundamental to considerations of tree mortality on a landscape scale is the assessment of differential mortality based on tree size (as a surrogate for age) and species. Hence, the diameter distribution is an important metric for establishing the demographic structure of a population of trees. The diameter distribution is one of the four inter-related components (species composition, quality, volume, and diameter distribution) of forest stands with which forest managers are concerned in planning silvicultural treatments and management activities (Leak 1964). It is commonly expressed as a histogram with the number of trees per unit area on the y-axis and diameter at breast height on the x-axis (Avery and Burkhart 2002). The shape of a diameter distribution depends on several factors including species composition, stand and tree age, and silvicultural treatments. It can range from unimodal and (almost) symmetric for pure, even-aged stands (Figure 2.1a), to reverse-J shaped for balanced, uneven-aged stands (Figure 2.1b), and to multimodal, rotated-sigmoid for irregular, mixed-species stands (Figure 2.1c) (Zhang *et al.* 2001).

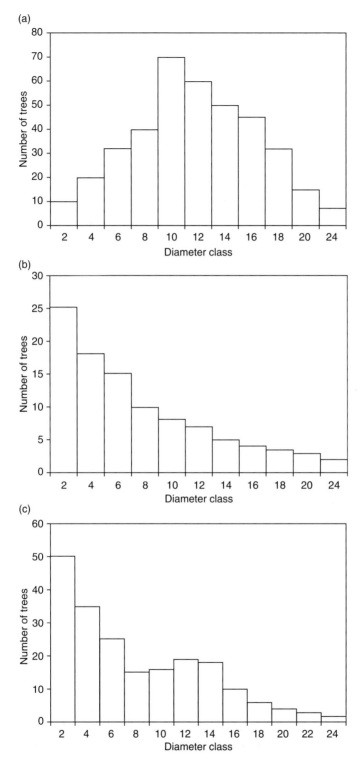

Figure 2.1 A typical diameter distribution for (a) pure, even-aged stands; (b) balanced, uneven-aged stands; and (c) rotated-sigmoid shape for irregular, mixed-species stands.

In the discipline of forest biometrics, the diameter distribution model is one of the three types of forest growth and yield models, including the whole stand model, the diameter distribution model, and the individual tree model. Since the 1980s, forest modelers have developed a number of diameter distribution models to describe and to quantify the diameter distributions of forest stands for different tree species and geographical regions (Clutter *et al.* 1992; Vanclay 1994; Avery and Burkhart 2002). In these diameter-distribution models the number of trees by diameter class is estimated using a probability density function (*pdf*). Mean tree height is predicted for each diameter class by a tree height-diameter model. Volume in each diameter class is calculated by substituting the predicted mean tree height and the diameter class midpoint into a tree volume equation. Yield estimates for a forest stand are obtained by summing over the diameter classes of interest. Thus, the diameter distribution models provide not only the growth and yield information on the total or average of the entire stand; but also more details on stand structure in terms of tree size, number, volume, product, and economic value for specified tree size classes. The information is valuable for forest managers to understand the dynamics of stand growth and yield, and to assess the effects of silvicultural treatments such as thinning and fertilizer application on stand structure (Hyink and Moser 1983).

One approach to describing a diameter distribution is to use a *pdf*, which is a continuous mathematical function defined by a vector of parameters. In probability theory and statistics, a *pdf* of a continuous random variable describes the relative likelihood or frequency for the variable to occur within a given interval in the observation space. In forestry, various *pdf*s have been used to model diameter distributions; such as normal, beta, gamma, lognormal, Weibull, and Johnson systems (Clutter *et al.* 1992; Vanclay 1994; Avery and Burkhart 2002). Over the last three decades many studies have been conducted to compare the goodness-of-fit and flexibility of those *pdf*s to represent different shapes and structures of diameter distributions for various tree species (Hafley and Schreuder 1977; Zhang *et al.*, 2003).

2.3. Diameter distribution of a sustainable forest

We define a **sustainable forest** as one that maintains a stable diameter distribution or structure, and a balanced relationship between growth and mortality (see Chapter 1, and Manion and Griffin 2001). This concept describes the size structure of forests with many small trees and fewer larger trees, which can be mathematically represented by a **negative exponential function** (Leak 1965; Rubin *et al.*, 2006). When this reverse-J relationship between tree density and diameter is plotted on log-linear axes, it becomes a linear relationship.

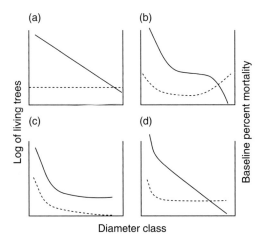

Figure 2.2 Diagram of different shapes of diameter distributions (solid lines – left axes) and corresponding baseline mortality per unit growth (dashed lines – right axes). (a) reverse-J. (b) rotated sigmoid. (c) negative power. (d) combination of negative power and reverse-J. (Adapted from Coomes *et al.* 2003 with permission.)

Therefore, the slope of this linear regression line defines the number of trees in a given diameter class that must die in order for the forest stand to maintain a stable diameter structure; i.e., baseline mortality (Manion and Griffin 2001).

Although the reverse-J shape traditionally has been considered an essential feature of balanced, uneven-aged diameter distributions (Meyer 1952; Leak 1996; Figure 2.2a), deviations from this descending, monotonic curve have been recognized and studied (Muller-Landau *et al.* 2006). One alternative is the **rotated-sigmoid shape** or **function** where the slope of the diameter distribution is steeper (i.e., higher mortality rates) for small- and large-sized trees than for mid-sized (co-dominant) trees (West *et al.* 1981; Lorimer and Frelich 1998; Zhang *et al.* 2001; Westphal *et al.* 2006; Figure 2.2b). Another alternative is a negative power model (Figure 2.2c, linear on a log-log plot), which is based on the theory of algometric scaling relationships and ignores the density-independent mortality (Midgley 2001). Recently, Coomes *et al.* (2003) suggested that many old-growth forests followed a negative power (scaling) relationship for small-diameter trees and negative exponential (reverse J-shaped) distributions for larger trees (Figure 2.2d). Although different shapes and structures of diameter distributions have been observed in practice, many factors may affect the resultant diameter distributions, such as sample size and sampling method, the number and width of diameter classes, data collection methods (e.g., prism points vs. fixed area plots, see Chapter 3), etc. (Rubin *et al.* 2006). Researchers attempt to find various mathematical functions or models to improve the fitting of the observed diameter distributions. Many of these alternative functions or models indeed are more flexible in fitting different diameter distributions. They include the Weibull function (Bailey and Dell 1973), the finite mixture model (Zhang *et al.* 2001), and the combined model of Coomes *et al.* (2003). However, these models are more complex and difficult to use than the negative exponential model. This makes them less practical for determining baseline mortality as discussed later in this chapter, but they can be used for calculation of baseline mortality (BM), and comparison of observed mortality to BM.

2.4 Theory and mathematical expression of baseline mortality

The oldest mathematical model used for a balanced, uneven-aged diameter distribution is the negative exponential function (de Liocourt 1898; Meyer 1952; Leak 1996). An important characteristic of this distribution is the constant rate of reduction in the number of trees from one diameter class to the next larger. Mathematically, the negative exponential function has the following *pdf* (Meyer 1952; Leak 1965):

$$N = \beta \cdot e^{-\beta \cdot D} \tag{2.1}$$

where β is a model parameter, D is the midpoint of a diameter class, and N is the number of trees in the diameter class D. Basically, the parameter β determines the rate of decrease of N as D increases. Let N_i and N_j be the number of trees for two adjacent diameter classes D_i and D_j, respectively. For a fixed and equal diameter class interval, a constant survival rate across all diameter classes can be expressed as follows (Manion and Griffin 2001):

$$\frac{N_j}{N_i} = \frac{\beta \cdot e^{-\beta \cdot D_j}}{\beta \cdot e^{-\beta \cdot D_i}} = e^{-\beta \left(D_j - D_i \right)} = e^{-\beta \cdot \Delta D} \tag{2.2}$$

where ΔD is the diameter class interval. Therefore, the baseline mortality (BM) is calculated by (Manion and Griffin 2001):

$$BM = 1 - e^{-\beta \cdot \Delta D} \tag{2.3}$$

For a given forest or stand, baseline mortality can be obtained once the parameter β of the negative exponential function is estimated from the available data.

2.5 Statistical methods for fitting diameter distributions

2.5.1 Brief review of simple linear regression

A **simple linear regression** describes a straight-line relationship between two quantities: one dependent or response variable Y, and one independent or predictor variable X:

$$Y = \beta_0 + \beta_1 \cdot X + \varepsilon \qquad\qquad [2.4]$$

where β_0 is an intercept coefficient, β_1 is a slope coefficient, and ε is the model error term whose distribution is assumed to follow a normal distribution with mean zero and constant variance. Both β_0 and β_1 can be zero, positive or negative. The intercept coefficient β_0 represents the value of Y when X equals zero. The slope coefficient β_1 indicates how much Y increases when X increases one unit if β_1 is positive, or how much Y decreases when X increases one unit if β_1 is negative. The model error term ε represents the random variation among the observations in the data.

One way to estimate the two regression coefficients β_0 and β_1 is to apply the least-squares method (Rawlings *et al.* 1998). For a given data set of n pairs (sample size) of observations (X_1, Y_1), (X_2, Y_2), ..., (X_n, Y_n), suppose the "best-fit" regression line to the data is

$$\hat{Y}_i = \hat{\beta}_0 + \hat{\beta}_1 \cdot X_i \qquad\qquad [2.5]$$

where $\hat{\beta}_0$ and $\hat{\beta}_1$ denote the numerical estimates of the coefficients β_0 and β_1, respectively, and $\hat{Y}_i$ is the model prediction of Y for any given value of X_i ($i = 1$, 2, ..., n). Then, the model error is defined by $\varepsilon_i = Y_i - \hat{Y}_i$ for each observation, in which Y_i is the observed value and $\hat{Y}_i$ is the computed value from eq. [2.5] for the same value of X_i. The least-squares principle chooses the coefficient estimates $\hat{\beta}_0$ and $\hat{\beta}_1$ such that the sum of squares of the model errors (SSE)

$$SSE = \sum_{i=1}^{n} \varepsilon_i^2 = \sum_{i=1}^{n} \left(Y_i - \hat{Y}_i\right)^2 = \sum_{i=1}^{n} \left(Y_i - \left(\hat{\beta}_0 + \hat{\beta}_1 \cdot X_i\right)\right)^2 \qquad [2.6]$$

is minimized over all n observations. Therefore, $\hat{Y}_i = \hat{\beta}_0 + \hat{\beta}_1 \cdot X_i$ is considered the "best-fit" regression model for the given data, and $\hat{\beta}_0$ and $\hat{\beta}_1$ are the "best" coefficient estimates for the model (Figure 2.3).

Mathematically, the estimators of β_0 and β_1 can be obtained by solving the normal equations of the least-squares, which are the derivatives of SSE (eq. [2.6]) with respect to the two coefficients. After the step-by-step derivations, the least-squares estimates of β_0 and β_1 are given by (Rawlings *et al.* 1998):

$$\hat{\beta}_1 = \frac{SS_{xy}}{SS_x} = \frac{\sum_{i=1}^{n}(X_i - \bar{X})(Y_i - \bar{Y})}{\sum_{i=1}^{n}(X_i - \bar{X})^2} \qquad\qquad [2.7]$$

$$\hat{\beta}_0 = \bar{Y} - \hat{\beta}_1 \cdot \bar{X} \qquad\qquad [2.8]$$

where SS_{xy} is the sum of squares of the product between X and Y, SS_x is the sum of squares of X, $\bar{Y}$ and $\bar{X}$ are the means of observed Y and X, respectively, in the sample data.

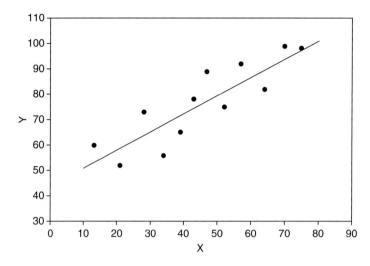

Figure 2.3 Scatterplot of Y vs. X. The solid line represents the "best fit" regression line of $\hat{Y} = \hat{\beta}_0 + \hat{\beta}_1 \cdot X$.

One measure to assess how well the model fits the data is to use the model R^2 ($0 \le R^2 \le$), which is computed as:

$$R^2 = 1 - \frac{SSE}{SST} = 1 - \frac{\sum\limits_{i=1}^{n} \left(Y_i - \hat{Y}_i\right)^2}{\sum\limits_{i=1}^{n} \left(Y_i - \bar{Y}\right)^2} \qquad [2.9]$$

where SST is the total sum of squares of Y. Basically, the model R^2 represents the percentage of total variation in the observed Y values that is explained by the regression model [2.5]. The higher the R^2, the better the model fits the data (Rawlings *et al.* 1998).

In order to determine if the observed mortality for a given diameter class is statistically significant from the baseline mortality, we use chi-square analysis. This technique compares observed values against expected values. The calculated chi-square value is then compared against a critical value obtained from a chi-square distribution table. This value is based on a single degree of freedom and an alpha value set for the statistical power needed (often 0.05). Because many times we are interested in the significance of multiple diameter classes, alpha correction is necessary. A Bonnferoni correction is commonly employed to adjust for the increased chance of falsely rejecting the null hypothesis. With this technique, the alpha value is divided by the number of comparisons to be made. The newly generated alpha value then can be used to obtain a critical chi-square value, as mentioned above.

2.5.2 Fitting the negative exponential function to sample stand data

When a diameter distribution is approximately a reverse-J shape, one commonly takes a logarithmic transformation on N to linearize the relationship between N and D. Thus, a simple linear regression model can be proposed to fit the negative exponential function (eq. [2.1]) as follows:

$$\ln(N) = b_0 + b_1 \cdot D \qquad\qquad\qquad [2.10]$$

where ln is natural logarithm. In eq. [2.10] $\ln(N)$ is the dependent or response variable (i.e., Y in eq. [2.4]) and D is the independent or predictor variable (i.e., X in eq. [2.4]). Both b_0 (intercept coefficient) and b_1 (slope coefficient) are estimated from the data using eqs. [2.7] and [2.8]. Then, the baseline mortality is calculated by -$BM = 1 - e^{-b_1 \cdot \Delta D}$, where ΔD is the diameter class interval used in the sample data.

Now we will use a real data set to demonstrate how to fit the negative exponential function (eq. [2.10]) using Microsoft® Excel®. The step by step procedure is shown in Appendix A. The sample data were collected from four tree species combined from Puerto Rico in the year 2000 (see the PR dataset.xls file in the Chapter 2 folder on the website). All tree observations were grouped by a 2-cm diameter class interval (i.e., $\Delta D = 2$). The data include diameter class (D), the number of live trees (N), the number of dead trees (M), and the total number of trees ($TN = N + M$). After the data were prepared into a desired format, it was important to draw a diameter histogram, and the relationship of $\ln(N)$-D in order to learn how much the diameter distribution of the available data deviated from the reverse-J shape, and how close the relationship between $\ln(N)$ and D was to the linear trend. In this case, the observed diameter distribution was basically a reverse-J shape form, and the relationship of $\ln(N)$-D was close to linear (Figure 2.4a).

Next we fit eq. [2.10], using $\ln(N)$ as the dependent variable, and D as the predictor variable. The regression results showed: (1) the "best-fit" simple linear regression model was: $\ln(N) = b_0 + b_1 \cdot D = 7.4217 - 0.0927 \cdot D$, (2) the model R^2 was 0.96, indicating that 96% of total variation in the observed $\ln(N)$ was explained by the linear model, and (3) the baseline mortality was calculated as $BM = 1 - e^{-b_1 \cdot \Delta D} = 1 - e^{-0.0927 \times 2} = 1 - 0.8308 = 0.1692 \approx 17\%$.

The last step is to draw the mortality chart with the diameter classes as the x-axis, $\ln(N)$ as the first y-axis (left), and the mortality rate as the second y-axis (right) (Figure 2.4b). The mortality chart shows the observed mortality across the diameter classes against the constant baseline mortality ($BM = 17\%$), as well as the observed relationship of $\ln(N)$-D with the linear trend line across the data range. The observed mortality also may be plotted on the same axes as baseline mortality for a visual comparison of observed to baseline mortality.

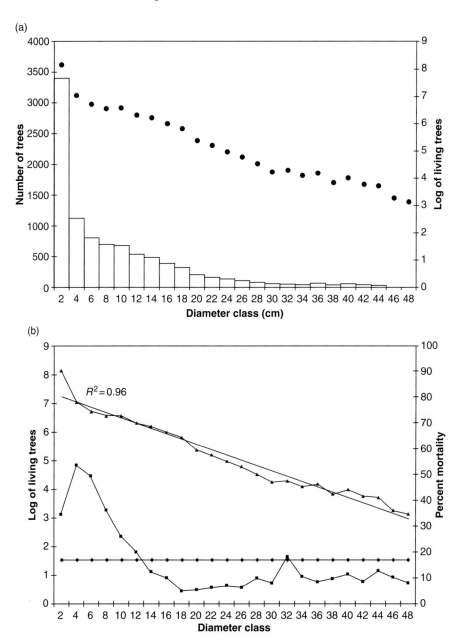

Figure 2.4 (a) Diameter histogram and relationship of ln(N)-D for the sample data of Puerto Rico in 2000 combining four tree species. (b) Mortality chart for (a), where squares are observed mortality, diamonds are baseline mortality, triangles are the natural log N, and the uninterrupted line is the linear trend of the data. (Data from the LFDP at the LUQ-LTER site in Puerto Rico funded by grants from the US National Science Foundation to the University of Puerto Rico in collaboration with IITF-USFS.)

2.5.3 Notes on model fitting

After having fit eq. [2.10] to a given data set, one may calculate the anti-logarithm to obtain the equivalent negative exponential form of $N = ae^{-b \cdot D}$, where the asymptotic parameter $a = e^{b_0}$ and the scale parameter $b = b_1$. However, it should be noted: (1) although the total number of trees in the stand is known, the model-fitting process estimates it as an independent and unknown asymptotic parameter, a; (2) the error structure of the model is assumed to be multiplicative, i.e., $N = ae^{-b \cdot D} \cdot \varepsilon$; and (3) the anti-logarithm transformation process will introduce biases into the negative exponential model.

An alternative approach to fitting a model to a reverse-J shaped diameter distribution is to apply a nonlinear least squares regression to directly fit $N = ae^{-b \cdot D}$ to the observed data. In this case, the error structure of the model is assumed to be additive, i.e., $N = ae^{-b \cdot D} + \varepsilon$, and no anti-logarithm process is involved. However, the total number of trees in the stand also is estimated as an independent and unknown asymptotic parameter in the model-fitting process. Statistical software (e.g., Statistical Analysis System [SAS]) other than Microsoft® Excel® is needed to fit the nonlinear least squares regression, and is beyond the scope of this text (Zhang et al. 2003).

An alternative model parameter estimation method is maximum likelihood estimation (MLE), which can be used to fit eq. [2.1] to the observed (continuous) diameter distribution in the form of either an individual tree list or grouped data. Again, statistical software (e.g., SAS) other than Microsoft® Excel® is needed to fit diameter distributions using MLE, and also is beyond the scope of this text (Zhang et al. 2003).

2.6 Alternative models of diameter distributions

2.6.1 Linear model vs. quadratic model for the ln(N)-D relationship

When the relationship of ln(N)-D is not linear, a quadratic model often is used instead of a linear model. Although the quadratic model may provide a better fit, it does not generate a constant survival or mortality rate across the diameter classes. For example, if a quadratic model $\ln(N) = b_0 + b_1 \cdot D + b_2 \cdot D^2$ is fitted to a data set, the anti-logarithm form of the model is $N = ae^{b_1 \cdot D} \cdot e^{b_2 \cdot D^2}$. Let N_i and N_j be the number of trees for two adjacent diameter classes D_i and D_j, respectively. The survival rate across all diameter classes can be expressed as follows:

$$\frac{N_j}{N_i} = \frac{ae^{b_1 \cdot D_j} \cdot e^{b_2 \cdot D_j^2}}{ae^{b_1 \cdot D_i} \cdot e^{b_2 \cdot D_i^2}} = e^{b_1\left(D_j - D_i\right)} \cdot e^{b_2\left(D_j^2 - D_i^2\right)} \qquad [2.11]$$

It is clear that $\left(D_j^2 - D_i^2\right) = (D_j - D_i)(D_j + D_i) = \Delta D(D_j + D_i)$ is not constant across the diameter classes. For the diameter classes with a 2-cm interval $2, 4, 6, 8, \ldots, 48, 50$ (i.e., $\Delta D = 2$), the term $\Delta D(D_j + D_i) = 2(D_j + D_i)$ is $2(4+2) = 12$, $2(6 + 4) = 20$, $2(8 + 6) = 28$, $2(10 + 8) = 36$, $\ldots$, $2(50 + 48) = 196$. Therefore, the constant survival rate across all diameter classes is not feasible, even if the diameter size interval ΔD is a constant.

A data set from the Luquillo forest dynamics plot in Puerto Rico was used to demonstrate the differences between the linear and quadratic models for fitting the ln(N)-D relationship. The data were collected in 1995 for all tree species in the plot, but here we will use data from only one, *Schefflera morototoni*. All tree observations were grouped by a 2-cm diameter class interval. The diameter distribution of the data indicated that it had a large number of small trees and few larger trees, thus the relationship of ln(N)-D was not linear (Figure 2.5a). Linear and quadratic models were fit to the data using Microsoft® Excel®. The resultant models were:

Linear model: $\ln(N) = 5.5561 - 0.1167 \cdot D$, with model $R^2 = 0.895$.

Quadratic model: $\ln(N) = 6.9039 - 0.2785 \cdot D + 0.00337 \cdot D^2$, with model $R^2 = 0.946$.

The quadratic model fit the observed diameter distribution better (higher R^2; Figure 2.5b). For the linear model, the baseline mortality was constant such that $BM = 1 - e^{-b_1 \cdot \Delta D} = 1 - e^{-0.1167 \times 2} = 1 - 0.7918 = 0.2082 \approx 21\%$. However, for the quadratic model, the baseline mortality ranged from 40.34% to -5.09% across the diameter classes (Figure 2.5c).

2.6.2 Other nonlinear functions

Besides the negative exponential function (eq. [2.1]), other mathematical functions are available to model diameter distributions such as the power function and Weibull function:

$$\text{Power function} : N = a \cdot D^b \tag{2.12}$$

$$\text{Weibull function} : \ N = \frac{\gamma}{\beta}\left(\frac{D}{\beta}\right)^{\gamma} e^{-\left(\frac{D}{\beta}\right)^{\gamma}} \tag{2.13}$$

where a, b, γ, β are model parameters to be estimated from data. However, these functions do not generate a constant survival or mortality rate across diameter classes. For example, denote N_i and N_j as the number of trees for two adjacent diameter classes D_i and D_j, respectively. The survival rate across all diameter classes can be expressed as follows:

$$\text{Power function} : \ \frac{N_j}{N_i} = \frac{aD_j^b}{aD_i^b} = \left(\frac{D_j}{D_i}\right)^b \tag{2.14}$$

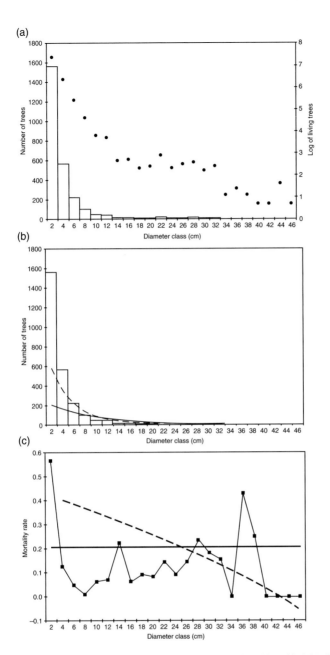

Figure 2.5 (a) The diameter histogram and relationship of ln(N)-D for the sample data of *Schefflera morototoni* 1995. (b) Observed diameter distribution and estimated number of trees by the linear and quadratic models for (a), where N is the observed frequency, N-Linear is the estimated number of trees by the linear model (solid line), and N-Quadratic is the estimated number of trees by the quadratic model (dash line). (c) Mortality chart for (a), where squares are observed mortality, baseline mortality by the linear model is the solid line, and baseline mortality by the quadratic model is the dashed line. (Data from the LFDP at the LUQ-LTER site in Puerto Rico funded by grants from the US National Science Foundation to the University of Puerto Rico in collaboration with IITF-USFS.)

$$\text{Weibull function}: \frac{N_j}{N_i} = \frac{\frac{\gamma}{\beta}\left(\frac{D_j}{\beta}\right)^{\gamma} e^{-\left(\frac{D_j}{\beta}\right)^{\gamma}}}{\frac{\gamma}{\beta}\left(\frac{D_i}{\beta}\right)^{\gamma} e^{-\left(\frac{D_i}{\beta}\right)^{\gamma}}} = \left(\frac{D_j}{D_i}\right)^{\Gamma} e^{-\frac{1}{\beta^{\gamma}}\left(D_j^{\gamma} - D_i^{\gamma}\right)} \qquad [2.15]$$

It is clear that the terms D_j/D_i and $\left(D_j^{\gamma} - D_i^{\gamma}\right)$ in eqs. [2.14] and [2.15] are not constant across the diameter classes. For the diameter classes with a 2-cm interval 2, 4, 6, 8, . . ., 48, 50, the ratio D_j/D_i is $4/2 = 2.00$, $6/4 = 1.50$, $8/6 = 1.33$, $10/8 = 1.25, \ldots, 50/48 = 1.04$. Therefore, a constant survival rate across all diameter classes is not feasible, even if the diameter size interval ΔD is constant.

Differences between the negative exponential function (linear model) and Weibull function for fitting to a diameter distribution can be demonstrated with data from another species in the Luquillo Forest, *Cecropia schreberiana*. Again, all tree observations were grouped by a 2-cm diameter class interval. The diameter distribution of the data indicated that it was unimodal and skewed to the right, rather than a reverse-J shape (Figure 2.6a). A linear model of $\ln(N)$-D and a Weibull function were fit to the data using the least squares method in Microsoft® Excel® and the MLE method in SAS, respectively (Zhang *et al.* 2003). The resultant models were:

Negative exponential (linear model): $\ln(N) = 7.4221 - 0.1809 \cdot D$, with model $R^2 = 0.88$.

Weibull function: $N = \frac{0.8368}{8.8694}\left(\frac{D}{8.8694}\right)^{1.8368} e^{-\left(\frac{D}{8.8694}\right)^{1.8368}}$, with model $R^2 = 0.95$.

The Weibull function had a higher R^2 and appeared to fit the observed diameter distribution much better (Figure 2.6b). This is not surprising because the Weibull function is known to be more flexible for fitting variously shaped diameter distributions (Avery and Burkhart 2002). For the linear model, the baseline mortality was a constant such that $BM = 1 - e^{-b_1 \cdot \Delta D} = 1 - e^{-0.1809 \times 2} = 1 - 0.6964 = 0.3036 \approx 30\%$. However, for the Weibull function, the baseline mortality ranged from -2.0223 to 0.8091 (-202% to 81%) across the diameter classes (Figure 2.6c).

It is evident that alternative models such as the quadratic model and the Weibull function may fit the observed diameter distributions and the relationships of $\ln(N)$-D better than does the negative exponential function – linear model (eq. [2.10]). It is worthy of noting that these alternative models may generate non-constant baseline mortalities across the diameter classes, which can nonetheless be utilized to assess the sustainability of a forest stand. However, these alternative models may produce negative baseline mortality values at one or more diameter classes. From a biological perspective, it is impossible to have negative mortality once a cohort (e.g., a size class) is established. Thus, a diameter distribution that requires negative mortality in order to be sustainable is illogical, and of no use.

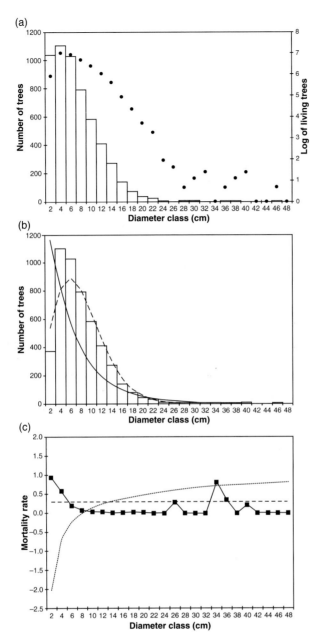

Figure 2.6 (a) Diameter histogram and relationship of ln(N)-D for the sample data of *C. schreberiana* 1995. (b) Observed diameter distribution and estimated number of trees by the negative exponential function (linear model) (solid line) and Weibull function (dashed line) for a). (c) Mortality chart for (a) where squares are observed mortality, the baseline mortality by the negative exponential function (linear model) is the dashed line, and the baseline mortality by the Weibull function is the dotted line. (Data from the LFDP at the LUQ-LTER site in Puerto Rico funded by grants from the US National Science Foundation to the University of Puerto Rico in collaboration with IITF-USFS.)

Furthermore, it is not uncommon that some unmanaged and uneven-aged forest stands may follow rotated sigmoid diameter distributions (Figure 2.1c) due to early disturbances and/or a mixture of species of different shade tolerances or age classes (e.g., Goff and West 1975; Lorimer and Frelich 1984; Leak 1996). The rates of tree growth and mortality are not uniform across size and age classes in such stands – high mortality in small and large size classes and lower mortality rates for medium sized/aged trees are characteristic of such stands. In this case, more complicated statistical models (e.g., a finite mixture function) and special computer software are required to adequately model rotated sigmoid diameter distributions (e.g., Zhang *et al.* 2001; Liu *et al.* 2002). However, it is inconvenient to fit this kind of diameter distribution model and to apply non-constant baseline mortality in forest management practices. In addition, foresters focus silvicultural treatments on trees between 5 cm (even 15 cm) and 70 cm dbh. The tails of the diameter distribution graph are not considered in most silvicultural prescriptions. For example, many stocking charts usually range from 15 to 50 cm dbh. Therefore, unless the diameter distribution of a forest stand is in an obviously rotated sigmoid shape, the negative exponential function is a good approximation for many uneven-aged forest stands, and the constant baseline mortality concept can be utilized for these stands.

What other methodologies are available to assess/evaluate the amount of mortality/disease/disturbance necessary to meet various management objectives. We discuss three examples below.

2.6.3 Stand profiling

Stand profiling is a methodology designed to determine how much disease is optimal for different management objectives. The method involves ordination to classify stands according to important variables for different management objectives. On this ordination, the location of desired conditions can be plotted (management targets) along with the location of individual stands. If the disease level at each stand is known, one can use the ordination to display whether stands with a given level of disease are located close to or far away from management targets.

One of the key concepts behind the idea of baseline mortality is that as long as it is not excessive, tree mortality can have ecological and economic benefits. Several papers have addressed this issue, and pointed out in theory that the benefits of mortality should include resources for regenerating trees, faster growth of survivors, and increased habitat availability for forest-dwelling animals (Castello *et al.*, 1995; Manion 2003; Holdenrieder *et al.*, 2004). Lundquist and Beatty (1999) developed and Lundquist *et al.* (2002) implemented

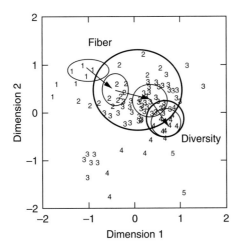

Figure 2.7 A multidimensional scaling ordination showing the locations of stands meeting two management objectives (fiber production and biodiversity: thick circles) and the location of stands with different average Hawksworth's dwarf mistletoe ratings (numbers 1 through 5) and the typical position of stands in each rating class (thin circles). (With permission from Lundquist *et al.* 2002.)

a system for identifying levels of disease most commonly associated with stands meeting a specified set of management objectives. The method involves defining a desired stand condition based on a series of descriptive variables or on expert opinion. Stands then are displayed in an ordination space using a multidimensional scaling (a multivariate ordination procedure), to create two dimensions that capture much of the variation in the original descriptive variables. Finally, an index of disease abundance or severity at each location is displayed on the ordination plot. For example, Hawksworth's (1977) dwarf mistletoe rating system (DMR), which classifies trees into classes from 0 for trees with no damage to 6 for severely damaged trees, was applied to a stand profiling ordination of 258 stands from the Rouge River National Forest in Oregon (Lundquist *et al.* 2002). Stands with average DMRs between 1 and 4 were most desirable for fiber production. Stands with an average DMR between 4 and 5 were most desirable to maximize biodiversity. Stands with the lowest level of disease (average DMR of 0 to 1) were present in the study area but were not the most desirable for either management objective (Figure 2.7). Thus, stand profiling provides a way to compare an index of disease to pre-defined management objectives, and demonstrates that the complete absence of disease may not be desirable.

Stand profiling is based on management objectives, therefore, it cannot say anything about forest sustainability. Also, stand profiling does not provide an easy method to integrate the impacts of several mortality agents, or if the study area is not divided into pre-defined areas for analyses (e.g., stands). As our thinking about baseline mortality expands to broader scales, this latter problem becomes more important. Data for large landscapes typically are collected or summarized by dividing the area into political subunits. However, there is usually no reason to expect that areas with mortality rates above, at, or below baseline levels will be accurately described by these political boundaries.

2.6.4 Spatial scan statistic

The **spatial scan statistic (SSS)** is designed to identify one or more spatial areas where disease or mortality rates are most likely to exceed background levels. Given a spatial array of disease or mortality levels measured at various locations throughout a region, the SSS can be used to determine if there is a subset of neighboring data locations in the region where the level of disease or mortality is statistically different from the corresponding level elsewhere.

One way to use baseline mortality is to look for subsets of an area where mortality levels or disease incidence are significantly higher than elsewhere. We need a statistical tool that can identify such subsets from the raw data alone, without relying on external information (e.g., where an expert might expect high mortality levels). Such a statistical tool has been developed to solve similar problems relating to human health. Drawing parallels between the fields of human medicine and forest pathology is not always entirely useful in large part because of the importance of mortality in forests. A good physician would prefer to cure all patients, whereas a good forest pathologist recognizes the benefit of letting some trees die. Public health practitioners do not attribute benefit to a baseline level of disease in a human population but, like forest pathologists, they accept a baseline level of disease as normal and focus their efforts on determining where, when, and why disease levels exceed baseline. For this reason, among the medical fields, public health probably has the most in common with forest pathology.

Kulldorff (1997) developed the SSS to identify areas with unusually high disease incidence. How SSS works is illustrated in the following hypothetical example. A public health official is confronted with data consisting of the number of cases of a certain disease, and the total population for all cities in a certain region. There will be some random variation in disease incidence (number of cases/population) that will likely be greater for cities with small populations than for large cities. In addition to this random variability, there may or may not be some underlying pattern (i.e., some city clusters where the

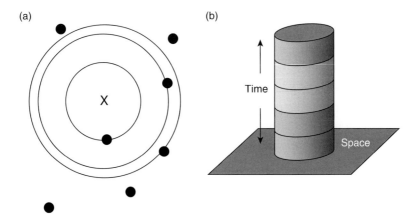

Figure 2.8 (a) A diagram of four potential clusters in the SSS. The cluster center (X) is considered a cluster on its own, and the three circles each include one additional location. The SSS will continue to consider larger clusters until a specified maximum size is reached, and then repeat the procedure at another cluster center. (b) A diagram of a space-time scan statistic where each circular cluster from a) is replaced with a series of cylinders such that the height of the cylinder is defined by a number of discrete, predefined time units between one and a specified maximum. (Adapted from Coulston and Riitters 2003 with permission.)

disease incidence within the cluster is higher than that outside the cluster). The ability to identify such a cluster could motivate an inquiry into the cause of the difference and thus be of value. The objective of the SSS is to determine whether or not such a cluster exists and, if so, then to identify its approximate size and location. The following description characterizes the essential features of the SSS. Several variants exist with different underlying statistical models, and different implementation options that are implemented using SaTScan, a freely available software package designed for spatial and space-time scan statistics (Kulldorff 2009, available at: www.satscan.org).

2.6.5 Description of the SSS

The SSS considers an array of potential cluster centers. Often these are the data locations (in the public health example, the cities themselves). For each potential cluster center, a series of concentric circles (potential clusters) is established such that the smallest potential cluster contains one data location, and each larger potential cluster adds one more location up to a specified maximum size (Figure 2.8a). A null and an alternative hypothesis are considered for each potential cluster. These hypotheses concern the underlying probability that an individual might have a disease (analogous to the probability of getting heads when tossing a coin) that can be estimated but not exactly known based on the percentage of individuals that have the disease (the percentage of heads observed in a finite series of tosses).

Null hypothesis: The underlying probability of each individual having the disease, p_{true}, does not depend on whether an individual is inside or outside of the potential cluster, and any difference between the observed rate of disease within and outside the potential cluster is attributed to sampling error (i.e., to chance). The underlying probability is estimated as the sum of the number of cases observed for all locations (C) divided by the sum of the population at all locations (N) ($p_{estimate} = C/N$, for locations inside and outside of a potential cluster).

Alternate hypothesis: Under the alternate hypothesis, the difference between the observed incidence of disease within the cluster, and that observed outside the cluster is attributed to a real difference in risk rather than to sampling error. For individuals within the potential cluster the probability of having the disease ($p_{true-inside}$) is estimated as the sum of the number of cases observed within the potential cluster (C_{inside}) divided by the number of individuals within the potential cluster (N_{inside}); thus, $p_{estimate-inside} = C_{inside}/N_{inside}$. For individuals outside the potential cluster the probability of having the disease ($p_{true-outside}$) is estimated as the sum of the number of cases observed outside the potential cluster divided by the sum of the population outside the potential cluster ($p_{estimate-outside} = C_{outside}/N_{outside}$). Thus, an individual's probability of having the disease is influenced by whether or not that individual is inside the potential cluster.

Next, the likelihood of the alternative hypothesis, L_1, is evaluated as the probability that one would observe values exactly equal to C_{inside} and $C_{outside}$ given the sample sizes (N_{inside} and $N_{outside}$), and given that $p_{true-inside} = p_{estimate-inside}$ (for individuals inside the potential cluster) and $p_{true-outside} = p_{estimate-outside}$ (for individuals outside the potential cluster). The likelihood of the null hypothesis L_0, is evaluated as the probability that one would observe values exactly equal to C_{inside} and $C_{outside}$ given the sample sizes (N_{inside} and $N_{outside}$) and given that the underlying probability of individuals for all individuals, $p_{true} = p_{true-inside} = p_{true-outside} = p_{estimate}$. The likelihood ratio for each potential cluster is evaluated as L_1/L_0.

A likelihood ratio of 1.0 implies that the null and alternative hypotheses are both equally plausible explanations for the observed data. A likelihood ratio above 1.0 indicates that there would be a higher probability of obtaining the observed data if the alternative hypothesis were true than if the null hypothesis were true. Therefore, the potential cluster with the highest likelihood ratio represents the most likely location where the null hypothesis has been violated (the potential cluster with the second highest likelihood ratio represents the second most likely location, etc.). Next, the SSS uses a randomized simulation technique known as Monte Carlo simulation to assign statistical *p*-values to each potential cluster based on the observed likelihood ratios (Kulldorff 1997; 2009).

2.6.6 Application of the SSS to forest pathology

Coulston and Riitters (2003) used a variant of the SSS that takes time into account by analyzing space-time clusters, which are "cylindrical" (i.e., circular in space with the height of the cylinder corresponding to a certain time-frame, see Figure 2.8b) to search for significant clusters of insect or pathogen damage as observed from annual forest health monitoring flights in the Pacific Northwest (Coulston and Riitters 2003).

The data for this application came from a series of annual aerial surveys, which mapped the extent of insect and pathogen damage. The survey region was divided into grid cells (locations). For each grid cell, the population was the number of hectares of forested land, and the number of cases was the number of hectares where damage was mapped.

The SSS is a potentially powerful tool for many forestry problems including searching for areas where observed tree mortality exceeds baseline levels. It has been used to search for hotspots of forest fires based on counts of the number of fires started within each of several administrative units (Tuia *et al.* 2008; Vadrevu 2008). It also has been used to search for areas where land protected for conservation is less abundant than elsewhere (Kamei and Nakagoshi 2006). In this example, the SSS is used to identify areas where the number of "cases" defined as conserved forest communities was unexpectedly low relative to the "population" of all forest communities. New variants of the SSS have been developed that can search for hot-spots using a continuous variable, rather than counts of cases (Huang *et al.* 2009); and which can search elliptical rather than circular windows (Kulldorff *et al.* 2006). The SSS cannot define a level of mortality that should be considered baseline, but can only identify subsets of a region where mortality or disease levels are significantly higher than elsewhere.

2.6.8 Space-time permutation scan statistic

The goal of the **space-time permutation scan statistic** (STPSS) is to define areas with similar diameter distributions that differ from the region as a whole. Often data are pooled from many forest inventory locations to form a diameter distribution that represents a region containing the locations. Often it is difficult to determine which groups of neighboring locations are homogeneous with respect to diameter distribution, and should therefore be combined to define regions of interest. One can modify a variant of the SSS (the space-time permutation scan statistic; STPSS) to define subsets within a larger region such that the diameter distribution of a subset is most different from the diameter distribution elsewhere.

When using diameter distributions to assess baseline mortality (either by calculating the mortality to sustain the distribution, or by looking for an expected shape) often data from individual plots must be combined because the sampled area at each location may be too small to accurately measure diameter distributions (Grenier *et al.* 1991; Rubin *et al.* 2006). The problem of knowing which plots to combine is analogous to the problem of knowing how to best combine data on disease incidence to detect hotspots where levels are significantly higher than elsewhere. The problem of deciding which locations to combine to describe diameter distributions can be solved by a modification of a variant of the spatial scan statistic (SSS described in the section above). The space-time permutation scan statistic (STPSS) is one version of a space-time scan statistic that searches for interaction effects in space and time. In other words, it controls for purely spatial (constant through time) or purely temporal (constant throughout space) patterns.

2.6.9 *Description of the STPSS*

The STPSS was originally designed as an early warning signal to detect outbreaks of disease based on data such as the number of emergency room visits where patients reported a specific set of symptoms (Kulldorff *et al.* 2005). In this example, it is not desirable to detect pure spatial trends as these would be expected if some emergency rooms are generally busier than others. Similarly, one would not wish to detect purely temporal trends because these would result if changes in weather, seasonality, days of the week or any other temporal factors influenced people's behavior in such a way as to change the likelihood that they would develop the symptoms or visit the emergency room. The beginning of an epidemic would be signaled when the number of emergency room visits at some subset of all locations was unexpectedly high for that time and place. The epidemic might ultimately spread throughout all locations, but since the goal is early detection, the STPSS should be designed to detect its initial stage.

The STPSS works in a similar manner to the SSS. First, a number of potential clusters are defined. In the SSS these were defined as a series of concentric circles around specified potential cluster centers such that successively larger circles each included one more location than the next smaller circle. In the STPSS, each circle is replaced by a series of cylinders where the height of each cylinder is defined as one or more consecutive time periods (e.g., days) up to a specified maximum height. Next for each potential cluster, the SSS described null and alternative hypotheses that the probability of an individual contracting the disease of interest inside the cluster, and the probability of contracting the disease outside the cluster were equal (H_0) or different (H_1). In the STPSS, the null hypothesis is that the number of cases within each cylindrical potential cluster is statistically dependent on the spatial and temporal extent of the cluster. In other words, the expected number of cases in the cluster is equal to the number of cases in the spatial extent of the clusters (the circular base of the cylinder) times the number of cases in the temporal extent (the "height" of the cylinder) divided by the overall number of cases. The null hypothesis is that the observed number of cases in the potential cluster is not significantly different from the expected number. The alternative hypothesis is that the observed and expected number of cases do differ significantly. The STPSS then calculates a likelihood ratio based on the likelihood of obtaining the observed data under the null or alternative hypothesis. Finally Monte Carlo simulations are used to assign *p*-values to potential clusters, just as in the SSS.

2.6.10 *Application of the STPSS to diameter distributions*

The STPSS can be used to detect subsets of a large area where the diameter distribution is different from the diameter distribution of the whole. Tree diameter is used in place of a time measurement in the statistic, and the number of trees in each forest plot is considered instead of the incidence of disease. The STPSS therefore looks for cylindrical clusters of tree density where the base of the cylinder is defined as a circle in space and the height is defined as a range of tree diameter. Purely spatial patterns (e.g., such as a change in the percent of forested land or the density of measurement plots throughout the study area) are controlled for, as are patterns purely related to diameter (e.g., small trees are more common than large trees throughout the entire region of interest). The result is that statistically significant clusters will have more or fewer than expected trees within a certain portion of the total diameter range of the population. The diameter distribution within a significant cluster will therefore differ from the diameter distribution outside of that cluster.

The STPSS has been applied to US Forest Service Forest Inventory and Analysis data from Pennsylvania (Rubin and MacFarlane 2008). They studied diameter distributions of three populations of trees: a group of oak (*Quercus*) species, red maple (*Acer rubrum*), and all species combined throughout Pennsylvania. Many significant clusters in all three populations were identified. Adjacent clusters were combined together into groups if they indicated similar diameter distributions. The statistical power of the STPSS (because use of a large maximum size considers large and small clusters while use of a small maximum is limited to only small clusters [Kulldorff *et al.* 2004]) could be decreased by reducing the maximum cluster size. By so doing, clusters would only be detected if the difference between the diameter distribution within and outside of the cluster were more pronounced. Thus, "core-zones" could be defined within each cluster group where the diameter distribution within the core zone was most different from that outside the zone. In Pennsylvania, the statewide distribution of oaks was concave indicating a lack of regeneration of oaks in the area, which has been widely reported and attributable to many factors including high deer density and fire suppression (Marquis et al. 1976; Abrams 1992). The STPSS identified two areas of Pennsylvania where the diameter distribution was more concave than expected and less concave then expected, indicating that in these areas the problem of oak regeneration was most and least severe, respectively (Figure 2.9). On the other hand, the state-wide diameter distribution of red maple was convex – perhaps typical of an increasing population (Abrams 1998). The STPSS identified two areas of the state where the convexity was more and less pronounced than expected (Figure 2.10).

2.7 Summary and conclusions

In summary then the following points are made:

1) Diameter distributions of forest stands provide valuable information on stand structures in terms of tree size, number, volume, product, and economic value for specified tree size classes. Various mathematical functions can be used to model the diameter distributions.

2) Traditionally, the negative exponential function, $N = \beta \cdot e^{-\beta \cdot D}$, has been used to establish baseline mortality. However, a linear regression model, $\ln(N) = b_0 + b_1 \cdot D$, is proposed to fit the relationship of $\ln(N)$-D for the given sample data. Once the slope coefficient b_1 is estimated from the data, the baseline mortality is calculated by $BM = 1 - e^{-b_1 \cdot \Delta D}$, where ΔD is the diameter class interval used in the sample data.

3) Microsoft® Excel® is easily used to fit the linear model above and to draw the necessary graphics such as the observed diameter histogram, the relationship of $\ln(N)$-D, and the mortality chart. In addition, chi-square analysis can be used to test the significance of differences between observed and baseline mortality.

4) Alternative models such as the quadratic model and the Weibull function can be used to improve the model fit to the observed diameter distributions, and the relationships of $\ln(N)$-D. However, these alternative models may generate non-constant baseline mortalities across the diameter classes, as well as biologically irrational values (e.g., negative values) of baseline mortality for some diameter classes.

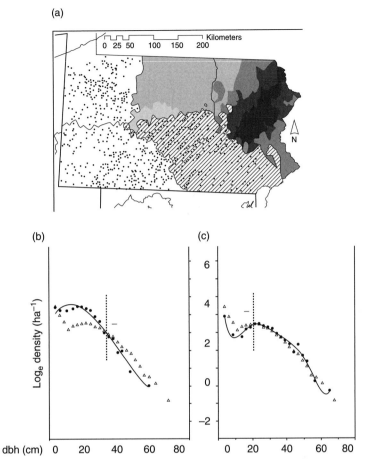

Figure 2.9 Map and diameter distributions resulting from the use of the STPSS to identify areas with anomalous diameter distributions of oaks in Pennsylvania. (a) Map of areas where anomalous diameter distributions were identified within each area. Successively darker colors represent areas of greater difference in diameter distribution, and the darkest color represents the "core zone" of each group. (b) and (c) show diameter distributions for the light and dark areas shown at top of (a), respectively. Open triangles represent the statewide diameter distribution of oaks, and black circles and regression line represent the diameter distribution within the core zone. (From Rubin and MacFarlane 2008, with permission.)

5)   Some of the newer techniques discussed here have been developed or greatly expanded within the past decade or two, but are still not used to their maximum potential. For example, spatial and space time scan statistics have a potentially broad range of applications in forestry and forest pathology problems, but at the time of writing the number of actual applications is very small.

(a)

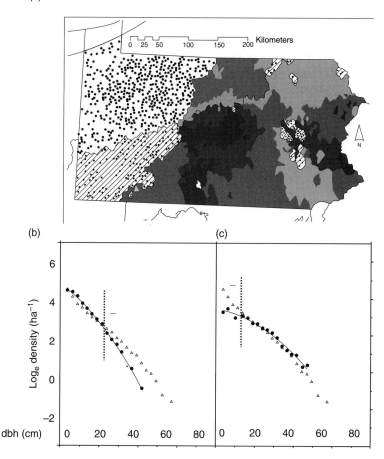

Figure 2.10 Map and diameter distributions resulting from the use of the STPSS to identify areas with anomalous diameter distributions of red maple in Pennsylvania. (a) map of areas where anomalous diameter distributions were identified. Within each area successively darker colors represent areas of greater difference in diameter distribution and the darkest color represents the "core zone" of each group. (b) and (c) show diameter distributions for the lighter and darker areas shown in (a), respectively. The open triangles represent the statewide diameter distribution of red maple, and the black circles and regression line represent the diameter distribution within the core zone. (From Rubin and MacFarlane 2008, with permission.)

6)   There also are some obvious needs in regards to assessing baseline mortality. Some of the concepts described here have been applied to levels of disease incidence, but not to actual mortality levels. For example, Lundquist *et al.* (2002) showed through stand profiling that moderate levels of disease are more consistent with management

objectives than very low levels. Can the same be shown for mortality levels? Similarly, Coulston and Riitters (2003) used the SSS to identify areas and times where disease incidence was higher than expected, but no one has yet tried this with observed mortality. Also, the work of Coomes *et al.* (2003) describing how a combination of reverse-J and negative power models offer better fits to some diameter distributions than either model alone and is potentially very powerful. If these results can be replicated, then perhaps a greater consensus can be reached as to what a stable diameter distribution for a large forest landscape should look like. Such consensus would make the modifications of the STPSS by Rubin and MacFarlane (2008) a more powerful tool.

7) There also is a great need to develop and empirically test cumulative liability indices that will accurately predict tree survival so that forests can be evaluated to see if the risk of mortality exceeding baseline levels is high before the mortality actually takes place (see Chapter 3).

Despite these needs, we conclude that baseline mortality is a useful tool to assess the health and sustainability of forest stands, by determining whether or not the forest can maintain a stable diameter distribution that balances reproduction, growth, and mortality.

References

Abrams, M.D. 1992. Fire and development of oak forests. *BioScience* **42**: 346–353.

Abrams, M.D. 1998. The red maple paradox. *BioScience* **48**: 355–364.

Alerich, C.L., Klevgard, L., Liff, C., and Miles, P.D. 2004. *The Forest Inventory and Analysis Database: Database Description and User's Guide Version 1.7. 193.US Forest Service Forest Inventory and Analysis Program*, Arlington, VA.

Avery, T.E. and Burkhart, H.E. 2002. *Forest Measurements*. 5th edition. McGraw-Hill, NY.

Bailey, R.L. and Dell, T.R. 1973. Quantifying diameter distributions with the Weibull function. *Forest Science* **19**: 97–104.

Boscoe, F.P., McLaughlin, C., Schymura, M.J., and Kielb, C.L. 2003. Visualization of the spatial scan statistic using nested circles. *Health & Place* **9**: 273–277.

Castello, J.D., Leopold, D.J., and Smallidge, P.J. 1995. Pathogens, patterns and processes in forest ecosystems. *BioScience* **45**: 16–24.

Clutter, J.L., Fortson, J.C., Pienaar, L.V., *et al.* 1992. *Timber Management: a Quantitative Approach*. Krieger Publishing Company. Malabar, FL.

Condit, R., Sukumar, R., Hubbell, S.P., and Foster, R.B. 1998. Predicting population trends from size distributions: a direct test in a tropical tree community. *American Naturalist* **152**: 495–509.

Coomes, D.A., Duncan, R.P., Allen, R.B., and Truscott, J. 2003. Disturbances prevent stem size-density distributions in natural forests from following scaling relationships. *Ecology Letters* **6**: 980–989.

Coulston, J.W. and Riitters, K.H. 2003. Geographic analysis of forest health indicators using spatial scan statistics. *Environmental Management* **31**: 764–773.

De Liocourt, F. 1898. De l'amenagement des sapinieres. *Bulletin Triemestriel Societe Forestriere de Franche Comte et Belfort, Besancon*: 396–409.

Dobbertin, M. 2005. Tree growth as an indicator of tree vitality and of tree reaction to environmental stress: a review. *European Journal of Forest Research* **124**: 319–333.

Duchesne, L., Ouimet, R., Moore, J.-D., and Paquin, R. 2005. Changes in structure and composition of maple-beech stands following sugar maple decline in Québec, Canada. *Forest Ecology & Management* **208**: 223–236.

Enquist, B.J. and Niklas, K.J. 2001. Invariant scaling relationships across tree-dominated communities. *Nature* **410**: 655–660.

Franklin, J.F., Shugart, H.H., and Harmon, M.E. 1987. Tree death as an ecological process: The causes, consequences, and variability of tree mortality. *BioScience* **37**: 550–556.

Gillis, M.D., Omule, A.Y., and Brierley, T. 2005. Monitoring Canada's forests: the National Forest Inventory. *Forestry Chronicle* **81**: 214–221.

Goff, F.G. and West, D. 1975. Canopy-understory interaction effects on forest - population structure. *Forest Science* **21**: 98–108.

Goodburn, J.M. and Lorimer, C.G. 1999. Population structure in old-growth and managed northern hardwoods: an examination of the balanced diameter distribution concept. *Forest Ecology & Management* **118**: 11–29.

Grenier, Y., Blais, L., and Lavoie, É. 1991. Aire minimum d'échantillonnage ou nombre se points de prisme nécessaires pour établir la structure d'un peuplement inéquienne. *Canadian Journal of Forest Research* **21**: 1632–1638.

Hafley, W.L. and Schreuder, H.T. 1977. Statistical distributions for fitting diameter and height data in even-aged stands. *Canadian Journal of Forest Research* **7**: 481–487.

Hansen, E.M. and Goheen, E.M. 2000. *Phellinus weirii* and other native root pathogens as determinants of forest structure and process in western North America. *Annual Review Phytopathology* **38**: 315–339.

Hartmann, H., Beaudet, M., and Messier, C. 2008. Using longitudinal survival probabilities to test field vigor estimates in sugar maple (*Acer saccharum* Marsh.). *Forest Ecology & Management* **256**: 1771–1779.

Hawksworth, F.G. 1977. The 6-class dwarf mistletoe rating system. *Gen. Tech. Rep. RM-48*. USDA Forest Service, Rocky Mountain Forest and Range Experiment Station., Ft. Collins, CO.

Hyink, D.M. and Moser, Jr., J.W. 1983. A generalized framework for projecting forest yield and stand structure using diameter distributions. *Forest Science* **29**: 85–95.

Hett, J.M. 1971. A dynamic analysis of age in sugar maple seedlings. *Ecology* **52**: 1071–1074.

Hett, J.M. and Loucks, O.L. 1968. Application of life-table analyses to tree seedlings in Quetico Park, Ontario. *Forestry Chronicle* **44**: 29–32.

Hett, J.M. and Loucks, O.L. 1971. Sugar maple (*Acer saccharum* Marsh.) seedling mortality. *Journal Ecology* **59**: 507–520.

Hett, J.M. and Loucks, O.L. 1976. Age structure models of balsam fir and eastern hemlock. *Journal Ecology* **64**: 1029–1044.

Holdenrieder, O., Pautasso, M., Weisberg, P.J., and Lonsdale, D. 2004. Tree diseases and landscape processes: the challenge of landscape pathology. *Trends in Ecology & Evolution* **19**: 446–452.

Huang, L., Tiwari, R., Zuo, J., Kulldorff, M., and Feuer, E.J. 2009. Weighted normal spatial scan statistic for heterogeneous population data. *Journal American Statistical Association* **104**: 886–898.

Kamei, M. and Nakagoshi, N. 2006. Geographic assessment of present protected areas in Japan for representativeness of forest communities. *Biodiversity Conservation* **15**: 4583–4600.

Kohira, M. and Ninomiya, I. 2003. Detecting tree populations at risk for forest conservation management: using single-year vs. long-term inventory data. *Forest Ecology & Management* **174**: 423–435.

Kulldorff, M. 1997. A spatial scan statistic. *Communication in Statistics – Theory & Methods* **26**: 1481–1496.

Kulldorff, M. 2009. *SaTScan User's Guide*. Version 8.0. 65.Online at: www.satscan.org [Accessed November 2010].

Kulldorff, M., Heffernan, R., Hartman, J., *et al.* 2005. A space-time permutation scan statistic for disease outbreak detection. *PLoS Medicine* **2**: e59.

Kulldorff, M., Huang, L., Pickle, L., and Duczmal, L. 2006. An elliptical spatial scan statistic. *Statistics in Medicine* **25**: 3929–3943.

Kulldorff, M., Tango, T., and Park, P.J. 2003. Power comparisons for disease clustering tests. *Computational Statistics and Data Analysis* **42**: 665–684.

Kulldorff, M., Zhang, Z., Hartman, J., *et al.* 2004. Benchmark data and power calculations for evaluating disease outbreak detection systems. *Morbidity & Mortality Weekly Report* **53**: 144–151.

Leak, W.B. 1964. An expression of diameter distribution for unbalanced, uneven-aged stands and forests. *Forest Science* **10**: 39–50.

Leak, W.B. 1965. The J-shaped probability distribution. *Forest Science* **11**: 405–409.

Leak, W.B. 1996. Long-term structural change in uneven-aged northern hardwoods. *Forest Science* **42**: 160–165.

Liu, C., Zhang, L., Davis, C.J., *et al.* 2002. A finite mixture model for characterizing the diameter distribution of mixed-species forest stands. *Forest Science* **48**: 653–661.

Lorimer, C.G. and Frelich, L.E. 1984. A simulation of equilibrium diameter distribution of sugar maple (*Acer saccharum*). *Bulletin Torrey Botanical Club* **111**: 193–199.

Lorimer, C.G. and Frelich, L.E. 1998. A structural alternative to chronosequence analysis for uneven-aged northern hardwood stands. *Journal Sustainable Forestry* **6**: 347–366.

Lundquist, J.E. and Beatty, J.S. 1999. A conceptual model for defining and assessing condition of forest stands. *Environmental Management* **23**: 519–525.

Lundquist, J.E., Goheen, E.M., and Goheen, D.J. 2002. Measuring positive, negative, and null impacts of forest disturbances: a case study using dwarf mistletoe on douglas fir. *Environmental Management* **30**: 793–800.

Manion, P.D. 2003. Evolution of concepts in forest pathology. *Phytopathology* **93**: 1052–1055.

Manion, P.D. and Griffin, D.H. 2001. Large landscape scale analysis of tree death in the Adirondack Park, New York. *Forest Science* **47**: 542–549.

Manion, P.D., Griffin, D.H., and Rubin, B.D. 2001. Ice damage impacts on the health of the northern New York State forest. *Forestry Chronicle* **77**: 619–625.

Manion, P.D. and Lachance, D. 1992. *Forest Decline Concepts*. American Phytopathological Society, St. Paul, MN.

Marquis, D.A., Eckert, P.L., and Roach, B.A. 1976. Acorn weevils, rodents, and deer all contribute to oak-regeneration difficulties in Pennsylvania. *Res. Pap. NE-356, 5.USDA Forest Service*, Upper Derby, PA.

Mathiasen, R.L., Nickrent, D.L., Shaw, D.C., and Watson, D.M. 2008. Mistletoes: pathology, systematics, ecology and management. *Plant Disease* **92**: 998–1006.

Meyer, H.A. 1952. Structure, growth, and drain in balanced uneven-aged forests. *Journal Forestry* **50**: 85–92.

Meyer, H.A. and Stevenson, D.D. 1943. The structure and growth of virgin beech-birch-maple-hemlock forests in northern Pennsylvania. *Journal Agricultural Research* **67**: 465–484.

Midgley, J.J. 2001. Do mixed-species mixed-size indigenous forests also follow the self thinning line? *Trends in Ecology & Evolution* **16**: 661–662.

Morin, R.S., Liebhold, A.M., and Gottschalk, K.W. 2004. Area-wide analysis of hardwood defoliator effects on tree conditions in the Allegheny Plateau. *Northern Journal Applied Forestry* **21**: 31–39.

Muller-Landau, H.C., Condit, R.S., *et al.* 2006. Comparing tropical forest tree size distributions with the predictions of metabolic ecology and equilibrium models. *Ecology Letters* **9**: 589–602.

Munck, I.A. and Manion, P.D. 2006. Landscape-scale impact of beech bark disease in response to slope and aspect in New York State. *Forest Science* **52**: 503–510.

OMNR. 2004. *Ontario Tree Marking Guide*. version 1.1. Ontario Ministry of Natural Resources, Toronto, ON.

Pulido, F.J., Díaz, M., and Hidalgo de Trucios, S.J. 2001. Size structure and regeneration of Spanish holm oak *Quercus ilex* forests and dehesas: effects of agroforestry use on their long-term sustainability. *Forest Ecology & Management* **146**: 1–13.

Rawlings, J.O., Pantula, S.G., and Dickey, D.A. 1998. *Applied Regression Analysis. A Research Tool*. 2nd edition. Springer-Verlag, New York.

Riitters, K.H. and Coulston, J.W. 2005. Hot spots of perforated forest in the eastern United States. *Environmental Management* **35**: 483–492.

Rouvinen, S. and Kuuluvainen, T. 2005. Tree diameter distributions in natural and managed old *Pinus sylvestris*-dominated forests. *Forest Ecology & Management* **208**: 45–61.

Rubin, B.D. and MacFarlane, D.W. 2008. Using the space-time permutation scan statistic to map anomalous diameter distributions drawn from landscape-scale forest inventories. *Forest Science* **54**: 523–533.

Rubin, B.D. and Manion, P.D. 2001. Landscape-scale forest structure in northern New York and potential successional impacts of the 1998 ice storm. *Forestry Chronicle* **77**: 613–618.

Rubin, B.D. and Manion, P.D. 2005. Characterizing regional forest health and sustainability from diameter distributions, baseline mortality, and cumulative liabilities. In: Lundquist, J.E. and Hamlin, R.C. (eds). *Forest Pathology: from Genes to Landscapes*. American Phyopathological Society Press, St. Paul, MN.

Rubin, B.D., Manion, P.D., and Faber-Langendoen, D. 2006. Diameter distributions and structural sustainability in forests. *Forest Ecology & Management* **222**: 427–438.

Schwartz, J.W., Nagel, L.M., and Webster, C.R. 2005. Effects of uneven-aged management on diameter distribution and species composition of northern hardwoods in Upper Michigan. *Forest Ecology & Management* **211**: 356–370.

Solberg, S. and Strand, L. 1999. Crown density assessments, control surveys and reproducibility. *Environmental Monitoring & Assessment* **56**: 75–86.

Song, C. and Kulldorff, M. 2003. Power evaluation of disease clustering tests. *Journal of Health Geographics* **2**: 1–8.

Steinman, J. 2000. Tracking the health of trees over time on forest health monitoring plots. In: *Proceedings of the IUFRO Conference Integrated Tools for Natural Resources: Inventories for the 21st Century, USDA Forest Service Gen. Tech. Rep. NC-GTR-212*. Hansen, M. and Burk, T. (eds).

Tuia, D., Ratle, F., Lasaponara, R., *et al.* 2008. Scan statistics analysis of forest fire clusters. *Communications in Nonlinear Science and Numerical Simulation* **13**: 1689–1694.

Vadrevu, K.P. 2008. Analysis of fire events and controlling factors in Eastern India using spatial scan and multivariate statistics. *Geografiska Annaler: Series A, Physical Geography* **90**: 315–328.

Vanclay, J.K. 1994. *Modeling Forest Growth and Yield: Application to Mixed Tropical Forests*. CAB International, Oxford, UK.

Weiss, N.A. 2008. *Introductory Statistics*. 8th edition. Pearson, San Fransisco.

West, D.C., Shugart, H.H., and Ranney, R.W. 1981. Population structure of forests over a large area. *Forest Science* **27**: 701–710.

Westphal, C., Tremer, N., von Oheimb, G., *et al.* 2006. Is the reverse J-shaped diameter distribution universally applicable in European virgin beech forests? *Forest Ecology & Management* **223**: 75–83.

Zhang, L., Packard, K.C., and Liu, C. 2003. A comparison of estimation methods for fitting Weibull and Johnson's S_B distributions to mixed spruce-fir stands in northeastern North America. *Canadian Journal of Forest Research* **33**: 1340–1347.

Zhang, L., Gove, J.H., Liu, C., and Leak, W.B. 2001. A finite mixture of two Weibull distributions for modeling the diameter distributions of rotated-sigmoid, uneven-aged stands. *Canadian Journal Forest Research* **31**: 1654–1659.

3

How do we do it, and what does it mean? Forest health case studies

J.D. CASTELLO, S.A. TEALE, AND J.A. CALE

3.1 Introduction and assumptions

In this chapter we take you through the process of calculating baseline mortality, and comparing it to observed mortality to assess the sustainability of four sample forests. We present four case studies, each of which utilizes a dataset from a different forest type and region of the world.

The use of the baseline mortality approach to assess forest health is dependent upon some important underlying assumptions that must be considered for appropriate use of the method and interpretation of results, and which include the following (we first mentioned these in Chapter 1, but it is worth repeating here): (1) The method generally is applicable only at the landscape scale to minimize the influence of individual stand peculiarities and sampling artifacts. It may, however, be appropriate at the stand level if the stand is fully stocked, and is properly sampled (i.e., sample plots are large enough or sufficiently numerous to provide an adequate representation of all diameter/size classes and species of trees in the forest. The plots must be randomly selected to remove sampling bias). (2) The method used to quantify observed mortality assumes that dead trees remain identifiable to species for about the same time that it takes for the living trees to grow into the next diameter class. Therefore, the decay rate and the growth rate must be taken into account when determining the optimum width of the diameter classes. (3) Observed mortality includes all mortality regardless of cause including cutting, fires, landslides, diseases, and insect pests, etc. (4) The management and disease/pest history of the forest should be known,

Forest Health: An Integrated Perspective, ed. John D. Castello and Stephen A. Teale. Published by Cambridge University Press. © Cambridge University Press 2011.

50

and the silvics and ecology of the species comprising the forest should be understood to interpret the results of these analyses in a meaningful ecological context.

What data are needed to conduct forest health assessments utilizing this approach? The field plot data needed to conduct these analyses include the number of all live and dead trees per unit area identified to species, as well as their dbh (diameter at breast height = 1.4 m above ground level). Such data usually are collected during routine forest inventories, forest health monitoring activities, or during research activities by foresters, forest ecologists, pathologists, or entomologists. Foresters and those conducting inventory or monitoring activities usually collect data from **prism plots** (i.e., variable-radius plots or point sampling), whereas ecological research activities typically utilize fixed-area plots. Both types of data can be used, but data from prism plots require calculation of expansion factors in order to convert tree numbers to densities by diameter class. In this chapter we provide four datasets, three of which utilize data obtained from fixed-area plots. The datasets from northern New York were obtained from prism plots. In Appendix B we provide step by step instructions for fitting a negative exponential model, calculating baseline mortality, and statistically comparing observed mortality (OM) to baseline mortality (BM).

3.2 The health of the forests of northern New York State

In Chapter 1, a few examples from northern New York State were introduced to illustrate the baseline mortality concept of forest health. We expand on those examples with this case study. We will utilize data from this area collected in 2001 by Paul Manion and his students.

The political and industrial history of this region is a key determinant of current forest conditions. The Adirondack Park is a 2.4 million ha patchwork of public and private lands located in northern New York State. The area was designated in 1892 by law to protect the region from unregulated forest clearing that was common during the late 1800s. It was the culmination of a preservation movement that grew out of concern about widespread tree cutting to support the lumber, paper, leather-tanning, and iron-smelting industries in the Adirondack Mountains that began in earnest in the 1850s. Preservation advocates championed the protection of the Adirondack region as a vast public park, and influential New York City merchants feared that continued logging would lead to reduced flows in the Hudson River and Erie Canal, the major regional transportation corridors of the day. The Park was originally conceived simply as an area in which additions to the Adirondack Park would be concentrated.

Today, the Park is a thriving mix of state and private forests, wetlands, waterways, and human settlement.

The Adirondack Forest Preserve (AFP) is the 1.0 million ha of state-owned land within the Adirondack Park. The New York State Constitution states that the timber in the AFP shall not be sold, removed, or destroyed. Thus, as lands within the Park are acquired by the state and added to the AFP, all timber harvesting and other forms of forest management as well as most kinds of development cease. What has been the impact of "protection" on the health of the state forests within the AFP? Is the forest returning to its virgin state, or have exploitative timber harvesting and other human influences left an indelible mark? Here, we will use the baseline mortality method to seek some insight into these questions.

In the 1890s, beech bark disease (BBD), an exotic disease complex of American beech (*Fagus grandifolia*) that involved an introduced scale insect and a possibly introduced canker fungus, spread into North America from Europe. By the 1960s it had moved into the Adirondack Mountains. The disease continues to spread throughout the range of American beech in the USA. Its ecological and economic impacts have been profound. How has the disease impacted the health of American beech in northern New York?

In 2001, Manion and his students established 154 randomly selected sampling points throughout state-owned forest lands in northern New York including within and outside the AFP. The online dataset contains the essential data to answer the questions below (i.e., measurements from approximately 8500 trees representing 77 species from 462 prism plots established on the 154 random sample points, 97 on state land not in the AFP (NNY dataset), and 57 within the AFP (AFP dataset). These data were compiled and analyzed using Microsoft® Excel®. Stepwise instructions for Excel 2007 for Windows are provided for your convenience in Appendix B.

3.2.1 Questions and instructions

a) Download the Excel workbook named NNY and AFP datasets from the web (in a folder named Chapter 3 datasets) onto your computer. Follow the detailed stepwise instructions in Appendix B for this dataset to graph a diameter-distribution plot for all tree species combined on the state forestlands in northern New York State (NNY) that are not within the AFP (Adirondack Forest Preserve). Use the sort and filter functions of MS Excel to separate those state lands within the AFP from those outside the AFP (i.e., the NNY state lands) to create two new worksheets. Label one worksheet NNY and the other AFP. Plot the diameter-distribution graphs on separate charts. These two sampling regions contained a

different number of prism plots. This difference is integral to the calculation of observed trees/acre and, subsequently, to the generation of the
correct region and species figures (Please see Appendix B, Section 6.1 for
the proper sampling plot numbers for each region).

b) Then, using the sort and filter functions of Excel again, separate out
the American beech (AB) and the yellow birch (YB) trees from each of the
two datasets (AFP and NNY). Graph the diameter distributions of AB in
NNY and the AFP on two charts, and those of YB in NNY and the AFP on
two more charts.

c) Generate and graph the first order linear regression lines (negative
exponential) for each of the six graphs in (a) and (b) above.

d) Is the diameter distribution of negative exponential form? How can you
tell? What are the R^2 values for each graph?

e) Following the stepwise instructions, calculate the BM for all tree species
combined in the NNY forest. In the AFP forest. Now calculate the BM for
AB and YB on the NNY and AFP forests. *Also calculate the BM using the slope
of the regression lines.*

f) Now calculate and graph the total OM by diameter class on each of the
six charts. Use chi-square analysis to determine if OM is significantly
different from BM. Is the OM for all species combined in the NNY forest
generally above or below BM? Is OM for all tree species combined on the
AFP forest generally above or below BM? If not, in which diameter classes
are the differences statistically significant?

g) Do the same analyses as in (e) above for AB and YB in both the NNY
and AFP forests. Is OM significantly different from BM for AB in the
NNY forests? In AFP forests? What about YB? If so, in which diameter
classes?

h) Are the forests of the AFP sustainable? What about the NNY forests? Do
the same for AB. Is the population of AB sustainable in the AFP forest?
In the NNY forest? What about YB?

3.2.2 Explanation of methodology

a) A diameter-distribution plot is a graph of the density of live trees (y-axis)
plotted against their dbh (x-axis). For a distribution to be sustainable, the
mortality in each diameter class must be equal to the difference in
density between each diameter class and the next larger diameter class.
The baseline mortality that will sustain a negative exponential distribution is constant across all diameter classes. You cannot simply tally the
total number of stems by diameter class and graph them on a chart of
the number of stems vs. diameter class because prism plots have a larger

radius (and therefore area) for large trees than for small trees. Therefore, for the New York State datasets you must generate multiple expansion factors (e.g., one for each 0.25 cm diameter class in this case study) that convert the number of trees per prism plot to the number of trees/acre (density) by diameter class. We have calculated the appropriate expansion factors for you for these data (Manion and Griffin 2001). Calculate the observed density of all stems (of all species combined) for both the AFP and NNY forests in each 2.5 cm diameter class. Then graph the natural log of that number on the y-axis, across diameter class on the x-axis.

b) Least squares regression analysis can be performed in Excel on the data used to create the diameter-distribution charts above. First, identify the dependent and independent variables.

c) Compute the R^2 value of the linear first order least squares regression equation generated by Excel. The linear first order regression model seems to fit these diameter distributions with a high correlation coefficient (generally 0.90 or greater), and the residuals appear to be randomly distributed. This means that the observed diameter distribution is negative exponential, and with the added benefit that the BM needed to maintain this distribution is constant across all diameter classes.

d) Baseline mortality then is calculated from the equation: $m = 1 - e^{a\Delta x}$ (Manion and Griffin 2001), where m = BM, a = slope of the best-fit regression line of the natural log of live stem density by diameter class distribution plot in a, Δx = width of each diameter class (1 in in this example), and e = base of the natural logarithm (i.e., 2.71). Graph it on the chart above. Use a separate y-axis for percent mortality on the right side of the chart for this purpose. (Alternatively, BM can be calculated simply by subtracting the density of the observed live trees in one diameter class from the density of the trees in the next lower diameter class, and dividing that number by the density of the lower diameter class multiplied by 100, across the entire distribution. This method should give the same BM as calculated from the above equation).

e) Using the appropriate datasets, graph total percent OM (percent observed mortality by diameter class (%OM) = number of dead trees in that diameter class divided by the total number of live and dead trees in that diameter class multiplied by 100) by diameter class on the chart (use the right y-axis for mortality in part d above for this purpose).

f) Statistically significant deviations of OM from BM in specific diameter classes are determined using chi-square contingency table analysis. Stepwise instructions are presented in Appendix B.

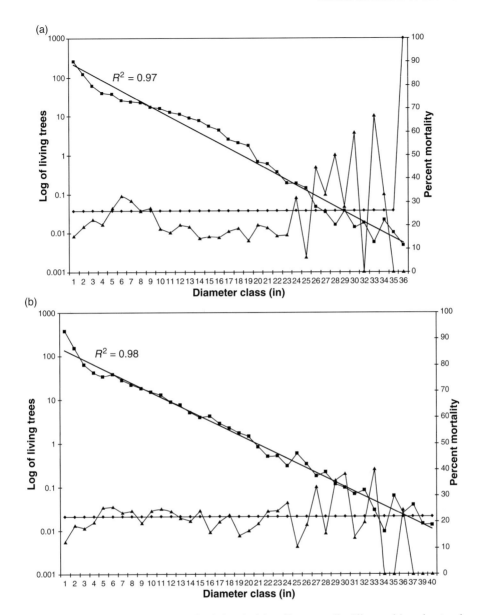

Figure 3.1 Observed mortality (triangles), baseline mortality (diamonds), and natural log of the observed (squares) and predicted (thick solid line) diameter distribution of all living trees on: (a) NNY (northern NY) state forest lands, and (b) AFP (Adirondack Forest Preserve) state forest lands. (Data with permission from P.D. Manion.)

3.2.3 Answers and interpretation

Figures 3.1a and b show the chart of the natural log of live stem density across diameter classes for all species combined in the NNY and AFP forests, respectively. The graphs show that the predicted and observed densities of living trees by diameter class fit a negative exponential model quite well with R^2 values = 0.97 and 0.98 for the NNY and AFP state forest populations, respectively. The NNY state forest lands are sustained by a BM of approximately 26%, while those of the AFP are sustained by a somewhat lower BM of approximately 22%. The difference may result from differences in species composition of the two forests that reflect past timber harvesting in the NNY forests, as well as different land use histories and management practices. Nonetheless, the close fit of the observed to the predicted diameter distribution suggests sustainability of both the NNY and AFP forests.

Sustainability of both populations is corroborated by an analysis of OM, which in both the NNY and AFP forests does not deviate significantly from BM except in a couple of the largest diameter classes (Figures 3.1a and b), which most likely reflects inadequate sampling in these larger diameter classes, which perhaps did not accurately describe the actual mortality in these size classes.

A comparison of the predicted and observed densities of AB on the NNY and AFP state forest lands again show a good fit to the negative exponential model with R^2 values of 0.92 and 0.97, respectively (Figures 3.2a and b). These diameter distributions are sustained by BMs of 35% and 28%, respectively.

The fate of American beech presents an interesting dilemma. What will become of it? There are two schools of thought. American beech is susceptible to BBD. The disease kills susceptible trees greater than 15 cm dbh. In the classical BBD scenario, susceptible beech trees are more likely to become infested with scale insects when they reach 15 cm dbh or larger, at which time they are infected and killed by the fungal pathogen *Neonectria faginata*. According to the first school of thought the dying and death of large, susceptible trees results in the formation of beech thickets of root-sprout origin, which typically become diseased when they reach the susceptible size classes (approximately 15 cm dbh or larger, Houston 1975). Thus, rather than removing beech from the forest, BBD induces a cycle of large tree mortality followed by dense disease-susceptible beech thickets, which represents the future of American beech in BBD "aftermath" forests. The dense beech thickets also shade out regeneration of the more commercially desirable sugar maple (Hane 2003). Thus, a northern hardwood forest dominated by thickets of young beech, with older dead or defective beech stems with minimal sugar maple regeneration is predicted.

The second school of thought presents a different scenario. Beech trees affected by BBD do not root sucker any more so than healthy beech trees (Jones and Raynal 1987). In fact, healthy disease-resistant trees produce many more (nine-fold) root suckers than diseased trees (MacKenzie 2005). Root suckering is

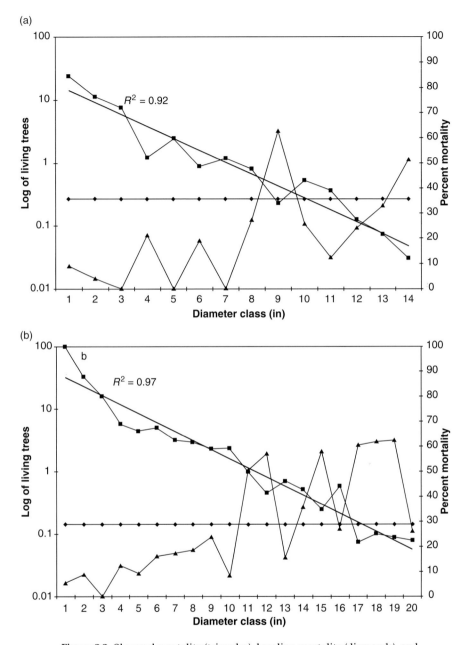

Figure 3.2 Observed mortality (triangles), baseline mortality (diamonds), and natural log of the observed (squares) and predicted (thick solid line) diameter distribution of the living American beech (AB) trees on: (a) NNY (northern NY) state forest lands, and (b) AFP (Adirondack Forest Preserve) state forest lands. (Data with permission from P.D. Manion.)

favored only by cutting. Although there is mortality of larger-diameter trees, this is compensated for by more than sufficient beech regeneration. Furthermore, there is evidence for resistance to BBD in the northern hardwood forest in the presence of large healthy beech trees in northern New England where the disease has been present for many decades, as well as in the AFP (Figure 3.2b). Thus, both beech and sugar maple will persist in the northern hardwood forest. Many of us who have worked in the northern hardwood forest can identify specific locations where each of these two scenarios is apparent. But which one represents the future of the northern hardwood forests of northern New York?

An analysis of the entire Adirondack region using the BM approach may provide a solution to this dilemma. We hypothesize that if the first school of thought is correct (i.e., significantly higher beech density in the smaller diameter classes coupled with significantly higher than baseline mortality in larger diameter classes); then this should be reflected in a rotated-sigmoid diameter distribution, rather than a negative exponential diameter distribution. Fitting both models to the AB diameter distribution data in the AFP and NNY datasets shows that both the negative exponential and the rotated-sigmoid models fit the AB diameter distribution in both the AFP and NNY state forests (Figures 3.2a and b) very well, as reflected in R^2 values of 0.92 and 0.97 for the NNY and AFP forests, respectively; versus R^2 values of 0.99 and 0.99 for the NNY and AFP forests, respectively, using the rotated-sigmoid model (calculations not shown).

The analysis supports both hypotheses because the closeness of the R^2 values makes it impossible to accept or to reject either hypothesis at this time. There is no unambiguous statistical test that can be used to determine which model provides the best fit to the diameter distribution given such close R^2 values. In reality, this scenario reflects our observations from 30 years of work in these forests. Some stands clearly are large thickets of American beech, and the diameter distribution of these stands best fits a rotated-sigmoid model. Other stands are not comprised of beech thickets, and thus fit a negative exponential diameter distribution. OM is significantly above BM in the largest diameter classes on the AFP, reflecting the impact of BBD; OM also is significantly below BM in the lowest diameter classes (Figure 3.2b). This pattern also is seen with AB on the NNY state forest lands (Figure 3.2a). This current pattern of OM, if sustained, suggests that small to midsize AB will become more prevalent while larger sizes will become less common in both forests. The greater slope of the regression line for living beech in comparison to other species clearly reflects this development. If conditions of the past continue, excess mortality in the larger classes will lead to a steeper density distribution line and a higher BM. This will ultimately lead to a different set of sustainability parameters. But, the presence of living beech in the 20 inch diameter class in the AB population of the

AFP suggests the presence of resistance to BBD, and thus perhaps lower mortality in the larger diameter classes of the future. We may be observing an incipient change in forest structure toward more prevalent beech thickets, but currently the problem is of insufficient scale to affect the diameter distribution on a landscape level. Only periodic, long-term monitoring can settle this issue. Presently, the excess mortality in the larger diameter classes is counterbalanced by lower mortality in the smaller diameter classes to result in a stable diameter distribution, and a sustainable beech population (Figure 3.2). The analysis suggests that the current structure of AB in the AFP and the NNY state forests are both sustainable at the current time, although perhaps not desirable from the viewpoint of management objectives (see below). An analysis of the sugar maple (we suggest that you do it for yourself) population in NNY and the AFP will show that it, too, has a sustainable diameter distribution with observed mortalities close to baseline, and an observed density distribution that closely fits the negative exponential model. Furthermore, cutting in the NNY forest does not seem to have negatively impacted the sustainability of either American beech or sugar maple.

A comparison of the predicted and observed densities of YB on the NNY and AFP state forest lands again show a reasonable fit to the negative exponential model with R^2 values of 0.85 and 0.86, respectively, (Figure 3.3a and b). These diameter distributions are sustained by BMs of 20 and 15%, respectively (Figure 3.3), once again probably reflecting the influence of different past management practices on the NNY forests compared to the AFP state lands. Both populations show an inexplicable deficit in the numbers of trees in the 3–4 in or 4–5 in diameter classes for the NNY and AFP lands, respectively (Figures 3.3a and b). OM of the YB population in the AFP forests is significantly above BM levels in almost all diameter classes, which is not observed in the NNY state forest lands. This level of mortality clearly is unsustainable. A 1996 survey of the Adirondacks (Manion and Griffin 2001) revealed the same excess in OM of YB. We believe that it is now appropriate to initiate research to uncover the cause of this mortality. In addition, the upper diameter limit of the YB in the NNY state forests is approximately half of the potential diameter for this species, which is a result of timber harvesting in these forests. The OM was more or less evenly distributed among the size classes suggesting that YB may decline in importance in the future. No consistent disease signs or symptoms were detected among living or dead trees that would explain the elevated observed mortality in the AFP population. The YB population of the NNY state forests is sustainable, whereas that in the AFP is not.

If we refer back to Table 1.1 in Chapter 1, we can try to determine whether these two forested landscapes are healthy. Is OM generally in line with BM? Yes, for both state forest lands of NNY and the AFP, with some exceptions for selected species as discussed above. So, despite cutting in the state forests of NNY, these

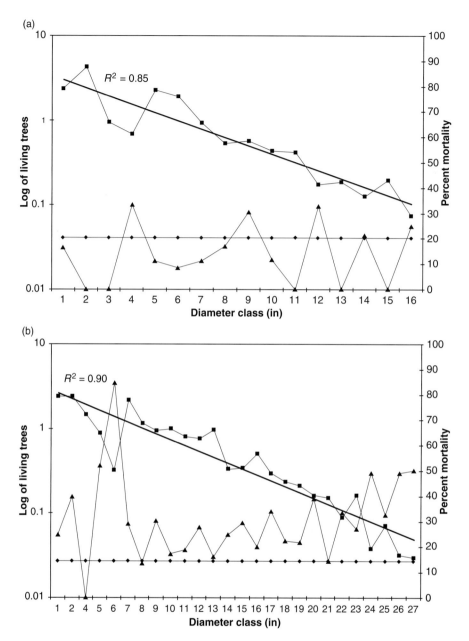

Figure 3.3 Observed mortality (triangles), baseline mortality (diamonds), and natural log of the observed (squares) and predicted (thick solid line) diameter distribution of the living yellow birch (YB) trees on: (a) NNY (northern NY) state forest lands, and (b) AFP (Adirondack Forest Preserve) state forest lands. (Data with permission from P.D. Manion.)

forests remain sustainable. OM generally approximates BM except for the top two or three largest diameter classes. But the BM needed to sustain them is different, 26 vs. 22% for the NNY and AFP state forests, respectively, which reflects past stand and management histories. The diameter distributions of all species combined on both the NNY and AFP forests is sustainable (Figure 3.1). Mortality in some species (e.g., YB Figure 3.3) is compensated for by growth in other species (e.g., AB Figure 3.2) to create an overall sustainable forest system. But are the forests in NNY and the AFP healthy (i.e., productive as well as sustainable. See Table 1.1 Do these forests meet their management objectives? The NNY state forest lands are producing small saw timber, so are meeting the management objectives set for them by the state. But besides commodity production, many forests must meet multiple management object-ives including the NNY and especially the AFP forest. Objectives may include timber, biodiversity conservation, recreation, wildlife management goals, etc. These objectives differ for the different state lands within the AFP and NNY. So, it is impossible to generalize with respect to the overall management object-ives, (i.e., the productivity, and thus the health) of these forests. But, we believe both forests are sustainable. Preliminary analysis has indicated that beech thickets significantly reduce understory herbaceous plant biodiversity (Cale *et al.* 2010).

It must be stressed that these analyses must be interpreted in an ecological context that includes the disturbance and management histories of the land-scape, as well as the ecology and silvics of the component species.

It is important to understand that these analyses do not characterize the health "potential" of a forest. Rather, sustainability is characterized based upon the current and past conditions of that forest. One approach to evaluating the future sustainability of a forest is to assess the cumulative liabilities present in the forest. In other words, is it possible to evaluate/assess the likelihood that a tree will grow into the next diameter class? Rubin and Manion (2005) developed and incorporated a cumulative liabilities index based on individual tree evalu-ation of key indicators of disease, dieback, and damage in relation to baseline mortality to make judgments on the health and sustainability of the New York forests. Their system first sums for each tree, the liability scores for main stem failure, four disease and injury indicators, crown class, dead branches, and twig dieback. Trees with no liability scores are healthy. Those with liability scores of 1 or 2 have slight liabilities. Those with a score greater than 8 are not likely to grow into the next diameter class. If the proportion of trees in each diameter class with severe liabilities is approximately equal to the BM, then this suggests a sustainable population structure. Alternatively, if the proportion of trees with severe liabilities is greater than the calculated BM, then mortality is likely to exceed BM in the near future. This system provides a forward-looking temporal dimension to forest health and sustainability assessment, and deserves to be further refined and tested.

3.3 Mountain beech in New Zealand

We selected this case study to demonstrate the use of the BM method of assessment on a landscape that is composed of a mosaic of even-aged stands. Mountain beech (*Nothofagus solandri* var. *cliffortioides*) dominates approximately 20% of the forests in New Zealand on both the North and South islands, and occurs mostly as a mosaic of even-aged, single-species stands on comparatively high and dry sites (Wardle 1984). Stand structure in these forests is influenced by large-scale disturbances that involve synchronous long-term cycles of dieback and regrowth over very large areas (Wardle and Allen 1983). The onset and magnitude of dieback may be related to factors that increase the susceptibility to disturbances (e.g., advanced stand age, low vigor, discrete disturbance events, pests, and pathogens).

In the 1970s, a network of 250 permanent plots (400 m^2 each) was established in three adjacent watersheds in the Craigieburn Research Area on the eastern slopes of the Southern Alps near Canterbury on the South Island to document a developing case of dieback. These forests occur between 650 and 1350 m elevation, and cover a total area of 5000–6000 ha. In each plot, the dbh of all trees was measured, and then tagged for a total of about 21 000 trees. Most of the trees on each of these plots have been remeasured eight times (1974, 1976, 1978, 1980, 1983, 1993, 1999, and 2004) at various intervals resulting in a 30-year dataset. The remeasurements continue. Two heavy snowfalls in 1968 and 1973 caused extensive damage in some of the beech forests of the Harper Watershed. Most of the damage involved crown breakage, but uprooting, tilting, and main bole breakage also were observed (Wardle and Allen 1983). Significant structural damage from the two storms was recorded in about 30% of the plots, mostly from those plots located at the lower elevations. By the time of the 1983 remeasurement, basal area was continuing to decrease substantially, and many trees were dying, even those that sustained little or no direct damage from the snowstorms. The mortality was associated with a pinhole beetle outbreak that caused the death mostly of the larger trees (Wardle and Allen 1983). Trees on 28 of the plots suffered notable dieback and mortality during and following this event. The watershed forest was relatively stable during the period from approximately 1983 to 1993, when disturbance consisted mostly of localized windthrow-associated mortality. In 1994, landslides caused by an earthquake resulted in widespread tree mortality (Allen *et al.*, 1999).

Important questions relating to the structure and sustainability of this forest are: What are the long-term effects of the mortality caused by the snow event and the earthquake on the health and sustainability of the montane *Nothofagus* forests on these watersheds, if any? Are all stands equally impacted? If not, why not?

For this analysis, we utilized a subset of 107 of the total 250 plot dataset because the remaining plots contained many dead trees for which no diameter measurements were available. Of these 107 plots, trees on 19 plots were damaged in the 1973 snow storm event, and those on the remaining 88 plots were undamaged in that event. These datasets (see the file named NZ mt. beech datasets in the folder named Chapter 3 datasets, on the website); were selected for you to evaluate the structural changes in damaged, undamaged, and all forest plots combined for the years 1983, 1993, and 1999 in relation to sustainability.

3.3.1 Questions and instructions

a) Open the file named NZmt.beechdataset.xls. Follow the detailed instructions beginning on p14 of Appendix B for this dataset (**Instructions for baseline mortality analysis of 1983 NZ mt. beech dataset using Microsoft® Excel® 2007**). Calculate and graph the BMs for the damaged, undamaged, and all plots combined datasets for 1983, as well as the natural logarithm of live trees by diameter class for each dataset, separately.

b) Calculate and graph the OM by diameter class for the combined plots dataset, as well as for the damaged and undamaged plots separately for 1983. Graph the OM on the charts in (a) above. Conduct the chi-square analysis, and determine if OM is significantly different from BM? If so, at what diameter classes? For which set of plots?

c) Plot the BM and OM data for the combined plots for the three years (1983, 1993, and 1999) on the same graph. Color code the lines so you can better see how BM and OM have changed from 1983 to 1999. What has happened to BM from 1983 to 1993 to 1999? What has happened to OM during the same time frame?

d) Are the mountain beech forests of the Harper Catchment sustainable or not? Is the observed mortality in the snow-damaged plots a management or sustainability concern? What was the impact of the region-wide mortality caused by the earthquake-induced landslides in 1994?

3.3.2 Answers and interpretation

a) The diameter distribution charts for all three datasets (damaged, undamaged, and all plots) show a good fit of the data to a negative exponential model (R^2 ranging from 0.88 to 0.98, Figures 3.4, 3.5, and 3.6).

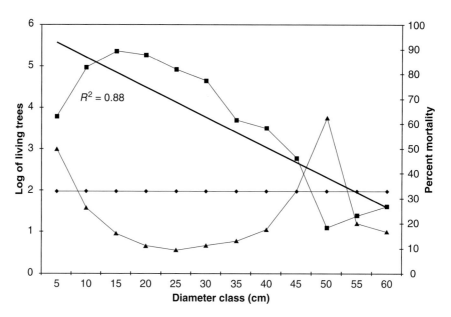

Figure 3.4 Baseline mortality (diamonds), observed mortality (triangles), and natural log of the predicted (thick solid line) and observed (squares) diameter distribution of living mountain beech trees in research plots damaged by the snowstorms of 1973 located within the Harper watershed on the South Island of New Zealand as calculated for 1983. (Data with permission from Rob Allen.)

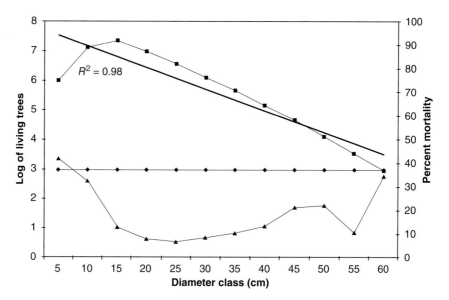

Figure 3.5 Baseline mortality (diamonds), observed mortality (triangles), and natural log of the predicted (thick solid line) and observed (squares) diameter distribution of living mountain beech trees in research plots undamaged by the snowstorms of 1973 located within the Harper watershed on the South Island of New Zealand as calculated for 1983. (Data with permission from Rob Allen.)

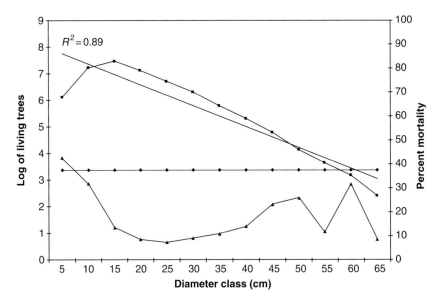

Figure 3.6 Baseline mortality (diamonds), observed mortality (triangles), and natural log of the predicted (thick solid line) and observed (squares) diameter distribution of living mountain beech trees in all research plots located within the Harper watershed on the South Island of New Zealand as calculated for 1983. (Data with permission from Rob Allen.)

The BM needed to sustain the observed diameter distributions is constant across all diameter classes, at approximately 33–37% in the three datasets) (Figures 3.4, 3.5, and 3.6). Figures 3.4, 3.5, and 3.6 all reveal 40–50% OM of trees in the smallest diameter class (5 cm) that we cannot explain, and which appears to result in lower than expected numbers of live trees in this diameter class, especially in the damaged plots where the OM is significantly different from BM (Figure 3.4). Alternatively, this situation may reflect a sampling problem in this diameter class, because it is impossible to increase the number of live trees in a diameter class once the cohort is established.

b) Although the observed diameter distribution for all three datasets (damaged, undamaged, and the total of all plots combined) fits the predicted diameter distribution closely, clearly there are sustainability issues in 1983 because the OM is significantly less than the BM needed to sustain the current diameter distribution (Figures 3.4, 3.5, and 3.6). With the exception of a large and significant level of mortality in the 50 cm diameter class in the damaged plots, due to the tree decline related to the snow events of 1968 and 1973, OM was otherwise significantly below BM in almost all other diameter classes. The mountain beech in these

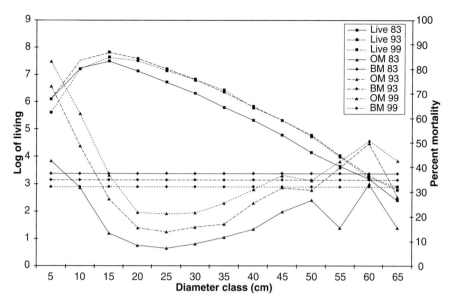

Figure 3.7 Baseline mortality (diamonds), observed mortality (triangles), and natural log of the observed diameter distribution (squares) of living mountain beech trees on plots located within the Harper watershed on the South Island of New Zealand as calculated for 1983 (solid lines), 1993 (dashed lines), and 1999 (dotted lines). (Data with permission from Rob Allen.)

watersheds appears to need mortality to restore sustainability to the system. These are dynamic systems and constantly changing. So, alternatively, perhaps the system was out of balance and the reduced mortality is restoring it to sustainability. Which is the correct interpretation? The following analysis provides a possible answer.

c and d) A combined graph of BM and OM for all plots combined for the time periods of 1983, 1993, and 1999 shows a progressive increase in OM in most diameter classes, and a concurrent decrease in BM during the same 16-year period (Figure 3.7). By 1999, the overall OM was not different from BM except in the very smallest and largest diameter classes (Figure 3.7); which might be expected in a light-demanding, early successional species such as mountain beech. Apparently, the ecosystem needed and got the large-scale mortality event in the form of an earthquake in 1994 that restored the ecosystem to sustainability.

In a recent study of size-specific tree mortality in the same watershed using the same dataset, Hurst *et al.* (in review) showed a reduced rate of mortality in the period from 1993 to 2004, which included the earthquake of 1994 when compared to the two time periods that preceded it (1974–1983 and 1983–1993). Although we did not explicitly measure rates of mortality in our analysis, it can be inferred as the gap between OM for small stems between the sampling years 1983, 1993, and 1999 that became smaller over time (Figure 3.7). The data presented in the study by Hurst *et al.* thus support our contention that landscape-level disturbances are important to sustain the negative exponential diameter distribution in some ecosystems (e.g., mountain beech in New Zealand), and that the approximate level of mortality needed to achieve it can be predicted.

The cause of the observed mountain beech mortality/decline subsequent to the storms of 1968 and 1973 in the largest diameter classes (Figures 3.4 and 3.7) is not known for certain, but certain essential factors are proposed to explain it. The researchers hypothesized the following scenario (Wardle and Allen 1983): First, the stands must be at a susceptible stage of development. In this case it seems either that old, even-aged stands; or dense, competing pole stands are required. Second, some form of predisposing disturbance or stress is needed, such as the snow storms in this instance. Third, a pest or pathogen outbreak could effect the necessary mortality. In this instance, there is evidence for the fungal pathogen *Sporothrix*, introduced into stressed trees by pinhole beetles of the genus *Platypus*. This proposed explanation, if true, represents a classic decline–disease scenario. Decline diseases and their relevance to forest health are discussed in detail in Chapter 4.

3.4 Hurricane damage and sustainability in the Luquillo Forest Dynamics Plot, Puerto Rico

3.4.1 Introduction

The Luquillo forest dynamics plot (LFDP) is a 16 ha (40 acre) forest plot located near El Verde field station in the Luquillo Mountains of northeastern Puerto Rico, 35 km southeast of San Juan. The plot is 500 m (N–S) by 320 m (E–W), and is divided into 400 20 × 20 m quadrats, with each subdivided into 16 5 × 5 m subquadrats. It is part of the global network of large, tropical forest plots of the Center for Tropical Forest Science (CTFS, Smithsonian); from which data are collected to improve our understanding of tropical forests, to predict their future, and to determine their response to environmental change and disturbance.

The LFDP was established in 1990. The LFDP is unique among all CTFS sites because of its history of land use disturbance and hurricane damage. These two disturbance types interact to influence community dynamics and species composition at the LFDP. The northern two-thirds of the plot was cleared and farmed until 1934, when it was purchased by the USDA Forest Service. The southern third was lightly selectively logged. Clear patterns in species distributions resulted from these disturbances. Major hurricanes struck the LFDP in 1928 and 1932, and then not again until hurricane Hugo in 1989, and Georges in 1998. Both of these hurricanes caused significant damage. On the LFDP three major censuses have been carried out, the first in the early 1990s, the second in the mid 1990s, and then again during 2000–2002. Individual stems greater or equal to 1 cm were tagged, identified, and diameter at 130 cm measured.

We include this dataset as one of our case studies to assess its usefulness for monitoring the impact of hurricane damage (pre and post hurricane Georges in 1998) on the sustainability of four common tropical forest tree species (*Dacryodes excelsa, Cecropia schreberiana., Schefflera [Didymopanax] morototoni,* and *Manilkara bidentata*).

Tropical tree species can be separated into two broad groups based on life history profiles: pioneer and non-pioneer (Swaine and Whitmore 1988). These two groups are distinguished based on the importance of a light cue for seed germination (pioneer group), and the ability of seedlings to withstand deep shade (non-pioneer group).

Both *C. schreberiana* and *S. morototoni* are well-known, fast-growing, large-leaved species in the pioneer group. *Schefflera* is common throughout the tropical Americas. Both *C. schreberiana* and *S. morototoni* are common in Puerto Rico, and both establish abundantly following hurricanes that damage the forests of the Luquillo Mountains. Both pioneer species are found in canopy openings caused by tree blowdowns in the same forest as *D. excelsa*, the mature or climax species of the subtropical wet forest in Puerto Rico. *Schefflera* may reach a height of 30 m and dbh up to 36 cm. But more commonly it reaches heights of 15–17 m and 20–22 cm dbh. Its maximum age is 35–50 years. *S. morototoni* is intolerant of shade, and grows best in full sunlight so it rapidly colonizes open areas; thus it is one of the first species to colonize hurricane-caused blowdowns. Wind commonly damages mature trees, uprooting them or breaking off branches. The wood is used primarily for matchsticks hence the specific name *morototoni*, general carpentry, and interior construction. Felled timber is very susceptible to decay.

C. schreberiana reaches heights of 20 m and 50 cm dbh, with few branches and deeply lobed leaves. It too typically lives 30–50 years. Forest soils contain a high density of *C. schreberiana* seeds, which lie dormant until canopy openings stimulate their germination. It grows rapidly in high light, but shaded trees suffer heavy mortality. Despite abundant regeneration following hurricanes, and heavy mortality of these colonizers as the forest closes, enough survive and grow so that this species is among the ten most common canopy trees in the tabonuco forest type. Its abundant regeneration and rapid growth capture and store nutrients following disturbance. The status of this species indicates the developmental status of the forest as a whole. Colonizing saplings may facilitate succession to mature forest by excluding grasses, herbs, and vines that hinder forest development. The biology of this species both reflects and helps to drive the dynamics of forests in the Luquillo Mountains.

Dacryodes excelsa (Tabonuco) and *M. bidentata* (Ausobo) are both primary, slow-growing, large, long-lived, canopy dominant trees of the non-pioneer group in the Luquillo Mountains. Both are shade tolerant, *Manilkara* (extremely) more so than *Dacryodes* (intermediate). They occur in association with one another, as well as with *Cecropia* and *Schefflera*. *Manilkara* can reach 300–400 years of age, 30 m in height, and a dbh of 140 cm. *Dacryodes* may reach heights of 35 m, 180 cm dbh, and up to 400 years of age. *D. excelsa* and *Manilkara* that survive hurricane disturbance usually suffer heavy crown damage.

3.4.2 Questions and instructions

a) Download the file named Puerto Rico datasets.xls from the Chapter 3 datasets folder from the website, and open in Microsoft® Excel® 2007. Use the stepwise Excel protocol detailed for the NZ mountain beech dataset in Appendix B (**Instructions for baseline mortality analysis of 1983 NZ mt. beech dataset using Microsoft® Excel® 2007**) as a guide. Graph the natural log of the living trees against diameter class, calculate and graph the BM for the two pioneer species *Schefflera* and *Cecropia* combined at each of the two time periods (1995 and 2000).

b) Do the same for the two non-pioneer species *Dacryodes* and *Manilkara* combined at each of the two time periods (1995 and 2000).

c) Graph OM by diameter class on each of the two graphs above at each time period.

d) Compare OM to BM at each diameter class using chi-square analysis (see Appendix B). Does OM differ significantly from BM for each set of species at each time period? If so, at which diameter classes? Which time period?

e) Which of the two sets of species show a sustainable diameter distribution?

f) What was the impact of hurricane Georges on the health/sustainability of the pioneer species? The non-pioneer species?

3.4.3 Answers and interpretation

The four species selected for analysis in this case study are native tropical species adapted to hurricane disturbance. They have evolved different strategies to survive recurring hurricane events. But are these different strategies reflected in different levels of baseline and observed mortalities?

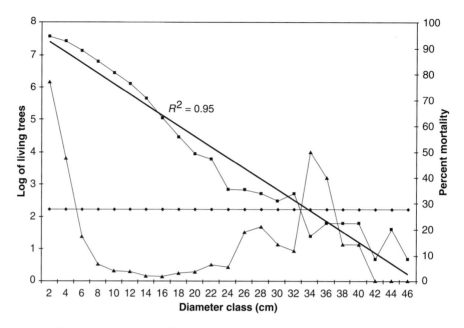

Figure 3.8 Natural log of live trees by diameter class (squares), the best-fit regression line (thick solid line), and baseline (diamonds) and observed (triangles) mortalities for the pioneer species *Cecropia* and *Schefflera* on the LFDP in the Luquillo Mountains of Puerto Rico in the year 1995, six years post Hurricane Hugo and three years pre Hurricane Georges. (data from the LFDP at the LUQ-LTER site in Puerto Rico funded by grants from the US National Science Foundation to the University of Puerto Rico in collaboration with IITF-USFS.)

a and b) The negative exponential model gives a good fit to the diameter distribution of both sets of species in both time periods with R^2 values ranging from 0.93–0.96 (Figures 3.8–3.11). The most obvious difference between the two pioneer species (*Cecropia* and *Schefflera*) and the non-pioneer species (*Dacryodes* and *Manilkara*) is that the BM needed to sustain the current diameter distribution of the two pioneer species on the LFDP is nearly three times that of the non-pioneer species. This was apparent in both the 1995 and 2000 datasets (28 vs. 11% for 1995 [Figures 3.8 and 3.10], and 29 vs 11% for 2000, respectively. Figures 3.9 and 3.11).

c and d) One caveat that must be considered in this particular analysis is that the small sample size, one 16 ha stand, may make a precise interpretation of the significance of these variations in OM difficult or impossible. This factor can be problematic when working with tropical datasets, which often are obtained from one or very few intensively sampled research plots to account for the high richness but low evenness, and often too few big trees in tropical forests.

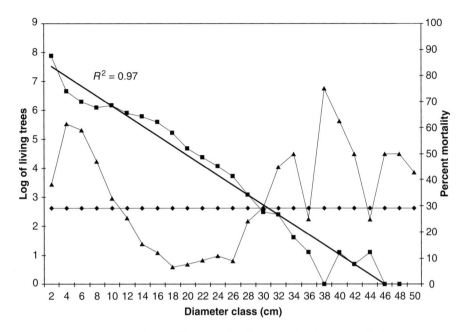

Figure 3.9 Natural log of live trees by diameter class (squares), the best-fit regression line (thick solid line), and baseline (diamonds) and observed mortalities (triangles) for the pioneer species *Cecropia* and *Schefflera* on the LFDP in the Luquillo Mountains of Puerto Rico in the year 2000, two years post Hurricane Georges. (Data from the LFDP at the LUQ-LTER site in Puerto Rico funded by grants from the US National Science Foundation to the University of Puerto Rico in collaboration with IITF-USFS.)

OM is significantly above BM in the youngest diameter classes for the pioneer species in both 1995 and 2000. OM is significantly below BM in the mid-diameter classes (10–24 cm in 1995 and 16–26 cm in 2000). OM is significantly above BM in the largest diameter classes (38–48 cm) in 2000, but significantly below BM in the larger diameter classes (40–46 cm) in 1995 (Figures 3.8–3.11). OM is significantly above BM in the smallest diameter classes for the non-pioneer species, but only in 1995. OM otherwise is not significantly different from BM.

e and f) The significant differences of OM from BM observed in the population of the two pioneer species in both 1995 and 2000 (Figures 3.8 and 3.9) initially suggests an unsustainable population. But we believe that it reflects a different life-history strategy for dealing with the impacts of recurrent hurricane disturbance, and that the population is indeed sustainable. The populations of these two species appear to peak and ebb in synchrony with hurricane disturbance.

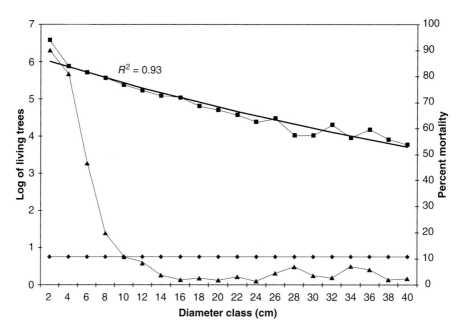

Figure 3.10 Natural log of live trees by diameter class (squares), the best-fit regression line (thick solid line), and baseline (diamonds) and observed (triangles) mortalities for the non-pioneer species *Dacryodes* and *Manilkara* on the LFDP in the Luquillo Mountains of Puerto Rico in the year 1995, six years post Hurricane Hugo, and three years pre Hurricane Georges. (Data from the LFDP at the LUQ-LTER site in Puerto Rico funded by grants from the US National Science Foundation to the University of Puerto Rico in collaboration with IITF-USFS.)

The population of the two non-pioneer species, *Dacryodes* and *Manilkara*, in 1995 is sustainable, even though the OM of the youngest trees is significantly greater than baseline (Figure 3.10). The mortality in these younger trees is most likely due to competition for resources (e.g., light) due to canopy closure because growth of seedlings and saplings of these species is slow, and very few survive to maturity. The diameter distribution also is clearly sustainable in the year 2000 dataset, because the OM does not differ significantly from BM, and there is a good fit of the observed to the predicted diameter distribution (Figure 3.11). Therefore, in our opinion this species component of the LFDP is sustainable. The OM well below baseline suggests that this population will gain in dominance in the future. The slope of the regression line will remain the same, but the line will move upwards.

The populations of the pioneer and non-pioneer species behave differently. The populations of the two pioneer species behave more like a disturbance-generated, even-aged system; and thus may not be appropriate for BM analysis, particularly at the stand level. The only way to properly assess even-aged systems

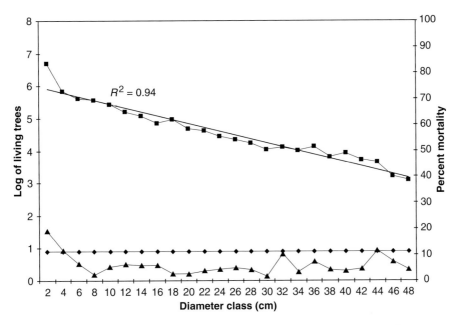

Figure 3.11 Natural log of live trees by diameter class (squares), the best-fit
regression line (thick solid line), and baseline (diamonds) and observed (triangles)
mortalities for the non-pioneer species *Dacryodes* and *Manilkara* on the LFDP in
the Luquillo Mountains in the year 2000, two years post Hurricane Georges.
(Data from the LFDP at the LUQ-LTER site in Puerto Rico funded by grants from
the US National Science Foundation to the University of Puerto Rico in
collaboration with IITF-USFS.)

is at the landscape level, which includes multiple cohorts of various age classes.
Conversely, the populations of the two non-pioneer species behave like an
uneven-aged system that fits a negative exponential model. The interpretations
that we make reflect these behaviors. We include both datasets to illustrate the
type of concerns to be considered when utilizing the BM analysis method to
assess forest health. Proper interpretation requires understanding of the silvics,
ecology, and life histories of the tree species of interest.

How did hurricane Georges in 1998 impact these four species? The two
non-pioneer species respond to hurricane damage by sprouting new branches,
and positioning themselves to quickly reclaim a position in the forest canopy
(Zimmerman *et al.* 1994). They are better able to resist stem breakage in high winds
due to slow growth, high wood density, and stronger less-flexible wood than that
of the pioneer species. Although mortality is lower, branch damage is more severe
in these species than in the pioneer species (Zimmerman *et al.* 1994). *Cecropia*
and *Schefflera* on the other hand are very susceptible to hurricane damage because
they grow quickly and their wood density is relatively low. There was a massive

recruitment of *Cecropia* following hurricane Hugo in 1989, which was followed by heavy mortality in the seedling and sapling size classes in both 1995 and 2000 (Figures 3.8 and 3.9). The life history strategy of these pioneer species is to invest more resources into new individuals after hurricane disturbance rather than having individual trees surviving each hurricane. Observed mortality above baseline was observed in 1995, and again in 2000, two years post hurricane Georges, at which time the difference was significant (Figures 3.8 and 3.9).

The hurricane caused extensive mortality of the pioneer species, especially the larger trees (Figures 3.8 and 3.9). But the presence of numerous seeds in the soil bank enables them to regenerate quickly following the storm, which opens the canopy and exposes the soil to light. In contrast, the non-pioneer species dominate the early recovery period because they do not suffer heavy mortality from the storm (Figures 3.10 and 3.11), and they sprout new branches that enable them to reclaim the canopy. Recruits of the pioneer species colonize large gaps in the canopy, or pulse through the ecosystem as cohorts of trees following hurricane disturbance, until they produce seed and then die at 35–50 years of age (Zimmerman *et al.* 1994; Brokaw 1998). The populations of the pioneer species also are sustainable because high mortality in the small and large diameter classes are counterbalanced by low mortality in the mid-diameter classes (Figures 3.8 and 3.9).

3.5 White spruce stand in Anchorage, Alaska

The Matanuska-Susitna Borough (MSB), Land Management Department (LMD) with support from the USDA Forest Service, State and Private Forestry Health and Protection proposes to undertake timber stand improvement and bark beetle suppression methods on forested lands within the Butte Community, AK. Aerial insect and disease surveys have identified several areas within the borough where forest pests, specifically the spruce bark beetle, are estimated to be causing new or expanded forest health problems that may increase forest fuels to hazardous levels due to spruce mortality. Aerial detection surveys in 2005, 2006, and 2007 identified an increase in beetle activity in the white spruce forests south of the Butte Community. Field reconnaissance in the fall of 2008 confirmed the presence of beetles there.

3.5.1 *Background and introduction*

The Borough wishes to "beetle proof" a forest at the wildland:urban interface within the Jim Creek Recreation Area before an eruptive bark beetle population takes hold (see Chapter 4, this volume). The proposed treatment areas are within this interface zone, and were selected in part for their accessibility.

We selected this case study to demonstrate how assessment of this forested area using the BM approach might assist in achieving the goals of this proposed treatment activity. Data have been collected to permit calculation of BM and OM, and are available in the file named named "Alaska white spruce dataset.xls" on the website. The stand is approximately 20 ha in size, uneven-aged, and consists of dense white spruce (*Picea glauca*) seedlings, saplings, and poletimber representing over 90% of the stand basal area. Most of the larger spruce has been selectively harvested leaving scattered residual saw-timber-sized spruce and *Populus*. Spruce bark beetles are present, and have caused mortality in many of the larger spruce. Spruce beetles appear to be at endemic levels due to the overall young age of the stand. Hopefully, careful thinning will keep the population at endemic levels.

3.5.2 *Questions and methodology*

a) Download the file named "Alaska white spruce dataset.xls" from the Chapter 3 dataset folder. Open it in Excel 2007 on your computer into a new worksheet. Follow the detailed Excel instructions for the NZ mountain beech dataset in Appendix B as a guide, and graph the natural log of the number of all living trees on the y-axis, by diameter class on the x-axis. Generate and graph the best fit first order linear regression line for this diameter distribution. What is the R^2 of the regression? Does the negative exponential function fit the data well?

b) Utilizing the equation presented in the detailed instructions, calculate the BM needed to sustain the current diameter distribution of trees in this stand. What is the BM?

c) Following the instructions, calculate and graph the OM in each diameter class, and plot it on the graph in (a) above. Now, use a chi-square analysis to determine if OM differs significantly from BM in each diameter class. Does OM differ significantly from BM? If so, in what diameter classes?

d) Is this white spruce stand sustainable? Does it require intervention to alter the diameter distribution? What needs to be done to beetle proof this stand?

3.5.3 *Answers and interpretation*

a) The diameter distribution of the living trees in this stand follows a negative exponential model with an $R^2 = 0.94$ (Figure 3.12).

b) The BM needed to sustain the current diameter distribution is approximately 35%.

c) The OM is below BM in all diameter classes, varying from 0 to approximately 30%. It differs significantly from BM at the small to mid-diameter size classes (Figure 3.12).

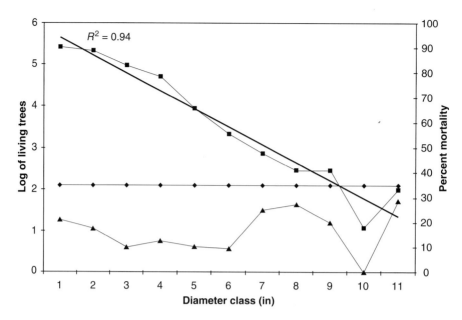

Figure 3.12 Natural log of live trees by diameter class (squares), the best-fit regression line (thick solid line), and baseline (diamonds) and observed (triangles) mortalities of white spruce in a stand near Anchorage, Alaska. (Data from J. Lundquist with permission.)

d) The significantly low OM suggests some sustainability issues in this stand of white spruce. Some cutting in this stand, particularly in the smaller size classes (5–15 cm diameter classes) may be needed to raise the mortality levels to bring them closer to BM.

The small sample size of this stand may result in an anomalous estimate of the relationship of OM to BM, especially if the stand is not fully stocked. If not fully stocked, then the trees may continue to grow in size with no need to balance OM and BM. Further thinning may not be appropriate in such stands. Alternatively, the MSB–LMD believes that thinning is necessary in these stands, and is prepared to carry it out. The question then is one of how much to thin. This scenario highlights the need to understand the management, disease, and pest histories of a forest to best interpret the results of baseline mortality assessment of forest sustainability.

From 1990 to 2000 the spruce beetle (*Dendroctonus rufipennis*) infested 1.19 million ha of forest in Alaska, 40% more area than that of the previous 70 years (Werner *et al.* 2006). The increase is attributed in part to increasing temperatures, which favors the survival of this beetle. Spruce beetles typically colonize severely stressed or dying trees weakened by drought, fire, ice, logging damage, root diseases, advanced age, and high stem densities. Periodic severe outbreaks occur at 30–50 year intervals, during which most healthy and mature spruce are killed. In parts of the Kenai Peninsula between 1976 and 1980 spruce beetles killed 29% of the white spruce. Mortality was greatest in the larger trees during the early stages of the infestation, but smaller trees were attacked once the larger ones had been killed. After 16 years, 51% of spruce larger than 20 cm dbh had been killed (this equalled 90% of commercial stand volume) (Werner *et al.* 2006). Silvicultural treatments to maintain vigorous growth are recommended in order to reduce losses to the spruce beetle. Treatments include thinning of stands approaching maturity, as well as stands younger than rotation age. Can we predict which spruce stands will be infested to help prioritize stand treatments? Hazard and risk models for management of the spruce beetle have been developed for south-central Alaska, and they suggest reducing residual basal area to 5–11 m^2/ha depending on site quality and beetle populaion densities. Our analysis suggests that the white spruce stand near Anchorage requires thinning to achieve sustainability. In the future, it will be interesting to follow-up the thinning treatments applied to this stand to see how they affected the subsequent BM, OM, sustainability, and beetle proofing of this forest.

References

Brokaw, N. V. L. 1998. *Cecropia schreberiana* in the Luquillo Mountains of Puerto Rico. *Botanical Reviews* **64**: 91–120.

Cale, J. A., McNulty, S. A., Teale, S. A., and Castello, J. D. 2010. Beech thickets impact northern hardwood forest biodiversity. *Journal of Forestry* **108**: 423.

Hane, E. N. 2003. Indirect effects of beech bark disease on sugar maple seedling survival. *Canadian Journal Forest Research* **33**: 807–813.

Houston, D. R. 1975. Beech bark disease: the aftermath forests are structured for a new outbreak. *Journal of Forestry* **73**: 660–663.

Hurst, J. M., Allen, R. B., Coomes, D. A., and Duncan, R. P. 2011 Size-specific tree mortality and neighbourhood interactions in montane *Nothofagus* forest. *Journal of Ecology* (in review).

Jones, R. H. and Raynal, D. J. 1987. Root sprouting in American beech: production, survival, and the effect of parent tree vigor. *Canadian Journal Forest Research* **17**: 539–544.

MacKenzie, M. 2005. Survival of the fittest – Beech bark disease-resistant beech will leave more offspring. In: *Beech Bark Disease: Proceedings of the Beech Bark Disease Symposium; 2004 June 16–18; Saranac Lake, NY. Gen. Tech. Rep. NE-331.* Evans, C. A., Lucas, J. A. and Twery, M. J., (eds). Newtown Square, PA: USA. Department of Agriculture, Forest Service, Northeastern Research Station.

Rubin, B. D. and Manion, P. D. 2005. Characterizing regional forest health and sustainability – A case study using diameter distributions, baseline mortality, and cumulative liabilities. In: *Forest Pathology: From Genes to Landscapes*. Lundquist, J. E. and Hamelin, R. C. (eds.). APS Press, St. Paul, MN.

Swaine, M. D. and Whitmore, T. C. 1988. On the definition of ecological species groups in tropical rain forests. *Vegetatio* **75**: 81–86.

USDA Forest Service. Yagrumo Macho. *Didymopanax morototoni*. Silvics Manual, Volume 2. http://www.na.fs.fed.us/pubs/silvics_manual/Volume_2/didymopanax/morototoni.htm [Accessed November 2010].

Wardle, J. A. and Allen, R. B. 1983. Dieback in New Zealand Nothofagus forests. *Pacific Science* **37**: 397–404.

Wardle, J. A. 1984. *The New Zealand Beeches: Ecology, Utilization, and Management*. New Zealand Forest Service, Christchurch.

Werner, R. A., Holsten, E. H., Matsuoka, S. M., and Burnside, R. E. 2006. Spruce beetles and forest ecosystems in south-central Alaska: A review of 30 years of research. *Forest Ecology & Management* **227**: 195–206.

Zimmerman, J. K., Everham III, E. M., Waide, R. B. *et al.* 1994. Responses of tree species to hurricane winds in subtropical wet forest in Puerto Rico: Implications for tropical tree life histories. *Journal of Ecology* **82**: 911–922.

Section II FOREST HEALTH AND ITS
ECOLOGICAL COMPONENTS

4

Regulators and terminators: the importance of biotic factors to a healthy forest

S.A. TEALE AND J.D. CASTELLO

Of all the extraordinary numbers of species of insects and other arthropods, nematodes, fungi, bacteria, and viruses that exist in the world's forests, only a relatively small percentage affect trees or forests to such an extent that they are considered to be problematic. Most have beneficial or at least harmless functions in the ecosystems in which they occur. What is it about this troublesome minority of species that makes them damaging to forests? The answers to this simple question are complex, and have far-reaching ramifications in the way we view forest ecology and management.

At the broadest level, the answer begins with recognizing that native organisms living in their natural environments are only problematic when a human dimension is introduced. The human role can take many forms including (1) management practices (e.g., commodity production) that create favorable conditions for insects and disease, (2) management objectives that view natural ecological processes as undesirable (e.g., insect outbreaks or diseases that damage forest resources) even though these processes occurred in the absence of human influence, and (3) the movement of insects, pathogens and/or trees out of their native ranges into new regions or continents; and thus the creation of new and often unpredictable interspecific interactions. Absent the human dimension, forest insects and pathogens act as natural thinning agents causing the tree mortality that is needed to cull the weak competitors and release resources that are needed to support the growth of the surviving trees (see Chapter 8).

Not so long ago, forest pathologists and entomologists viewed diseases and insects as exerting only negative impacts in a forest, and as such, they needed to

Forest Health: An Integrated Perspective, ed. John D. Castello and Stephen A. Teale. Published by Cambridge University Press. © Cambridge University Press 2011.

81

be eliminated or at least managed. The forest industry paradigm at that time was based upon the sustainable yield of commodities. This paradigm, however, has now shifted from one of sustainable yield to sustainable productivity, health, and multiple uses (see Chapter 8) that recognizes the importance of the ecological and societal values of a forest, (e.g., biodiversity, preservation of natural processes, resilience, recreation, etc.). With this new paradigm, we have come to understand that natural disturbances (i.e., fire, wind, insects, and diseases) are not only integral, but essential, components of forest ecosystems. In other words, natural disturbances are not always a bad thing.

4.1 Biotic agents of tree stress

We begin with a discussion of forest diseases and insects, and their effects on the health of a forest. **Disease** is a chronic condition or irritation that prevents the affected host from reaching its maximum genetic potential. The chronic nature of the irritation is critical to distinguish disease from **injury**, which is an acute or short-term irritation, or **damage** which is measurable loss associated with injury. The impact of disease is invariably negative when viewed from a human health perspective where the individual host is of paramount importance. But this is not necessarily the case with regard to forest health, where the health of an individual tree is less important than that of the population of trees. The term **forest insect pest** refers to those insects that have a negative effect on trees and forests. The term pest itself has no biological meaning, but refers to organisms that interfere with human objectives. Thus, insects that reduce the amount of food, fiber, or other resources available for human use are labeled as pests. Insects and other animals that transmit pathogens from one tree to another are **vectors**, also considered as pests. Most insects that live in forests do not adversely affect trees, and many do not even feed on trees. Although these insects could be viewed as "forest insects," the term forest insect is usually used in reference to those that are pests.

The study of forest insect pests is called **forest entomology**, and the study of tree diseases is called **forest pathology**; both are applied sciences that deal with solving practical forest management problems related to tree pests and diseases (Boyce 1961; Manion 1991). There are many different types of tree diseases. Diseases can be caused by biotic causal agents (i.e., living agents). Examples include fungi, bacteria, viruses, nematodes, and dwarf mistletoes. Such causal agents are called **pathogens**. Thus, the terms disease and pathogen are not interchangeable: disease is a syndrome and pathogens are causal agents. You might be wondering if insect pests also might be considered pathogens because they too are biotic agents that can cause problems in the host. Most pathologists and entomologists do not think of them as pathogens. Two possible reasons for this apparently artificial distinction may help to explain it. One is based on the historical separation of the disciplines of entomology and pathology because of taxonomic and life history differences, and the other is based on the idea that insect pest activity usually is short term or acute, and not long term (i.e., chronic).

Disease also can be caused by abiotic (non-living) causal agents. Examples include diseases caused by nutrient deficiencies, drought, flooding, unfavorable site conditions, chronic air pollutant exposure, etc. These factors are considered separately in Chapter 7. **Declines** are a third category of disease that affects populations of mature trees, and are caused by an interacting, specifically ordered, set of causal agents grouped into predisposing, inciting, and contributing factors (Manion 1991 and Figure 4.1).

The precise set of predisposing, inciting, and contributing factors will vary from one specific decline disease to another, yet the disease always involves mature populations of trees, not individual trees, and not young trees. Pathogens and insect pests may act as predisposing, inciting, or contributing factors. The terms **dieback** and decline often are incorrectly used synonymously. Individual trees may display crown dieback for a variety of reasons, and may or may not die as a result. Crown dieback may be reversible. Crown dieback, however, often is a symptom of decline. Once a population of mature trees has been acted upon by the proper set of predisposing, inciting, and contributing factors, death is the end result. Declines are difficult to diagnose because too often the predisposing, inciting, and/or contributing factors involved are not known, and the temporal dimension cannot be replicated in attempted experiments. Decline diseases have an important ecological function. They are responsible for "thinning the forest from above." Specifically, they serve an analogous function to that of competition for resources, which is responsible for "thinning forests from below." Both processes serve to keep a balanced diameter distribution in the forest (Manion and Lachance 1992), and serve an important role in maintaining a healthy forest.

How does one recognize an unhealthy tree? A diseased tree usually produces a specific set of **symptoms** that progress over time, and is known as the **disease syndrome**. Diseases are diagnosed by recognizing specific signs and symptoms. **Signs** are visible evidence of the pathogen itself (e.g., a mushroom of a fungal root-infecting fungus), whereas **symptoms** are the response of the tree to the causal agent (e.g., leaf spots caused by a foliage pathogen). The effects of insect feeding are typically described as feeding damage, not as symptoms. Skill at recognition of specific syndromes leads to a diagnosis, which is the identification of the causal agent or factors. Symptoms of tree disease can vary from a slight reduction in growth rate without any obvious external symptoms, to death. Although insects and disease do not always kill trees, they often reduce the competitive ability of the affected tree. Thus, trees affected by insects and

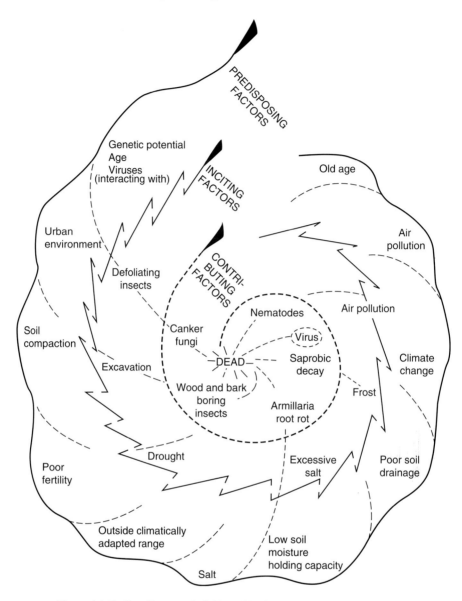

Figure 4.1 Decline disease spiral. (From Manion 1991, with permission.)

diseases often are outcompeted by healthy trees for growing space in the forest. Conversely, trees that do not compete well due to genetic or microsite factors are generally more susceptible to insects and pathogens.

4.1.1 The roles of disease and insects in forested ecosystems

The impacts of insects and pathogens vary from natural thinning to extraordinary levels of tree mortality. The most severe impacts are typically caused by non-native pests and pathogens. For instance, the American chestnut (*Castanea dentata*) was eliminated as a canopy- dominant species in eastern North America by the introduced fungal pathogen (*Cryphonectria parasitica*) that causes a disease known as chestnut blight. Other, less widespread, though nearly as severe, examples are all too common. Non-native, invasive species are such a pernicious, rising, and global problem that an entire chapter of this book (Chapter 5) is devoted to them. In the remainder of this chapter, we will restrict our discussion to native insects and pathogens.

That insects and pathogens kill trees does not necessarily make them enemies of the forest. Biologists widely recognize that some trees in a forest naturally die, and that this is a normal ecological process (Haack and Byler 1993; Castello *et al.* 1995). However, recognizing how much mortality is natural, and how much is excessive, is an important task for forest managers, pathologists, and entomologists. Similarly, it is important for these people to recognize when observed mortality is caused by anthropogenic disturbance. For example, the pristine forests of the Sierra San Pedro Martir in northern Baja, Mexico have been largely unaffected by human activity, yet trees there still die from disease and insects. More importantly, the mortality is associated with tree density, which leads to the conclusion that the pathogens and insects are natural thinning agents that reduce competition among trees in these mixed-conifer stands, and thereby maintain tree vigor (Maloney and Rizzo 2002). In this instance, tree mortality is not a problem in need of management.

Native insects that cause minor injury can become pests when the forest is disturbed. In a study of humid evergreen forests in Cameroon, seven species of trees in undisturbed stands experienced minor levels of leaf feeding, shoot boring, sap sucking, and wood boring. Disturbed stands experienced greater levels of injury and some mortality (Foahom 2003). In undisturbed forests, insect injury may or may not lead to mortality, but the same species that act as natural thinning agents in an undisturbed forest can respond to tree stress following disturbance and cause elevated levels of damage.

Temperate and boreal forests sometimes experience massive outbreaks of native insects that cause widespread tree mortality. The spruce beetle (*Dendroctonus rufipennis*) in Alaska and the Yukon (see Chapter 3), the mountain pine beetle (MPB; *D. ponderosae*) in interior western USA and Canada, and the southern pine beetle (*D. frontalis*) in the southeastern USA are native bark beetles that have caused breathtaking levels of tree mortality. These insects kill trees by girdling *en masse* in the phloem and cambium of tree stems and introducing pathogenic fungi. Defoliators, such as the eastern and western spruce budworms (*Choristoneura fumiferana* and *C. occidentalis*) also kill large numbers of trees over extensive areas from time to time. They injure their host trees by consuming much or all of the foliage; unlike many hardwoods, the conifer hosts of these budworms have little capacity to survive heavy defoliation and often succumb to secondary insects and pathogens. Historical records indicate that these outbreaks have occurred for centuries and thus appear to be long-standing components of the ecosystem (Swetnam and Lynch 1993; Krause 1997). However, the frequency and extent of especially the MPB have increased in recent decades due to fire suppression and drought (see Chapter 7). These outbreaks can alter the direction and rate of forest succession. When tree mortality is extensive, and canopy loss allows increased light to reach the ground, the forest may be returned to an early seral state if the seed source consists of pioneer species; thus, succession may be reset. If there is advance regeneration consisting of later successional species, then succession may be accelerated as the early stages are removed and species of a later stage are released. While these outbreaks and their consequences may be natural, they invariably wreak havoc on management objectives.

Tropical forests typically do not experience these large-scale outbreaks, and this is generally believed to be due to high species diversity of trees. Tropical forests may contain over 100 tree species per hectare and several hundred species regionally (Whitmore 1998). Temperate and boreal forests include substantially fewer species overall, and often are dominated by a small handful of species. It is widely held that this difference in tree diversity is the reason for the difference in the occurrence of pest outbreaks (Vehviläinen *et al.* 2006). Low tree diversity favors pests because dispersal from host to host is facilitated and dispersal-related mortality is low. This is one of the major reasons why monocultures typically have more severe pest problems. At the other extreme, tropical forests with such high tree species diversity are unaccommodating places for insect herbivores searching for new host trees. An alternate viewpoint is that higher diversity of vegetation supports greater populations of natural enemies (parasitoids and predators), which limit herbivore population growth by causing elevated levels of mortality (Root 1973). Regardless of the mechanism, tree diversity plays a major role in insect outbreaks. Tropical forest plantations (monocultures) are subject to serious pest and disease problems, as are low-diversity temperate forests, presumably for the same reason.

Forest insect pest damage is frequently less severe than the extensive outbreaks of bark beetles and budworms. Insects are an extraordinarily diverse group of animals, and their feeding habits are varied. Forest insect pests can be categorized as folivores (including external feeders, skeletonizers, and miners), shoot feeders, bark and wood borers, seed and cone pests, sap-sucking insects, and root feeders. While modes of feeding and life history details vary widely among different species and groups of forest insects, there are commonalities in the behavior of populations that are of critical importance to forest managers.

4.2 Forest pest and disease management

The management of diseases and pests in forests often is made difficult by economic limitations. The value of individual trees in a forest managed, for example, for saw timber is often quite modest. This is unlike the situation in a fruit orchard, where each tree has great value. The monetary value of a stand of timber lies in the number of valuable trees per hectare at the stand or landscape level. For this reason, economic considerations often limit direct control of pest and disease problems to forests of exceptionally high value. It is not usually economically feasible to apply pesticides to control insect or disease outbreaks in many forest ecosystems. So a reasonable question might be, is it always necessary, or even desirable, to control or to manage diseases in forests? If so, then is it possible to determine objectively when management intervention is warranted? Of course, the answer to this question depends upon the landowner's management objectives. But are there guidelines, especially with regard to the health, productivity, and sustainability of the forest in question that we can provide to guide decision making? Can we predict with any degree of accuracy when pathogens or insect pests already present in the forest are likely to become problematic, and what their impacts might be?

There are many answers to these important questions, and which answers are the most appropriate depends on the management objectives. The framework within which management decisions are made is **Integrated Pest Management (IPM)**, which uses an array of management activities, including habitat manipulation, biological control, chemical control, and others, that balance expenses with the value of the resource, while also minimizing adverse environmental effects.

In a forest setting, habitat manipulation is better known as silviculture. Silviculture (see Chapter 8) is the forest manager's most important tool for minimizing pest and disease impacts by maintaining tree vigor. Vigorous, healthy trees are generally more resistant to insect feeding and pathogen infection. Trees that are growing at high densities must allocate their resources (photosynthate, nitrogen, phosphorus, etc.) to growth in order to compete with other trees, and therefore have fewer resources to allocate to chemical defense against pests and pathogens. Silviculture includes a wide array of tactics including thinning, controlled burning, fire suppression, planting, and others. An example of the positive effects of thinning was shown in a study of Scots pine on the Karelian Isthmus on the border of Finland and the Russian Federation (Veteli *et al.* 2006). Stands that received periodic thinning for several decades had lower tree densities and lower levels of damage caused by defoliators and bark beetles compared to the unthinned stands. In stands that are unthinned by foresters, the thinning is caused by pests and pathogens, and the trees that are killed decompose in the forest. In such a case, the pests and diseases become the forest managers, as they kill (i.e, the terminators) susceptible trees, and regulate which trees reach the canopy (i.e., the regulators) by reducing the growth rate of those they infect or infest (Castello *et al.* 1995). These decomposing trees are known as **coarse woody debris**, and provide important microhabitats for many kinds of organisms. The presence of coarse woody debris, while untidy in appearance, is important in preserving forest biodiversity (see Chapter 9). When stands are thinned to promote tree growth and vigor, the trees that are removed may be used for commodity production, or may be left in the forest as coarse woody debris. In either case, the diameter distribution of the growing forest tends to approximate the negative exponential function, or reverse-J curve (see Chapter 8).

Biological control is the use of natural enemies (predators, parasites, pathogens of pests) to limit or suppress pest populations. It is a top-down process; that is, the regulation of the herbivore population comes from a higher trophic level. Habitat manipulation is a bottom-up process where the herbivore population is limited by the availability of suitable plants. In **classical biological control**, a non-native natural enemy is brought from elsewhere and released with the expectation that it will become established and attack the target pest, which is usually also non-native. For example, the larch casebearer (*Coleophora laricella*) in Canada and the northern USA was a serious defoliator of native eastern larch (*Larix laricina*) after its introduction from Europe in the 1880s. Two parasitic wasps, *Agathis pumila* and *Chrysocharis laricinellae*, were introduced into eastern North America from Europe in the 1930s and 1940s (Long 1988) and have reduced casebearer populations to the point where only relatively minor outbreaks now occur. The advantage of classical biological control is that it is self sustaining and lasting. As long as a classical biological control agent does not harm native, non-target species, then there is no environmental harm.

Neoclassical biological control is the use of non-native natural enemies to control native pests, and is occasionally used in agriculture but less often in forests. **Augmentive** or **inundative biological control** involves the release of large numbers of laboratory-reared natural enemies. They may be predators, but more often are **parasitoids** – parasites that kill their hosts as larvae but are free living as adults and thus affect their host population numbers more like predators than true parasites. Augmentive releases generally have a short-term effect because the environment does not support a high predator population. This technique has seen limited use in forestry because the land areas involved are so great. *Trichogramma* spp. are egg parasitoids of many folivores and have been used extensively in agriculture and occasionally in forestry.

Conservation biological control involves manipulation of the environment in a manner that favors natural enemies of a pest. This may involve the preservation of flowering plants that provide energy in the form of nectar for foraging parasitoids, or leaving coarse woody debris in the forest as refugia for both vertebrate and invertebrate predators.

The balance of resources expended on management against the value of the resource is a cornerstone of IPM. It makes no sense to spend more controlling an insect or disease problem than the affected trees are worth. Applying values to natural resources is not easy, and can be quite complicated and imprecise. In agriculture, the value of a crop is fairly straight-forward, but in forests there are many values. Minimally, one can use the "stumpage" value of the trees, that is, the value that a logger will pay to the landowner, but there are many other, less easily quantified values. The monetary value of a tree resulting from its aesthetic, recreational, wildlife, or biodiversity values is difficult to assess.

4.2.1 Insect outbreaks

Low level or endemic pest populations are usually of little concern to forest managers. Exceptions include species in which very few individuals can cause economic damage. For instance, the offspring of a single gravid terminal weevil (*Pissodes strobi*) can destroy two to four years of height growth and cause substantial deformity and value loss to some species of conifers. However, the small proportion of native forest insects whose populations increase by orders of magnitude over a brief time span, i.e., outbreaking species, are generally of greater concern to forest managers. Because these are native insects, one might presume that the forest ecosystem is adapted to the effects of these outbreaks. This may be true in many instances, but anthropogenic disturbances such as past timber harvest practices, climate change and fire suppression, among others, may play a substantial role in promoting outbreaks. Regardless of the root cause of a pest outbreak, the consequences to the forest invariably impinge on management objectives and can rarely be ignored. Thus, it is important to understand the mechanisms that cause pest outbreaks in order to prevent them, or at least to respond to them effectively.

Population biologists have struggled for decades to determine the causes of outbreaks as well as the factors that lead to population declines. Outbreaking insect populations typically have a low-density phase, in which their numbers are sparse and their effect on the forest is slight. Then they exhibit a building phase, in which reproduction and immigration surpass mortality, and emigration and the density of the population increases. This is followed by the outbreak phase, where pest population density peaks and the impacts on the forest can be severe. Lastly, there is a decline phase, in which mortality and emigration exceed reproduction and immigration. Of interest to population biologists are the factors that regulate low-density populations, factors that release the population, and factors that terminate the outbreak.

Of all the outbreaking insect pests, there is a subset that enters the outbreak phase at fairly regular intervals of around 8 to 11 years from peak to peak. The regularity of these events is an additional feature that has eluded explanation for some time. Additionally, outbreaks often occur synchronously over large geographic areas. This, too, requires an explanation, which has remained largely elusive.

Pest populations are influenced by several factors, many of which can be controlled or influenced by forest managers. Abiotic factors that influence pest populations include some that can be managed (e.g., soil fertility, fire, site suitability for a given species) and those that cannot (e.g., weather). The biotic factors influencing pest populations are primarily trophic interactions. "Bottom-up" trophic interactions involve herbivores and their plant hosts (i.e., consumers and producers) and include strategies employed by each for avoiding the adverse effects of the other. Plants are adapted to alter their physical and chemical properties to minimize loss of fitness due to herbivory. Physical properties involved in plant defense include hairs, thorns, and, perhaps more importantly, raw fiber content. Chemical properties involve the production of secondary plant metabolites that may have a variety of adverse effects on the herbivore. The diversity of secondary plant metabolites is immense, and the kinds of effects on herbivores range from affecting the herbivore's food choices by decreasing plant tissue palatability to reducing the digestibility of ingested plant material by compounds such as condensed tannins to outright toxicity involving alkaloids, cyanohydrins, cardenolides and others.

Plants are not passive participants in these interactions. They control their nutritive quality and toxicity both temporally and spatially. The production of defensive chemicals requires resources (e.g., energy, C, N) which the plant must allocate among growth, reproduction, and defense. Plants or plant parts that are highly defended are generally more resistant to herbivore attack. Plants that are stressed are generally (but not always) less well defended and more susceptible to herbivory. For example, drought-stressed trees are typically more prone to insect attack. The relationship between drought and bark beetle outbreaks has long been observed by foresters and entomologists. Similarly, trees stressed by crowding become suppressed, and are more susceptible to colonization by insects and pathogens.

Top-down interactions affecting forest insect populations involve the next higher trophic level – a herbivore's natural enemies, e.g., parasitoids and predators. Natural enemies have widely varying effects on herbivore populations, but from a population standpoint, the important measures of a natural enemy's impact are its **functional response** and its **numerical response**. The functional response is the increase in the number of prey killed per predator per unit time as the prey

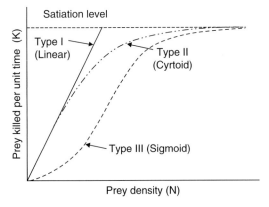

Figure 4.2 Functional responses of natural enemies of insects. Type I
functional responses are typical of ambush predators such as orb-weaving
spiders, Type II functional responses are typical of arthropod predators and
parasitoids, and Type III functional responses are typical of vertebrate predators
such as birds and mice. (From Berryman 1986, with permission.)

population density increases. The functional response may result from the predator
spending less time searching for prey, developing a search image to improve
foraging efficiency, or any other behavioral mechanism that results in an increased
kill rate. Natural enemies have characteristic functional responses; for instance, sit-
and-wait, or ambush predators such as spiders display a linear (Type I) response
(Figure 4.2) as prey densities increase. Many arthropod natural enemies such as
parasitoids tend to respond rapidly to prey population density increases at low
densities (Type II functional response). Generalist vertebrate predators respond to
increasing prey densities by learning to search for more abundant prey. This
"learning curve" results in a Type III functional response, in which the kill rate
does not increase substantially until the prey density has reached moderate levels.

The numerical response of a natural enemy is simply an increase in the
natural enemy population density in response to an increase in the prey population. The increase in food abundance may cause an increase in the birth rate of a
natural enemy, which results in increased natural enemy numbers. Similarly, an
increase in immigration by natural enemies into an area of greater prey abundance may also result in a local increase in the natural enemy population. Thus,
the numerical response is a function of both the reproductive response and the
migratory response.

Favorable conditions for a pest include either or both an increase in the food
supply, and a decrease in the natural enemy population. The food supply may
increase as a result of environmental factors that increase the number of trees
that are susceptible to herbivorous insect feeding due to reduced chemical or

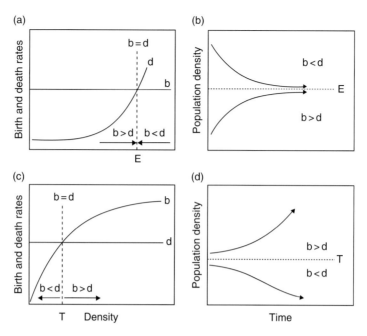

Figure 4.3 The effects of increasing population density on birth and death rates of forest insect populations. Negative density-dependent feedback (a and b) is associated with the depletion of food resources at high densities, an increasing death rate (or decreasing birth rate – not shown) with an increase in population density, and a stable equilibrium density (e) for a given set of environmental conditions. Positive density-dependent feedback (c and d) is associated with an advantage in numbers, an increasing birth rate with increasing population density (or decreasing death rate – not shown), and an unstable equilibrium or outbreak threshold (T) above which the population density increases. (From Berryman 1986, with permission.)

physical defenses (see Textbox 4.1). This can result from adverse weather conditions that cause physiological stress (e.g., drought) or breakage (e.g., wind or ice storms). Competition among trees also can induce stress by limiting the water, light and nutrients available to the weaker competitors. When the population of trees that is susceptible to pest colonization increases, opportunistic herbivore populations also tend to increase, but the herbivores will consume the finite food supply that results in a population decline. This simple dynamic is seen in certain "secondary" bark beetles whose populations build up on logging slash, winter breakage, or windthrown trees. These "outbreaks" are simply short-lived responses to favorable environmental conditions. The increase in mortality or decrease in birth rate that is associated with over consumption of the food supply is called **negative density-dependent feedback** (Figure 4.3a, b). This means that as the pest population density increases, the increased density causes deterioration of the environmental conditions that caused the initial increase. Pest populations exhibiting negative density-dependent feedback tend to self-regulate near an equilibrium density determined largely by the food supply. The role of density-dependent processes in a general theory of insect population dynamics is the foundation of this section and was developed by Berryman (1981; 1986; 1987; 1999), Isaev *et al.* (1984), and Berryman and Kindl-mann (2008).

Textbox 4.1 Asian longhorned beetle in China

Anoplophora glabripennis, known as the Asian longhorned beetle (ALB), in the West, but as *guang jian xing tian niu* (smooth-shouldered, white-spotted longhorned beetle) to Chinese entomologists, is an important pest of hardwoods in Asia, Europe and North America. It is native to China and the Korean Peninsula and is a very serious invasive in Europe and North America, where it has gained considerable notoriety in recent years.

Because damage has been so severe in North America, the question is often asked: How can there be any trees left in China and Korea where ALB has been known since at least the Qing Dynasty? The answer to this question begins with a comparison of the situations in China and Korea. In Korea, ALB populations are sparse and cause relatively little damage. This appears to be due to a variety of factors including the natural resistance of native tree species to ALB colonization, relatively high diversity of tree species (at least by temperate standards), effective regulation by natural enemies, and a narrower host range (Williams *et al.* 2004).

In stark contrast to the situation in Korea, in China losses due to ALB have been staggering. ALB is widely distributed in China, but the severe damage has occurred primarily in the "Three Norths Region" which includes most of the northern tier of provinces and Inner Mongolia. In an effort to confront the problem of desertification in this arid and semi-arid region, massive afforestation programs were mounted, the largest of which is known as the Three Norths Shelter Forest System Project. This project includes 30.6 million ha of afforestation distributed in nearly 43% of the land surface of China. In spite of this herculean effort to stem the expansion of the northern deserts, desertification has intensified, sandstorm frequency has increased and the majority of planted trees have died (Cao 2008). In the interest of producing wood for commercial use, 80% of the trees planted were fast growing species such as *Populus tremula*, established in monocultures. These fast-growing trees had significantly higher water demands than the native vegetation causing water tables to drop, resulting in drought-stress to the trees making

Textbox 4.1 (cont.)

them susceptible to ALB colonization and subsequent mortality (Cao 2008). In Ningxia Autonomous Region alone, approximately 80 million infested trees were felled in an effort to control the infestation and another 11 million trees were lost in Inner Mongolia (Yang 2005).

ALB also has been a serious urban forest problem in Chinese cities. For instance, 70 000 *Acer negundo* were killed in the northeastern city of Harbin in 2004 (Li 2008). Since *A. negundo* is native to North America, not Asia, it is not surprising that it has not evolved resistance to ALB. However, in these urban settings, many native tree species are also infested by ALB raising the question of why native tree species have been so severely damaged. Perhaps urban trees which are often stressed by heat, droughty conditions and physical damage are less resistant to insect attack. There may also be frequency-dependent factors involved such as escape from natural enemy regulation or Allee effects (when reproduction or survival increase with population density [Yamanaka and Liebhold 2009]).

In some cases, the negative effect of an increasing pest population occurs after a time lag. This can be caused by natural enemies whose populations grow in response to the increased pest density, but do so only after one or more generations of the pest have passed. The production of **induced secondary metabolites** (defensive chemicals produced in response to herbivory) in plants may also cause a delayed negative effect on herbivore populations by effectively reducing food quality and herbivore fecundity. Entomopathogenic fungi, bacteria, and viruses also increase in abundance when their host populations increase, and this can cause the termination of an outbreak by causing an outbreak of disease on the pest itself. Because all of these biotic agents respond to increased pest density with a time lag, they tend to cause outbreak cycles that occur at fairly regular intervals typically around 8–11 years in length. This is called delayed negative density-dependent feedback. It is likely that these agents interact or affect different phases of the pest population cycle (Dwyer *et al.* 2004).

As we have just discussed, an increase in the population density of a pest often results in negative feedback that causes the pest abundance to decrease. However, in some cases, an increase in the pest population causes **positive density-dependent feedback**, which results in a further increase in the pest population density (Figure 4.3c, d). In general, this involves some sort of "advantage in numbers" mechanism. For instance, a natural enemy with weak numerical and functional responses may quickly become overwhelmed by the sheer numbers of prey in the building phase of an outbreak; and while the natural enemy may kill a greater number of prey, they kill smaller and smaller proportions of the prey population as the prey density increases. Similarly, aggressive species of bark beetles form mass aggregations on their hosts, which quickly overwhelm the resin defenses of the tree (in the case of conifers). If a small number of bark beetles attack a reasonably healthy tree, they will be expelled and killed by copious resin flow as they bore into the inner bark tissues and breach the resin canals. However, if a sufficiently large number of beetles attack *en masse*, then they can cause the tree to "bleed out" and be colonized and killed. A successful bark beetle attack on a healthy tree requires the recruitment of enough beetles to overwhelm the tree's defenses, which makes a healthy tree that is usually unsuitable for colonization available as a food source that supports additional bark beetle population growth. As the bark beetle population grows, there are more and more individuals available for recruitment to mass attacks, which results in ever-increasing numbers of living trees that are converted to beetle food further favoring a continued increase in the bark beetle population.

Pest populations that display positive density-dependent feedback have density thresholds above which the birth rate is greater than the death rate, and the population increases toward outbreak levels. Below the threshold, the birth rate is lower than the death rate and the population declines toward extinction. This threshold is known as an **outbreak threshold**. An easily observed characteristic of this population behavior is that they spread from an epicenter. At the epicenter, environmental conditions including abiotic factors, cause a localized population increase. For example, in the southeastern USA, the southern pine beetle (SPB), *Dendroctonus frontalis*, normally occurs at low densities, but colonizes lightning-struck pines that are unhealthy and unable to defend against bark beetle attack. The attacking SPB reproduce in the damaged tree and the population grows. The new generation of beetles that emerges from the killed tree along with others that are attracted to the area by the aggregation pheromone produced by these beetles then attack neighboring trees and raise the population density of surrounding areas above the outbreak threshold. As this process continues, the outbreak spreads outward from the epicenter and the area of dead and dying trees grows in size.

Recognizing the population processes underlying an outbreak is a critical component of forest pest management decision-making. Fortunately, there are observable characteristics of forest insect outbreaks that forest managers can use for this purpose. The geospatial dynamics of an outbreak are an important feature distinguishing gradient outbreaks (those with negative density-dependent feedback mechanisms) from eruptive outbreaks (those with positive density-dependent feedback). Outbreaks that, once initiated, spread from an epicenter are of the latter type, as discussed above. Outbreaks that arise over a broad area defined by the presence of weakened host trees are of the gradient type.

Temporal dynamics of an outbreak also provide important clues as to the underlying population processes. Long-term data sets on pest population densities are used to determine if a certain pest's population cycles at regular intervals, remains high for a brief period, or is sustained at a high level. The regularity of the interval between cycling outbreaks varies. Some display remarkably uniform periodicity, while others show greater variation in the interval from outbreak to outbreak. The larch budmoth (*Zeiraphera diniana*) in Central Europe and the Alps has cycled every eight or nine years for approximately 1200 years. Only in the past 30 years has this periodicity changed, apparently in response to climate change (Esper *et al.* 2007). Rarely are such long-term records available, but in trees with observable annual growth rings, dendrochronological methods typically enable one to detect evidence of outbreaks for several decades prior to sampling. Non-cycling outbreaks may be short-lived pulses, which are the result of temporary environmental disturbances such as drought, windstorms, or ice damage. They also may be sustained over a relatively long period of time, which typically results from chronic environmental conditions favoring the pest including overstocking of stands or poor site conditions for the tree species growing there. Thus, there are three temporal patterns of pest outbreaks, each with different underlying causes and ramifications for management.

4.2.2 Combining spatial and temporal characteristics allows for a practical classification of forest insect outbreaks (Table 4.1).

1. **Sustained-gradient outbreak** dynamics are the result of forest insects responding to favorable environmental conditions over an extended period of time. Environmental conditions that favor forest insects are varied but may include conditions related to site history. For example, reforested agricultural lands have highly disturbed soils that may not support the native tree species that were original to the site. Trees growing on such sites may attain some size before the stress resulting from soil conditions becomes sufficient to weaken the trees and make them susceptible to insect (or disease) problems. Similarly, overstocked stands suffer from high levels of inter-tree competition, and are likely to experience elevated levels of insect- and disease-caused mortality.

2. **Pulse-gradient outbreaks** are similar to sustained gradients in that they are the result of environmental conditions favoring insect populations. They differ, however, in being short-lived. Pulse gradients are typically caused by abiotic disturbances such as wind or ice storms, drought, or temperature anomalies that create an abundance of damaged or stressed trees. These ephemeral resources can be exploited by herbivorous insects

Table 4.1. *Classification of insect outbreaks based on temporal and spatial characteristics (modified from Berryman 1987)*

Temporal characteristics	Spatial characteristics	
	Does not spread from epicenter (negative density dependent feedback)	Spreads from epicenter (positive density dependent feedback)
Population density remains high for extended time (site & stand conditions)	Sustained gradient	Sustained eruptive
Population density remains high for short time (environmental disturbance)	Pulse gradient	Pulse eruptive
Population density peaks in regular cycles (delayed density-dependent feedback)	Cyclical gradient	Cyclical eruptive

whose populations increase and remain high until the resource is depleted, at which time they return to a lower equilibrium density. An example is *Hylobius abietis*, variously known as the large pine weevil, the large brown trunk beetle, or snytbagge (in Sweden). It is a serious pest of conifers throughout Europe where it breeds in cut stumps following timber harvesting. The adults feed on the bark of seedlings causing extensive mortality and thereby creating regeneration difficulties. As the suitability of cut stumps declines over time, so does the weevil population.

3. **Cyclical-gradient outbreaks** result from delayed density-dependent feedback mechanisms (i.e., numerical functional responses) involving host defenses or natural enemies (predators, parasitoids, pathogens) that are associated with site conditions. Cyclical-gradient outbreaks persist for about two to three generations and recur at regular intervals (8–11 generations). They are typically exhibited by defoliators that do not cause excessive tree mortality. The larch budmoth in the Swiss Alps

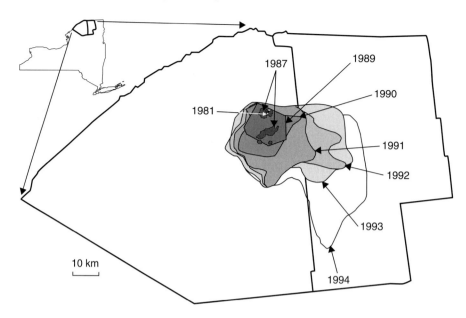

Figure 4.4 A forest pest outbreak that spread from an epicenter. The pine false webworm (*Acantholyda erythrocephala*) in northern New York. This outbreak began in 1981 in a 30 ha stand of Scots pine (white area at center) and spread every year until it infested 5440 ha of pine hosts in a total area of 231 000 ha. (Photo courtesy of D.A. Allen.)

is a well-studied example of a defoliator that exhibits very regular population cycles. While previously thought to be due to the delayed response of induced host defenses (Baltensweiler and Fischlin 1988; Berryman 1999), the delayed numerical responses of parasitoids have recently been shown to be a more likely cause (Turchin *et al.* 2003).

4. **Sustained-eruptive outbreaks** spread from an epicenter and persist for several years. All eruptive outbreaks involve positive density-dependent feedback associated with cooperative behavior or outstripping the killing capacity of natural enemies. Many defoliators exhibit sustained eruptive outbreaks and do not cause extensive mortality directly, but may cause sufficient stress to the host tree to cause attack by secondary pests or pathogens that are the direct cause of tree death. The pine false webworm (*Acantholyda erythrocephala*) is a conifer-feeding sawfly native to Europe and introduced to northeastern North America around 1920. In 1985 a small (30 ha) outbreak occurred in a pine plantation in northern New York that spread every year until 1995, by which time it infested 5440 ha of pine in a total area of 231 000 ha (Figure 4.4). As it spread, populations remained high near the epicenter and host trees (*Pinus sylvestris*, *P. strobus*, and *P. resinosa*) sustained considerable growth loss

and mortality. The outbreak subsided in 1998–2000 as a result of extensive harvesting of the host trees (Asaro and Allen 2001).

5. **Pulse-eruptive outbreaks** also spread from an epicenter, but have a brief duration. They cause extensive localized mortality and then subside as the host resource is depleted or pathogens, parasitoids or predators cause mortality rates to exceed birth rates. Aggressive bark beetles in the genus *Dendroctonus* regularly undergo pulse-eruptive outbreaks in North America as their population densities increase in response to temporary environmental stressors including lightning and drought. These insects form mass aggregations on their hosts using a system of chemical communication (pheromones) to coordinate their activities, and when they are able to recruit a sufficient number of conspecifics they overwhelm the chemical defenses of healthy host trees normally able to repel smaller numbers of beetles.

6. **Cyclic-eruptive outbreaks** are not common but show the same temporal pattern as cyclical gradients but also spread from epicenters. A species of jumping plant lice (*Cardiaspina albitextura*) that feeds on eucalyptus trees in Australia is the only known example.

4.3 Control of forest insects

Recognizing the underlying causes and types of insect outbreaks can enable forest managers to make pest management decisions that will lead to cost effective and sustainable solutions. Failure to understand the factors that initiate and sustain outbreaks can lead to suppression tactics that bring short-term relief but exacerbate the root causes of the outbreak and make the problem worse in the long run.

Sustained-gradient outbreaks are maintained by favorable site conditions, so direct suppression of the pest population can provide only a temporary benefit. It is better to identify the specific factors such as the site conditions that favor a given pest and then to alter the conditions in such a way as to bring the pest to a lower equilibrium density that limits damage to tolerable levels. The western pine shoot borer (*Eucosma sonomana*) is a moth that mines both lateral and terminal shoots of managed lodgepole (*P. contorta*) and ponderosa pines (*P. ponderosa*) in western North America. It can damage its hosts for 25–30 years and is more prevalent on faster-growing trees than on slower-growing trees. Unfortunately, management practices such as intensive site preparation and brush control, which favor faster tree growth, also favor the shoot borer. In this case, prevention by mixed planting with Douglas-fir can reduce damage, but direct suppression of the pest with insecticides or pheromones also is used to reduce damage.

Pulse-gradient outbreaks are, by definition, short lived and in many instances, direct control of the pest population may not be necessary. However, when the damage caused during the pulse interferes with management objectives, then management intervention is warranted. The damage to regeneration caused by *H. abeitis* is short lived, but often severe because reduced recruitment into a new cohort leads to reduced stocking density or expensive replanting. Consequently, chemical or biological control is frequently used to suppress weevil populations to protect young seedlings during the period of high weevil densities.

The Douglas-fir tussock moth (*Orgyia pseudotsugata*) is a widespread defoliating moth of Douglas-fir in western North America that exhibits cyclical-gradient outbreaks. Defoliation by *O. pseudotsugata* weakens the host tree and makes it susceptible to attack by secondary insect pests and pathogens. Most notably, the Douglas-fir beetle (*Dendroctonus pseudotsugae*) frequently attacks and kills Douglas-fir trees that have been defoliated by *O. pseudotsugata*. During outbreak years of *O. pseudotsugata*, a spray formulation of a pathogenic virus is effective in suppressing population growth and reducing tree mortality (Otvos *et al.* 1999) during the peak of the cycle. A treatment that augments natural enemy populations (including pathogens) is effective in this case because the population cycles are driven by natural enemies, not induced defenses of the host. In pests exhibiting cyclical-gradient outbreaks that are regulated at low density by induced host defenses, population suppression by application of chemical or microbial insecticides would interfere with the induction of the host defenses by reducing defoliation. In such cases the pest population may continue to increase after the insecticide treatments are ceased.

Sustained-eruptive outbreaks must be managed using a dual strategy. It is important to correct the underlying environmental conditions that favor pest population build up (when possible), and also to suppress the population below the outbreak threshold in order to return the pest to a low-density equilibrium. The European woodwasp (*Sirex noctilio*) is an example of a forest pest that exhibits sustained-eruptive outbreaks. Outbreaks in the southern hemisphere are typically associated with overstocked, unthinned plantations of radiata pine (*Pinus radiata*). The inter-tree competition leaves the trees weakened and susceptible to insect attack. When the woodwasp population builds up on this resource, it reaches high population densities where probing of healthy trees by numerous female woodwasps results in a toxin load in the tree that weakens it. Thus, the high population benefits itself by making healthy trees susceptible. Suppression of the woodwasp population with biological control agents keeps it below its outbreak threshold, but maintaining tree vigor through silviculture (especially timely thinning) eliminates the initial cause of the population increase.

The environmental conditions (e.g., weather, drought) that favor the initiation of pulse eruptives are usually beyond the ability of forest managers to influence. Thus the management options are either to do nothing or, if the forest damage caused by such outbreaks is considered unacceptable, then suppression of the pest below its outbreak threshold may be a viable alternative. The mountain pine beetle (*D. ponderosae*) in western North America is an intensively studied species of outbreaking pest with pulse-eruptive dynamics. The environmental conditions that favor population build up are drought and even-aged stands of overmature trees. While drought conditions cannot be avoided, overmature trees, in many instances, can be harvested to reduce the population of trees on which bark beetles can build up. However, a very effective strategy of population management has been developed and implemented in western Canada that involves the felling of infested trees together with a pheromone-trapping treatment to further reduce the beetle population below the outbreak threshold. This technique has been used effectively to minimize damage to lodgepole pine in western Canada, but the extent of the recent damage due to climate change (See Textbox 7.1, Chapter 7) has overwhelmed forest managers' ability to keep up with the problem.

4.4 Disease

Biotic disease results when the interaction of the host, the pathogen, and the environment are favorable in time and space. In other words, the host must be susceptible to the particular pathogen present, the pathogen must be virulent on that particular host, the environmental factors must be favorable for disease development, and all of these factors must come together in the correct temporal and spatial dimensions for disease to occur. Plant pathologists refer to this concept as the **disease triangle**, or as the **disease pyramid** if you include the temporal dimension. For these reasons, biotic disease is the exception rather than the rule in populations of plants, including trees. Nevertheless, disease does occur in populations of trees, and the impacts can be significant. The concept of the disease pyramid is important because if one understands the specific details, it is possible to design effective disease control/management strategies based on breaking the weakest leg of the triangle/pyramid. Some examples of control options based on this concept include the use of tree varieties resistant to a given strain or race of the pathogen, the removal of **inoculum** (the agent of pathogen dispersal whether it be a fungal spore, virus particle, or bacterial cell, etc.) from the soil by stump removal, fungicides to kill spores of a virulent fungal leaf pathogen, increasing or decreasing moisture to prevent infection, or delayed planting of tree seedlings to avoid the inoculum release period of a pathogen.

In addition, for biotic disease to result the pathogen must complete the following seven steps referred to as the **disease development cycle**. The cycle involves an interaction of the host and the pathogen life cycles. A detailed knowledge of the specifics of the disease development cycle for a specific host-pathogen interaction can facilitate effective disease management strategies. The first step is inoculation during which the inoculum of the pathogen must contact the host plant. The second step, penetration occurs when the inoculum contacts an infection court (in trees these can be wounds, natural openings, or via an insect vector). Infection occurs when pathogen-host cell contact is made. This step is followed by incubation, which is the time interval between infection and symptom development. In trees, this period can be decades long, and often is referred to as the latent period. Step five is invasion, which involves movement of the pathogen away from the initial infection site. The next step is reproduction during which the pathogen produces more inoculum. Lastly, dissemination involves inoculum spread to infect new hosts. If one can disrupt this cycle at any point, then biotic disease will not develop. Therefore, the more pathologists know about the details of these seven steps, the easier it will be to prevent disease development. You may be shocked to learn how little we really know about these details for many (most?) diseases. There is much work for future forest pathologists.

It is not a trivial matter to prove that a suspect pathogen causes a specific disease. A set of rules, called **Koch's Postulates**, named after Robert Koch (1843–1901), the famous German physician and one of the founders of microbiology, must be followed to do so. The four postulates are as follows: First, there must be a constant (100%) association of the suspect pathogen and the specific disease syndrome. Second, the suspect pathogen must be isolated from the diseased host and grown in pure culture. Third, when inoculated into healthy plants, the suspect pathogen must induce the disease symptoms. Fourth, re-isolation from the inoculated host must yield the same pathogen. These postulates apply to all biotic diseases whether the host is a human, pig, petunia, or microorganism. There are obvious problems applying these rules to trees. Trees are long-lived organisms, in and on which many biotic agents may occur at any point in time. Therefore, isolation of the proper suspect causal agent can be problematic. To generate disease, the suspect pathogen must interact with both the host and a suitable environment at the proper time (i.e., disease triangle concept). Often, forest pathologists do not know the proper environmental conditions or timing necessary for infection of the host, and thus even though the suspect pathogen may be correct, no disease results upon inoculation of the host. Decline diseases, which are diseases of mature trees caused by specifically ordered sets of interacting factors, are not readily amenable to these postulates because the specific factors are not known or cannot be artificially recreated in time or space; and therefore are difficult to diagnose.

There are many closely allied disciplines upon which forest pathology is closely linked. Disease development is a dynamic, not a static, process because the host is actively involved in the interaction. Thus, a major subdiscipline of forest pathology involves the study of host-pathogen interactions that requires detailed knowledge of biochemistry, genetics, tree physiology, molecular biology, and other disciplines, and is beyond the scope of this book. Discoveries in this area of forest pathology research have lead to great advances in our knowledge of how diseases develop in trees, how pathogens spread, the development of effective disease management strategies, as well as the development of specific and sensitive diagnostic techniques (Lundquist 2005).

How does disease spread in populations of trees? The study of how diseases spread in populations is called **epidemiology**. It, too, is another important subdiscipline of plant/forest pathology. Forest land managers most often need to manage disease in populations of trees. Therefore, one strategy to manage disease involves limiting spread. Very few control measures completely stop a disease. If, however, we can slow disease spread such that replanting or regeneration compensates for the trees lost, then we have been successful. A plant disease **epiphytotic** is an increase in disease in time. Some epiphytotics increase rapidly, and some slowly. There are two basic types of disease increase: Simple and compound. In compound increase, each infected host contributes inoculum to infect other healthy hosts. This usually is not true for simple disease increase. Obviously then, disease increase in a compound manner can be explosive. If one plots the accumulated disease increase against time, called the disease-progress curve, either a sigmoid curve (compound) or a straight line (simple) will result. It is important to realize that compound spread is not normal for most natural populations because natural populations of plants and pathogens have coevolved over time to reach a balance that prevents domination of one over the other. Various features of the disease cycle will allow rapid short-term change, but will generally act to limit long-term change. This type of disease increase is more common in an artificial population such as an agricultural field or a plantation, or when a native population of plants is invaded by an exotic pathogen (see Chapter 5). Mathematical models based on the shape of the disease-progress curve can be used to recognize exotic pathogen introductions, management activities that have changed the natural balance between native hosts and pathogens, identify environmental factors that trigger disease increase, etc.

Early epidemiological studies, such as the above discussion illustrates, have focused on the temporal dynamics of disease spread. But diseases also spread and increase in space as well as in time. Forest diseases are key determinants of forest health. Both forest diseases and forest health are spatial as well as temporal phenomena; and thus can be assessed at many spatial scales including the individual tree, stand, community, and landscape.

Landscape pathology integrates the disciplines of landscape ecology and plant pathology, and thus is concerned with how ecological and pathological factors vary in space, how this variability influences biotic and abiotic interactions within the ecosystem, and how these interactions can be managed to achieve specific objectives (Dobson and Crawley 1994) (see Chapter 2 for discussion of various techniques developed by landscape pathologists to identify and/or monitor disease/mortality in space, etc.).

As discussed below, diseases impact forest health by altering community structure and spatial heterogeneity by killing trees, enhancing susceptibility to secondary stresses and insect pests, or preventing the establishment of regeneration. A few examples of diseases that impact forest health and alter spatial heterogeneity at the landscape level include chestnut blight, white pine blister rust, jarrah dieback (see Chapter 5), oak wilt, and Metrosideros decline (Lundquist 2005). Because forest pathology aims to solve practical management problems, it seems logical that disease management information and forest health assessments are more likely to be useful to forest managers if they address the same spatial scales at which management decisions are made. Increasingly stand-scale management, traditionally the focus of silviculturists, is being supplemented or replaced by landscape-scale management, particularly as the range of resources that are managed in extensive forest lands has increased (multiple-use management) (Shea 1998). An important need is to develop a set(s) of spatial metrics to characterize these impacts or changes. Many such metrics have been developed (e.g., Lundquist *et al.* 2002, Lundquist and Beatty 2002, see Chapter 2). Characterizing the state of a landscape using numerical spatial metrics simplifies comparative analyses, disease monitoring, forest health assessments, and ultimately management decisions. Spatial heterogeneity has traditionally been considered a barrier to effective disease management. But increasingly, it is coming to be viewed as a quality that increases management options. Spatial metrics have expanded the view of disease management beyond simple reduction or elimination of disease, to an understanding that diseases play more complex roles in forests when managers restore, conserve, or otherwise manipulate ecosystems.

> 4.4.1 *Diseases may have a positive, negative, or no impact on overall forest health; and thus on management decisions.*

How does disease affect the health of a forest? Diseases influence forest dynamics, and thus forest health, in many ways. Their influence is exerted primarily through the mechanism of tree mortality, which can occur at either the broad landscape scale, or at the scale of the individual tree or small groups of trees (Castello *et al.* 1995). Mortality, whatever the cause, is essential to permit forest succession to proceed (see Chapters 6 and 8), as well as to maintain a sustainable forest (a forest with a stable size and age class structure; see Chapters 1, 2, and 3). Silviculturists have known this fact for a long time. They manage mortality and light levels with a chainsaw. But disease also can affect forest structure and species composition, succession, biodiversity, and landscape pattern. Such changes can, in turn, affect disease development and spread. Diseases are effective regulators of species distributions (Augspurger 1984; Burdon and Shattock 1980; Dinoor and Eshed 1984; Grubb 1977; Read 1968). A dramatic example of the impact of disease on forest structure and composition is chestnut blight in North America. This disease eliminated chestnut from the overstory in eastern deciduous forests, relegating it to an understory shrub (Keever 1953; Mackey and Sivec 1973. McCormick and Platt 1980; Stephenson 1986). Although the species replacing chestnut varies with location, oak-hickory forests now are replacing many forests once dominated by chestnut (also see Chapter 5). Fungal root diseases have altered structure, composition, and community patterns in coniferous forests of the Pacific Northwest of North America (Boone *et al.* 1988; Byler *et al.* 1990; Kile *et al.* 1991 Shaw and Kile 1991; van der Kamp 1991). Root rot has dramatically altered the structure and composition of the dry and wet sclerophyll eucalypt forests of Australia (Weste 1986). Diseases also are important in the dynamics of old-growth forests through the formation of canopy gaps (McCauley and Cook 1980, Worrall and Harrington 1988). Mortality, however, is not the only mechanism by which diseases can exert an influence on forest development. By direct mortality or by slowing the growth of susceptible genotypes in concert with competition for resources, pathogens can influence which individuals will grow into the canopy. These examples illustrate that diseases can profoundly impact forest development, and thus forest health.

Insects and diseases are natural, indeed essential, components of all forest ecosystems. They serve important functions as discussed above. The mortality that they induce normally is essential to the proper functioning of a forest ecosystem. So why worry about them? The critical question is not one of *if*, but *how much* disease or insect-induced mortality is necessary to maintain a healthy forest (see Chapters 1, 2, and 3). Thus, all forests require a "healthy amount of mortality." When, then, does disease become problematic? By establishing objectively the specific amount of mortality needed to maintain a healthy forest (i.e., baseline mortality) it is possible to determine when there is too little mortality and thereby predict when a forest is likely to experience a significant mortality event, and actions taken to prepare for it. It is important

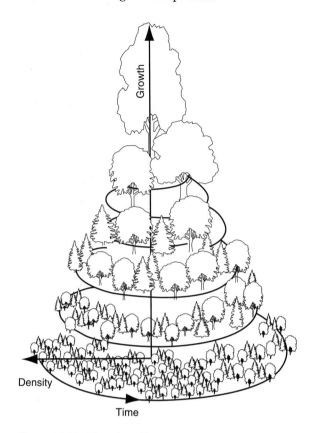

Figure 4.5 The Phoenix Helix concept. (From Manion and Griffin 2001, with permission.)

to know which insect pests and pathogens are operating within a forest ecosystem, and under what circumstances they are likely to become problematic. If we do not, then the pathogens and pests in the ecosystem become the real forest managers.

The concept of the **Phoenix Helix** (Manion and Griffin 2001) helps to put this discussion of mortality into the proper context. The premise of the concept is that the forest, like the mythical bird, derives life from death. The forest forms an upwardly spiraling population of increasingly larger, but fewer trees (Figure 4.5) where diameter growth, tree density, and time interact to form the upward and inwardly directed helix. At time zero, the forest consists of a large population of small seedlings at high density. The density vector is long, and at the base of the growth vector. Over time the density vector rotates around the growth vector as seedlings die shortening the density vector, and the survivors grow in diameter and height. In this way, the rotating vector rises above its base, and the tip follows an upward and inwardly rotating helix. Thus, a healthy (balanced growth and mortality) forest evolves from a continuous dynamic process involving multiple cohorts with a predictable relative mortality across diameter classes to produce a forest with a stable age and size-class structure.

We propose that insect pests and pathogens become problematic when the mortality that they induce is greater than the baseline mortality determined for that particular forest, thus disrupting its sustainability (i.e., the current age and size class structure). Furthermore, this situation typically occurs when stable and healthy forest ecosystems are disturbed as a consequence of human activities. Human-induced disturbances include, but are not limited to: fire, fire suppression, climate change, pollutants, land-use history, site disturbances such as logging or mismanagement, introduction of exotic pests and pathogens, salinization, grazing by domesticated animals, etc.

Textbox 4.2 Fusiform rust

A classic example that effectively illustrates the role of anthropogenic disturbance in setting-up a disease problem is provided by fusiform rust in the southeastern United States. Fusiform rust is caused by the rust fungus *Cronartium quercuum* f.sp. *fusiforme*. It is a major obstacle to intensive forest management in the southern United States. Significant annual losses result from direct mortality and defect resulting from stem infection of young trees (seedlings to about 8 years old) resulting in galls and cankers. Almost 100% infection often is observed within 5–10 years in plantations established in high-hazard areas. The pathogen is complex and requires five spore stages and two hosts (pine and oak) to complete its life cycle. The most susceptible and economically important pine hosts are loblolly (*P. taeda*) and slash (*P. elliottii*) pines, although many other species are susceptible. The most important natural alternate hosts are water (*Quercus nigra*) and laurel (*Q. imbricaria*) oaks, but at least 22 oak species are susceptible.

The disease, native to the southern USA but a rarity at the turn of the 20th century, has expanded rapidly in geographic range, incidence, and severity in large areas of the South since about 1940. Why? The explanation involves a combination of many factors some of which include past land abuse, fire suppression, the increasing intensity of forest management, poor forestry practices, and the initial genetic selection of pines for rapid growth and better form without regard for susceptibility to rust. The disease was first described in 1896, at which time it was relatively scarce. Colonization of the land and early attempts at forest management disrupted the balance between the pathogen and its hosts. The pine forests of this region were a fire sub-climax, i.e., maintained by natural and native-set fires. Fire-resistant

Textbox 4.2 (cont.)

longleaf pine (*P. palustris*) grew on the higher and drier sites, the less fire-resistant slash pine on the low areas and swamp margins, and loblolly pine on the upper coastal plain and on moist inland sites not frequently burned. Following the Revolutionary War in 1789, there were several cycles of land clearing for agriculture followed by land abandonment. The abandoned fields were invaded by loblolly and slash pines. But disease-resistant longleaf pine was preferred for timber up until the early 20th century, but after harvest it was not replanted because of regeneration problems attributed to another disease in combination with fire-suppression practices. Fire suppression also favored the regeneration of slash and loblolly pines, as well as to release the suppressed oak (alternate host) understory. Beginning in about 1920, abandoned lands were planted with slash and loblolly pine seedlings raised in nurseries that were unknowingly distributing rust-infected seedlings. This situation was attributed, in part, to the development of mechanized seedling lifting equipment that circumvented inspection and culling of individual seedlings, thus allowing the fungus to be introduced into new areas where it did not yet occur. Regional rust surveys that began in 1930 showed that the rust spread from southern Louisiana and Mississippi essentially throughout the range of slash and loblolly pines by the 1960s, where rust incidence varied from 1–100%.

The disease affects nurseries, plantations, and natural stands, and trees of all ages and size classes from seedlings to sawtimber-sized trees more than 50 years of age. Infections decrease as the trees age, and progress of the disease slows as trees gain size. Infection in the later stages of a rotation causes very little mortality and little loss of wood through defect. The greatest mortality and defect occur in plantations up to five years of age. Sections of trees with galls or cankers are unacceptable for either lumber or pulpwood, and must be culled. Young trees with numerous stem and branch cankers are so deformed that they are worthless even for pulpwood. The growth rate of infected trees is reduced. Mortality is more frequent in slash pine, whereas slow growth is more common in loblolly pine as a result of multiple stem cankers. A measure of the incidence of infection is not the best measure of the economic impact of this disease. The reduction in stand productivity caused by the amount of space occupied by deformed and dwarfed trees also must be considered in addition to losses caused by death or windthrow of infected trees.

This disease has altered the size and age-class structure of the plantations and natural stands in which it occurs. By causing greater

Textbox 4.2 (cont.)

mortality and the need to cull smaller trees it results in decreased stocking levels (in plantations), and higher baseline mortality in the lower size and age classes (in natural stands), and thus an unhealthy (i.e., unstable and unsustainable) forest.

In nurseries, disease management is focused on proper timing and spraying with effective fungicides. In plantations, disease management must begin with the planting of non-infected seedlings. Disease management using silvicultural methods can lessen the impact of the disease in plantations and natural stands, but essentially once the disease is established in a plantation or natural stand, practical and effective control measures are almost non-existent. The management of this disease will depend upon the development and planting of disease-resistant cultivars of slash and loblolly pines, which are well underway.

Textbox 4.3 Oak decline in Central Europe

Oaks (*Quercus* spp.) have been experiencing episodic mortality from the stand to the regional level in many countries around the world for nearly 300 years. It appears on the basis of historical records, and a review of the literature, that episodes of mortality may have different causes so that a comparison of the impacts of each episode on overall forest health or the detection of trends in forest response, are difficult to evaluate. Global oak mortality problems may provide a test case to evaluate the usefulness of the baseline mortality concept for evaluation and comparison of forest health around the world. Although this discussion focuses on oak decline as it currently exists in Central Europe, oak mortality also occurs in the Far East, the southern and western United States, and Mexico. Therefore, the concepts/ principles generated here should apply equally well to other locations.

Oak species (*Q. petraea* and *Q. robur*) in combination with European beech (*Fagus sylvatica*) are arguably the most important broad-leaved forest tree species in Europe (Muesel *et al.* 1965). Oak decline has been reported from many European countries including Russia, Romania, Poland, Slovakia, the Czech Republic, Hungary, Austria, Germany, the Netherlands, Sweden, UK, Belgium, France, Italy, Spain, and Portugal (Thomas *et al.* 2002). It has been attributed to the single or combined effects of climatic extremes, defoliating insects, and pathogenic fungi (Thomas *et al.* 2002). The specifics of these factors vary in time

Textbox 4.3 (cont.)

and space. A combination of severe insect defoliation in at least two successive years coupled with climatic extremes is the most significant complex of factors that explain most episodes of oak decline in Central European oak stands on acidic sites (Thomas *et al.* 2002). In northwestern Germany, the most prevalent episodes of oak mortality are characterized by rapid and severe mortality that occur in local but widespread centers followed by decreasing and slower mortality. These episodes may last for up to 10 years, and are sometimes preceded by reduced growth. In this region, such episodes have occurred several times between 1910 and 1940, and then again after 1987 and 1997 (Wachter 2001). This syndrome is different from the general forest decline symptoms noted on oaks since the early 1990s (Eichhorn and Paar 2000). Standardized European monitoring of crown condition does not satisfactorily detect this type of oak decline with high mortality in localized centers because of the coarse and systematic sampling grid used in the European forest health monitoring system (see Chapter 10 for details). In addition, the capacity of this monitoring system to reveal trends is limited to about 10 years, which is too short in relation to temporal gradations in defoliation and extreme weather episodes to be useful (Altenkirch 1991).

It is likely that the occurrence and intensity of the factors that lead to oak decline in Central Europe will occur again in the future. What then are the consequences for forest health and forest management? On selected sites (e.g., hydromorphic sites) oak decline can result in a long-term change in forest structure, because natural oak regeneration will be prevented by grasses and sedges (Delb 1999). The death of mature oaks may lead to a community dominated by water-tolerant species such as birch, pine, and alder (Delb 1999). Tree species diversity in this scenario may increase, but overall species diversity may decrease. Is the forest in its current state sustainable or not? Are these changes desirable or not? Is it healthy or not? Is another episode of severe mortality likely in the near future? Where is forest management intervention needed? What type of an intervention is needed? How does the health of this forest compare to the health of oak forests experiencing mortality problems elsewhere? The elaboration of reliable criteria for the recognition of endangered stands is indispensable (Hartmann and Blank 1998). Management practices in decline-prone sites then should aim to maintain an adequate age-class distribution (Thomas *et al.* 2002; 2008). The baseline mortality concept of forest health allows us to address these questions, to provide those criteria, and then to permit the development of sound management procedures.

But are there guidelines, especially with regard to the health, productivity, and sustainability of the forest in question that we can provide to guide management decision making? Can we predict with any degree of accuracy when pathogens or insect pests, already present in the forest, or expected abiotic factors are likely to become problematic and what their impacts on the health of the forest might be?

4.5 Summary and conclusion

In summary, native forest insects and pathogens impact the health of forests in many ways. In natural, forested ecosystems they may determine which trees survive and grow, and which trees are naturally culled; they may determine which trees reach the canopy and become dominant; which ones will linger in the understory; and they may determine when it's time for old trees to make room for young ones. The baseline mortality approach to assessing forest health allows us to compare actual, observed levels of mortality with the amount of mortality that is needed in order for a forest to grow and to develop. In this way, we can distinguish between healthy impacts of insects and pathogens and unhealthy amounts of mortality.

We view forest insects and pathogens as problems when they interfere with management objectives, whether they are ecologically based or commodity-based. Very often, the environmental conditions that favor insect and disease problems are the result of past or ongoing human activity. The subdisciplines of forest pathology and forest entomology are critically important to the discipline of forest health because they lead to a better understanding of the ecological relationships between these organisms and the forest; and because they help forest managers monitor, control and plan for insect and disease problems that interfere with management objectives.

References

Altenkirch, W. 1991. Zyklische Fluktuationen beim Kleinen Frostspanner (*Operophthera brumata* L.). *Allg. Forst-u. Jagdz.* **162**: 2–7.

Asaro, C. and Allen, D. C. 2001. History of a pine false webworm (Hymenoptera: Pamphiliidae) outbreak in northern New York. *Canadian Journal Forest Research* **31**: 181–185.

Augspurger, C. K. 1984. Seedling survival of tropical tree species: Interactions of dispersal distance, light-gaps, and pathogens. *Ecology* **65**: 1705–1712.

Baltensweiler, W. and Fischlin, A. 1988. The larch budmoth in the Alps In: *Dynamics of Forest Insect Populations: Patterns, Causes, Implications*. Berryman, A. A. (ed.). Plenum Press, New York.

Berryman, A. A. 1981. *Population Systems: A General Introduction*. Plenum Press, New York, USA.

Berryman, A. A. 1986. *Forest Insects: Principles and Practice of Population Management*. Plenum Press, New York.

Berryman, A. A. 1987. The theory and classification of outbreaks, In: *Insect Outbreaks*. Barbosa, P. and Schultz, J. C. (eds). Academic Press, New York.

Berryman, A. A. 1999. *Principles of Population Dynamics and their Application*. Stanley Thornes, Cheltenham.

Berryman, A. A. and Kindlmann, P. 2008. *Population Systems: A General Introduction*. Springer, Dordrecht.

Boone, R. D., Sollins, P., and Cromack, Jr., K. 1988. Stand and soil changes along a mountain hemlock death and regrowth sequence. *Ecology* **69**: 714–722.

Boyce J. S. 1961. *Forest Pathology*. 3rd edition. Mc-Graw-Hill Book Co., Inc. New York, USA.

Burdon, J. J. and Shattock, R. C. 1980. Disease in plant communities. *Applied Biology* **5**: 145–219.

Byler, J. W., Marsden, M. A., and Hagle, S. K. 1990. The probability of root disease on the Lolo National Forest, Montana. *Canadian Journal Forest Research* **20**: 987–994.

Cao, S. 2008. Why large-scale afforestation efforts in China have failed to solve the desertification problem. *Environmental Science & Technology* **42**: 1826–1831.

Castello, J. D., Leopold, D. J., and Smallidge, P. J. 1995. Pathogens, patterns, and processes in forest ecosystems. *BioScience* **45**: 16–24.

Coulson, R. N., Hennier, P. B., Flamm, R. O., *et al.* 1983. The role of lightning in the epidemiology of the southern pine beetle. *Z. Ang. Entomol.* **96**: 182–193.

Delb, H. 1999. Folgewirkungen der Schwammspinner-Kalamitaet 1992 bis 1995 (*Lymantria dispar* L.) in einem mitteleuropaeischen Eichenwaldgebiet am Beispiel des Bienwaldes in Rheinland-Pfalz. *Thesis*, Goettingen, Germany: University Goettingen, Faculty of Forest Sciences.

Dinoor, A. and Eshed, N. 1984. The role and importance of pathogens in natural plant communities. *Annual Review Phytopathology* **22**: 443–466.

Dobson, A. and Crawley, M. 1994. Pathogens and the structure of plant communities. *Trends Ecology & Evolution* **9**: 393–398.

Dwyer, G., Dushoff, J., and Harrell Yee, S. 2004. The combined effects of pathogens and predators on insect outbreaks. *Nature* **430**: 341–345.

Eichhorn, J. and Paar, U. 2000. Oak decline in Europe. Methods and results of assessments in the ICP forests. In: *Recent Advances on Oak Health in Europe*. Oszako, T. and Delatour, C. (eds). Forest Research Institute, Warsaw.

Esper, J. U. Buntgen, D. C. Frank, D. *et al.* 2007. 1200 years of regular outbreaks in alpine insects. *Proceedings Royal Society* **274**: 671–679.

Foahom, B. 2003. Preliminary investigations on insect pest attacks in a disturbed evergreen forest of south Cameroon. *International Forestry Review* **6**: 195–200.

Grubb, P. J. 1977. The maintenance of species richness in plant communities: The importance of the regeneration niche. *Biol. Rev. Camb. Philos. Soc* **52**: 107–145.

Haack, R. A. and Byler, J. W. 1993. Insects and pathogens: regulators of forest ecosystems. *Journal Forestry* **91**: 32–37.

Hartmann, G. and Blank, R. 1998. Aktuelles Eichensterben in Niedersachsen-Ursachen und Gegenmaßnahmen. *Forst Holz.* **53**: 733–735.

Isaev, A. S., Khlebopros, R. G., Nedorezov, L. V., *et al.* 1984. *The Dynamics of Forest Insect Populations*. Nauka, Novosibirsk.

Keever, C. 1953. Present composition of some stands of the former oak-chestnut forest in the southern Blue Ridge Mountains. *Ecology* **34**: 44–54.

Kile, G. A., McDonald, G. I., and Byler, J. W. 1991. Ecology and disease in natural forests. In: *Armillaria Root Disease. USDA Forest Service Agriculture Handbook No. 691.* Shaw III, C. G., and Kile, G. A. (eds). USDA Forest Service, Fort Collins, CO.

Krause, C. 1997. The use of dendrochronological material from buildings to get information about past spruce budworm outbreaks. *Canadian Journal Forest Research* **27**: 69–75.

Li, H. 2008. *J. Heilongjiang Vocational Inst. Ecol. Eng* **21**: 23–24.

Long, G. E. 1988. The larch casebearer in the intermountain northwest, In: *Dynamics of Forest Insect Populations, Patterns, Causes, Implications.* Berryman, A. A. (ed.). Plenum Press, New York.

Lundquist, J. E. and Hamelin, R. C. (eds.) 2005. *Forest Pathology – From Genes to Landscapes.* APS Press, St. Paul, MN.

Lundquist, J. E. 2005. Landscape pathology: Forest pathology in the era of landscape ecology. In: *Forest Pathology – From Genes to Landscapes.* Lundquist, J. E. and Hamelin, R. C. (eds). APS Press, St. Paul, MN.

Lundquist, J. E. and Beatty, J. S. 2002. A method for characterizing and mimicking forest canopy gaps caused by different disturbances. *Forest Science* **48**: 582–594.

Lundquist, J. E., Goheen, E. M., and Goheen, D. J. 2002. Measuring positive, negative, and null impacts of forest disturbances: A case study using dwarf mistletoe on Douglas-fir. *Environmental Management* **30**: 793–800.

Mackey, H. E., Jr. and Sivec, N. 1973. The present composition of a former oak-chestnut forest in the Allegheny Mountains of western Pennsylvania. *Ecology* **54**: 915–919.

Maloney, P. E. and Rizzo, D. M. (2002). Pathogens and insects in a pristine forest ecosystem: The Sierra San Pedro Martir, Baja, Mexico. *Canadian Journal Forest Research* **32**: 488–457.

Manion, P. D. 1991. *Tree Disease Concepts.* Prentice-Hall Inc. Englewood Cliffs, NJ.

Manion, P. D. and Griffin, D. H. 2001. Large landscape scale analysis of tree death in the Adirondack Park, New York. *Forest Science* **47**: 542–549.

Manion, P. D. and D. Lachance (eds). 1992. *Forest Decline Concepts.* APS Press, St. Paul, MN.

McCauley, K. J. and Cook, S. A. 1980. *Phellinus weirii* infestation of two mountain hemlock forests in the Oregon Cascades. *Forest Science* **26**: 23–29.

McCormick, J. F. and Platt, R. B. 1980. Recovery of an Appalachian forest following the chestnut blight or Catherine Keever – you were right! *American Midland Naturalist* **104**: 264–273.

Muesel, H., Jaeger, E., and Weinert, E. 1965. *Vergleichende Chorologie der zentraleuropaeischen Flora.* Jena, Germany: VEB G. Fischer.

Otvos, I. S., Cunningham, J. C., MacLaughlan, L., *et al.* 1999. The development and operational use of a management system for control of the Douglas-fir tussock moth, *Orgyia pseudotsugata* (Lepidoptera:Lymantriidae), populations at pre-outbreak levels. In: *Proceedings: Population Dynamics, Impacts, and Integrated Management of Forest Defoliating Insects. General Technical Report NE-27.* McManus, M. L. and Liebhold, A. M. (eds). USDA Forest Service. Radnor, Pennsylvania.

Read, D. J. 1968. Some aspects of the relationship between shade and fungal pathogenicity in an epidemic disease in pines. *New Phytologist* **67**: 39–48.

Root, R. B. 1973. Organization of a plant-arthropod association in simple and diverse habitats: the fauna of collards (*Brassica oleracea*). *Ecological Monographs* **43**: 94–125.

Shaw, C. G. III and Kile, G. A. 1991. *Armillaria Root Disease. USDA Forest Service Agriculture Handbook No. 691*. USDA Forest Service, Fort Collins, CO.

Shea, K. 1998. Management of populations in conservation, harvesting, and control. *Trends Ecology & Evolution* **13**: 371–375.

Stephenson, S. L. 1986. Changes in a former chestnut-dominated forest after a half century of succession. *American Midland Naturalist* **116**: 173–179.

Swetnam, T. W. and Lynch, A. M. 1993. Multicentury, regional-scale patterns of western spruce budworm outbreaks. *Ecological Monographs* **63**: 399–424.

Thomas, F. M., Blank, R., and Hartmann, G. 2002. Abiotic and biotic factors and their interactions as causes of oak decline in Central Europe. *Forest Pathology* **32**: 277–307.

Thomas, F. M. 2008. Recent advances in cause-effect research on oak decline in Europe. *CAB Reviews: Perspectives in Agriculture, Veterinary Science, Nutrition and Natural Resources* 2008 **3**, No 037.

Turchin, P., Wood, S. N., Ellner, S. P., *et al.* 2003. Dynamical effects of plant quality and parasitism on population cycles of larch budmoth. *Ecology* **84**: 1207–1214.

Van der Kamp, B. J. 1991. Pathogens as agents of diversity in forested landscapes. *Forestry Chronicle* **67**: 353–354.

Vehviläinena, H., Koricheva, J., Ruohomäki, K. *et al.* 2006. Effects of tree stand species composition on insect herbivory of silver birch in boreal forests. *Basic and Applied Ecology* **7**: 1–11

Veteli, T. O., Koricheva, J., Niemelä, P., and Kellomäki, S. 2006. Effects of forest management on the abundance of insect pests on Scots pine. *Forest Ecology & Management* **231**: 214–221.

Wachter, H. 2001. *Untersuchungen zum Eichensterben in Nordrhein-Westfalen. Teil 2 (1951–2000). Schriftenr. Landesforstvwerw. Nordrhein-Westfalen 13*. Arnsberg/Germany: Forstl. Dokumentationsstelle.

Weste, G. 1986. Vegetation changes associated with invasion by *Phytophthora cinnamomi* of defined plots in the Brisbane Ranges, Victoria, 1975–1985. *Australian Journal Botany* **34**: 633–648.

Whitmore, T. 1998. *An Introduction to Tropical Rain Forests*. Oxford University Press, New York.

Williams, D. W., Lee, H. P., and Kim, I. K. 2004. Distribution and abundance of *Anoplophora glabripennis* (Coleoptera: Cerambycidae) in natural *Acer* stands in South Korea. *Environmental Entomologist* **33**: 540–545.

Worrall, J. J. and Harrington, T. C. 1988. Etiology of canopy gaps in spruce-fir forests at Crawford Notch, New Hampshire. *Canadian Journal Forest Research* **18**: 1463–1469.

Yamanaka, T. and Liebhold, A. M. 2009. Mate-location failure, the Allee effect, and the establishment of invading populations. *Population Ecology* **51**: 37–340.

Yang, H. K. 2005. Review of the Asian longhorned beetle: research, biology, distribution and management in China. *For. Dep. Work. Pap., FBS/6E*, Food Agriculture Organization, Rome.

5

Alien invasions: the effects of introduced species on forest structure and function

D. PARRY AND S.A. TEALE

Invasive species are among the greatest threats to forested ecosystems globally (Liebhold *et al.* 1995; Vitousek *et al.* 1996; Pimental *et al.* 2000), ranking behind only deforestation and land use conversion (Walker and Steffen 1997; Wilcove *et al.* 1998). Shifting patterns of trade, globalization of economies (e.g., Hulme *et al.* 2009; Meyerson *et al.* 2007), and climate change have ensured that even the most remote and pristine forests are not immune to this threat.

Recognition of the threat to forests posed by invasive species is universal among biologists and forestry professionals, yet despite the frequency with which the term *invasive species* is used, operational definitions vary widely among disciplines. Indeed, use of this term is so imprecise that some have advocated for its elimination from ecological literature (Colautti and MacIssac 2004). Here, the term is retained for continuity and defined as a non-indigenous species whose introduction was directly or indirectly facilitated by anthropogenic forces and causes or is likely to cause significant ecological or economic harm in natural and managed ecosystems. This definition separates a select group of species from a much larger pool of introduced and naturalized species that are relatively benign ecologically and economically, and also from those whose geographic distribution has changed in response to natural phenomena.

5.1 Ecology and mechanisms of invasion

The spread of an invasive species from donor to recipient region always involves a stepwise process of transport, establishment, and spread (Richardson

Forest Health: An Integrated Perspective, ed. John D. Castello and Stephen A. Teale. Published by Cambridge University Press. © Cambridge University Press 2011.

(a)

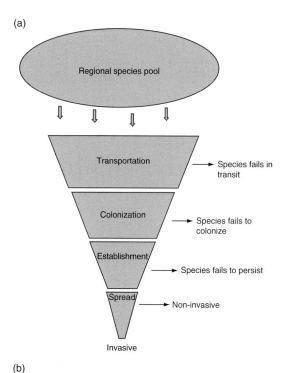

(b)

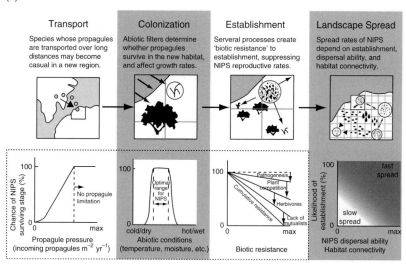

Figure 5.1 (a) The diminishing cascade as a framework for understanding biological invasion. The pathway from donor to recipient geographical region can be viewed as an inverted triangle with a series of transitional steps. At each transitional step, a portion of the original species pool does not succeed and is removed from the pathway. As a result, a very small number of the original species pool becomes a serious invader. (b) Abiotic and biotic factors regulating the likelihood of a potential invasive species transitioning through each of the phases of the diminishing cascade. (From Theoharides and Dukes 2007, with permission.) Although shown here for plant invasions, processes apply equally to other organisms. NIPS = Non-indigenous plant species.

et al. 2000; Kolar and Lodge 2001; Colautti and MacIssac 2004), often visualized as an inverted triangle (Figure 5.1a). An inverted triangle captures the diminishing cascade of potential invasive species that survive each step along the pathway from transport to actual invasive species. At each step, species are faced with extrinsic and/or intrinsic environmental and biological barriers (Figure 5.1b). Success rate in transitioning between stages varies among different groups of organisms, but irrespective of taxonomic designation, only a very small proportion of the original species pool become invasive species (Kolar and Lodge 2001; Williamson and Fitter 1996).

Successful transport, establishment, and spread of introduced species depend on many interacting factors. One of the most critical of these is **propagule pressure**, which incorporates estimates of the absolute number of individuals involved in any given release event (propagule size) and the number of discrete release events (propagule number) (Lockwood *et al.* 2005; Reaser and Waugh 2007; Simberloff 2009). Positive correlations between propagule pressure and successful establishment have been shown for a diverse array of organisms (Lockwood *et al.* 2005; Simberloff 2009), and even seemingly resilient ecosystems can be invaded if propagule pressure is sufficiently high (Colautti *et al.* 2006).

Disturbance encompasses any natural or anthropogenic perturbation to an ecosystem that increases the availability of limiting resources such as space, light, or nutrients, or alters trophic interactions (Von Holle and Simberloff 2005). Logging, fire, windthrow, drought, insect outbreak, or climate change are all examples of disturbances that can influence invasions at scales ranging from local to landscape (Hobbs and Huenneke 1992; Vitousek *et al.* 1997). Many invasive species, especially plants, appear to be disturbance adapted, and thus readily invade ecosystems following perturbation (Mack *et al.* 2000). In tandem, disturbance and propagule pressure are potent facilitators of many biological invasions (Lozon and MacIssac 1997) although it is often difficult to tease apart the interactive effects of these processes (Eschtruth and Battles 2009a).

The patterns and nature of invasive species introductions are perpetually in flux because they are a product of human trade and transportation. Thus, vectors (the method of conveyance, not to be confused with biotic vectors of pathogens discussed in Chapter 4) and **pathways** (routes on which invasive species travel) change as trade shifts between nations and regions, as specific goods and commodities fall in and out of favor, and as different modes of transportation and cargo management wax and wane (Lonsdale 1999). Long oceanic journeys aboard sailing ships, for example, precluded species that could not withstand the rigor of the voyage, but the advent of rapid

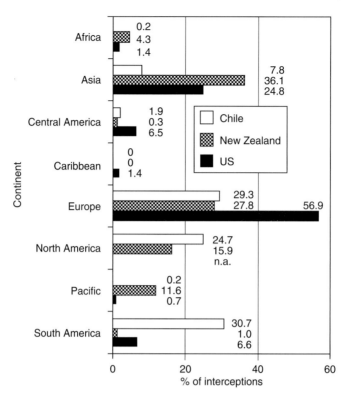

Figure 5.2 Source regions for exotic bark beetles established in three countries (USA, Chile, and New Zealand). (From Haack 2006, with permission.) Bark beetles are important targets for inspections and thus serve as useful indicators of the source countries, vectors, and pathways for introductions.

container-based sea or air cargo shipping has removed that barrier, leading to a new suite of introductions (Ruiz and Carlton 2004). Not only do donor and recipient regions change over time, so to do the organisms entrained in transit. Thus, shifting transportation vectors and pathways bring about wholesale changes in the types of organisms that are introduced. For example, many early introductions of exotic organisms to North America were associated with the movement of horticultural goods from Europe whereas contemporary introductions are dominated by species associated with containerized shipping (Ruiz and Carlton 2004). A change in trading partners or regional patterns can rapidly change the nature of introductions (Figure 5.2, Meyerson and Mooney 2007). Furthermore, legislative changes that restrict movement of goods or associated products may reduce invasive species associated with a particular region or commodity but increase invasive species introductions from elsewhere as substitute pathways and/or vectors are adopted. The introduction of legislation and the accompanying inspection and quarantine system has had a positive effect on some groups, with the rate of new establishments peaking in the early to mid 20th century for insects and plants, respectively (Meyerson and Mooney 2007; Langor *et al.* 2009).

Analysis of invasions in forests suggests great disparity in the number of introductions among various trading regions. Among insects, for example, historic trading patterns coupled with biogeographic history resulted in a large asymmetry between Europe and North America with at least 400 European species of woody plant feeding insects established in North America, while only 57 species have gone the other way (Mattson *et al.* 2007). Furthermore, most adventive North American species in Europe utilize introduced North American trees in contrast to the adoption of native Nearctic trees by insects from Europe (Mattson *et al.* 1994; Niemela and Mattson 1996). A similar asynchrony between North America and Europe exists for invasive plants (Van Kleunen and Fischer 2009), again reflecting both human and geologic history. It has been hypothesized that the asymmetry is due to a greater prevalence of generalist insect herbivores in Europe compared to North America. These generalists are better able to utilize North American woody plant species upon introduction compared to North American insect herbivores, which tend to be more specialized and fare worse upon introduction to Europe. Niemela and Mattson (1996) further hypothesized that host breadth is greater among European herbivorous insects due to extinction events that occurred when Pleistocene glaciers moved southward into the east–west oriented Alps. In North America, the principal mountain ranges are oriented north–south and when the glaciers advanced, the flora and fauna moved southward ahead of them. Rather than causing extinctions, this likely increased species diversity and specialization.

Tropical regions, especially where forests remain intact, appear to be much less invaded, although it is unclear if lower propagule pressure or greater resiliency of tropical forests due to higher tree diversity explains this pattern (Lonsdale 1999; Fine 2002; Martin *et al.* 2009). However, the importance of this threat is increasing in tropical forests while the impact of invasive species remains best documented in temperate forests (Wright 2005).

5.2 Important groups of invasive organisms in forests

5.2.1 Microorganisms

As with other invasive species, the effects of exotic pathogens on forest ecosystems depend on their mode of action, host specificity, and virulence (e.g., Lovett *et al.* 2006; Loo 2009). Thus, invasive pathogens can be viewed along a continuum ranging from reductions in tree growth, to sudden and extensive mortality across large landscapes or even continents. Introduced pathogens that have had the largest impact on natural forests generally are those with high host specificity and virulence, and that affect trees that occupy prominent ecological roles. Important pathogens originating in North America are relatively few, especially considering the extensive export of wood and horticultural products to Europe following European settlement.

Many of the most important invasive pathogens are host-specific, attacking only a single species or a group of closely related species. For example, widespread mortality has occurred in butternut (*Juglans cinerea*), white pines (five-needle *Pinus* spp.), dogwood (*Cornus florida*, *C. nuttalli*), and American beech (*Fagus grandifolia*) in North America (Loo 2009). Each of these epidemics has been associated with fungal pathogens with relatively narrow primary host specificity, as was also the case with Dutch elm disease.

Not all pathogens have narrow host ranges and some, in fact, infect a broad array of species. Perhaps one of the most important pathogen threats to forests is from several species of *Phytophthora*. These pathogens are water molds in the Kingdom Stramenopila, Phylum Oomycota, more closely related to algae than to fungi (Hansen 2008). They are characterized by a motile infectious zoospore and resting oospores, which allow them to survive conditions not suitable for growth. *Phytophthora* spp. are found throughout the world, primarily in poorly drained soils where they infect a variety of agricultural and woody plants. Most cause root diseases but on trees, a number of species are associated with cankers. Some species of *Phytophthora* have very broad host ranges.

5.2.2 Insects

With the advent of wood products for transportation by early humans, be it log rafts or travois, it is likely that insects were assisted in colonizing novel habitats. This accelerated with the domestication of woody plant crops some 12 000 years ago, and was facilitated with early trade. As continual improvements in the speed and distance of shipping occurred, so too did the volume of trade and the diversity of products carried between disparate regions. Colonization of the New World and Australasia by Europeans removed biogeographic barriers present for millions of years allowing free interchange of species from climatically similar regions and among forests composed of congeneric trees. The advent of Asian nations as major exporters of consumer goods to western countries has amplified these patterns and allowed interchange of a new suite of species.

Insect defoliators exemplify the need to use quantitatively based assessments of forest health. Because outbreaks of defoliating insects are among the most spectacular and visible examples of invasive species, attention paid to them is often disproportionate to their apparent effects on forest health. Taken as a whole, defoliators have not been particularly successful invaders, especially in continental ecosystems. Furthermore, the direct effects of introduced defoliators on forest health often are not as detrimental as other feeding guilds of insects because their effects often are ecologically similar to those of native species (see Mattson *et al.* 1991 and Chapter 4). Thus, recipient ecosystems may be pre-adapted and the relationship between exotic defoliator and host tree may be categorically similar to interactions with native insects already found in those forests.

Hardwoods generally are more resilient to defoliation than conifers, where even a single severe defoliation event can cause tree mortality, because a much greater portion of carbon reserves resides in conifer needles than in deciduous leaves (Kulman 1971). In addition, hardwoods can refoliate by developing a second set of leaves within the same season following severe defoliation. Defoliation is a significant stressor especially when repeated or chronic and if coupled with other stressors, such as drought or poor site conditions, dieback and whole tree mortality can be significant.

Introductions of new defoliators appear to have peaked in the early part of the 20th century and recent introductions to North America have been rare (Aukema *et al.* 2010). Few exotic defoliators have become established in Europe and Asia, but this is not the case for islands such as New Zealand where introductions of defoliators have accelerated over the last 15 years with a series of Asian and Australian species becoming established. Although eradication was successful for two invasive tussock moth (Lymantriidae) species, *Uraba lugens* (Nolidae), a defoliator of eucalypts introduced from Australia appears to be well established in New Zealand with unknown effects on forest health (Suckling 2005; Kay 2008; Brokerhoff *et al.* 2010).

Worldwide, the three most significant defoliator introductions have been the gypsy moth (*Lymantria dispar* L.) from Europe to North America (Textbox 5.1), the fall webworm (*Hyphantria cunea*) from North America to Asia and Europe, and the spread of horsechestnut leafminer, (*Cameraria ohridella*) from Macedonia through Western Europe and England.

In contrast to the gypsy moth, the effects of other introduced hardwood defoliators on forest health have generally been poorly studied, beyond simple metrics, such as area defoliated. For example, despite becoming widespread throughout Europe and Asia since its introduction from North America in the 1940s (Gomi 1997; Yang *et al.* 2008), the effects of even chronic defoliation by the

Textbox 5.1 Gypsy moth

The introduction of gypsy moth (*Lymantria dispar*) from Europe to North America in 1867–68 and its effects on hardwood forests have received more attention than any other exotic forest insect. Accidentally released in Medford, Massachusetts, by the entrepreneurial French astronomer Leopold Trouvelot, it has since spread north into Canada, south to North Carolina and west to Minnesota. Numerous natural enemies including parasitoids, predators, and pathogens have been released over the past century in futile attempts to check its range expansion (Elkinton and Liebhold 1990). It is likely that its geographic range will eventually encompass all hardwood forest types within its environmental envelope. The introduction of the fungal pathogen *Entomophaga maimaiga* (Hajek *et al.* 1995) in the late 1980s has reduced the intensity, frequency, and duration of regional outbreaks, at least in northeastern North America. Extensive outbreaks still occur in a variety of different forest types, predominantly those with a high oak or aspen (*Populus tremuloides*) component.

The effect of gypsy moth defoliation on trees varies with species, site, intensity, and duration of outbreaks (Figure 5.3a–d). These factors can interact to predispose trees to attack by secondary pathogens and opportunistic wood-boring beetles. The effects of gypsy moth defoliation are often greater during the first widespread outbreak in a region than during subsequent outbreaks (Figure 5.3e). In an extensive review, Davidson *et al.* (1999) suggested that already stressed trees are eliminated during the first outbreak and that remaining oak trees are more tolerant of, or resistant to, defoliation.

Because the effect of gypsy moth on forests depends on a matrix of interactions between site conditions, climate, and biotic factors, the net effect on the sustainability of the afflicted forests will likely vary in different forest types, and different regions. In areas where significant oak mortality has occurred, the basal area of oaks decreases as overstory trees and seedlings die, seed production diminishes, and the proportion of less preferred hosts such as red maple (*Acer rubrum*) or black cherry (*Prunus serotina*) increases (Campbell and Sloan 1977; Gottschalk *et al.* 1998; Jelinka and Vandermeer 2004). Many mature oak-dominated forests in the eastern United States are already changing in composition due to fire suppression, recruitment failure, and intense vertebrate herbivory on seedlings, and defoliation of canopy trees may just speed up an ongoing conversion of these stands as oak recruitment fails to keep pace with mortality (Allen and Bowersox 1989; Ganser *et al.* 1993). In areas where gypsy moth is a more recent arrival and where defoliation has

Textbox 5.1 (cont.)

been less frequent or intense following the arrival of the gypsy moth
pathogen *E. maimaiga* in the mid-1980s, species composition has probably not
been changed dramatically by this insect.

Gypsy moth defoliation is lethal to susceptible conifer species and the
frequent interception and occasional establishment of the Asian biotype, a
geographic race of the same species, is of great concern to land managers
because it prefers conifers. Successful establishment of this gypsy moth
biotype in North America might have more severe consequences for long-
term sustainability of some conifer systems. Nonetheless, to date, the
resources and effort spent controlling this insect are highly disproportionate
to the observed effects that it has had on forests in North America.

fall webworm on stand health, productivity, mortality, or other measures of
long-term sustainability have not been described in the literature.

The apparent lack of pervasive effects to forest health from introduced defoliators is likely a product of two factors. First, hardwood trees are remarkably
resilient to the direct effects of even chronic defoliation, and secondly, most, if
not all defoliator population dynamics are governed to a large extent by top-
down factors (primarily parasitoids and pathogens) rather than tree resistance.
Thus, defoliators are often more amenable to biological control than some other
guilds of insect herbivore and once successfully established, natural enemies
tend to reduce the amplitude and frequency of population outbreaks. For
example, winter moth (*Opherophtera brumata*), browntail moth (*Euproctis chrysor-
rhoea*), and several European conifer-feeding sawflies (e.g., *Diprion, Neodiprion*)
were all viewed as major threats to the health of natural and managed forests
in North America in the early 20th century but have been reduced to occasional
minor pests following successful biological control campaigns (Cunningham and
Entwhistle 1979; Elkinton *et al.* 2006; Roland and Embree 1995).

In tropical regions, native defoliators have successfully adopted exotic trees as
hosts and can be problematic, especially in plantation settings, but invasive
defoliators do not appear to be important in either natural or intensively
managed native tropical forests (Nair 2007).

While defoliators generally function as stressors, reducing tree vigor and
increasing susceptibility to opportunistic secondary insects or pathogens, the
direct effects of some invasive wood-boring insects can be rapid and substantive.
Lack of strong host plant defenses in unadapted host species may contribute to
the lethality of some wood borer introductions (e.g., Anulewicz *et al.* 2008). Wood

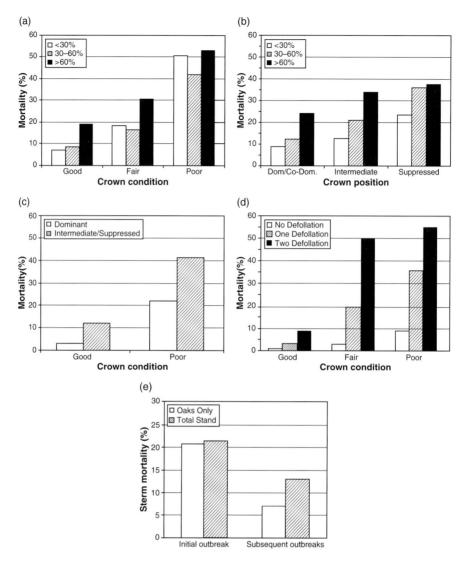

Figure 5.3 Oak mortality following gypsy moth defoliation in the northeastern United States. The effect of defoliation severity on mortality of oaks relative to (a) crown health and (b) canopy position prior to insect outbreak. (Adapted from Gottschalk *et al.* 1998.) (c) Interaction between defoliation and crown condition and (d) the number of defoliation events on mortality of oaks in Massachusetts. (Adapted from Campbell and Sloan 1977.) (e) Mortality of oaks and total stand mortality following initial and subsequent gypsy moth outbreaks. (Adapted from Davidson *et al.* 1999, with permission.)

borers (insects feeding in the cambium or xylem) are found in the orders Coleoptera, Lepidoptera, Diptera, and Hymenoptera. The most important of these are beetles (Coleoptera), comprising more than 84% of interceptions of wood borers in Canada (Langor *et al.* 2009), USA (Haack 2001), Chile (Beeche-Cisternas 2000) and New Zealand (Bain 1977). With changes in shipping methods, commodities traded, the rise of Asia in the global economy, and a series of high profile introductions, wood borers have achieved prominence as the insect group of greatest concern in forest health. Increased diligence by inspection agencies and a diminishment in the movement of untreated wood objects such as dunnage and spools appears to have reduced the rate of new incursions in New Zealand and Canada (Ridley *et al.* 2000; Langor *et al.* 2009) although establishment rates do not appear to have plateaued in the USA yet (Aukema *et al.* 2010).

Introductions of exotic longhorned beetles (Cerambycidae) have increased over the last few decades. A common vector for cerambycids is untreated, solid wood-packing materials including shipping crates, pallets, wire spools and dunnage. In North America and Europe, inspection and biomonitoring authorities frequently intercept several species of *Anoplophora*. Of these, the Asian long horned beetle (*A. glabripennis*, see Textbox 4.1) is of greatest concern as populations have become established in several areas of North America as well as in Austria, France, Germany, and Italy (Carter *et al.* 2010). Native to China and Korea, this large beetle primarily attacks trees in the genera *Acer*, *Salix*, and *Populus*, although its host range appears to be larger where it is invasive (Sawyer 2003). Tree death caused by the beetle or tree removal during eradication efforts will hasten a wholesale turnover in tree species composition and age classes in afflicted urban areas. In North America, ironically many of the favored tree species were themselves planted as replacements for elms decimated by Dutch elm disease.

Bark and ambrosia beetles (Curculionidae: Scolytinae; Platypodinae) represent the most frequently intercepted forest insects at ports of entry. In New Zealand, 98 species from these subfamilies were intercepted from 1952–2000 and 11 species were documented as established (Brokerhoff *et al.* 2010). In only a 20-year period (1985–2005), at least 16 species of bark and ambrosia beetles became established in the USA (Haack 2006).

Although the majority of bark beetles are secondary agents in tree decline and death, a number of species in the genus *Dendroctonus* and to a lesser extent, *Ips*, *Tomicus*, and *Scolytus*, are primary causes of tree mortality. Thus, frequent interception and establishment of these insects is of great concern to forest health professionals. Given the high rate of accidental movement between biogeographic regions, it is somewhat surprising that more species have not become

established. Nonetheless, there are several examples of exotic bark beetles causing extensive mortality in both natural and managed forests.

An important introduction to North America was the European *Scolytus multi-
striatus*, which was subsequently introduced to Australia and New Zealand
(Lanier and Peacock 1979). Although the beetle itself is of little consequence to
its host trees, it is an effective vector of the fungi *Ophiostoma ulmi* and *O. novo-ulmi*,
the causative agents for Dutch elm disease that decimated elms across Europe
and North America.

Another feeding guild well represented among introduced insects are the sap
feeders. Sap feeders extract nutrients from trees by utilizing piercing/sucking
mouthparts to access phloem in vascular tissues. Major groups of insects using
this feeding strategy are found in the Orders Hemiptera (Suborder Sternor-
rhyncha: aphids, whiteflies and scale insects), and Thysanoptera (thrips). In
Europe, Hemiptera comprise the largest proportion of tree-feeding insect introductions (42%) and rank second in North America (30%) (Niemela and Mattson
1996; Mattson *et al.* 2007). These insects also rank high among introductions to
Australasia and South America. Many are cryptic and/or minute, factors that may
contribute to the high rate of transit and frequency of introduction for this
group. Relative to their high rate of interchange among regions, few sap feeders
cause significant impact, either ecologically or economically, to forested ecosystems. Among those that do, however, are some of the most destructive invasive
species in forests.

5.2.3 Invasive plants

Widespread tree mortality or dieback driven by an insect or pathogen
are obvious consequences of invasion, the effects of plant introductions on forest
structure and function can be just as important. Forests, especially when intact,
have been viewed historically as resistant to invasion, in large part because deep
shade is an establishment barrier difficult to surmount. The validity of this view
has come under recent scrutiny and there are several reasons to suggest that it
may not necessarily be true (Martin *et al.* 2009). The likelihood that invasions of
shade-tolerant and intolerant species alike will succeed, and the speed at which
they will occur, are greatly enhanced by disturbance (Lugo 2004; Vanhellemont
et al. 2009). This is increasingly important, as globally, few forests of any type are
now free from extensive anthropogenic influence.

An obvious challenge to the idea that forests are biotically resistant to
invasion is that propagule pressure from shade-tolerant invaders is very low
relative to early successional, shade-intolerant plant species that have dominated deliberate and accidental introductions (Martin *et al.* 2009). Second,
shade-tolerant invaders may require much longer periods of time to become

competitively dominant because their life-history strategies are necessarily different than shade-intolerant species. Finally, a disproportionate amount of research effort has focused on early successional plants and on ecosystems that are already invaded (Brothers and Spingarn 1992), thus our knowledge about invasive plants in intact temperate and tropical forests is incomplete.

5.3 Impacts of invasive species

The devastating impacts of invasive species in forests are undeniable, especially those rendering wholesale changes to the structure and function of an ecosystem. For many other introductions, even for well-established species with wide geographical distributions, quantifying changes to forest ecosystem processes is difficult, with effects not manifest for decades or even centuries. Such dynamics, while less dramatic in the short term, may ultimately cause changes on a similar scale to those wrought by faster-acting species, and we must be cautious in assuming that an introduction is innocuous. Surprisingly, empirical data on changes to forest health driven by species introductions have been shown in relatively few cases (Kenis *et al.* 2009). In many systems, long-term studies are lacking and a central role of invasive species in forest dynamics is inferred rather than measured. It is clear that a greater emphasis needs to be placed on the development of standardized quantitative methods to assess changes in forest dynamics and ecosystem function driven by invasive species. To this end, the concept of baseline mortality has considerable utility in providing an unbiased assessment of the overall effects of invasive species on forest health.

While a few taxonomic groups of invasive species, herbivorous insects, and pathogenic fungi, for example, have historically had the greatest impact on forested ecosystems, there is increasing recognition that other taxa can also directly or indirectly influence the function, productivity, composition, or dynamics of natural and/or managed plantation forests. These range from pathogenic microbes such as bacteria and viruses to nematodes and even vertebrates. The effects of exotic plant invasions have been underappreciated in forest ecosystems (Martin *et al.* 2009), but there is increased recognition that they can impart significant changes to forest dynamics through competitive interactions or changes to nutrient cycling, fire regimes, or hydrologic properties. Finally, there is growing awareness that below-ground processes driven by exotic soil dwelling invertebrates may play significant roles in changing biogeochemical cycles and forest structure (Bohlen *et al.* 2004; Coyle *et al.* 2008).

From the standpoint of forest health, not all introductions are equal. In fact, the majority of introductions, even when successful, appear to cause little or no discernible damage, either economically or ecologically. This does not suggest that we should be complacent or fail to allocate significant resources to prevention, because we currently lack the ability to predict which exotic introductions will subsequently become major invasive species. Many species exhibit significant lag between when establishment occurred and when they were observed to be problematic (Crooks and Soule 2001).

In an attempt to move beyond the simplistic native or invasive dichotomy, Lovett *et al.* (2006) developed a conceptual framework incorporating the magnitude of the effects of invasive insects and pathogens in forest ecosystems. Using three attributes, (1) mode of action, (2) host specificity, and (3) virulence for a given non-indigenous species, coupled with the importance, uniqueness, and community relationships of the affected tree species, they proposed a predictive framework for assessing new introductions. A weakness of this approach, however, is that it does not capture more insidious, yet potentially equally as important effects of invasive species, such as plants. For example, the model would rightfully assign high risk to the fungal pathogen *(Cryphonectria parasitica)* responsible for chestnut blight but would greatly underrate some invasive plants, which given sufficient elapsed time, may have categorically similar effects on stand composition through their effects on recruitment. Thus, a metric such as baseline mortality might better capture the effects of invasive species on forest health than qualitative rankings because it reduces bias associated with assigning invasive species to particular categories based on subjective anthropocentric assessment.

5.3.1 Elimination of a tree species

Rarely does an invasive organism cause the complete removal of a tree species from the landscape, but when one does, the effect is tragic and irreversible. A few notable examples are chestnut blight (caused by *Cryphonectria parasitica*) and the emerald ash borer, *Agrilus planipennis*, (Textbox 5.2) both in eastern North America, pine wilt disease in Japan (Textbox 5.3; Figure 5.4), and jarrah dieback in Australia (Figure 5.5). While chestnut blight and jarrah dieback ran their course several decades ago, we are currently witnessing the seemingly unstoppable progression of the emerald ash borer. In the wake of such an event, the forest may be left with a significant, or even dominant, tree species extirpated.

The loss of an important tree species presents a conundrum from the perspective of forest health assessment. Can the forest ever be considered healthy after the removal of a native tree species? Forests usually adapt to conditions that

Textbox 5.2 Emerald ash borer

The arrival of the buprestid, *Agrilus planipennis* (emerald ash borer, hereafter EAB) ranks among the most devastating exotic introductions ever. First discovered in 2002 in Michigan, USA and adjoining Ontario, Canada, it dispersed rapidly by both natural means and extensive inadvertent anthropogenic movement (Poland and McCullough 2006). All North American species of *Fraxinus* appear susceptible and it attacks virtually all size classes in urban, suburban, and natural forests (Poland and McCullough 2006; Anulewicz *et al.* 2008; Pureswaran and Poland 2009). By 2007, an estimated 53 million native ash had succumbed to the beetle (Kovacs *et al.* 2010).

The natural range of EAB encompasses eastern Russia, northern China, Korea, and Japan, where it is a minor pest on Manchurian and Chinese ash (*F. mandshurica* Rupr. and *F. chinensis* Roxb., respectively) (Wei *et al.* 2004; Wei, *et al.* 2007). This insect is difficult to detect at low density and often has been established for several years before symptoms become apparent (McCullough *et al.* 2009). Although some management techniques exist and biological control organisms are being released, the short- and perhaps long-term prognosis for ash in much of North America is grim. Illustrating the global nature of introductions, EAB has recently colonized Moscow, Russia, well beyond its eastern Asian distribution (Baranchikov *et al.* 2008).

In the presence of this insect, unadapted ash populations are simply not sustainable. Barring successful biological control, native species of *Fraxinus* in North America will likely be eliminated from most natural and urban forests. Although ash can sprout from stumps, EAB will attack and kill even small diameter trees and ash seeds appear to have a short residual time in seed banks suggesting that total elimination of the species may occur, at least locally. We do not yet know if ash will persist at some basal area or density threshold below what will sustain ash borer populations across a landscape or if the beetles will eventually eliminate all individual trees within a forest. The wholesale removal of ash from forests will have important economic and ecological effects. The cost of continued expansion of the infestation has been estimated at more than a billion dollars per year (Kovacs *et al.* 2010). Because of the recent and ongoing nature of this introduction, it is still unclear how loss of ash across entire landscapes will affect forested ecosystems and whether associated tree species will colonize the gaps or if replacement will be by other native or exotic species (e.g., Gandhi and Herms 2010). It is certain, however, that EAB will substantively alter both urban and natural forests, perhaps permanently.

Textbox 5.3 Pine wilt disease

Pine wilt is a serious disease of old world pines caused by the pine wilt nematode (PWN), *Bursaphelenchus xylophilus* (Steiner). Infection of susceptible pine species such as *Pinus densiflora*, *P. thunbergii*, and *P. sylvestris* causes extensive tree mortality (Kondo *et al.* 1982). PWN is thought to be native to North America and was first found in Japan in the early 20th century (Iwahori *et al.* 1998). Historically, pines composed about 10% of Japan's standing forest. Losses to PWN have been staggering. After two abnormally dry years (1978 and 1979), the annual loss to pine wilt was 2.4 million m³ (Mamiya 1988). Between 2000 and 2005, annual losses ranged from 663 500 to 835 200 m³. Since its introduction into Japan, the pinewood nematode has spread to Korea, Taiwan, and China. In China, a cluster of 256 trees were found dying from pine wilt in 1982; by 2000 more than 50 million trees are estimated to have died over an area of 80 000 ha. PWN arrived in Portugal in 1999 where an intensive campaign has been mounted to prevent its further spread in Europe (Mota *et al.* 1999).

PWN is vectored by wood-boring cerambycid beetles in the genus *Monochamus* (Sousa *et al.* 2001). These beetles are attracted to dying and recently dead conifers where females oviposit. Adults of both sexes feed on the bark of living twigs and the feeding wounds provide access points for the nematode, which has a complex life cycle intricately linked with beetle development. Juvenile nematodes colonize developing cerambycid larvae and pupae. After beetles emerge from the tree, the dispersing juvenile nematodes exit the trachea, and then leave the beetle to colonize the feeding wounds left by the adult beetles.

Once PWN becomes established in a stand, mortality rises until most pines succumb to the disease (Figure 5.4). Tree mortality is highest in an epicenter and spatially radiates outwards as emerging adult beetles vector nematodes away from their host trees (Togashi and Shigasada 2006). As mortality increases, the loss of mature pines hastens the conversion of stands to deciduous or evergreen hardwoods. Fujihara *et al.* (2002) found that four different vegetational trajectories occurred following pine death and these were dependent on aspect and elevation. Accompanying an increase in basal area by deciduous tree oaks like *Quercus serrata*, was a shift from light-demanding plants to shade-tolerant species in the lower vegetation strata. Soils became significantly moister once the overstory pines had succumbed to the disease. In some areas of Japan, declining *P. densiflora* forests have been replaced by evergreen hardwood forests dominated by species such as *Quercus glauca* and *Castanopsis cuspidata* (Fujihara 1996).

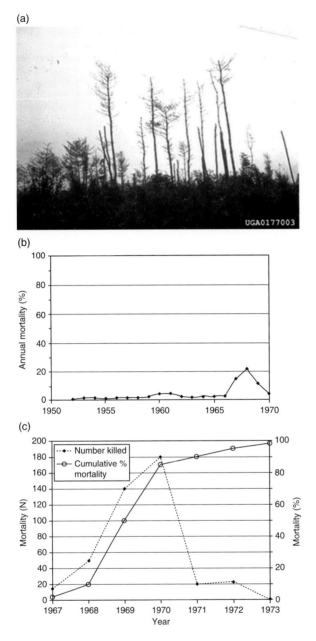

Figure 5.4 (a) Death of overstory *Pinus densiflora* in Japan following attack by pine wilt nematode (with permission Institut National de la Recherche Agronomique, France). Without the pine overstory, a dense hardwood stratum is growing up in the absence of competitors for light and space. (b) Annual tree mortality for a Japanese pine stand prior to the arrival of pine wilt nematode. The two peaks represent increased tree death following typhoons. (c) Pine mortality in a stand following the arrival of pine wilt nematode. (Adapted from Kobayashi 1988, with permission.)

(a)

(b)

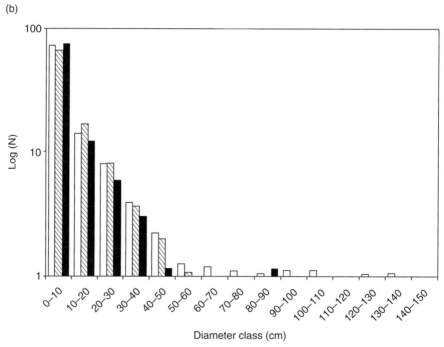

Figure 5.5 (a) Overstory death and severe dieback in jarrah forest following infection with *Phytophthora cinnamomi* (with permission of Ray Willis). (b) Diameter distribution of *Eucalyptus marginata* in sites with no infection (white bars), 20 years post infection (black bars), and 50 years post-infection (striped bars). (Adapted from McDougall *et al.* 2002, with permission.)

prevail following disturbance, though the species composition, successional trajectory, and many other factors and processes may be different than occurred prior to the disturbance. Is it necessary to restore the missing species before the forest can be regarded as healthy? What if no means of restoring the missing species is available? Is the affected forest forever unhealthy? An assessment based on baseline mortality can tell us about the sustainability of the size structure of the forest, but the inherent value of the altered forest is ultimately a judgment call, which is to say that it depends on the landowners' management objectives. If those objectives include a forest in its pristine condition, then a forest that is missing a native tree species would be considered unhealthy, even if sustainable. If the adapted forest meets the landowner's management objectives, even though it has lost a tree species, then there is no reason to consider it as unhealthy.

A case in point is chestnut blight, which arguably represents the most complete and geographically widespread instance of the removal of a native tree species from the landscape by an invasive pathogen and yet the forests of eastern North America have adapted. Red oaks have filled the void left where chestnut once existed, and these forests appear to be sustainable (although significant recruitment problems in red oak suggest further changes lie ahead), productive in terms of forest products, and support abundant wildlife, and remain one of the most biologically diverse temperate ecosystems in the world. These are hardly the characteristics one would associate with an unhealthy ecosystem unless one desires the most pristine, if unattainable, conditions.

5.3.2 Alteration of forest structure

One of the most important limiting resources in forests is light, especially for plants growing beneath an overstory canopy. The development of extensive, exotic-dominated, below-canopy strata where none previously existed intercepts a large portion of the already limited light, precluding recruitment of native tree seedlings and herbaceous understory plants. For mature forest trees, this may substantially decrease recruitment and may fundamentally change, or at least significantly delay, successional patterns (Duncan and Chapman 2003).

Despite the seeming resilience of many tropical forests to invasions, exotic woody plants have become dominant in a variety of systems, especially on islands. The proliferation of invasive woody plants can fundamentally alter the three-dimensional canopy structure of afflicted forests through the formation of light-intercepting mid-level strata or from increased foliar density at the canopy level. In either scenario, recruitment and establishment of native herbaceous and woody species may be impossible once light transmission falls below a certain threshold, further altering the structure and function of afflicted stands. In some cases, these changes may be ephemeral, an intermediate successional stage along a pathway to a climax community, whereas such changes appear to be more durable in other forest types. In Puerto Rico, exotic species appear to facilitate the regeneration of some native trees (Lugo 2004), presumably because they act as nurse plants, providing shelter and reducing erosion in these heavily degraded sites. In contrast, invasive dominated forests in the Hawaiian Islands do not appear to have any positive effects on native plant diversity (Mascaro et al. 2008).

Exotic-dominated Hawaiian forests appear to have a very different canopy profile from the native forests they replace (Figure 5.6). Depending on the forest type, the canopy position of the dominant invasive plants ranges from large upper canopy trees like tropical ash (Fraxinus uhdei) with diameters of greater than 120 cm, to persistent mid-and understory species like strawberry guava (Psidium cattleianum).

The fundamental change in the availability of light at different strata may underlie the profound and persistent change in native species diversity in these forests (Figure 5.7). Relatively shade-intolerant native tree and shrub seedlings are unable to recruit under the dense mid and upper canopy exotics. In mature tropical ash or fire tree-dominated (M. faya) forests, canopy volume may increase by more than 50% at the upper levels with light reaching the forest floor reduced to 2% from the 9–13% in the replaced native forests (Asner et al. 2008). Furthermore, Morella (Myrica) faya and Falcataria moluccana are nitrogen-fixers, and their presence facilitates the growth of other nitrogen-demanding invasive plants in the poor soils characteristic of these forests. The long-term stability of these novel assemblages of plant species is unknown and will present significant management challenges irrespective of objectives, whether they be conservation of Hawaiian endemics or wood products from trees like tropical ash.

Shading of competitors is frequently viewed as one of the most important mechanisms leading to dominance of invasive plants in forests as seen in the examples above. However, shading might actually be an outcome rather than the cause of competitive domination. Increasingly, research is focusing on below-ground processes as a potential mechanistic basis for explaining competitive relationships between invasive and native plants. Two below-ground processes thought to influence competition are allelopathy, the production of secondary chemical compounds that negatively influence other plants in a community (e.g., Inderjit and Callaway 2003), and changes to mycorrhizal associations (Pringle et al. 2009).

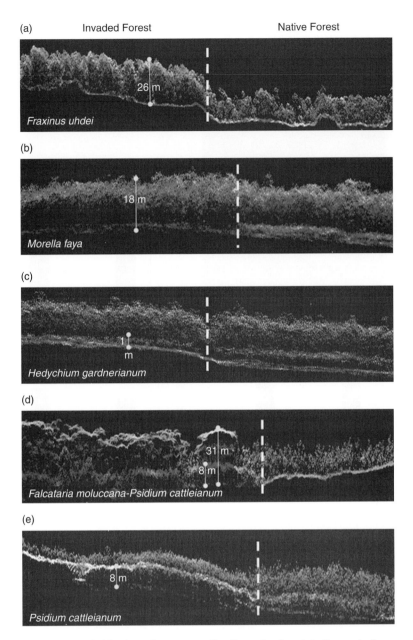

Figure 5.6 (a–e) Side view of canopy profiles for native forests before and after invasion by exotic plants in Hawaii. (from Asner *et al.* 2008, with permission.)

Hardwood forests in temperate North America have been the recipient of several shade-tolerant invasive plants that can exert significant change to the structure and function of the afflicted forest including Japanese stilt-grass, garlic mustard (Textbox 5.4), and several species of Asian bush

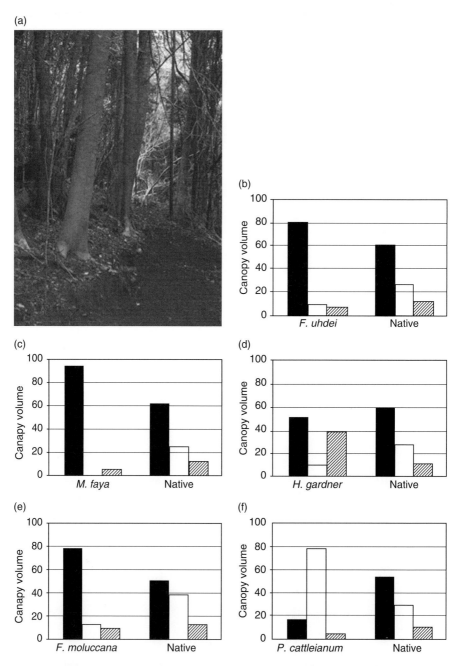

Figure 5.7 (a) Large tropical ash (*Fraxinus uhdei*) cast deep shade on the understory reducing recruitment and growth of native species. (With permission from Forrest and Kim Starr.) (b–f) The effect of five different invasive plants (*F. uhdei*, *Morella (Myrica) faya*, *Hedychium gardnerianum*, *Falcataria moluccana*, and *Psidium cattleianum*) on the canopy structure of native Hawaiian forests. Each of these species significantly alters the 3-dimensional structure of the canopy and changes light availability in lower strata. Black bars are upper canopy, white bars are mid-canopy, and striped bars are understory. (Adapted from Asner *et al.* 2008, with permission.)

honeysuckles (*Lonicera* spp.). Honeysuckle shrubs form a persistent and dense layer underneath forest canopies that can competitively exclude herbaceous and woody native species. Honeysuckle has a negative effect on survival of tree seedlings including important tree species in the northeastern and midwestern USA deciduous forests such as red oak, black cherry, and sugar maple (Inderjit and Callaway 2003). Furthermore, there is accumulating evidence from dendrochronological studies that *Lonicera* can significantly decrease the growth of native canopy trees. At 18 even-aged, mixed species sites in Ohio, *L. maackii* invasion was found to reduce radial growth of overstory trees by 58% and the growth of basal area by 53%. The first significant growth reductions were detectable six years after invasion with the greatest negative growth changes occurring after 20 years (Hartman and McCarthy 2007). When the overall effects of honeysuckle invasions on forest ecosystems are integrated, changes to succession may be profound. Hartman and McCarthy (2008) found that the older an invasion of *L. mackii* was in a temperate forest understory, the less the composition (diversity and density of herbaceous layer, tree seedling, and seed bank) of the substrata resembled uninvaded sites, suggesting a new successional trajectory for the stands.

Textbox 5.4 Garlic mustard

Alliaria petiolata (Brassicaceae) is a biennial herbaceous plant introduced from Eurasia in the mid-1800s for its medicinal and culinary properties. After naturalizing, it has become an aggressive colonizer of the forest floor in eastern and midwestern North America (Blossey *et al.* 2001, Figure 5.8). Dense infestation of garlic mustard suppresses the establishment and growth of other herbaceous plants as well as tree seedlings (Stinson *et al.* 2007 and Figure 5.9a–d). The propensity of this species to invade the understory and thrive in undisturbed deciduous forests is both unusual and concerning, and considerable effort has been devoted to understanding the basis for its competitive advantage (Rodgers *et al.* 2008).

Garlic mustard has an array of secondary metabolites known as glucosinolates, sulfur-based molecules that inhibit unadapted herbivores and fungi. One of the mechanisms underlying this species overwhelming success may be the suppression of arbuscular mycorrhizal fungi (AMF) used by other plants. Garlic mustard itself does not rely on AMF and research suggests that secondary phytochemicals exuded from its leaves and roots inhibit AMF on competing species (Stinson *et al.* 2006).

Textbox 5.4 (cont.)

Differential herbivory also appears to contribute to the success of this species. In stands invaded by garlic mustard, generalist herbivores such as the hyper-abundant white-tailed deer disproportionately browse the foliage and twigs of native species (Figure 5.9e), further enhancing the success of this species (Eschtruth and Battles 2009b; Knight *et al.* 2009).

Some of the direct effects on understory species by *Lonicera* spp. result from light competition but in addition, allelopathic compounds have been identified in the extracts that inhibit germination and growth of competitors (Dorning and Cipollini 2007). Another important invasive shrub in temperate North American forests, glossy buckthorn *(Frangula alnus)*, appears to delay succession through vigorous competition for light with other understory species, but does not prevent it entirely, and as succession proceeds, its influence and prevalence diminishes (Cunard and Lee 2009). It is unclear what the long-term consequences of invasions by woody shrubs like honeysuckle are in forest ecosystems, but slowed growth and decreased recruitment may pave the way for structural and compositional change.

In more than 60 countries throughout the Old World tropics, *Lantana camara*, a woody shrub of South American origin, has become a major problem in many different forest types (Day *et al.* 2003). As with dense shrub strata in temperate forests, lantana shuts off light to the forest floor and severely curtails recruitment for most native species (Gooden *et al.* 2009). As was shown for bush honeysuckles above, lantana also reduces growth of the overstory trees in forests where it is abundant. Invasion and dominance by lantana appears to be facilitated by strong allopathic capabilities (Sharma *et al.* 2005).

5.3.3 Addition of a tree species

The addition of tree species to a forest or region is often intentional and done to provide commodity products such as wood or fruit, erosion control, aesthetic qualities and shade. The list of invasive tree species worldwide is long and includes some species, such as *P. radiata* in many Southern Hemisphere countries, that exist primarily in plantations and others such as the Australian *Casuarina equisetifolia* and *C. cunninghamiana* that have become widely distributed and naturalized in the Caribbean Region.

Often, non-indigenous trees are "found" by their native insect herbivores or pathogens. Extensive plantings of exotic *Eucalyptus* have enjoyed a lengthy time period without significant natural enemies in California. Multiple different

(a)

(b)

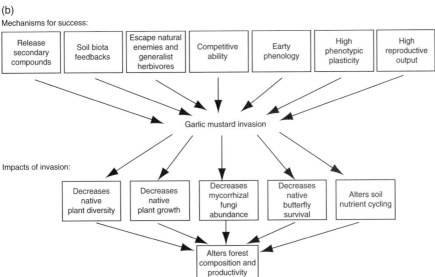

Figure 5.8 (a) Garlic mustard can form a monodominant herbaceous layer in northeastern North American hardwood forests (with permission of Victoria Nuzzo). (b) Competitive mechanisms and effects of garlic mustard on forest ecosystem processes. (From Rodgers *et al.* 2008, with permission.)

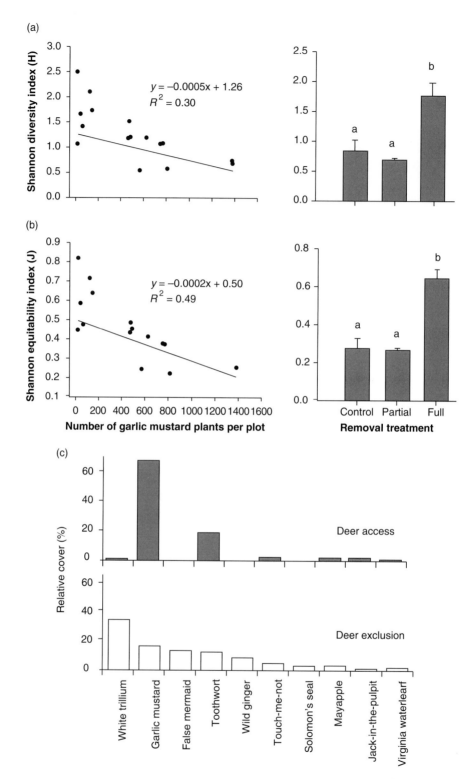

(a)

(b)

(c)

Figure 5.9 Garlic mustard effects on Shannon diversity and equitability indices for (a) competing native species (b) and the effects of garlic mustard removal.

species, cultivars, and hybrids have been planted and several have naturalized, with at least one recognized as an invasive plant. In California, the establishment of two exotic cerambycids, *Phoracantha semipunctata* and *P. recurva* in 1985 (Paine *et al.* 2000; Paine and Miller 2002) presents an interesting conundrum. The advent of these longhorned beetles represents a re-association with their native hosts, but in an exotic environment. For weedy eucalypts, *Phoracantha* may act as an unintentional form of biological control, but at the same time, a significant forest health issue for high value landscape plantings. These beetles are particularly lethal for eucalypts under drought stress, as they are seasonally in southern California, and will necessitate a shift in planting recommendations to more drought-tolerant species and cultivars, which tend to be more beetle resistant (Hanks *et al.* 1995).

In other cases, exotic trees growing in plantation settings remain viable economically only in the absence of their natural enemies. For example, the cypress aphid, *Cinara cupressivora*, has a distribution spanning the northern hemisphere (Watson *et al.* 1999) but colonized plantation-grown cypress trees in Africa. It was found first in Malawi in 1986 and by the early 1990s was causing millions of dollars of damage to *Cupressus lusitanica* throughout eight countries in southern and eastern Africa (Murphy 1996). To provide perspective, in Kenya, this tree species represents nearly 50% of all plantation-grown forest. Ironically, *C. lusitanica* was extensively planted as a replacement for *C. macrocarpa*, which had become uneconomical due to repeated and severe infestation by the canker pathogen *Rhynchosphaeria cupressi* (Cock 2003).

Severe infestations by *C. cupressivora* can cause significant mortality and chronically attacked trees suffer dieback and major reduction in radial growth (Ciesla 1991; Orondo and Day 1994), necessitating changes to the management of these plantations. Over a 30-year rotation, 50% of the trees in a plantation may succumb to cypress aphid infestation (Orondo and Day 1994; Cock 2003). Outbreaks of *Cinara* are associated with poorer soil and declines in growth rate of *C. lusitanica* as they mature, so better site selection for plantations coupled with shorter rotations are recommended for reducing the impact of the insect (Ciesla 2003). A biological control program has been developed and has shown promise in reducing the intensity of outbreaks (Day *et al.* 2003).

Caption for Figure 5.9. (*cont.*) (c) The facilitative effect of white-tailed deer on the abundance of garlic mustard and nine native plants. Deer exclusion cages were in place for 5 years. (From Knight *et al.* 2009, with permission.)

Similarly, the disease red band needle blight, caused by *Dothistroma* spp. has little effect on pines growing in natural environments but in exotic pine plantations, this pathogen can cause substantial growth loss and even extensive mortality (van der Plas 1981). Outbreaks of *Dothistroma* in *P. radiata* plantations have been severe in New Zealand and Chile, but in East Africa, the disease was so prevalent that widespread abandonment of *P. radiata* occurred in favor of species like *P. patula*, which is relatively resistant to infection (Gibson 1974).

5.3.4 Alteration of a fire regime

Exotic plants can have significant effects on the frequency and intensity of disturbances like fire, which in turn facilitates their competitive superiority (Mack and D'Antonio 1998; Brooks *et al.* 2004). Fire-tolerant species may promote and increase the frequency and/or severity of fires, whereas the converse is true for some fire-intolerant invasive plants. Exotic grasses, in particular, can hasten conversion of woodlands to monoculture grasslands, by greatly increasing the frequency of fires while simultaneously increasing fuel load and thus intensity (Levine *et al.* 2002). In contrast, some fire-intolerant species have the effect of dampening fire intensity and frequency, thus facilitating their own survival. The Brazilian pepper tree, *Schinus terebinthifolius*, is an important invader of pine forests in the southeastern USA. Dense populations of this species reduce the probability of fire in a stand, facilitating their growth at the expense of fire-tolerant pine (Stevens and Beckage 2009). This will likely hinder natural fire regimes in pine savannahs and the application of prescribed fire in plantation-grown pines where burning to control hardwood competitors is an important management tool.

5.3.5 Alteration of nutrient cycling processes

Invasive plants can have profound effects on carbon and nitrogen cycles in forested systems as well as in grasslands and wetlands. Large variation in the ecophysiological traits of various invading plants makes it difficult to predict the effects in any given situation. However, certain trends are evident. When woody plants invade an ecosystem, they generally increase the carbon pool in the system more than do herbaceous invaders. Similarly, nitrogen-fixing invaders increase the nitrogen pool more than do non-nitrogen fixing plants, but in general, the nitrogen concentration of plants and the soil concentration of ammonium and nitrate all increase in invaded ecosystems over those of native ecosystems. Furthermore, the above-ground net primary production and litter decomposition of invaded ecosystems has been shown to increase between 50% and 120% compared to those of native ecosystems. This results in positive feedback in systems altered by invasive plants where increased availability of carbon and nitrogen support plant growth, which results in yet more carbon and nitrogen and so on (Liao *et al.* 2007).

5.3.6 Effects on hydrology

Hydrology can be affected when a native forest community is invaded by non-indigenous tree species with deeper roots or higher transpiration rates than native species. For example, in the western USA, *Tamarix* spp. a woody plant native to Asia, has replaced native trees and shrubs in riparian forests consequently lowering water tables and changing stream hydrology (De Tomaso 1998). The invasion of native grasslands by exotic trees also fundamentally changes ecosystem function. In Mediteranean grasslands and savannahs world-wide, *Eucalypus* spp. invasions have lowered water tables and changed nutrient cycling. The paperbark tree (*Melaleuca quinquenervia*) has similarly converted substantial areas of the grass-dominated Everglades in Florida to an invasive forest and has modified rainfall interception, surface flow, evapotranspiration rates, and possibly water table levels in this sensitive and critically important watershed (Gordon 1998).

5.3.7 Interactions among introduced species

Non-indigenous organisms interact in many ways with each other, with native organisms and with abiotic agents in the ecosystem, but two notable interactions are of particular importance to forest health. First, a non-indigenous tree species may be subsequently colonized by a herbivorous insect or a patho-gen from its native range. The introduction of the eucalyptus longhorned beetles (*Phoracantha* spp.) in California and their establishment on exotic *Eucalyptus* as discussed above is one example. In a variation of the theme, Scots pine (*P. sylvestris*) in the northeastern USA. has been widely planted for a variety of purposes, not the least of which is its tolerance for a wide range of soil types. It too has been followed by a number of insect pests from its native range including the European woodwasp (*Sirex noctilio*) (Textbox 5.5), the pine shoot beetle (*Tomicus piniperda*) and the European pine sawfly (*Neodiprion sertifer*) among others. The European woodwasp and the pine shoot beetle have not only damaged Scots pine in North America, but Scots pine may facilitate the susceptibility of native pines to these insects. Thus, Scots pine has been a stepping stone for invasive insect pests on native North American pines.

The second type of interaction among invaders involves a complex cascade of interactions among invading organisms as has plagued the hardwood forests of the eastern USA. Chestnut blight ranks among the worst invasive species ever recorded. A lethal disease caused by the fungal pathogen *Cryphonectria parasitica* had unparalleled effects on forest ecosystems, particularly in

Textbox 5.5 European woodwasp

The global spread of the European woodwasp (*Sirex noctilio*) epitomizes the nature of modern economies, the complexity of trade, and the international movement of wood and wood products. The native range of *S. noctilio* encompasses central and southern Europe and portions of North Africa where it is only occasionally a minor pest of pines (Hurley *et al.* 2007; Madden 1988). Successful colonization of trees involves a mutualistic fungus (*Amylostereum areolatum*) and toxic mucus, both of which are provided by the ovipositing female (Figure 5.10a). The combination of the fungus and mucus rapidly kills susceptible trees. Larvae feed on the fungus within galleries bored within the tree. Adults emerge the following year. While of minor consequence within its native range, its arrival in Australia, followed by New Zealand, several South American countries, and South Africa (Hurley *et al.* 2007; Carnegie *et al.* 2006; Figure 5.10b) devastated high value plantations of exotic pines, especially *P. radiata*, that are an economically important resource in these countries. In the southern hemisphere, *Sirex* populations build up in low quality, suppressed trees. Once a population becomes sufficiently large, when coupled with stress factors such as drought or overstocking, *Sirex* can successfully colonize and kill large healthy trees.

In 2004, *S. noctilio* was found to be established in North America. Since its first detection in New York State, delimitation surveys suggest that it is widespread throughout parts of northeastern USA and adjoining Canada. Thus far, attacks are focused on the non-native Scot's pine (*P. sylvestris*) and to a lesser extent, native red pine (*P. resinosa*) (Dodds *et al.* 2008). A concern is the potential effect of *S. noctilio* in the southeastern USA where pine is extensively grown in plantations and in western North America where vast areas of even-aged pines grow naturally.

From a pest management perspective, *Sirex* is a serious threat that can generally be reduced to low levels with judicious silvicultural prescriptions and/or biological control (Tribe and Cillie 2004). The effects of *Sirex* in Australia, in particular, changed silvicultural recommendations for pine plantations growing where this insect occurs. On-time first thinning is a key to minimizing risk from this insect because vigorously growing pines are resistant. The largest of the *Sirex* outbreaks in New Zealand and Australia were associated with overstocked stands and drought (Madden 1988). *Sirex noctilio* needs stressed, weakened and suppressed trees for rapid population growth and to reach outbreak populations. Thinned stands may sustain some damage during droughts or other stresses, but the lack of sufficient

Textbox 5.5 (cont.)

host material precludes the initiation of major outbreaks. Preventing outbreaks is critical because *Sirex* has killed up to 12% of merchantable volume across wide areas and mortality rates upwards of 60% have been recorded in some overstocked stands.

Within a stand, pines exhibit a range of susceptibility with some trees completely resistant, while others are capable of recovery following attack. Female woodwasps utilize stressed and suppressed trees first. As the population grows, the availability of suppressed and weak trees dwindles and attacks are initiated on healthy trees. Outbreaks collapse when resistant trees become numerically dominant in a plantation, greatly reducing successful reproduction of the woodwasp (Figure 5.11a, b).

In addition to silviculture, an effective biological control agent, the parasitic nematode *Deladanus siricicola* and several hymenopteran parasitoids have further reduced the threat of *Sirex* to *P. radiata* forests in Australia. However, biological control appears to be less effective in South Africa and in some South American countries for a variety of reasons including climate, different pine species (extensive use of *P. patula* in South Africa for example), and perhaps incompatibility between strains of nematode and biotypes of the woodwasp (Hurley *et al.* 2007). In South Africa, higher stocking densities in plantations managed for pulpwood rather than sawlogs may also contribute to *Sirex* problems.

North America where as many as 1.5 billion chestnut trees were killed (Hardin *et al.* 2001). Not only was the scale unprecedented, chestnut occupied a prominent and ecologically distinct place in eastern North American forests (Paillet 2002). In 1904, chestnut blight first appeared in the USA on an American chestnut in the Bronx Zoological Park, New York (Merkel 1906). The disease was transported to North America on nursery stock of Asian chestnuts (Roane *et al.* 1986). Within four years it was established throughout the Northeast and by the 1920s occurred throughout the Southeast (Woods and Shanks 1959; Gibbs 1978). Within 40 years of its introduction, the range of chestnut blight had encompassed that of its host, decimating a species that once composed 25% of the canopy in some eastern deciduous forests (Roane *et al.* 1986).

A full understanding of the effects that the loss of chestnut as a functional canopy tree has had on forest ecosystems is not possible in large part because the forests where chestnut was dominant at the time of the blight epiphytotic were

(a)

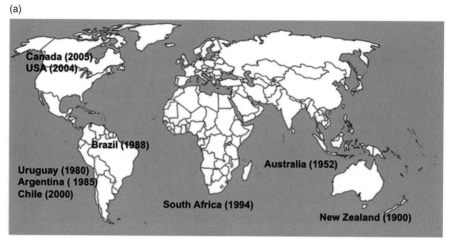

(b)

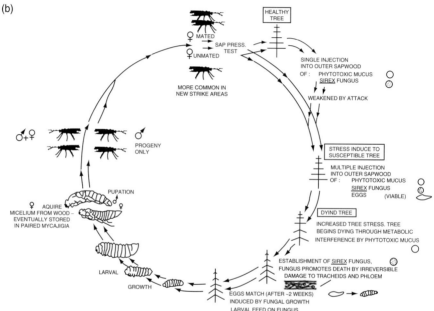

Figure 5.10 (a) Global spread of *Sirex noctilio*. (Data from Hurley *et al.* 2007; Hoebeke *et al.* 2005.) (b) lifecycle of *Sirex noctilio* and the mutualistic fungus, *Amylosterum aereolatum*. (With permission NCT Forestry Cooperative.)

already fundamentally altered from their composition prior to European colonization. Thus the super-abundance of chestnut was partly an artifact of historical land use patterns in the region. Historical reconstruction of eastern forests suggest that oaks, particularly white oak (*Quercus alba*), were much more abundant prior to European settlement, then declined as chestnut rose to

(a)

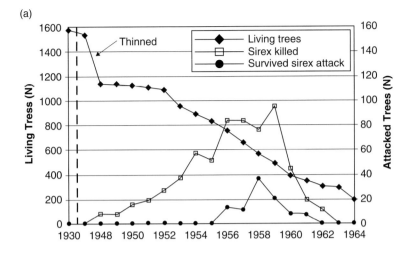

(b)

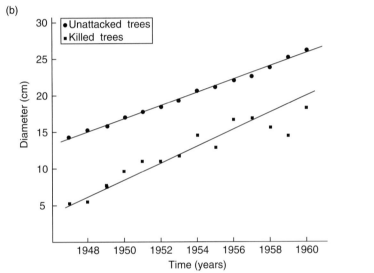

Figure 5.11 (a) Survival of a cohort of *Pinus radiata* in an Australian plantation. Annual mortality from *S. noctilio* increases until the availability of susceptible trees diminishes. As a greater portion of the attacked trees survive, the infestation declines. (b) Growth rate in *Sirex*-killed trees prior to attack relative to unattacked trees in the same stand. (Adapted from data in Madden 1975, with permission.)

prominence following extensive logging and clearing. As the blight removed American chestnut from the canopy, red and chestnut oaks (*Q. rubra* and *Q. prinus*), hickories (especially *Carya glabra*), red maple (*Acer rubrum*), and tulip tree (*Liriodendron tulipifera*) increased in abundance (Paillet 2002). Thus, the ecological effects of the loss of chestnut were likely mitigated somewhat by an increase in the abundance of oak and hickory, which fill ecologically similar roles (Woods and Shanks 1959; Loo 2009). The indirect ecosystem consequences of the increase in oak-hickory forest types following the decline of chestnut have not been well investigated. However, it is possible that high oak mortality associated with gypsy moth defoliation (see Textbox 5.1) in some areas (e.g., Gottschalk *et al.* 1998) may be in part due to oaks growing outside of their historical niche or at higher density or basal area than they were prior to European settlement (Allen and Bowersox 1989).

5.4 Management of invasive species

The idiosyncrasies of individual invasive species will dictate the specific management tools to be used for controlling them. However, there are common strategies used in the management of invasive species regardless of their biological characteristics or taxonomic group. These strategies are the prevention of new introductions, the detection of new arrivals, and the management of invasive species after their introduction.

5.4.1 The prevention of new introductions

The prevention of all new introductions is impossible. However, some introductions may be prevented by identifying the organisms that are at high risk of being introduced to a given country or other geographic area, identifying the pathways by which these organisms may enter, and then taking steps to block the pathways. The first step, identifying the high risk organisms most likely to be introduced presents some problems. Many of the worst invasives are quite innocuous in their native ranges and would never be ranked as being of high risk for introduction. The list of examples is long, but three more notorious examples are the European woodwasp (see Textbox 5.5) which is insignificant in Europe, but devastating in pine plantations across the southern hemisphere, the hemlock woolly adelgid (*Adelges tsugae*) which does not harm native Asian hemlocks or western North American species but is very destructive to native hemlocks in eastern North America (Textbox 5.6), and the pinewood nematode from North America which has killed millions of pines in Asia (see Textbox 5.3). None of these species would have or could have been predicted to have such severe impacts when introduced. This illustrates some major limitations in developing threat lists and trying to prioritize decisions about the allocation of resources to newly discovered introductions.

Identification of new invasive species is important in another sense. Newly arrived invasive species are often unfamiliar to biologists in the country or region being invaded. Thus, it is important to have taxonomic expertise available to carry out this critically important step in an effective response to an invasion. For example, jarrah dieback is perhaps the most devastating of the *Phytophthora* disease epiphytotics from an ecological perspective. Extensive dieback and mortality were recorded in *E. marginata* (jarrah)-dominated ecosystems in Australia as early as 1920, but the causative agent, *Phytophthora cinnamomi*, was not identified until 1965. Jarrah decline is not limited to a few species or genera, but rather it is an epidemic affecting the majority of woody plants in this ecosystem thus initiating a wholesale transformation in species diversity and function. In some forests, 50–75% of the woody plant species were lost over a period of 3–5 years (Weste *et al.* 2002). Non-susceptible species, primarily sedges, grasses, and ruderals proliferate approximately three years after an epiphytotic begins and in 20 years replace many of the *Phytophthora*-susceptible species. This has shifted infected areas from a forest to shrub- or grass-dominated communities. The changes wrought to plant communities are persistent for extended time periods, 50 years or more (McDougall *et al.* 2002; Weste *et al.* 2002, see Figure 5.5), and it is unclear if partial or full recovery of forest communities is possible following an epidemic, or whether a new disease cycle will initiate once susceptible species begin to become more abundant.

The second part of the prevention equation is blocking the pathway of movement. This involves such actions as inspecting international shipments of goods at ports of entry, inspecting traveler's baggage at customs upon entry into a country, and prohibiting the importation of certain materials and goods that are known conduits for invasive species. This seems like a rational approach, but the problem is that the volume of international trade and transportation has become so vast that anything more than a token level of inspection is beyond the capabilities of the government agencies charged with these tasks. The political will needed to support meaningful rates of inspection is more the exception than the rule.

The International Plant Protection Convention (IPPC) sets phytosanitary standards for the purpose of preventing the spread of plant pests. Undoubtedly, the adoption of these standards by participating countries has prevented the spread of many pests since the inception of the IPPC in 1952. The numbers of pests that have not been transported due to the implementation of phytosanitary standards will never be known. For example, the adoption of a ban on unprocessed solid wood-packing materials, which are significant vectors for wood-boring insects such as the Asian longhorned beetle and the emerald ash borer, will substantially stem the flow of this group of forest pests to countries that adopt the standard.

5.4.2 Detection

Prevention of establishment through detection of new arrivals is the first step in managing them, but is also a difficult step. Routine surveys around ports of entry are important, but modern domestic transportation networks are so efficient and diffuse that exotic hitchhikers can be quickly carried to points far from ports of entry. Nonetheless, greater effort in survey and detection effort will invariably be cost-effective because the likelihood of successful eradication increases when an invader is found while it remains in a limited geographic area. All too often, invasive organisms are not detected until they are well established and have spread.

Many invasive species have been detected more or less by accident by the public; fewer have been detected by government agencies or ministries charged with the task. In the case of plants, it is usually the plant itself that is apparent whereas for tree pathogens and forest insects, it is usually the signs, symptoms, and damage that call attention to the problem. Because insects are mobile (at least at some stage in their lives) and must seek out host trees or mates, considerable effort has been invested in developing traps combined with chemical attractants for detection and monitoring. A challenge with this strategy is that most insect chemical attractants are fairly species-specific which means that the attractants for each new invasive insect must be identified before they can be deployed. For insects that have not yet been introduced to a new area, trap and lure technologies are usually not available. After an insect has been introduced to a country or region and has been detected, the development of trap and lure technology is often initiated. This is a time-consuming process which delays or fails to enhance the implementation of other management activities that rely on detection.

In addition to the initial detection of a new invasive species, **delimitation surveys** are needed to determine the exact geographic distribution of the organism in its new environment. The specific survey methods used are dictated by the nature of the organism. They may be visual surveys based on observation of the organism itself, or of its signs, symptoms, or damage; they may be aerial surveys if observable indications are visible from aircraft. In the case of insects, traps and lures are the most cost-effective and sensitive tools for delimitation surveys. Without the information gathered from delimitation surveys, no effective management can be implemented because it would not be known where the control measures should be applied.

Once an invasive species has become established and is documented as causing economic or ecological harm, control strategies may need to be applied. Eradication, the removal of all viable propagules of the species from its introduced range, is the best option but is only possible or cost-effective if the geographic extent is well defined and relatively small. Another requisite for eradication is that there must be a means of locating, containing, and destroying the target organism. While several eradication efforts have been successful, most have failed. If eradication is not attempted or has failed, then the invasive organism may be managed through containment, mechanical, chemical, or biological control methods (see Chapter 4). With the exception of successful biological control, other approaches must be continued in perpetuity for mitigation of ecological or economic costs to continue. In many, if not most cases, there is no attempt to mitigate the negative effects and the ecological or economic damage is tolerated.

5.5 Conclusion

Few forests remain unaffected by invasive species, and many secondary forests are dominated by exotics. Further introductions are inevitable. Lag-times ensure that some seemingly innocuous exotic species present in forests today will become invasive species in the future. As economies grow and change, new pathways and vectors will give rise to new threats while reducing old ones. A great challenge will be the continued pressure to log and develop areas within contiguous forests as these disturbances enhance both propagule pressure and opportunities to colonize. Some aspects of biological invasions have yet to be assessed in detail. For example, the effects of below ground invaders such as earthworms and root-feeding insects may have important long-term effects on the structure, function, and diversity of forest ecosystems, but have only recently begun to be studied. Finally, we need to make better use of existing data sets and collect the data necessary to understand and quantify the effects of introduced species on forest ecosystem processes.

Textbox 5.6 The hemlock woolly adelgid (HWA)

Adelges tsugae, was first found in eastern North America in 1951 likely arriving on ornamental hemlocks. Spreading at a rate of 8–30 km/yr, HWA now ranges from New York State to the southern Appalachians (Morin *et al.* 2009). Hemlock woolly adelgid occurs on all nine species of *Tsuga* worldwide, but is only problematic on *T. caroliniana* and *T. canadensis* in eastern North America where host resistance is weak and natural enemies lacking, allowing for persistent high population densities (Havill *et al.* 2006). Until recently, the biogeography of HWA was not well understood.

Textbox 5.6 (cont.)

Molecular studies using mitochondrial DNA indicate that the eastern North American population likely originated in southern Japan, arriving independently from populations in western North America, which are not closely related (Havill *et al.* 2006).

Hemlocks have been described as foundation species as they play a unique ecological role in forests where they are dominant (Lovett, *et al.* 2006; Ellison *et al.* 2005). The effects of HWA on eastern North American hemlock forests have been catastrophic and both native species of *Tsuga* will disappear entirely from much of their ranges unless effective control is achieved. Depending on site, mortality can occur in as few as four years, or over time periods as protracted as 15 years (Orwig *et al.* 2002; Figure 5.12).

Following the decline and death of overstory hemlock, stands undergo fundamental change in species and stand structure. These successional patterns vary across the geographic range of each of the hemlock species (Ellison *et al.* 2005). In the southern Appalachians, two distinct trajectories have been suggested for replacement forests; those dominated by rhododendron (an evergreen shrub), or early successional deciduous hardwoods such as *Liriodendron tulipifera* (Nuckolls, *et al.* 2009). Rhododendron thickets can be persistent and prevent the establishment of tree seedlings for extended time periods thus delaying transition to a hardwood forest (Roberts *et al.* 2009). In the northern part of the range of hemlock, a variety of deciduous trees (*Acer* spp., *Quercus* spp., *Prunus serotina*), but especially black birch (*Betula lenta*) have been the major beneficiaries of the loss of overstory hemlock, at least in the short term.

Longer-term studies illustrate how forest structure and function change following the decline of hemlock stands infested with HWA (Ellison, *et al.* 2005; Lovett *et al.* 2006; Ellison *et al.* 2010). Sequential sampling across a ten-year period showed a doubling of transmitted light, large increases in percentage cover and species richness of vascular plants, and the colonization of invasive plants (Ellison *et al.* 2005). Substantive changes to soil composition and biogeochemistry are associated with declining hemlock stands (Eschtruth *et al.* 2006). In particular, soil temperature and decomposition rates increase as does available nitrogen and nitrification (Stadler *et al.* 2005). These changes may facilitate the transition from a hemlock-dominated system to one of deciduous woody plants.

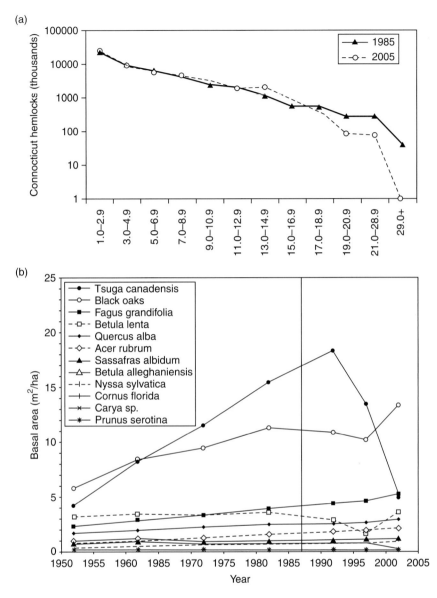

Figure 5.12 (a) Change in diameter distribution of eastern hemlock in Connecticut for the time periods before and after the arrival of hemlock woolly adelgid (from Ward, 2008) with permission. (b) Basal area of eastern hemlock and associated trees near New London, CT before and after the arrival of HWA in 1987. (From Small *et al.*, 2005, with permission.)

References

Allen, D. and Bowersox, T. W. 1989. Regeneration in oak stands following gypsy moth defoliation. In: *Proceedings of the 7th Central Hardwood Forest Conference. USDA Forest Service General Technical Report NC-132*, Rink, G. and Budelsky, C. A. (eds).

Anulewicz A. C., McCullough, D. G., Cappaert, D. L., and Poland, T. M. 2008. Host range of the Emerald ash borer (*Agrilus planipennis* Fairmaire) (Coleoptera: Buprestidae) in North America: Results of multiple-choice field experiments. *Environmental Entomology* **37**: 230–241.

Asner, G. P., Hughes, R. F., Vitousek, P. M., *et al.* 2008. Invasive plants transform 3-D structure of rainforests. *Proceedings National Academy Sciences* **105**: 4519–4523.

Aukema, J. E., McCullough, D. G., Von Holle, B., *et al.* 2010. Historical accumulation of non-indigenous forest pests in the continental US. *BioScience* **60**: 886–897.

Bain, J. 1977. Overseas wood- and bark-boring insects intercepted at New Zealand ports. *New Zealand Forest Service Technical Paper No. 63*.

Baranchikov, Y., Mozolevskaya, E., Yurchenko, G., and Kenis, M. 2008. Occurrence of the emerald ash borer, Agrilus planipennis in Russia and its potential impact on European forestry. *OEPP/EPPO Bulletin* **38**: 233–238.

Beeche-Cisternas, M. A. 2000. Riesgos cuarentenarios de insectos asociados a embalajes de madera y maderas de estiba de cargas de internacion en Chile. In: *Proceedings of the International Conference on Quarantine Pests for the Forestry Sector and their Effects on Foreign Trade, 27–28 June 2000, Concepcion, Chile*. Concepcion, Chile, CORMA.

Blossey, B., Nuzzo, V., Hinz, H., and Gerber, E. 2001. Developing biological control of *Alliaria petiolata* (M. Bieb) Cavara and Grande (garlic mustard). *Natural Areas Journal* **21**: 357–367.

Bohlen. P. J., Groffman, P. M., Fahey, T. J., *et al.* 2004. Ecosystem consequences of exotic earthworm invasion of north temperate forests. *Ecosystems* **7**: 1–12.

Brockerhoff, E. G., Liebhold, A. M., Richardson, B., and Suckling, D. M. 2010. Eradication of invasive forest insects: concepts, methods, costs and benefits. *New Zealand Journal Forest Science* **40 suppl.**: S117–S135.

Brockerhoff, E. L., Knízek, M., and Bain, J. 2003. Checklist of indigenous and adventive bark and ambrosia beetles (Curculionidae: Scolytinae and Platypodinae) of New Zealand and interceptions of exotic species (1952–2000). *New Zealand Entomologist* **26**: 29–44.

Brooks, M. L., D'Antonio, C. M., Richardson, D. M., *et al.* 2004. Effects of invasive alien plants on fire regimes. *BioScience* **54**: 677–688.

Brothers, T. S. and Spingarn, A. 1992. Forest fragmentation and alien plant invasion of central Indiana old-growth forests. *Conservation Biology* **6**: 91–100.

Campbell, R. W. and Sloan, R. J. 1977. Forest stand responses to defoliation by the gypsy moth. *Forest Science Monographs* **19**: 1–34.

Carnegie, A. J., Matsuki, M., and Haugen, D. A. 2006. Predicting the potential distribution of *Sirex noctilio* (Hymenoptera: Siricidae), a significant exotic pest of *Pinus* plantations. *Annals Forest Science* **63**: 119–128.

Carter, M., Smith, M., and Harrison, R. 2010. Genetic analyses of the Asian longhorned beetle (Coleoptera, Cerambycidae, *Anoplophora glabripennis*), in North America, Europe and Asia. *Biological Invasions* **12**: 1165–1182.

Ciesla, W. M. 1991. Cypress aphid, *Cinara cupressi*, a new pest of conifers in eastern and southern Africa. *FAO Plant Protection Bulletin* **39**: 82–93.

Cock, M. J. W. 2003. Biosecurity and forests: an introduction with particular emphasis on forest pests. *Forest Health and Biosecurity Working Paper FBS/2E*. Rome, FAO, www.fao.org/DOCREP/006/J1467E/J1467E00.HTM [Accessed November 2010].

Colautti, R. A., Grigorovich, I. A., and MacIsaac, H. J. 2006. Propagule pressure: a null model for biological invasions. *Biological Invasions* **8**: 1023–1037.

Colautti, R. I. and MacIssac, H. J. 2004. A neutral terminology to define 'invasive' species. *Diversity and Distributions* **10**: 135–141.

Coyle, D. R., Mattson, W. J., and Raffa, K. F. 2008. Invasive root feeding insects in natural forest ecosystems of North America. In: *Root Feeders: An Ecosystem Perspective*. Johnson, S. and Murray, P. (eds). CABI Press, London.

Crooks, J. A. and Soulé, M. E. 2001. Lag times in population explosions of invasive species: Causes and implications. In: *Invasive Species and Biodiversity Management*. Sandlund, O. T., Schei, P. J., and Viken, A. (eds). Kluwer Academic Press. Dordrecht.

Cunard, C. and Lee, T. D. 2009. Is patience a virtue? Succession, light, and the death of invasive glossy buckthorn (*Frangula alnus*). *Biological Invasions* **11**: 577–586.

Cunningham, J. C. and Entwistle, P. F. 1981. Control of sawflies by baculoviruses. In: *Microbial Control of Pests and Plant Diseases*. Burges, H. D. (ed.). Academic Press. Inc., New York.

Davidson, C. B., Gottschalk K. W., and Johnson, J. E. 1999. Tree mortality following - defoliation by the European gypsy moth (*Lymantria dispar* L.) in the United States: a review. *Forest Science* **45**: 74–84.

Day, M. D., Wiley, C. J., Playford, J., and Zalucki, M. P. 2003. *Lantana: Current Management, Status and Future Prospects*. Australian Centre for International Agricultural Research: Canberra.

Day, R. K., Kairo, M. T. K., Abraham, Y. J., *et al.* 2003. Biological control of homopteran pests of conifers in Africa. In: *Biological Control in IPM Systems in Africa*. Neuenschwander, P., Borgemeister, C., and Langewald, J. (eds). Wallingford, UK, CAB International.

Dodds, K. J., Cooke, R. R., and Gilmore, D. W. 2007. Silvicultural options to reduce pine susceptibility to attack by a newly detected invasive species, *Sirex noctilio*. *Northern Journal Applied Forestry* **24**: 165–167.

Dorning, M. and Cipollini, D. 2006. Leaf and root extracts of the invasive shrub, *Lonicera maackii*, inhibit seed germination of three herbs with no autotoxic effects. *Plant Ecology* **184**: 287–296.

Duncan, R. S. and Chapman, C. A. 2003. Tree-shrub interactions during early secondary forest succession in Uganda. *Restoration Ecology* **11**: 198–207.

Elkinton, J. S. and Liebhold, A. M. 1990. Population dynamics of gypsy moth in North America. *Annual Review Entomology* **35**: 571–596.

Elkinton, J. S., Parry, D., and Boettner, G. H. 2006. Implicating an introduced generalist parasitoid in the enigmatic demise of the invasive browntail moth. *Ecology* **87**: 2664–2672.

Ellison, A. M., Barker-Plotkin, A. A., Foster, D. R., and Orwig, D. A. 2010. Experimentally testing the role of foundation species in forests: the Harvard Forest Hemlock Removal Experiment. *Methods Ecology Evolution* **1**: 168–179.

Ellison, A. M., Bank, M. S., Clinton, B. D., *et al.* 2005. Loss of foundation species: consequences for the structure and dynamics of forested ecosystems. *Frontiers in Ecology and the Environment* **9**: 479–486.

Eschtruth A. K., Cleavitt, N. L., Battles, J. J., *et al.* 2006. Vegetation dynamics in declining eastern hemlock stands: 9 years of forest response to hemlock woolly adelgid infestation. *Canadian Journal Forest Research* **36**: 1435–1450.

Eschtruth, A. K. and Battles, J. J. 2009a. Assessing the relative importance of disturbance, herbivory, diversity, and propagule pressure in exotic plant invasion. *Ecological Monographs* **79**: 265–280.

Eschtruth, A. K. and Battles, J. J. 2009b. Acceleration of exotic plant invasion in a forested ecosystem by a generalist herbivore. *Conservation Biology* **23**: 388–399.

Di Tomaso, J. M. 1998. Impact, biology, and ecology of saltcedar (*Tamarix* spp.) in the southwestern United States. *Weed Technology* **12**: 326–336.

Fine, P. V. A. 2002. The invasibility of tropical forests by exotic plants. *Journal Tropical Ecology* **18**: 687–705.

Fujihara, M. 1996. Development of secondary pine forests after pine wilt disease in Western Japan. *Journal Vegetation Science* **7**: 729–738.

Fujihara, M., Hada, Y., and Toyohara, G. 2002. Changes in the stand structure of a pine forest after rapid growth of *Quercus serrata* Thunb. *Forest Ecology & Management* **170**: 55–65.

Gandhi, K. J. K. and Herms, D. A. 2010. Direct and indirect effects of alien insect herbivores on ecological processes and interactions in forests of eastern North America. *Biological Invasions* **12**: 389–405.

Ganser, D. A., Arner, S. L., Widman, R. H., and Alerich, C. L. 1993. After two decades of gypsy moth is there any oak left? *Northern Journal Applied Forestry* **10**: 184–186.

Gibbs. J. N. 1978. Intercontinental epidemiology of Dutch elm disease. *Annual Review Phytopathology* **16**: 287–307.

Gibson, I. A. S. 1974. Impact and control of Dothistroma blight of pines. *European Journal Forest Pathology* **4**: 89–100.

Gomi, T. 2007. Seasonal adaptations of the fall webworm *Hyphantria cunea* (Drury) (Lepidoptera: Arctiidae) following its invasion of Japan. *Ecological Research* **22**: 855–861.

Gooden, B., French, K., Turner, P. J., and Downey, P. O. 2009. Impact threshold for an alien plant invader, *Lantana camara* L., on native plant communities. *Biological Conservation* **142**: 2631–2641.

Gordon, D. R. 1998. Effects of invasive, non-indigenous plant species on ecosystem processes: lessons from Florida. *Ecological Applications* **8**: 975–989.

Gottschalk, K. W., Colbert, J. J., and Feicht, D. L. 1998. Tree mortality risk of oak due to gypsy moth. *European Journal Forest Pathology* **28**: 121–132.

Haack, R. A. 2001. Intercepted Scolytidae (Coleoptera) at U.S. ports of entry: 1985–2000. *Integrated Pest Management Review* **6**: 253–282.

Haack, R. A. 2006. Exotic bark- and wood-boring Coleoptera in the United States: recent establishments and interceptions. *Canadian Journal Forest Research* **36**: 269–288.

Hajek, A. E., Humber, R. A., and Elkinton, J. 1995. Mysterious origin of *Entomophaga maimaiga* in North America. *American Entomologist* **41**: 31–42.

Hanks, L. M., Paine, T. D., Millar, J. G., and Hom, J. L. 1995. Variation among Eucalyptus species in resistance to Eucalyptus longhorned borer in California. **74**: 185–194.

Hansen, E. M. 2008. Alien forest pathogens: *Phytophthora* species are changing world forests. *Boreal Environment Research* **13**: 33–41.

Hardin, J. W., Leopold, D. J., and White, F. M. 2001. *Harlow and Harrar's Textbook of Dendrology*. 9th edition. McGraw-Hill, Boston, Massachusetts.

Hartman, K. M. and McCarthy, B. C. 2007. A dendro-ecological study of forest overstorey productivity following the invasion of the non-indigenous shrub *Lonicera maackii*. *Applied Vegetation Science* **10**: 3–14.

Hartman, K. M. and McCarthy, B. C. 2008. Changes in forest structure and species composition following invasion by a non-indigenous shrub, Amur honeysuckle (*Lonicera maackii*). *Journal Torrey Botanical Society* **135**: 245–259.

Haugen, D. A. 1990. Control procedures for *Sirex noctilio* in the Green Triangle: Review from detection to severe outbreak. (1977–1987). *Australian Forestry* **53**: 24–32.

Haugen, L. 2001. How to identify and manage Dutch elm disease In: *Shade Tree Wilt Diseases*. Ash, C. L. (ed.). APS Press. St. Paul, MN.

Havill, N. P., Montgomery, M. E., Yu, G., *et al.* 2006. Mitochondrial DNA from hemlock woolly adelgid (Hemiptera: Adelgidae) suggests cyrptic speciation and pinpoints the source of the introduction to eastern North America. *Annals Entomological Society*, **99**: 195–203.

Hobbs, R. J. and Huenneke, L. F. 1992. Disturbance, diversity, and invasion: implications for conservation. *Conservation Biology* **6**: 334–337.

Hobbs, R. J., Arico, S., Aronson, J., *et al.* 2006. Novel ecosystems: theoretical and management aspects of the new ecological world order. *Global Ecology and Biogeography* **15**: 1–7.

Hoebeke, E. R., Haugen, D. A., and Haack, R. A. 2005. *Sirex noctilio*: discovery of a Palearctic siricid woodwasp in New York. *Newsletter of the Michigan Entomological Society* **50**: 24–25.

Hulme, P. E. 2009. Trade, transport and trouble: managing invasive species pathways in an era of globalization *Journal Applied Ecology* **46**: 10–18.

Hurley, B. P., Slippers, B., and Wingfield, M. J. 2007. A comparison of control results for the alien invasive woodwasp, *Sirex noctilio*, in the southern hemisphere. *Agricultural and Forest Entomology* **9**: 159–171.

Inderjit and Callaway, R. M. 2003. Experimental designs for the study of allelopathy. *Plant and Soil* **256**: 1–11.

Iwahori H., Tsuda K., Kanzaki N., *et al.* 1998. PCR-RFLP and sequencing analysis of ribosomal DNA of *Bursaphelenchus* nematodes related to pine wilt disease. *Fundamentals Applied Nematology* **21**: 655–666.

Jelinka, J. and Vandermeer, J. 2004. Gypsy moth defoliation of oak trees and a positive response of red maple and black cherry: An example of indirect interaction. *American Midland Naturalist* **152**: 231–236.

Kay, M. K. 2008. Are island forests vulnerable to invasive defoliators? In: *Invasive Forest Insects, Introduced Forest Trees, and Altered Ecosystems*. Paine, T. D. (ed.). Springer. Dordrecht.

Kenis, M., Auger-Rozenberg, M., Roques, A., *et al.* 2009. Ecological effects of invasive alien insects. In: *Ecological Impacts of Non-Native Invertebrates and Fungi on Terrestrial Ecosystems*. Langor, D. W. and Sweeney, J. (eds). Springer, Dordrecht.

Knight T. M., Dunn, J. L., Smith, L. A., *et al.* 2009. Deer facilitate Invasive plant success in a Pennsylvania forest understory. *Natural Areas Journal* **29**: 110–116.

Kobayashi, F. 1988. The Japanese pine sawyer. In: *Dynamics of Forest Insect Populations*. Berryman, A. A. (ed.)., Plenum Publishing, New York.

Kolar, C. S. and Lodge, D. M. 2001. Progress in invasion biology: predicting invaders. *Trends Ecology Evolution* **16**: 199–204.

Kondo, K., Foundin, A., Linit, M., *et al.* 1982. Pine wilt disease-nematological, entomological, and biochemical investigations. *Univ Missouri-Columbia Agric. Exp. Stn. SR* **282**: 1–56.

Kovacs, K. F., Haight, R. G., McCullough, D. G., *et al.* 2010. Cost of potential emerald ash borer damage in U.S. communities, 2009-2019. *Ecol. Econ.* **69**: 569–578.

Kulman, H. M. 1971. Effects of insect defoliation on growth and mortality of trees. *Annual Review Entomology* **16**: 289–324.

Langor, D., DeHaas, L., and Foottit, R. 2009. Diversity of non-native terrestrial arthropods on woody plants in Canada. *Biological Invasions* **11**: 5–19.

Lanier, G. N. and Peacock, J. W. 1981. Vectors of the pathogen. *Compendium of Elm Diseases*. Stipes, R. J. and Campana, R. J. (eds). APS Press. St. Paul, MN.

Levine, J. M., Adler, P. B., and Yelenik, S. G. 2002. A meta-analysis of biotic resistance to exotic plant invasions. *Ecology Letters* **10**: 975–989.

Liao, C., Peng, R., Luo, Y., *et al.* 2007. Altered ecosystem carbon and nitrogen cycles by plant invasion: a meta-analysis. *New Phytologist* **177**: 706–714.

Liebhold A. M., Macdonald, W. L., Bergdahl, D., and Maestro V. C. 1995. Invasion by exotic forest pests – A threat to forest ecosystems. *Forest Science* **41**: 1–49.

Lockwood, J. L., Cassey, P., and Blackburn, T. 2005. The role of propagule pressure in explaining species invasions. *Trends Ecology Evolution* **20**: 223–228.

Lonsdale, W. M. 1999. Global patterns of plant invasions and the concept of invasibility. *Ecology* **80**: 1522–1536.

Loo, J. L. 2009. Ecological impacts of non-indigenous invasive fungi as forest pathogens. *Biological Invasions* **11**: 81–96.

Lovett G. M., Canham, C. D., Arthur, M. A., *et al.* 2006. Forest ecosystem responses to exotic pests and pathogens in eastern North America. *BioScience* **56**: 395–405.

Lozon, J. D. and MacIssac, H. J. 1997. Biological invasions: are they dependent on disturbance? *Environmental Reviews* **5**: 131–144.

Lugo, A. E. 2004, The outcome of alien tree invasions in Puerto Rico. *Frontiers Ecology and the Environment* **2**: 265–273.

Mack, M. C. and D'Antonio C. M. 1998. Impacts of biological invasions on disturbance regimes. *Trends Ecology Evolution* **13**: 195–198.

Mack, R. N., Simberloff, D., Lonsdale, W. M., *et al.* 2000. Biotic invasions: Causes, epidemiology, global consequences, and control. *Ecological Applications* **10**: 689–710.

Madden, J. L. 1975. An analysis of an outbreak of the woodwasp, *Sirex noctilio* F.
(Hymenoptera, Siricidae), in *Pinus radiata*. *Bulletin Entomological Research* **65**: 491–500.

Madden, J. L. 1988. Sirex in Australasia. In: *Dynamics of Forest Insect Populations*.
Berryman, A. A. (ed). Plenum Publishing, New York.

Mamiya, Y. 1988. History of pine wilt disease in Japan. *Journal Nematology* **20**: 219–226.

Martin, P. H., Canham, C. D., and Marks, P. L. 2009. Why forests appear resistant to
exotic plant invasions: intentional introductions, stand dynamics, and the role of
shade tolerance. *Frontiers Ecology Environment* **7**: 142–149.

Mascaro J., Becklund, K. K., Hughes, R. F., and Schnitzer, S. A. 2008. Limited native plant
regeneration in novel, exotic-dominated forests on Hawai'i *Forest Ecology &
Management* **256**: 593–606.

Mattson, W. J., Herms, D. A., Witter, J. A., and Allen, D. C. 1991. Woody plant grazing
systems: North American outbreak folivores and their host plants. In: *Forest Insect
Guilds: Patterns of Interactions with Host Trees. USDA Forest Service General Technical
Report NE-153*. Baranchikov, Y. N., Mattson, W. J., Hain, F. P., and Payne, T. L. (eds).

Mattson W., Niemelä, P., Millers, I., and Inguanzo Y. 1994. Immigrant phytophagous
insects on woody plants in the United States and Canada: An annotated list. *USDA
Report no. NC-169*. St. Paul, MN, USA.

Mattson W., Vanhanen H., Veteli T., Sivonen S., and Niemela P. 2007. Few immigrant
phytophagous insects on woody plants in Europe: legacy of the European
crucible? *Biological Invasions* **9**: 957–974.

McCullough D. G., Poland, T. M., Anulewicz, A. C., *et al*. 2009. Emerald Ash Borer
(Coleoptera: Buprestidae) attraction to stressed or baited ash trees. *Environmental
Entomology* **38**: 1668–1679.

McDougall, K. L., Hobbs, R. J., and St Hardy, G. E. 2002. Vegetation of *Phytophthora
cinnamomi*-infested and adjoining uninfested sites in the northern jarrah
(*Eucalyptus marginata*) forest of Western Australia. *Australian Journal Botany*
50: 277–288.

Mckimm, R. J. and Walls, J. W. 1980. A survey of damage caused by the Sirex woodwasp
in the radiata pine plantations at Delatite, north-eastern Victoria, between 1972–
1979. *For. Comm. Vic* **28**: 3–11.

Merkel, H. W. 1906. A deadly fungus on the American chestnut. *Annual Report NY
Zoological Society* **10**: 97–103.

Meyerson, L. A. and Mooney, H. A. 2007. Invasive alien species in an era of
globalization. *Frontiers Ecology Environment* **5**: 199–208.

Morin, R. S., Liebhold, A. M., and Gottschalk, K. W. 2009. Anisotropic spread of hemlock
woolly adelgid in the eastern United States. *Biological Invasions* **11**: 2341–2350.

Mota, M. M., Braasch H., Bravo M. A., *et al*. 1999. First report of *Bursaphelenchus xylophilus*
in Portugal and in Europe. *Nematology*, **1**: 727–734.

Murphy, S. T. 1996. Status and impact of invasive conifer aphid pests in Africa. In:
*Impact of Diseases and Insect Pests in Tropical Forests. Proceedings of the IUFRO Symposium
23–26 November 1993, Peechi, India*. Nair, K. S. S. Sharma, J. K., and Varma, R. V. (eds).
Kerala, India, Kerala Forest Research Institute and Forestry Research Support
Programme for Asia and the Pacific.

Nair, K. S. S. 2007. *Tropical Forest Insect Pests: Ecology, Impact, and Management*. Cambridge University Press, Cambridge.

Niemela P. and Mattson W. J. 1996. Invasion of North American forests by European phytophagous insects: Legacy of the European crucible? *BioScience* **46**: 741–753.

Nuckolls, A. E., Wurzburger, N., Ford, C. R., *et al.* 2009. Hemlock declines rapidly with hemlock woolly adelgid infestation: impacts on the carbon cycle of southern Appalachian forests. *Ecosystems* **12**: 179–190.

Orondo, S. B. O. and Day, R. K. 1994. Cypress aphid (*Cinara cupressi*) damage to a cypress (*Cupressus lusitanica*) stand in Kenya. *International Journal Pest Management* **40**: 141–144.

Orwig, D. A., Foster, D. R., and Mausel, D. L. 2002. Landscape patterns of hemlock decline in New England due to the introduced hemlock woolly adelgid. *Journal Biogeography* **29**: 1475–1488.

Paillet, F. L. 2002. Chestnut: history and ecology of a transformed species. *Journal Biogeography* **29**: 1517–1530.

Paine, T. D. and Millar, J. G. 2002. Insect pests of eucalypts in California: implications of managing invasive species. *Bulletin Entomological Research* **92**: 147–151.

Paine, T. D., Hanks, L. M., Millar, J. G., and Paine, E. O. 2000. Attractiveness and suitability of host tree species for colonization and survival of *Phoracantha semipunctata* F. (Coleoptera: Cerambycidae). *Canadian Entomologist* **132**: 907–913.

Pimentel D., Lach L., Zuniga R., and Morrison D. 2000. Environmental and economic costs of nonindigenous species in the United States. *BioScience* **50**: 53–65.

Poland, T. M. and McCullough, D. G. 2006. Emerald ash borer: Invasion of the urban forest and the threat to North America's ash resource. *Journal Forestry* **104**: 118–124.

Pringle, A. J. D., Bever, M., Gardes, J. L., *et al.* 2009. Mycorrhizal symbioses and plant invasions. *Annual Review Ecology, Evolution Systematic* **40**: 699–715.

Pureswaran, D. S. and Poland, T. M. 2009. Host selection and feeding preference of *Agrilus planipennis* (Coleoptera: Buprestidae) on Ash (*Fraxinus* spp.). *Environmental Entomology* **38**: 757–765.

Reaser J. K. and Waugh, J. A. 2007. *Denying Entry: Opportunities to Build Capacity to Prevent the Introduction of Invasive Species and Improve Biosecurity at US Ports*. IUCN-World Conservation Union, Washington, DC Panel.

Richardson, D. M., Pysek, P., Rejmanek, M., *et al.* 2000. Naturalization and invasion of alien plants: Concepts and definitions *Diversity and Distributions* **6**: 93–107.

Ridley, G. S., Bain, J., Bultman, L. S., *et al.* 2000. Threats to New Zealand's indigenous forests from exotic pathogens and pests. *Science for Conservation* **142**: 1–68.

Roane, M. K., Griffin, G. J., and Elkins, J. R. 1986. *Chestnut Blight, Other Endothia Diseases, and the Genus Endothia*. APS Press. St. Paul, MN.

Roberts, S. W., Tankersley, Jr., R., and Orvis, K. H. 2009. Assessing the potential impacts to riparian ecosystems resulting from hemlock mortality in Great Smoky Mountains National Park. *Environmental Management* **44**: 335–345.

Rodgers, V. L., Stinson, K. A., and Finzi, A. C. 2008. Ready or not, garlic mustard is moving in: *Alliaria petiolata* as a member of eastern North American forests. *BioScience* **58**: 426–436.

Roland, J. and Embree, D. G. 1995. Biological control of the winter moth. *Annual Review Entomology* **40**: 475–492.

Ruiz, G. and Carlton, J. 2003. *Global Pathways of Biotic Invasions*. Island Press, New York, USA.

Sawyer, A. J. 2003. Annotated categorization of ALB host trees. USDA-APHIS-PPQ, Otis Plant Protection Laboratory. http://www.uvm.edu/albeetle/hosts.htm. [Accessed November 2010].

Sharma G. R., Raghubanshi, A. S., and Singh, J. S. 2005. Lantana invasion: An overview. *Weed Biology & Management* **5**: 157–165.

Simberloff, D. 2009. The role of propagule pressure in biological invasions *Annual Review Ecology Systematic* **40**: 81–102.

Small, M. J., Small, C. J., and Dreyer, G. D. 2005. Changes in a hemlock-dominated forest following woolly adelgid infestation in southern New England. *Journal Torrey Botanical Society* **132**: 458–470.

Sousa, E., Bravo, M. A., Pires, J., *et al.* 2001. *Bursaphelenchus xylophilus* (Nematoda; Aphelenchoididae) associated with *Monochamus galloprovincialis* (Coleoptera; Cerambycidae) in Portugal. *Nematology* **3**: 89–91.

Stadler, B., Muller, T., Orwig, D., and Cobb, R. 2005. Hemlock woolly adelgid: transforming ecosystem processes and landscapes. *Ecosystems* **8**: 233–247.

Stevens, J. T. and Beckage, B. 2009. Fire feedbacks facilitate invasion of pine savannas by Brazilian pepper (*Schinus terebinthifolius*). *New Phytologist* **184**: 365–375.

Stinson K. A., Campbell, S. A., Powell, J. R., *et al.* 2006. Invasive plant suppresses the growth of native tree seedlings by disrupting belowground mutualisms. *PLoS Biology* **4**: 727–731.

Stinson, K. A., Kaufman, S. K., Durbin, L., and Lowenstein, F. 2007. Impacts of garlic mustard invasion on a forest understory community. *Northeastern Naturalist* **14**: 73–88.

Suckling, D. M., Gibb, A. R., Dentener, P. R., *et al.* 2005. Gum leaf skeletoniser *Uraba lugens* in New Zealand: pheromone trapping for delimitation and phenology. *Journal Economic Entomology* **98**: 1187–1192.

Theoharides, K. A. and Dukes J. S. 2007. Plant invasion across space and time: factors affecting nonindigenous species success during four stages of invasion. *New Phytologist* **176**: 256–273.

Togashi, K. and Shigasada, N. 2006. Spread of the pinewood nematode vectored by the Japanese pine sawyer: modeling and analytical approaches. *Population Ecology* **48**: 271–283.

Tribe, G. D. and Cillié, J. J. 2004. The spread of *Sirex noctilio* Fabricius (Hymenoptera: Siricidae) in South African pine plantations and the introduction and establishment of its biological control agents. *African Entomologist* **12**: 9–17.

Van der Pas, J. B. 1981. Reduced early growth rates of *Pinus radiata* by *Dothistroma pini*. *New Zealand Journal Forest Science* **11**: 210–220.

Vanhellemont, M., Wauters, L., Baeten, L., *et al.* 2010. *Prunus serotina* unleashed: invader dominance after 70 years of forest development *Biological Invasions* **12**: 1113–1124.

Van Kleunen, M. and Fischer, M. 2009. Release from foliar and floral fungal pathogen species does not explain the geographic spread of naturalized North American plants in Europe. *Journal Ecology* **97**: 385–392.

Vitousek, P. M., D'Antonio, C. M., Loope, L. L., and Westbrooks, R. 1996. Biological invasions as global environmental change. *American Scientist* **84**: 468–478.

Vitousek, P. M., D'Antonio C. M., Loope, L. L., *et al.* 1997. Introduced species: A significant component of human-caused global change New Zealand. *Journal Ecology* **21**: 1–16.

Von Holle, B. V. and Simberloff, D. 2005. Ecological resistance to biological invasion overwhelmed by propagule pressure. *Ecology* **86**: 3212–3218.

Walker, B. and Steffen, W. 1997. An overview of the implications of global change for natural and managed terrestrial ecosystems. *Conservation Ecology* **1**: 2.

Ward, J. 2008. The historical and future Impacts of exotic insects and diseases on Connecticut's forests. In: *Proceedings of the 4th Symposium on Hemlock Woolly Adelgid in the Eastern United States. Hartford, CT.* Onken, B. and Reardon, R. (eds). USDA Forest Service FHTET-2008-01.

Watson, G. W., Voegtlin, D. J., Murphy, S. T., and Foottit, R. G. 1999. Biogeography of the *Cinara cupressi* complex (Hemiptera: Aphididae) on Cupressaceae, with description of a pest species introduced into Africa. *Bulletin Entomological Research* **89**: 271–283.

Weeks, E. P., Weaver, H. L., Campbell, G. S., and Tanner, B. D. 1987. Water use by saltcedar and by replacement vegetation in the Pecos River floodplain between Acme and Artesia, New Mexico. *United States Geological Survey Professional Paper 491-G.*

Wei, X., Reardon D., Wu, Y., and Sun, J. H. 2004. Emerald ash borer, *Agrilus planipennis* Fairmaire (Coleoptera: Buprestidae), in China: a review and distribution survey. *Acta Entomologica Sinica* **47**: 679–685.

Wei, X., Wu, Y., Reardon, R., *et al.* 2007. Biology and damage traits of emerald ash borer (*Agrilus planipennis* Fairmaire) in China. *Insect Science* **14**: 367–373.

Weste, G., Brown, K., Kennedy, J., *et al.* 2002. *Phytophthora cinnamomi* infestation – a 24-year study of vegetation change in forests and woodlands of the Grampians, Western Victoria. *Australian Journal Botany* **50**: 247–274.

Wilcove, D. S., Rothstein, D., Dubow, J., *et al.* 1998. Quantifying threats to imperiled species in the United States. *BioScience* **48**: 607–615.

Williamson, M. and Fitter, A. 1996. The characters of successful invaders. *Biological Conservation* **78**: 163–170.

Woods, F. W. and Shanks, R. E. 1959. Natural replacement of chestnut by other species in the Great Smoky Mountains National Park. *Ecology* **40**: 349–361.

Wright, S. J. 2005. Tropical forests in a changing environment. *Trends Ecology Evolution* **20**: 553–560.

Yang, Z. Q., Wang, X. Y., Wei, J. R., *et al.* 2008. Survey of the native insect natural enemies of *Hyphantria cunea* (Drury) (Lepidoptera: Arctiidae) in China *Bulletin Entomological Research* **98**: 293–302.

6

Out of sight, underground: forest health, edaphic factors, and mycorrhizae

R.D. BRIGGS AND T.R. HORTON

6.1 Introduction

The introductory chapter recognizes that tree mortality is both inevitable and desirable in a functioning forest. Imagining the development of a forest in the absence of mortality leads to the implausible scenario in which thousands of stems initially present attain increasingly larger diameters and grow outward to the point where they physically begin to interfere with their neighbors. The finite resources (sunlight, air, water, nutrients) available to individual trees would be insufficient to support continued growth and development. Severe competition between stems would constrain growth because all of the carbon fixed would be allocated for maintenance respiration, "freezing" the stand at this maximum attainable stem size in perpetuity – the ultimate stagnation. In reality, competition among individual trees leads to decline and ultimate death of those unable to compete. Site resources are focused on a smaller number of more vigorous competitors, and the implausible scenario is averted.

As the less competitive stems succumb to mortality and the stand thins out, the slope of the relationship (described in Chapters 1–3) between number of stems plotted against diameter (logarithmic scale) approaches $-3/2$. The multiple factors that contribute to mortality do not dissipate; a tenuous balance between site resources and the number of competing stems manifests itself through a sustainable diameter distribution. Catastrophic disturbances such as fire, windstorms, and attack by pests and pathogens may periodically upset the balance. As those disturbances subside and time passes, the balance tends to be

Forest Health: An Integrated Perspective, ed. John D. Castello and Stephen A. Teale. Published by Cambridge University Press. © Cambridge University Press 2011.

re-established. This leads to the fundamental premise of this book: the health of a forest can be evaluated within the framework of a sustainable diameter distribution.

At the stand level, the diameter distribution is the ultimate expression of the outcome of competition among individuals for resources (light and CO_2 from above-ground, nutrients, water and O_2 from soil). As trees effectively compete for those limited resources, they increase in size at the expense of those that succumb to mortality. In the absence of catastrophic disturbance, the diameter distribution is "buffered"; large changes are resisted. The number of stems gradually declines as those remaining increase in size. There are no precipitous declines in stand growth. A sustainable diameter distribution reflects the balance in resource acquisition and allocation between two scales: the individual tree and the stand. Mortality links the two scales, mediating the balance between them. Nowak *et al.* (Chapter 8) describe how competition is managed in both even- and uneven-aged stands to constrain mortality within baseline limits. The diameter distribution, and thus the current stand structure, is "sustainable". Coupled with maintenance of productivity, this is characteristic of a healthy forest, in accordance with Table 1.1.

Those abiotic resources, for which individual trees fiercely compete, are encompassed in the concept of site. Resources are finite; there is an upper limit on the supply of moisture and nutrients that constrains net primary production (NPP). With respect to vegetation, NPP (gross primary production – respiration) is the ultimate measure of productivity because it is an expression of carbon assimilation. Although we recognize that there are other important roles and management objectives for forests beyond vegetative production (e.g., source of high quality water, biodiversity, etc.), the capacity for sustained biological production requires a functioning soil system. Any disturbance that impacts the soil system will affect NPP and will ultimately impact the diameter distribution. Consequently, substantial and/or sudden declines in NPP manifest themselves through increased mortality, potentially an indicator of declining forest health.

Recognition of constraints on NPP posed by resource limitations leads to the concept of **site quality**, which is defined as the capacity for vegetative production on a given site for a specific purpose. High-quality sites have a large capacity to provide effective supplies of moisture and nutrients, generating high NPP (Figure 6.1). Low-quality sites can be limited by nutrients or moisture alone or in combination, reducing NPP relative to a high-quality site. Changes in NPP on a given site in response to disturbance may serve as an indicator of altered soil function. Soil function refers to the capacity of the soil system, the ultimate biogeochemical membrane, to maintain fluxes of energy, water, and gases among the hydrosphere, lithosphere, and atmosphere.

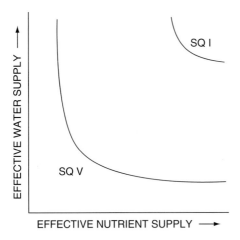

Figure 6.1 Influence of effective moisture and nutrient supply on site quality. High
site quality (SQ 1) requires a relatively large effective water supply as well as a
relatively large effective nutrient supply. Low site quality can result from either
limited effective water alone or in combination with limited effective nutrient supply.
(From Stone 1984, with permission.)

The use of productivity as a *de facto* measure of soil function has a long history.
Our dependence on soil to produce food and fiber has shaped the way that we
assess or value soil as a resource. Observations of high crop production on soils
with good physical properties date back to ancient Greece, in the writings of
Aristotle and Theophrastus (Fisher and Binkley 2000). The need to increase food
and fiber production to meet the needs of an exponentially increasing population has driven much research and advanced our understanding of how soil
properties affect plant productivity. Currently, attention devoted to function
equals or exceeds that devoted to production. In fact, the two are inseparable
in the context of sustainability.

A healthy forest could be construed as one in which NPP does not precipit-
ously decline within a given time period. A sudden decline in NPP would be
accompanied by a noticeable increase in baseline mortality. Utilization of
change in productivity as an indication of forest health requires an understanding of forest productivity *per se*. Burger's (1994) model provides an excellent
foundation for this purpose. He partitioned forest productivity into three components: biotic, abiotic, and cultural. The biotic component, which encompasses
the capacity of various species to grow and to compete, is determined by geno-
type, ecophysiology, and community dynamics. Introduction of exotic pests may
be considered a negative aspect of this component. Mycorrhizal fungi, which are
critical for root uptake of moisture and nutrients, are an important positive
element of this component.

The abiotic component, previously introduced as the concept of site, encompasses disturbance, climate, physiography, and soils. Lundquist *et al.* (Chapter 7) provide a detailed analysis of climate and disturbance which will not be repeated here, where the focus is on the soil system. The cultural component refers to anthropogenic control of water (irrigation), nutrients (fertilization), and pests (integrated pest management). In forestry, manipulation of the cultural component is often referred to as intensive management.

Burger's model of forest productivity has three important implications for forest health. First, changes in productivity (either increase or decrease) can be effected by a number of factors. Second, increases in productivity due to one component can counteract or mask decreases due to another. For example, short-term increases in tree growth obtained by fertilization could mask negative long-term impacts of alteration of soil pore size distribution by soil compaction. Third, the three components are not entirely independent. The interaction of the biotic and abiotic components can be illustrated by the influence of soil moisture regime (SMR) on species distribution in Ontario, Canada (Sims *et al.* 1996). Those species (balsam poplar, black ash, and tamarack) that have the capacity to grow in poorly aerated soils commonly occur on soils with a wet SMR. Trembling aspen and white birch, species that require higher levels of soil aeration and generally have higher rates of growth, are dominant on soils with better aerated fresh and moist SMRs. Another example of the interaction between biotic and abiotic factors also is apparent below-ground. Increases in N-deposition (fertilizers or pollution) have been associated with a loss in species richness in the ectomycorrhizal fungal communities (Peter *et al.* 2001; Lilleskov *et al.*, 2002). Even without local extinction of some mycorrhizal fungi, those that remain on a site tend to be less mutualistic or even parasitic as evidenced by changes in fitness (flower number and size) in the host plants (Johnson 1993). We will return to the role of mycorrhizal fungi in forest health below.

The complex interaction between species and site quality has a strong impact on diameter distribution through its impact on both species composition and growth rates. High-quality sites favor nutrient-demanding species with relatively high growth rates so that stand composition shifts more towards site-demanding species. Increased tree growth accelerates stand development by increasing the rate of self thinning, resulting in fewer stems, which tend to be larger in height and diameter relative to those on lower quality sites. The complex microtopography associated with forest systems plays a role in species composition on a fine scale. Tree growth and development are most certainly rooted in the soil (pun intended).

Our purpose is to explore the influence of site on forest health within the context established in Chapter 1. We begin with an examination of soil as a system at the global scale, successively refining the level of resolution to the local scale. Ultimately, we consider the influence of soil on baseline mortality, and provide an analytical framework for recognizing potential soil-based impacts on forest health. Within this chapter we address an emerging front in research focused on how plants access nutrients from soils – through their interactions with mycorrhizal fungi.

6.2 From global to local: soil in an ecosystem context

The premise that forest health can be viewed in the context of ecosystem function and/or productivity was established in Chapter 1. In order to appreciate the role of soil, it is useful to consider its position relative to other components. At the global scale, functioning ecosystems can be conceptually partitioned into three interacting subsystems: atmosphere, hydrosphere, and lithosphere. The atmosphere is the source of O_2, a fundamental requirement for aerobic organisms responsible for processing organic detritus into humus while releasing nutrients to the soil solution via the process of mineralization. The hydrosphere consists of an interconnected system of surface waters (lakes, rivers, and streams), ground water, and the oceans. The lithosphere is the solid portion of the earth's crust.

Knowledge of each of these subsystems has grown exponentially in the past decades. While much of the research has been confined within the individual disciplines (e.g., hydrologists focus on water systems while atmospheric scientists study the atmosphere in great detail), biogeochemists and modelers have been reaching across disciplinary boundaries to address broader issues that involve their interaction (e.g., mercury contamination, global climate change). Efforts to link global atmospheric models with those detailing ocean circulation have produced a new generation of sophisticated global climate circulation models (GCMs) (Flato *et al.* 2000) that continue to evolve (e.g., GCM2, the second generation coupled global climate model, Environment Canada 2008). These efforts demonstrate increased attention devoted to understanding the complex interactions among the atmosphere, lithosphere, and hydrosphere at a coarse scale. Since these interactions play a key role in forest health, it is informative to consider where these interactions are physically concentrated. The key role that soil plays in mediating these interactions has been recently highlighted in an issue of the journal *Applied Geochemistry* that focuses on the Soil Geochemical Landscapes Project (Smith 2009).

Considered within the realm of global subsystems, soil itself is a system that is physically positioned at the interface of the atmosphere, hydrosphere, and lithosphere. Consequently, the soil system functions as a biogeochemical membrane, mediating exchanges of energy, water, and gases among the three global subsystems. A portion of the solar energy transmitted through the atmosphere reaches the plant canopy and drives photosynthesis. The portion of solar energy that reaches the soil surface raises soil temperature, and drives evaporation during the daylight hours. At night, heat energy is released back to the atmosphere in the form of long wave radiation. Precipitation infiltrates the soil and is either stored, transpired, or transported to the hydrosphere.

The "ideal" soil system, from the perspective of plant production, would be comprised of approximately 45% mineral particles, 5% organic matter, and 50% pore space, with air and water equally distributed among the pore volume (25% each). Examination of the role of soil at the local scale requires a focus on the interdependent nature of fluxes of energy, water, and gases. Those fluxes are the mechanistic underpinnings for effective supply of moisture and nutrients to plant roots. Gas exchange occurs in pores that are not occupied by water. The conduction of energy occurs rapidly through soil solids, but is inhibited by air-filled pores. However, the addition of water to air-filled pores increases thermal conductivity. The fluxes of energy, water and gases are influenced by a combination of temperature, precipitation, and organism activity interacting with soil physical properties that imparts a unique morphology to the soil. Spatial and temporal variability are expressed through soil morphology, which can be readily observed in a soil pit.

Excavation of a soil pit exposes horizontally oriented layers referred to as horizons. Horizon development is a consequence of the fact that fluxes of energy, water, and gases are greatest at the surface and decrease with increasing depth. Differences in soil morphology reflect corresponding differences in physical and chemical characteristics. As a result, horizon description and soil classification are based on morphological features. A brief review of the fundamentals of soil profile morphology is provided below.

One of the primary variables used to classify soils on a coarse scale is carbon. An organic C concentration of 20% differentiates organic from mineral horizons, with the latter having less than 20% on a gravimetric basis. This is particularly important in forest soils, because continual inputs of litter (leaves, twigs, etc.) produce a layer of organic material referred to as the forest floor or duff on the soil surface. The organic horizons are further classified on the basis of degree of decomposition. The relatively undecomposed material that can still be identified (e.g., foliage, bark, etc.) is designated as Oi. As the biota process organic matter, which provides them with energy and C, organic matter becomes increasingly more amorphous, proceeding from partially decomposed (Oe) to highly decomposed (Oa) material, which is also referred to as humus. It is important to realize that this attempt to define discrete layers across a continuum of decomposition

Table 6.1. *Master horizon designations used for soil profile descriptions*

Horizon	Properties
O	Organic horizon in varying states of decomposition ranging from undecomposed plant litter to highly decomposed humus
A	Dark colored (due to incorporation of organic matter) mineral horizon commonly referred to as topsoil
E	Gray color due to leaching of organic matter and sesquioxides from mineral particles
B	Subsurface mineral horizon undergoing change (e.g., deposition of organic matter, clay, sesquioxides from percolating water, loss of carbonates, etc.)
C	Subsurface soil horizon characterized by minimal soil formation processes and organism activity
R	Bedrock

sometimes makes it difficult to precisely determine the boundary among the Oe and Oa horizons.

Proceeding downward from the surface, the dominance of organic material gives way to mineral particles that comprise mineral soil horizons, which also are designated by capital letters (Table 6.1). While all of the master horizons are listed in Table 6.1, every horizon may not be present in any given soil profile. The dark-colored surface horizon comprised of an intricate mixture of mineral and organic matter (less than 20%), designated as the A horizon, is what most people think of as top soil which is easily seen on freshly plowed fields. Organic matter is a source of nutrients and provides capacity to hold both water and nutrients. Consequently, the A horizon is the "richest" part of the soil profile. An A horizon develops naturally as biota actively incorporate organic matter into the upper mineral soil, or can be formed when soil is plowed, mixing organic and mineral horizons.

The process of organic matter decomposition generates organic acids, which dissolve and move downward with percolating water in those regions where precipitation exceeds evapotranspiration. These acids strip organic matter and mineral coatings from the soil particles, leaving quartz and feldspar mineral particles, giving a visually striking morphology to the E horizon. This bundle of acidic leaching processes is commonly referred to as **podzolization**, a term that originated with Dokuchaev, the famed Russian geographer, in the late 1800s. The E horizon is distinguished by the light gray color, a stark contrast to the overlying O or A horizons and the underlying B or C horizons. The B horizon, a subsurface horizon that underlies an O, A, or E horizon, is defined as actively undergoing **pedogenesis** (soil formation). The C horizon, in contrast, is characterized by the relative absence of pedogenic processes. Ultimately, a soil profile terminates in bedrock, providing one has the energy and will to excavate to that depth. This system of letters (capital for master horizons, lower case for subordinate distinctions, such as i, e, and a, provides a standard framework that is used for description of soil profiles.

While soil formation processes are expressed through soil morphology, soil physical properties play a key role in exchange of energy, water, and gases through the soil system, which is constrained by the size and distribution of the system of pores. Two fundamental physical properties that influence pore size distribution are soil texture and soil structure. **Soil texture** is defined as the relative proportion of sand (2–0.05 mm), silt (0.05–0.002 mm) and clay ($<$ 0.002 mm) particles. Sandy soils are characterized by a high proportion of macropores, which allow water to drain under the force of gravity (in the absence of an impermeable layer). Sandy soils do not hold water and tend to be droughty. Clay soils, on the other hand, are dominated by micropores, which do not drain under the force of gravity. They tend to be poorly aerated. Loam-textured soils, which are comprised of a mixture of sand, silt and clay, tend to exhibit a range in pore sizes that facilitate both water movement and water storage, the best of both worlds from the perspective of aerobic soil organisms.

Soil structure, the aggregation of sand, silt and clay-sized particles into secondary units, modifies the effects of texture. Soil structure is promoted by organic matter. The presence of aggregates provides large pores between the aggregates allowing for *both* water movement *and* storage in the small pores within aggregates. The presence of macropores is critical for soil aeration because exchange of O_2 and CO_2 requires air-filled pores. Soil texture and structure play an equally important role in soil nutrient and water-holding capacity. Clay-organic matter complexes adsorb water and attract cations (positively charged ions), an important mechanism for nutrient retention in the soil system. The "ideal" texture, a silt loam, promotes a balanced distribution between macropores and micropores. Together, soil texture, structure, and organic matter play an important role in the capacity of soil to support biological activity.

The biota provide the link between the soil and forest health. Biological activity is constrained by fluxes of energy, water, and gases through the soil system. Altering those fluxes may result in shortages (or in some cases, excesses) of water, energy, and specific gasses and consequent reduction in biological activity. Applied to trees, such alterations apply stress, eliciting allocation of resources to alleviate impacts on tree growth and development. Consider the consequences of reducing the flux of water from the soil. A classic, well-known example is provided by the multitude of roads that were built in the mid 1950s during the expansion of highway construction in the USA that resulted in localized saturation in low-lying forest stands due to impeded drainage. The subsequent increase in soil moisture restricted aeration. Species capable of effectively competing under poorly aerated conditions (e.g., red spruce, red maple) thrived at the expense of those that could not compete (i.e., red pine, sugar maple). The large numbers of dead stems occupying those landscapes provide a continual reminder of the impact of that altered flux of water.

The flux of water can be altered from the other end as well. Reducing the flux of water to the soil or reducing moisture storage capacity would create a moisture deficit, reducing organism activity and vigor, favoring species that could more effectively compete (e.g., red pine) under droughty conditions. Reducing the flux of energy (thermal conductivity) can result in excessive (both high and low endpoints) soil temperature, which reduces organism activity and contributes to tree mortality. While these fluxes ultimately constrain NPP, substantial alteration of these fluxes regardless of their cause (i.e., human impacts or natural disturbance) may have a tremendous impact on species composition, tree vigor and by extension, mortality. When NPP declines abruptly and excess mortality begins to appear, the soil is the first place to look for causes of reduced tree vigor. The interaction of site quality, species composition, and mortality is illustrated with several examples.

6.3 Site quality and stand development – towards the elusive sustainable diameter distribution

6.3.1 Spruce and fir in Maine

In the rolling hills and small mountains of northern Maine in the USA, site quality is strongly impacted by, and thus associated with landscape position. As soil drainage class becomes progressively wetter, site quality declines and species composition shifts dramatically.

Textbox 6.1 Spruce and fir in Maine

Schiltz and Grisi (1980) building on earlier work of Young (1954) sampled 105 even-aged spruce-fir stands and analyzed the impact of soil drainage class on tree growth. Williams (1986) extended that work by adding data collected from an additional 21 plots. Briggs (1994), drawing on his work in young, intensively managed stands, synthesized the information and developed a site classification field guide that uses soil drainage class as an indicator of above-ground production for spruce and fir stands.

Textbox 6.1 (cont.)

The relationship between landscape position and site quality is based on effective potential depth of aerated soil. Thin, excessively drained soils on ridge tops give way to higher quality sites consisting of well and moderately well-drained soils on the upper convex slopes with greater effective rooting depth (Figure 6.2). Saturated conditions associated with poor drainage restrict soil aeration, limiting effective soil depth. The consequent reduction in effective moisture and nutrient uptake progressively reduces site quality to its lowest point on the very poorly drained soils at the toe slopes and valley bottoms.

The topographic impact on site quality is reflected in species composition, individual tree growth rates, and stand development. Stands dominated by red spruce, which can effectively compete and subsist on minimal soil resources provided by shallow, excessively drained soils at ridge tops, gives way to site-demanding northern hardwoods, which are more effective competitors on the deeper and moderately well-drained soils. As soils become progressively wetter further downslope, red spruce and balsam fir outcompete hardwood species and attain a greater presence. At the very poorly drained lower slope positions, spruce and fir form densely stocked stands, often referred to as "dog-hair thick"; very few hardwood species are capable of competing under very poorly drained conditions.

While the changes in species composition are visually apparent, the impacts of decreasing site quality on individual tree growth and stand dynamics are even more interesting. The reduction in site quality associated with decreasing effective soil depth (as little as a few centimeters in very poorly drained soils) is reflected in individual tree growth. Height growth for spruce at a given age diminishes as soil drainage class becomes successively wetter (Figure 6.3). While reduced height growth is quite noticeable for individual trees, the collective impacts on stand development are enormous. The process of self thinning sometimes referred to as "race for the sky" is delayed. Consequently, stands on the more poorly drained soils are characterized by dense stands of shorter, smaller diameter stems. This provides a contrast to the fewer numbers of larger trees on the better-drained soils (Figures 6.3 and 6.4). The shift in tree height, stocking, and diameters from well- to poorly drained soils is as visually apparent as the shift in species composition.

Textbox 6.1 (cont.)

Despite the apparent differences in tree growth and stand development, the individual stands that were studied by Williams (1986) would be considered healthy on the basis of their diameter distributions (*sustainability*) and their capacity to meet landowner objectives (*productivity*), a premise established in Chapter 1 of this volume. Abrupt changes in the number of stems (either excess or deficiency) for a given diameter class would suggest an unhealthy condition. One of the common biotic agents that could induce such a change is the spruce budworm (*Choristoneura fumiferana*). The majority of stands from which those data were collected originated in the 1920s in response to severe budworm infestation, a clearly unhealthy situation. However, with the passage of time, those stands recovered; seedlings and saplings took advantage of the newly available site resources made available by the death of the overstory.

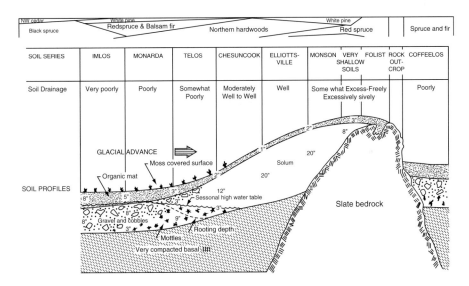

Figure 6.2 Illustration of topographic changes in soil depth, drainage class, and species composition for spruce-fir forests in north-central Maine, USA. (After Ferwerda and Young 1981; Schiltz and Grisi 1980, with permission.)

6.3.2 Sugar maple decline

Sugar maple, an economically important species in the Northeast USA, has exhibited declines in response to a combination of biotic and abiotic stresses. Decline is characterized by crown thinning, which may proceed to tree mortality

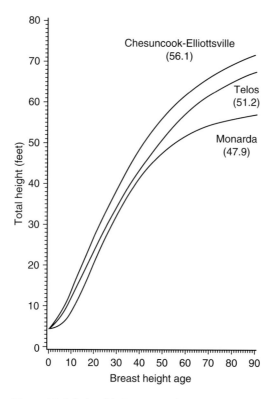

Figure 6.3 Relationship between red spruce height growth and age for spruce growing on soils differing in drainage class. (From Williams 1986, with permission.) Chesuncook-Eliottsville soils are moderately well- and well drained, Telos soils are somewhat poorly-drained, and Monarda soils are poorly to very poorly drained. Numbers in parentheses are site index values for each soil series.

(Chapter 4). Houston (1999) pointed out that the majority (29 of 31) of reported sugar maple decline episodes for forest and roadside situations occurred in the latter half of the 20th century, coinciding with sugar maple attaining the age of increased susceptibility to stress. Decline syndromes in two regions, South-central Canada and northwestern PA, are among those that have been studied most intensively.

Sugar maple decline in the Allegheny plateau region of northwestern PA and southwestern NY has been attributed to a combination of repeated insect outbreaks, climatic stress, and low-site quality. The most recent episode inspired an international symposium (Horsley and Long, 1999). Research continues and results have been synthesized by Horsley *et al.* (2002, 2008), providing the basis for current understanding of decline with respect to the interaction of site quality and biotic stress.

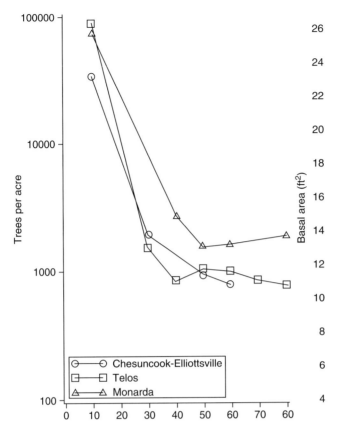

Figure 6.4 Soil drainage class impacts on the relationship between stand density (No. trees per acre) and age (years) for even-aged spruce-fir stands in Maine. (From Williams 1986, with permission.) Chesuncook-Eliottsville soils are moderately well- and well drained, Telos soils are somewhat poorly drained, and Monarda soils are poorly to very poorly drained.

Textbox 6.2 Sugar maple decline

The highly weathered soils of the unglaciated portion of the Allegheny plateau in PA are limited in their capacity to supply Ca and Mg. Consequently, site quality is relatively poor for sugar maple, which is a nutrient-demanding species. Extensive clearcuts, commonly used around the turn of the 20th century to support the wood chemical industry, favored sugar maple advance regeneration that developed under the protection of large slash piles. It is interesting to note that increased recruitment of sugar maple recently has been reported for oak-hickory forests in Indiana (Lin and Augsperger 2008). The harvest history in PA ultimately increased the

Textbox 6.2 (cont.)

proportion of sugar maple stems in the secondary forest as compared to the pre-settlement forests on soils that are less than ideal for sugar maple.

Understanding of the role of site quality in sugar maple decline was advanced as a result of a liming experiment conducted by the US Forest Service. One of the original purposes of this experiment was to gain an understanding of why lime applications seldom had any impact on northern hardwood productivity in the Northeast. In many cases those application rates were relatively small and the plot sizes were small; the new experiment attempted to address those past short comings. High rates (22.4 Mg/ha) of dolomitic lime were applied to large plots of Allegheny hardwoods in the unglaciated portion of northwest and north central PA in 1985 to assess impacts on tree growth. The response was not immediately apparent: three to eight years passed before the positive impacts on tree growth and development were realized (Long, et al., 1997).

Results of that experiment, which continue to inform our understanding of maple decline, clearly demonstrate the role of site quality in the context of its interaction with stand history and silvical characteristics of the species. Declining stands were located in upper slope positions (summit, shoulder, upper backslope). Sugar maple trees on lower slope positions, which receive nutrient inputs in water flowing down slope laterally through the soil, generally did not exhibit decline. Evaluation of foliar nutrient concentration data for healthy trees relative to trees in decline quantitatively supported the impact of site quality. Foliar concentration thresholds differentiating healthy from declining trees were identified. Trees in decline exhibited foliar Mg concentrations < 700 mg/kg, Ca < 5500 mg/kg, and Mn > 2000 mg/kg (elevated Mn is an indicator of stress). The increased presence of sugar maple coupled with sites of low fertility contributed to reduction in vigor. As those stands were challenged repeatedly by a combination of defoliating insects and periodic droughts, sugar maple trees exhibited crown dieback and excess mortality on low quality sites. Although results of these studies were not presented in terms of baseline mortality, it is clear that mortality is excessive.

Results of another, smaller-scale liming study in Quebec provided further evidence for the impact of site quality on sugar maple decline. Moore and Ouimet (2006) varied the rate of dolomitic limestone (0, 0.5, 1, 2, 5, 10, 20, and 50 Mg/ha) applied to individual sugar maple trees in a stand in Quebec. Ten years after application, crown dieback for treated trees (0.5–4.5%) was

Textbox 6.2 (cont.)

substantially lower than for control trees (23.7%). In addition, basal area increment for limed trees exceeded that of control trees. For both crown dieback and basal area increment, there were no differences among application rates. Foliar Ca concentration data for trees from all application rates exceeded 5500 mg/kg, the putative threshold that differentiates healthy from declining trees.

Sugar maple decline may have a subtle impact on site quality over time due to changes in species composition. Duchesne, *et al.* (2005), in one of the few papers explicitly dealing with baseline mortality, documented the impacts of maple decline on stand structure in Quebec. Although they did not isolate site quality, they recognized its contribution to decline in combination with disturbance history and differential shade tolerance of species. They evaluated inventory data over a 10-year period for 12 unmanaged uneven-aged maple-beech stands varying in decline severity. Mortality of sugar maple trees in the pole size class was partially (but not completely) offset by increased numbers of American beech, which were positioned to take advantage of the resources relinquished by the dying sugar maple (Figure 6.5). The surviving-fraction for all species combined was insufficient to ensure that the original diameter distribution would be maintained. Increased American beech density had a negative impact on site quality, reducing exchangeable soil Ca as beech foliar litter replaced that of sugar maple. Duchesne, *et al.* (2005) concluded that this negative feedback loop of diminishing site quality would continue, contributing to competitive success of beech over sugar maple.

6.3.3 *Eucalyptus in Australia*

The impact of site quality on tree growth and stand development in Australian forests has been a topic of great interest. Duncan *et al.* (2000) studied early growth (10–12 years) for 36 *Eucalyptus* species in plantations across a wide array of site conditions in Gippsland, Victoria. Not surprisingly, moisture proved to be an important factor in tree growth. Volume production was most rapid on sites with rainfall > 900 mm/yr and least on sites with <700 mm/yr rainfall. Limitations resulting from too little moisture provide an interesting contrast to the spruce-fir systems where excess soil moisture was associated with reduction in site quality due to the negative impact on effective soil depth, constraining uptake of water and nutrients. In both cases (moisture excess in spruce-fir vs. deficit in *Eucalyptus*) site quality was reduced due to a lack of effective supply of moisture and/or nutrients. The interaction between site quality and species affects

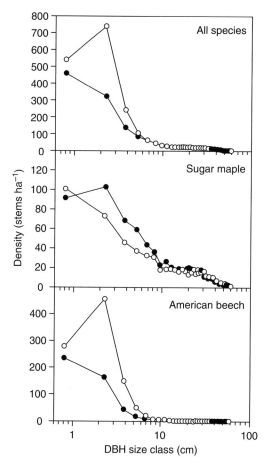

Figure 6.5 Initial (black dots) and final (white dots) stand structure after 10 years for all species, sugar maple, and American beech for 12 stands impacted by sugar maple decline in Quebec. (From Duschesne, *et al.* 2005, with permission.)

above-ground production. *Eucalyptus nitens* exhibited the highest volume production on high quality sites while *E. botryoides* was the highest-producing species on low quality sites. *E. globulus* was the most productive species on all other sites.

Florence (1996), in a detailed text devoted to Australian *Eucalyptus* forests, documented the influence of species and site quality on the relationship between stem density and stand age for seven fast-growing Eucalypt species (Figure 6.6). The graphs exhibited patterns similar to those displayed for the spruce-fir systems of northern Maine. Mountain ash (*E. regnan*) one of the fast-growing species, exhibited a high rate of self thinning characterized by a relatively large instantaneous slope for stem density as a function of stand age. Florence attributed the high growth rate of this species to crown structure (conical crown shape and strong apical growth).

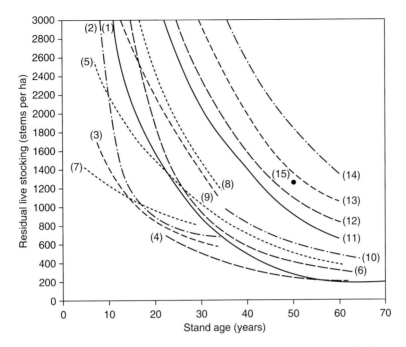

Figure 6.6 Patterns of self-thinning in stands of *Eucalyptus* species compiled by Florence 1996: (1)–(4) *E. regans* (Ashton 1976b, Borough, *et al.* 1978); 5) *E. diversicolor* (M. Rayner, CALM, West. Aust., pers comm.); (6) *E. delegatensis* (Borough, *et al.* 1978); (7) *E. grandis* plantation in Australia (Borough, *et al.* 1978); (8) and (9) *E. grandis* plantations in South Africa (Bredenkamp, 1984); (10) *E. maculata*, high quality site, south coast New South Wales (Forestry Comm. NSW; (11) *E. pilularis* on moderate quality site (Queensland Forestry Dept. records); (12)–(14) *E. sieberi* on sites of high (12) to low (14) quality (Borough, *et al.* 1978); (15) Stocking in *E. marginata* regrowth at 50 years. (From Florence 1996 with permission.)

The influence of site quality was visually apparent in a graphical comparison of self thinning curves for silver top ash (*E. sieberi*) growing on low, medium, and high quality sites (Figure 6.6). Stand density for a given age decreased with increasing site quality. Low-quality sites exhibited less standing volume, greater stem density with slower rates of stand development (lower instantaneous slope for density vs. stand age) relative to high-quality sites. These patterns paralleled those reported for spruce-fir stands in northern Maine, where soil drainage class constrained site quality. Physical conditions associated with the various site qualities for Eucalyptus were not described. Mortality rates were greater on high-quality sites where dominance was expressed earlier.

The general applicability of the self-thinning rule was documented in an extensive review by Westoby (1984). The slope of average individual plant biomass plotted against average plant density (both on logarithmic scale) approximated −3/2 for 31

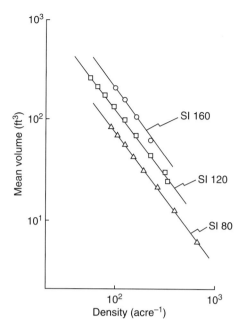

Figure 6.7 Influence of site quality, as measured by site index of *Pinus ponderosa*, on the relationship between volume and density. (From Westoby 1984, with permission.)

species ranging from annual grasses/herbs to trees/shrubs. That general relationship, averaged across a variety of species and site conditions, obscures the role of site quality. Westoby pointed out two important implications of this universal relationship: (1) mortality is solely a function of biomass accumulation, and (2) mortality occurs more slowly as conditions for growth become less favorable; slower-growing trees require more time to attain a given biomass relative to faster-growing trees. Several examples were provided to empirically illustrate the complex role of site quality in stand development and production. Tree growth and stand development were compared across a range of site qualities. Reduced individual tree growth for spruce and fir in Maine and for Eucalyptus in Australia on poor quality sites was expressed through delayed stand development relative to higher-quality sites. The positive impacts of site quality in individual tree growth are readily apparent. Westoby (1984) documented increased average tree volume for a given stand density as Ponderosa pine **site index** increased from 80 to 160 (Figure 6.7). Site index, the average height of dominant and co-dominant trees at index age of 100 years, provides a useful expression of site quality. Higher resource availability associated with high-quality sites supports greater production.

Morris (2003) used an analytical approach to more formally explore the potential impacts of site quality (expressed as fertility level) on the rate of self

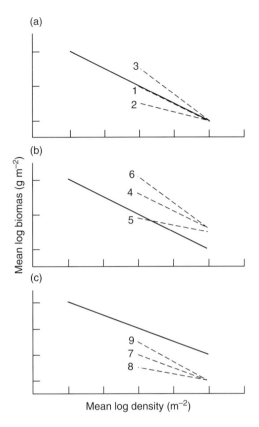

Figure 6.8 Hypothetical combinations of self-thinning lines for populations sown at the same density and grown at higher (solid line) or lower (dashed line) fertility level. Self-thinning begins at: (a) the same biomass in both stands; (b) a lower biomass in the higher fertility stand; (c) a lower biomass in the lower fertility stand. Numbers beside the low fertility lines represent options 1–9 (i.e., 1, 4, and 7 show slope of self thinning line on high quality site = low quality site; 3, 6, and 9 depict greater slope for low quality site; 2, 5, and 8 depict reduced slope for low quality site (From Morris 2003, with permission.)

thinning (Figure 6.8). He considered the potential self thinning patterns that might be possible for two contrasting fertility levels (low and high). The two causes for variation in self thinning patterns are (1) slope of the biomass vs. density line, and (2) the level of biomass at which self thinning is initiated (Figure 6.8). Self thinning on low quality sites may begin at a level of biomass that is (1) higher than, (2) lower than, or (3) the same as the level of biomass for a high-quality site. For each of those initial scenarios, there are three possibilities: the slope of the self thinning line for the low quality site could be (1) greater than, (2) less than, or (3) equal to that for the high quality site. Morris' survey of the published literature identified evidence for six of the nine possible combinations described (Figure 6.8). However, no unifying theory has been offered that would make it possible to predict which outcome would occur; i.e., the classification is descriptive rather than predictive. The issue of how competition changes along a productivity gradient remains unresolved.

Site quality clearly influences both the level of biomass that can be supported, and the rate of stand development with respect to self-thinning. Mortality, partly the result of severe competition among individuals in a system where resources are limiting, is the ultimate link between individual tree and stand growth. The differential development of below- vs. above-ground competition likely plays an important role in the process of stand development. The logistical difficulties in quantifying below-ground competition challenge our ability to develop a theoretical underpinning that can be used to predict outcomes on sites varying in quality.

6.4 The role of mycorrhizal fungi

As we begin to think more in depth about sustained production of food and maintenance of soil function, it is critical to consider the biotic component of soil, specifically the role of microorganisms. Plant root nutrient and water uptake capacity is highly dependent on the presence of mycorrhizal fungi; their role in maintaining soil function and production has become increasingly more apparent. Consequently, it is worthwhile to explore mycorrhizae in greater detail.

The term mycorrhizae was first coined by A.B. Frank (Trappe 2005). Dr. Robert Hartig, recognized as the father of forest pathology, had identified fungal hyphae in and among root cells of forest trees as pathogens. It was A.B. Frank who first recognized that some of these fungi were beneficial. Over 120 years later, we have reached a point where most foresters agree that mycorrhizal fungi are important. However, the role these fungi play in forest health remains difficult to document in the field. Readers are encouraged to consult recent comprehensive treatments by Smith and Read (1997), Peterson *et al.* (2004), and Brundrett *et al.* (1996). After a brief introduction to mycorrhizal fungi in general, several case studies are presented.

Mycorrhizal fungi are beneficial mutualistic symbionts that colonize the roots of most of the world's plant species, playing the critical role of acquisition and transfer of soil nutrients and water to the plants (Smith and Read 1997). The fungi produce extensive networks of hyphae that physically increase the volume of soil utilized by plants. But it is too simple to leave it as a physical extension of the roots. These fungi bring with them unique enzymatic capabilities that increase the forms of nutrients available to the plants. For instance, phosphorus is typically present in forest soil, but not in forms that are available to plants.

Textbox 6.3 Mycorrhizal types

Mycorrhizae: This word is constructed of two Greek roots, myc meaning mushroom and rhiz meaning root. The singular form is mycorrhiza and the plural form is variously given with a Latin (mycorrhizae) or English ending (mycorrhizas).

Arbuscular mycorrhizae: Named for the treelike hyphal structures that form within walls of cortex cells in the roots, the arbuscules. The plant cell membrane is not penetrated by the hyphae, but rather grows in close contact with the arbuscule, increasing the contact area for nutrient transfer. Formerly known as endomycorrhizae.

Ectomycorrhizae: Named because a fungal sheath covers the outside of the feeder roots and hyphae that surround the cortex cells of those roots do not penetrate the plant cell wall. The hyphae surrounding the cortex cells is called the Hartig net in honor of Dr. Robert Hartig, and is where nutrients are transferred.

Cortex cells: These are root cells that occur between the epidermis and endodermis of the plant root. The transfer of nutrients between fungi and plants occurs in the cortex layer.

Mycorrhizal fungi access these recalcitrant forms of phosphate (e.g., Al-PO$_4$, Fe-PO$_4$) through the production of phosphotases. Fungi are also capable of accessing forms of soil nitrogen that are unavailable to plants. We now know that in addition to uptake and transfer to hosts of NO$_3^-$ and NH$_4^+$ from soil pools, mycorrhizal fungi are competitive with other microorganisms for organic forms of nitrogen such as amino acids (Smith and Read 1997). Interestingly, a common source of nitrogen transferred to ectomycorrhizal hosts from the fungi is whole amino acids such as glutamine. Ecosystem scientists have recently become aware of the importance of mycorrhizal fungi in direct access to organic nitrogen for plant uptake (Schimel and Bennett 2004). In addition to nitrogen and phosphorus, mycorrhizal fungi have varying capabilities to access and transfer other minerals including calcium, magnesium, iron, nickel, etc. (Smith and Read 1997). Further, the fungi impart resistance to soil pathogens and heavy metals (Marx 1969; Tichelen *et al.* 2001). In exchange for all of these services, the heterotrophic fungi acquire energy from the plants in the form of photosynthetic products. Mycorrhizal fungi are not carbon limited – they have direct access to recently fixed carbon from their hosts. This gives them a competitive advantage over many other heterotrophic microbes that must compete for sources of energy before they can obtain other nutrients.

About 90% of the world's plant species belong to families that are typically mycorrhizal; many of them are obligate mycorrhizal plants and will die as seedlings without compatible mutualists (Molina *et al.* 1992; Peterson *et al.* 2004). Mycorrhizal types can be defined by their root anatomy. The two main types will be treated here, arbuscular mycorrhizae and ectomycorrhizae. Other types include those that occur with orchids, three types with plant species in the family Ericaceae (ericoid, arbutoid, monotropoid), and other root endophytes with unclear symbiotic interactions with their hosts. It is estimated that fully 70–80% of the world's plants associate with arbuscular mycorrhizal (AM) fungi (Peterson *et al.* 2004; Smith and Read 1997). Important AM forest trees in temperate forests include maple, ash, and redwood. Many tropical trees also associate with arbuscular mycorrhiza, but most have not been adequately assessed for AM fungi in their roots. Estimates vary, but about 10–14% of the world's plants associate with ectomycorrhizal fungi. This is a relatively small proportion of the world's plants but these trees are dominant members of many forests including all species of pine, oak, birch, eucalyptus, and dipterocarps.

6.4.1 What happens when there are no compatible mycorrhizal fungi for a tree?

The clearest examples of the importance of mycorrhizal fungi to tree health are found in failed attempts to establish plantations outside the natural range of the trees. For instance, multiple attempts have been made to plant pine species in the southern hemisphere and eucalypt species in the northern hemisphere, but without compatible mycorrhizal fungi the seedlings typically die after a few months (Grove and Le Tacon 1993). Vozzo and Hacskaylo (1971) review attempts to establish pine in Puerto Rico: only when compatible mycorrhizal fungi were introduced in soils or on seedlings did the seedlings survive and grow well. Those that died were found to lack mycorrhizal root tips, and those that survived were fully colonized by mycorrhizal fungi. It is now clear that compatible fungi are not present on a global scale, and must be introduced in some situations for a specific host (Nuñez *et al.* 2009).

Another example of what happens when mycorrhizal fungi are not available for trees was documented in the Pacific Northwest of the United States. Douglas-fir (*Pseudotsuga menziesii*) is native to the region and a major lumber crop. After a clearcut harvest, the typical management practice is to use herbicides to reduce competition with successional shrub species in the genus *Arctostaphylos*. In some instances, Douglas-fir seedlings were planted onto harvested sites several years after the initial harvest and herbicide treatment. These sites had converted to grass-dominated fields in the interim. Apparently, the Douglas-fir seedlings from the nurseries were non-mycorrhizal and there where no compatible mycorrhizal fungi in the grassland soils (grasses are associated with arbuscular mycorrhizal fungi). Interestingly, *Arctostaphylos* forms mycorrhizal associations with many of the same fungi as Douglas-fir (Molina and Trappe 1982b). When researchers added soil that was removed from beneath the canopy of local *Arctostaphylos* shrubs, Douglas-fir seedlings planted into the grasslands established and grew well. This led to a model in which the soil microbial community associated with mature Douglas-fir was supported by the so-called competing shrubs after disturbance (Perry *et al.* 1989). The model is supported by data from a successional community where establishment of one-year old Douglas-fir seedlings that had germinated in the field was facilitated by the mycorrhizal fungi associated with mature *Arctostaphylos* (Horton *et al.* 1999).

6.4.2 How do mycorrhizal fungi move nutrients below-ground?

In the previous example, successional shrubs were killed to reduce competition for light and soil nutrients. One can argue that after a fire, the canopy is wide open and light competition is minimal for several years. But even as the canopy closes, mycorrhizal fungi may ameliorate competition for light. For instance, although birch and Douglas-fir compete for light, fixed carbon is transferred between the competing hosts via the ectomycorrhizal networks below-ground (Simard *et al.* 1997a; Simard *et al.* 1997b). Carbon transfer between competing hosts also has been documented in the field for a spring perennial trout lily (*Erythronium americanum*) and maple, two arbuscular mycorrhizal plants (Lerat *et al.* 2002). Precisely how do trees compete for soil nutrients? Our current understanding does not take mycorrhizal fungi into account. Yet, we have found that roughly 100% of the primary feeder roots of ectomycorrhizal trees growing in undisturbed locations are covered by ectomycorrhizal fungi (the fungal sheath), and one rarely finds root hairs on the roots. Similarly, fungi colonize roughly 100% of the root systems of arbuscular mycorrhizal trees in undisturbed settings. This suggests that it is not the plants but the fungi that pick up the soil nutrients, delivering them directly to the cortex layer of the primary roots. Plant competition for soil nutrients then becomes one between competing mycorrhizal fungi. But most of the fungi show low host specificity, and actually connect competing plant species in a mixed stand (Molina *et al.* 1992; Horton and Bruns 1998; Horton *et al.* 1999; Dulmer 2006). This may explain why the Douglas-fir seedlings discussed above benefited from the mycorrhizal fungi associated with the competitor *Arctostaphylos* – some of the soil nutrients acquired by the fungi supported by *Arctostaphylos* were probably transferred to the Douglas-fir seedlings with little investment by the seedlings. Mycorrhizal fungi probably alter competitive outcomes in other ways and this is a topic that begs more attention.

Humans are now the dominant force in the nitrogen cycle with resultant major impacts on aquatic and terrestrial ecosystems (Vitousek *et al.* 1997). Records of fruiting patterns in Europe over the last several decades indicate that ectomycorrhizal fungi are negatively impacted by human-induced atmospheric nitrogen deposition (Arnolds 1991). In areas with atmospheric deposition, the community of ectomycorrhizal fungi is altered and species richness can decline (Peter *et al.* 2001; Avis *et al.* 2003; Lilleskov *et al.* 2002; Parrent and Vilgalys 2007). How these changes in the mycorrhizal community will impact forest health is unclear, but some forest declines resulting from nitrogen-deposition have been attributed to mycorrhizal dysfunction (Meyer 1988; Mejstrik 1989). A survey of the 24 most common tree species of the eastern United States shows a range of responses to nitrogen deposition with three species showing declines in biomass (Quinn *et al.* 2010). Interestingly, this study also showed that growth and survival of arbuscular mycorrhizal trees are favored in areas experiencing anthropogenic nitrogen deposition.

Forest decline in areas affected by acid deposition was thought to be the result of sulfur biogeochemistry, but long-term recovery appeared to be restricted due to base cation losses in the ecosystem, especially calcium (Likens *et al.* 1996). Acid deposition appeared to enhance losses of base cations from soil pools. Sources of calcium from the forest ecosystem such as atmospheric deposition and mineral weathering did not account for losses measured in streams at Hubbard Brook Experimental Forest in New Hampshire, USA. Blum *et al.* (2002) showed that apatite rock deep in the soil represented a significant pool of calcium, and that this calcium pool was directly utilized by ectomycorrhizal fungi, which demonstrates that mycorrhizal fungi are directly involved in forest health through their nutrient acquisition and subsequent transfer to their hosts. Indeed, leaves of ectomycorrhizal trees (spruce and birch) showed higher levels of calcium than leaves of the dominant arbuscular mycorrhizal host (maple). There is an intriguing lesson here. By incorporating mycorrhizal fungi as an important part of the biogeochemical cycle, the calcium budget was resolved. The role of the fungi was not apparent before because apatite rock in the shallow soil horizons is depleted but in this case, the fungi transfer calcium derived from deep soil apatite directly to the plants without passing it into the soil pool. As we pursue a working definition of forest health, it can only help to contemplate the role of mycorrhizal fungi.

6.4.3 Are mycorrhizae related to forest health as we define it?

As we described above, the importance of mycorrhizal fungi for plant health in general is well known today. However, it is still extremely difficult to assess how specific mycorrhizal fungi affect forest stand health over time. We can now confidently identify the players from below-ground structures using molecular techniques and we are beginning to understand the role some of these fungi play in nutrient cycling. For example, in a monodominant conifer stand of 0.1 ha, one can easily expect 30–100 species of fungi interacting with the hosts, and they are patchily distributed below ground at a fine scale (Horton and Bruns 2001). Most individuals colonize soils and roots over about 1 m^2 of soil (Redecker et al. 2001), although some species produce large perennial individuals covering tens of meters (Kretzer et al. 2004; Lian et al. 2006). We still do not know whether the distribution of most species, and certainly individuals within a species, is a function of edaphic factors, hosts, or a lottery, but it is probably a combination of all three.

Although many studies have shown that mycorrhizal fungi are critical for tree seedling establishment (reviewed in Horton and van der Heijden 2008), we are not aware of any studies that allow one to investigate the role of mycorrhizal fungi on forest health per se. One can conduct a laboratory study to test the effect on plant growth of some mycorrhizal fungi across a nutrient gradient (e.g., N or P). But in a forest stand, entire communities of fungi are involved, and these communities are quite fluid on an annual basis. So, while we are presently unable to address how mycorrhizal fungi impact forest health in terms of sustainable diameter distributions, we know that they provide plants with increased access to soil nutrients and damage to that function adversely affects the health of trees, as may be occurring with forest decline with anthropogenic nitrogen-deposition.

Today, a variety of technologies have given us unprecedented abilities to sample mycorrhizal fungi and to understand their roles in forest health. We can now identify most ectomycorrhizal fungi from root tip samples using molecular techniques leading to a much clearer understanding of the roles these fungi play in plant community dynamics (Horton and Bruns 2001). Molecular typing of arbuscular mycorrhizal fungi is not as well developed, but is still contributing to our understanding of the role these fungi play in plant communities. The use of isotopes has given researchers insights into how the fungi access and move nutrients between hosts and throughout the forest ecosystem (Simard et al. 1997b; Hobbie and Colpaert 2003; Hobbie et al. 2005). Incorporating mycorrhizal fungi into studies investigating the biogeochemistry of our forest ecosystems has elucidated interesting and important roles the fungi play (Blum et al. 2002). These and other approaches will continue to enlighten our view of the roles of mycorrhizal fungi in forest health.

6.5 Soil quality

Soil physical properties ultimately define the limit of biological activity. Soil systems characterized by a balance in particle and pore sizes have the greatest potential (or minimal constraints) for productivity; that provides for water and nutrient movement and storage. As those conditions depart from optimal, potential productivity is necessarily reduced. Consequently deep soils with high nutrient and water supplying capacity will have a high potential for above-ground production compared to shallow soils or other soils where either micropores (limiting aeration) or macropores (limiting moisture storage) dominate. Regardless of the maximum level of site quality for a given site, an important goal is continued maintenance of productivity over the long term, often referred to as sustainability; any reduction in productivity is undesirable. A healthy forest could be construed as one in which the inherent level of productivity is not reduced.

The application of the term health to ecosystems is not unique to forest pathologists; soil scientists have been wrestling with it for over a decade. Soil health is defined as the ability of the soil to perform according to its potential (Mausbach and Tugel, 1995). In that sense, soil scientists debate the term health with the same degree of subjectivity and attempts at clarity as forest pathologists applying the term to forests. Soil scientists have taken a slightly different approach, introducing the concept of "soil quality". **Soil quality**, is 'the capacity of a soil to function within ecosystem boundaries, to sustain biological productivity, maintain or enhance water and air quality, and support human health and habitation' (Karlen *et al.* 1997). Johnson *et al.* (1997) further refined the soil quality concept by associating it with meeting requirements of a group of species or a single purpose.

Many attempts to develop a numerical soil quality index (SQI) to rate and compare different soils, or to assess soil quality over time have been tried. None are entirely useful. While the objective is laudable, the "devil is in the details"; the results have generated vigorous discussion. Variation in management objectives or end products (e.g., crops, forest products, potable water, biological waste processing, etc.) is a fundamental issue. Soil properties selected as indicators of quality are land-use specific; there is no universal set of soil quality indicator variables applicable to all situations.

Recognizing the influences of land use change or management impacts on a variety of soil properties, the Natural Resources Conservation Service proposed a minimum data set (NRCS 1999) that encompasses physical, chemical, and biological soil properties. They produced a test designed for use on agricultural lands. Even within this single land use category, differences in climate and physiography influence selection of soil properties that would serve as useful indicators of quality. For example, soil electrical conductivity (a measure of salinity) would be useful in regions of low rainfall where accumulation of salts can be problematic compared to regions where rainfall is plentiful.

Table 6.2. *Soil variables used as indicators of soil quality for the Soil Quality Test Kit (NRCS 1999; Seybold,* et al. *2001)*

Soil Variable	Description
Site characterization	Soil series, management history, slope and topographic conditions, field location, and climatic information provide physical context
Soil CO_2 efflux	Combined heterotrophic and autotrophic respiration reflects rate of biological activity
Infiltration	Rate of water movement into the soil (unsaturated conditions suggested)
Bulk density	Mass per unit volume of dry, undisturbed soil
Electrical conductivity	Measure of salinity using a portable EC probe in 1:1 soil:solution
pH	Active acidity measured using portable probe in 1:1 soil:solution
Nitrate	Water filtered through soil sample measured using a test strip (colorimetric)
Aggregate stability	Proportion (mass) of aggregates remaining after wet sieving
Slake test	Structural integrity of aggregates placed in water for five minutes indicates potential for disruption by rapid wetting.
Earthworms	No. earthworms per unit volume of soil. Their presence as a positive indicator in agricultural fields
Physical observations	A horizon thickness, rooting depth, soil structure, and soil texture are associated with productive potential

The soil variables used for the NRCS soil quality index kit are summarized in Table 6.2. It is interesting to note that the kit does not provide for measurement of organic carbon, which many soil scientists feel is an important variable (Karlen *et al.* 1997). Seybold *et al.* (2001) described use and application of the soil test kit: (a) assessing soil quality: comparison of management systems on the same soil type (e.g., till vs. no till), (b) monitoring changes on the same soil over time, and (c) evaluating impacts from individual management activities within a single site (i.e., machine traffic). Changes in those variables over time or differences between impacted vs. non-impacted sites were used as an indication of change in soil quality. Reductions in infiltration, aggregate stability, and earthworms suggest diminished soil quality while increases in electrical conductivity and bulk density are associated with reduced soil quality.

Attempts to assess soil quality have not been restricted to agriculture. The US Forest Service has begun to routinely characterize and sample soils on plots associated with the Forest Inventory and Analysis (FIA) program. Amacher *et al.* (2007) computed a SQI to represent soil data collected from FIA plots. The variables include bulk density, coarse fragment content, pH, organic carbon, total nitrogen, and extractable nutrient concentrations. Results from each measured variable were assigned a discrete score ranging from −1 to 2, indicating values optimal and severely deficient, respectively, for tree growth. For example, pH values ≤ 3 (strongly acidic and adverse for most plant species) received a score of −1 while pH values ranging from 5.5 to 7.2 received a score of 2. The SQI was computed as the summation of individual scores for the 19 variables. As more soil data are collected and associated with corresponding data for tree growth and forest condition, it may be possible to develop empirical relationships between stand growth and soil quality indices. At this early stage of development, eliciting a relationship between baseline mortality and SQIs is a goal that will require continued monitoring and refinement.

References

Amacher, M. C., O'Neil, K. P., and Perry, C. H. 2007. Soil vital signs: A new soil quality index (SQI) for assessing forest soil health. *Research Paper RMRS-RP-65WWW*. Fort Collins, CO, USDA Forestry Service Rocky Mountains Research Station.

Arnolds E. 1991. Decline of ectomycorrhizal fungi in Europe. *Agriculture Ecosystem & Environment* 35: 209–244.

Avis, P. G., McLaughlin, D. J., Dentinger, B. C., and Reich, P. B. 2003. Long-term increase in nitrogen supply alters above- and below-ground ectomycorrhizal communities and increases the dominance of *Russula* spp. in a temperate oak savanna. *New Phytologist* 160: 239–253.

Blum, J. D., Klaue, A., Nezat, C. A., *et al.* 2002. Mycorrhizal weathering of apatite as an important calcium source in base-poor forest ecosystems. *Nature* 417: 729–731.

Briggs, R. D. 1994. Site classification field guide. *CFRU Tech. Note 6, Maine Ag. and For. Exp. Stn. Misc. Pub.* 724. University of Maine, Orono.

Brundrett, M., Bougher, N., Dell, B., *et al.* 1996. *Working with Mycorrhizas in Forestry and Agriculture*. ACIAR Monograph, Canberra.

Burger, J. A., 1994. Cumulative effects of silvicultural technology on sustained forest productivity. In: *Assessing the Effects of Silvicultural Practices on Sustained Productivity. Proceedings of the IEA/BE Workshop'93, May 16–22, Fredericton, NB, Canada. IEA/BA Task IX, Activity 4, Report 3, Info. Rep. M-X-191*. Mahendrappa, M. K., Simpson, C. M., and Smith, C. T. (Compilers). Canadian Forest Service – Maritimes Region, Natural Resources Canada, Fredericton, NB.

Duchesne, L., Ouimet, R., Moore, J. D., and Paquin, R. 2005. Changes in structure and composition of maple-beech stands following sugar maple decline in Quebec, Canada. *Forest Ecology & Management* 208: 223–236.

Dulmer K, 2006. *Mycorrhizal Associations of American Chestnut Seedlings: a Lab and Field Bioassay, Environmental and Forest Biology*. W. S. thesis SUNY-ESF, Syracuse, New York.

Duncan, M. J., Baker, T. G., Appleton, R., and Stokes, R. C. 2000. Growth of Eucalypt plantation species across twelve sites in Gippsland, Victoria. *CFTT Report No.:99/056, Department of Natural Resources and Environment*.

Environment Canada. 2008. *Models The Second Generation Coupled Global Climate Model (CGCM2)* http://www.cccma.bc.ec.gc.ca/models/cgcm2.shtml [Accessed November 2010].

Ferwerda, J. A. and Young, H. E. 1981. The relationship between spruce and fir biomass production and four soil series of a major soil catena in Maine. In: *Proceedings of the 1981 IUFRO World Congress Kyoto, Japan, 6–17 September*.

Fisher, R. F. and Binkley, D. 2000. *Ecology and Management of Forest Soils*. 3rd edition. John Wiley & Sons, Inc, New York.

Flato, G. M., Boer, G. J., Lee, W. G., *et al.* 2000: The Canadian Centre for Climate Modeling and Analysis Global coupled model and its climate. *Climate Dynamics* **16**: 451–467.

Florence, R. G. 1996. *Ecology and Silviculture of Eucalypt Forests*. CSIRO Publishing, Collingwood, VIC.

Grove, T. S. and Le Tacon F. 1993. Mycorrhiza in plantation forestry. *Advances in Plant Pathology* **23**: 191–227.

Hobbie, E. A. and Colpaert, J. V. 2003. Nitrogen availability and colonization by mycorrhizal fungi correlate with nitrogen isotope patterns in plants. *New Phytologist* **157**: 115–126.

Hobbie, E. A., Jumpponen, A., and Trappe J. 2005. Foliar and fungal 15N:14N ratios reflect development of mycorrhizae and nitrogen supply during primary succession: testing analytical models. *Oecologia* **146**: 258–268.

Horsley, S. B. and Long, R. P. (eds.). 1999. *Sugar Maple Ecology and Health: Proceedings of an International Symposium*. USDA Forest Service, NE Res. Stn., GTR NE-261.

Horsley, S. B., Long, R. P., Bailey, S. W., *et al.* 2002. Health of eastern North American sugar maple forests and factors affecting decline. *Northern Journal Applied Forestry* **19**: 34–44.

Horsley, S. B., Bailey, S. W., Ristau, T. E., *et al.* 2008. Linking environmental gradients, species composition, and vegetation indicators of sugar maple health in the northeastern United States. *Canadian Journal Forest Research* **38**: 1761–1774.

Horton, T. R. and Bruns, T. D. 1998. Multiple-host fungi are the most frequent and abundant ectomycorrhizal types in a mixed stand of Douglas fir (*Pseudostuga menziesii*) and bishop pine (*Pinus muricata*). *New Phytologist* **139**: 331–339.

Horton, T. R. and Bruns, T. D. 2001. The molecular revolution in ectomycorrhizal ecology: peeking into the black-box. *Molecular Ecology* **10**: 1855–1871.

Horton, T. R., Bruns, T. D., and Parker, T. 1999. Ectomycorrhizal fungi associated with *Arctostaphylos* contribute to *Pseudotsuga menziesii* establishment. *Canadian Journal Botany* **77**: 93–102.

Horton, T. R. and van der Heijden, M.G.A. 2008. The role of symbiosis in seedling establishment and survival. In: *Seedling Ecology and Evolution*. Leck, M., Parker, V. T., and Simpson, B. (eds). Cambridge University Press, Cambridge, UK.

Houston, D. R. 1999. History of sugar maple decline. In: *Sugar Maple Ecology and Health: Proceedings of an International Symposium*. Horsley, S. B. and Long, R. P. (eds.). USDA Forest Service, NE Res. Stn., GTR NE-261.

Johnson, D. L., Ambrose, S. H., Bassett, T. J., *et al.* 1997. Meanings of environmental terms. *Journal Environmental Quality* **26**: 581–589.

Johnson, N. C. 1993. Can fertilization of soil select less mutualistic mycorrhizae. *Ecological Applications* **3**: 749–757.

Karlen, D. J., Mausbauch, M. J., Doran, J. W., *et al.* 1997. Soil quality: A concept definition, and framework for evaluation. *Soil Science Society America Journal* **61**: 4–10.

Kretzer, A., Dunham, S., Molina, R., and Spatafora, J. W. 2004. Microsatellite markers reveal the below ground distribution of genets in two species of *Rhizopogon* forming tuberculate ectomycorrhizas on Douglas fir. *New Phytologist* **161**: 313–320.

Lerat, S., Rachel, R., Catford, J. G., *et al.* 2002. 14C transfer between the spring ephemeral *Erythronium americanum* and sugar maple saplings via arbuscular mycorrhizal fungi in natural stands. *Oecologia* **132**: 181–187.

Lian, C. L., Narimatsu, M., Nara, K., and Hogetsu, T. 2006. *Tricholoma matsutake* in a natural *Pinus densiflora* forest: correspondence between above- and below-ground genets, association with multiple host trees and alteration of existing ectomycorrhizal communities. *New Phytologist* **171**: 825–836.

Likens, G. E., Driscoll, C. T., and Buso, D. C. 1996. Long-term effects of acid rain: response and recovery of a forest ecosystem. *Science* **272**: 244–246.

Lilleskov, E. A., Fahey, T. J., Horton, T. R., and Lovett, G. M. 2002. Belowground ectomycorrhizal fungal community change over a nitrogen deposition gradient in Alaska. *Ecology* **83**: 104–115.

Lin, Y. and Augspurger, C. K. 2008. Long-term spatial dynamics of Acer saccharum during a population explosion in an old-growth remnant forest in Illinois. *Forest Ecology Management* **256**: 922–928.

Marx, D. H. 1969. The influence of ectotrophic ectomycorrhizal fungi on the resistance of pine roots to pathogenic infections. I. Antagonism of mycorrhizal fungi to pathogenic fungi and soil bacteria. *Phytopathology* **59**: 153–163.

Mejstrik, V. 1989. Ectomycorrhizas and forest decline. *Agriculture, Ecosystems and Environment* **28**: 325–337.

Meyer, F. H. 1988. Ectomycorrhiza and decline of trees. In: *Ectomycorrhiza and Acid Rain*. Jansen, A. E., Dighton, J., and Bresser, A.H.M. (eds). Berg en Dal.

Molina, R., Massicotte, H., and Trappe, J. M. 1992. Specificity phenomena in mycorrhizal symbioses: Community-ecological consequences and practical implications. In: *Mycorrhizal Functioning an Integrative Plant-fungal Process*. Allen. M. F. (ed.). Chapman and Hall, New York.

Molina, R. and Trappe, J. M. 1982a. Lack of mycorrhizal specificity by the ericaceous hosts *Arbutus menziesii* and *Arctostaphylos uva-ursi*. *New Phytologist* **90**: 485–509.

Molina, R. and Trappe, J. M. 1982b. Patterns of ectomycorrhizal host specificity and potential among pacific northwest conifers and fungi. *Forest Science* **28**: 423–458.

Moore, J. D. and Ouimet, R. 2006. Ten-year effect of dolomitic lime on the nutrition, crown vigor, and growth of sugar maple. *Canadian Journal Forest Research* **36**: 1834–1841.

Morris, E. C. 2003. How does fertility of the substrate affect intraspecific competition? Evidence and synthesis from self thinning. *Ecological Research* **18**: 287–305.

NRCS. 1999. *Soil Quality Test Kit Guide*. USDA Agricultural Research Service, Natural Resource Conservations Service, Soil Quality Institute. August 1999.

Nuñez, M.T.A., Horton, T. R., and Simberloff, D. 2009. Lack of belowground mutualisms hinders Pinaceae invasions. *Ecology* **90**: 2352–2359.

Parrent, J. L. and Vilgalys, R. 2007. Biomass and compositional responses of ectomycorrhizal fungal hypahe to elevated CO_2 and nitrogen fertilization. *New Phytologist* **176**: 164–174.

Perry, D. A., Amaranthus, M. P., Borcher, J. G., *et al.* 1989. Bootstrapping in ecosystems. *BioScience* **39**: 230–237.

Peter, M., Ayer, F., and Egli, S. 2001. Nitrogen addition in a Norway spruce stand altered macromycete sporocarp production and below-ground ectomycorrhizal species composition. *New Phytologist* **149**: 311–325.

Peterson, L. R., Massicotte, H. B., and Melville, L. H. 2004. *Mycorrhizas: Anatomy and Cell Biology.* NRC Research Press, Ottawa, Ontario.

Quinn, R. Q., Canham, C. D., Weathers, K. C., and Goodale, C. L. 2010. Increased tree carbon storage in response to nitrogen deposition in the U.S. *Nature Geoscience* **3**: 13–17.

Redecker D., Szaro, T. M., Bowman, R. J., and Bruns, T. D. 2001. Small genets of *Lactarius xanthogalactus, Russula cemoricolor* and *Amanita francheti* in late-stage ectomycorrhizal successions. *Molecular Ecology* **10**: 1025–1034.

Schimel J. P. and Bennett J, 2004. Nitrogen mineralization: challenges of a changing paradigm. *Ecology* **85**: 591–602.

Schiltz, H. M. and Grisi, B. F. 1980. *Soil-site Relationships of Spruce-Fir Stands on the Chesuncook Catena Soils.* Soil Conservation Service, Orono, Maine, USA.

Seybold, C. A., Dick, R. P., and Pierce, F. J. 2001. USDA Soil quality test kit: Approaches for comparative assessments. *Soil Survey Horizons* **42**: 43–52.

Simard S. W., Jones, M. D., Durall, D. M., *et al.* 1997a. Reciprocal transfer of carbon isotopes between ectomycorrhizal *Betula papyrifera* and *Pseudotsuga menziesii. New Phytologist* **137**: 529–542.

Simard S. W., Perry, D. A., Jones, M. D., *et al.* 1997b. Net transfer of carbon between ectomycorrhizal tree species in the field. *Nature* **388**: 579–582.

Sims, R. A., Baldwin, K. A., Kershaw, H. M., and Wange, Y. 1996. Tree species in relation to soil moisture regime in northwestern Ontario, Canada. *Environmental Monitoring and Assessment* **39**: 471–484.

Smith, D. B. 2009. Geochemical studies of North American soils: Results from the pilot study phase of the North American Soil Geochemical Landscapes Project. *Applied Geochemistry* **24**: 1355–1356.

Smith S. E. and Read, D. J. 1997. *Mycorrhizal Symbiosis.* 2nd edition. Academic Press, London.

Sojka, R. E. and Upchurch, D. R. 1999. Reservations regarding the soil quality concept. *Soil Science Society America Journal* **63**: 1039–1054.

Stone, E. L. 1984. Site quality and site treatment. In: *Forest Soils and Treatment Impacts. Proc. of the Sixth North American Forest Soils Conference, Knoxville, TN.* Stone, E. L. (ed.).

SSSA. 1997. *Glossary of soil science terms 1996.* Soil Science Society of America, Madison, WI, USA.

Tichelen K.K. Van, Colpaert J. V., and Vangronsveld, J. 2001. Ectomycorrhizal protection of *Pinus sylvestris* against copper toxicity. *New Phytologist* **150**, 203–213.

Trappe J. M., 2005. On the nutritional dependence of certain trees on root symbiosis with belowground fungi [Translation of Frank A. B. (1885) Ueber die auf Wurzelsymbiose beruhende Ernährung gewisser Bäume durch unterirdische Pilze. Berichte der Deutschen Botanischen Gesellschaft 3: 128–145.] *Mycorrhiza* **15**: 267–275.

Tugel, A. J., Wills, S. A., and J. E. Herrick. 2008. Soil change guide: Procedures for soil survey and resource inventory, version 1.1. *USDA, Natural Resources Conservation Service, National Soil Survey Center, Lincoln, NE. http://soils.usda.gov/technical/soil_change/ [Accessed November 2011].*

Vozzo, J. A and Hacskaylo, E, 1971. Inoculation of *Pinus caribaea* with ecomycorrhizal fungi in Puerto Rico. *Forest Science* **17**: 239–245.

Warkentin, B. P. 1992. Soil science for environmental quality- how do we know what we know? *Journal Environmental Quality* **21**: 163–166.

Westoby, M. 1984. The self-thinning rule. *Advances in Ecological Research* **14**. Macfadyen, A. and Ford, E. D. (eds). Academic Press, London.

Williams, R. A. 1986. Comparison of site index and biomass production on four soil drainage classes from the Chesuncook catena for spruce-fir stands in northwestern Maine. PhD dissertation, University of Maine, Orono.

Young, H. E. 1954. Forest soils-site index studies in Maine. *Soil Science America Proc* **18**: 95–87.

7

Earth, wind, and fire: abiotic factors and the impacts of global environmental change on forest health

J.E. LUNDQUIST, A.E. CAMP, M.L. TYRRELL, S.J. SEYBOLD, P. CANNON, AND D.J. LODGE

7.1 Introduction

Trees do not just die; there is always a primary cause, and often contributing factors. Trees need adequate quantities of water, heat, light, nutrients, carbon dioxide, oxygen, and other abiotic resources to sustain life, growth, and reproduction. When these factors are deficient or excessive, they cause mortality. According to the concept of baseline mortality (Chapters 1, 2, and 3), a certain number of trees must die as a forest ages to maintain a healthy condition. Abiotic factors kill trees in different ways, e.g., starvation, desiccation, uprooting, or stem breakage. The patterns of mortality and how the forest responds determine how changing stand structures impact sustainability and productivity. Here, we discuss abiotic factors, and how they influence diameter and age class distributions. We conclude this chapter by suggesting general principles about the impacts of abiotic disturbances on stand structures within forest ecosystems.

7.2 Weather events

Weather is the set of all phenomena occurring in a given atmosphere at a given time. Weather phenomena include wind, clouds, rain, snow, fog, dust storms, ice storms, hurricanes, tornadoes, and others. Some weather events can reset forest succession directly by killing trees. Weather events also can influence the rate and direction of forest succession indirectly by increasing fuels to enhance fire risk or by predisposing trees to other stresses. Previous assessments of annual forest impacts (Dale *et al.* 2001) show that ice storms are the least

Forest Health: An Integrated Perspective, ed. John D. Castello and Stephen A. Teale. Published by Cambridge University Press. © Cambridge University Press 2011.

extensive (> 180 000 ha) and costly (> US$10 million), whereas wind events (hurricanes and tornadoes) are the most extensive (> 1 600 000 ha) and costly (> US$800 million) weather phenomena.

7.2.1 Drought

Drought is an extended period (months or years) of water supply deficiency. Generally, this occurs when a region receives consistently below average precipitation, although land use practices (overfarming, excessive irrigation, massive water diversion, deforestation, or erosion) can trigger a drought. Cessation of rainfall may be related to reductions in the amount of water vapor in the atmosphere, or reduction in upward forcing of the air mass containing that water vapor. Both can be caused by more frequent high pressure systems, winds carrying continental, rather than oceanic air masses (i.e., reduced water content), and ridges of atmospheric high pressure that restrict local thunderstorm activity or rainfall. Although humans tend to be most cognizant of the impact of drought in the context of food production and desertification of agricultural lands, drought stress can also have significant impacts on forested landscapes, especially in concert with tree-killing bark beetles (see case study below). Drought reduces net primary production and water use in forests; plants can die during moderate (seedlings, saplings) or severe droughts (large trees) (Dale *et al.* 2001). Drought can also reduce nutrient cycling and decomposition, which result in a buildup of flammable organic matter that can increase the frequency and/or intensity of fires (Dale *et al.* 2001).

For many trees, water is the most limiting resource. Different tree species respond differentially to water stress. Coder (1999) categorized the various responses of plants, short of death, to drought of increasing severity: "1) recognizing ("sensing") soil/root water availability problems; 2) chemically altering (osmotic) cell contents; 3) closing stomates for longer periods; 4) using food storage reserves; 5) closing-off or closing-down root activities (suberizing roots); 6) initiation of foliage, branch and /or root senescence; 7) setting-up abscission and compartment lines; and 8) sealing-off (allowing to die) and shedding tissues/ organs that are unable to maintain health." Under extreme conditions of intensity or duration or both, drought stress can kill trees, but exactly how is not well defined. Two hypotheses of how tree death occurs in response to drought have been frequently recognized (McDowell *et al.* 2008): (1) the *carbon-starvation hypothesis* states that when stomata close, photosynthesis stops, resulting in a carbohydrate deficit in metabolizing living tissues and eventual starvation and death of a tree, and (2) the *hydraulic-failure hypothesis* states that cavitation of the water column in the xylem leads to desiccation of tree tissues and eventual tree death.

Trees display many mechanisms to avoid drought impacts. Drought avoiders close their stomata under low moisture, whereas drought endurers continue to

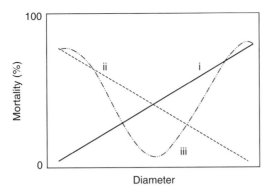

Figure 7.1 Stylized curves corresponding to various patterns of mortality reported in studies of drought in forest stands. The curve marked i, for example, shows heaviest mortality in larger diameter classes. The curve marked ii shows just the opposite with heaviest mortality occurring in the smallest diameter classes. Curve iii shows peaks of mortality in both the small and large diameter classes.

transpire. Certain species are more vulnerable than others, and in mixed stands, these species tend to be replaced by more drought-hardy trees.

The relationship between tree age and drought-associated mortality depends on many interacting variables, including among others: intensity and duration of the drought event/s, previous drought history, topography, species, stand structure, and previous harvest history. Studies examining the impacts of drought on age distribution have shown that drought can have a major impact on mortality and that usually trees of either young or old ages or both die during extreme drought episodes (Mueller *et al.* 2005). The small root volume of seedlings and young trees limits their ability to acquire soil water, making them relatively vulnerable to drought damage or death. Large trees require more water to maintain their relatively large crowns, making these age classes also relatively vulnerable to drought damage or death.

The interaction of drought, diameter class, and tree mortality has been recently studied in many different forest types worldwide. Mueller *et al.* (2005) examined the effects of age on mortality during a severe summer drought in 2003 in pinyon-juniper woodlands in the southwestern USA. They found that mortality impacts differed between the two co-dominant tree species (*Pinus edulis* and *Juniperus monosperma*), and that mortality was positively correlated with diameter (Figure 7.1i). The authors speculate that because *P. edulis* was more severely impacted than *J. monosperma*, the latter would eventually gain dominance in affected stands, resulting in a species shift at the stand level. Nepstad *et al.* (2007) came to the same conclusions when they examined drought effects on mortality of tropical forest stands in experimental dry and wet plots in the

Amazon basin in Brazil (Figure 7.1i). In contrast, following droughts in 1985 and 1994, Lloret *et al.* (2004) reported more mortality among smaller trees than larger (i.e., older) trees in holm oak (*Quercus ilex*) forests in Spain (Figure 7.1ii). Vygodskaya *et al.* (2002) describe mortality of both small and large trees in *Picea abies* forests of the southern taiga in Russia over a 30-year observation period (Figure 7.1iii). Slik (2004) found a disproportionate number of dead trees in large diameter classes and an increase in abundance of newly established small diameter classes in drought-stricken dipterocarp forests in Borneo(Figure 7.1ii to 1iii). These studies illustrate how drought can have a significant effect on age class distribution, and that the effects vary among different forest ecosystems.

A third hypothetical mechanism for drought-caused tree mortality is the *biotic agent demographic hypothesis*, which states "drought drives changes in demographics of mortality agents that subsequently drive forest mortality" (McDowell *et al.* 2008). The direct effects of drought leading to mortality are usually minor compared to the indirect effects that result from enhanced vulnerability to other abiotic stresses, insect pests, and pathogens, or other secondary disturbances (Rouault *et al.* 2006). The effects on age class distribution depend on the nature, extent, and magnitude of these interactions within a complex environment.

Textbox 7.1 Drought, forest dieback, and bark beetles in Western North America

Conifers such as piñon pine, ponderosa pine, lodgepole pine, and Engelmann spruce died in large numbers throughout western North America as a consequence of an historically severe drought in 2000–2004. On the Colorado Plateau alone, 1.5 million ha of piñon pine and 1.0 million ha of ponderosa pine were affected by drought-catalyzed population increases of piñon ips (*Ips confusus*[LeConte]) and a complex of *Dendroctonus* spp. and *Ips* spp., respectively (CIRMOUNT Committee 2006). Over a longer time period centered on this turn-of-the-century drought, nearly 15 million ha of lodgepole pine were killed in Alberta and British Columbia by the mountain pine beetle (*Dendroctonus ponderosae* Hopkins) (Nealis and Peter 2008). In the San Bernardino Mountains of southern California, Grulke, *et al.* (2009) report a long-term correlation between below-average annual precipitation and regional pest report records of bark beetle outbreaks in the mixed conifer forest, dominated by Coulter, Jeffrey, and ponderosa pines (Figure 7.2). The mechanism that explains the role of drought stress and successful colonization, reproduction, and population increase by bark beetles on conifers is an area of intensive study.

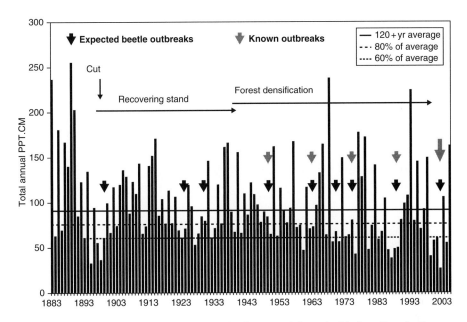

Figure 7.2 Long-term (123 yr) precipitation record from the Big Bear Dam in the eastern San Bernardino Mountains, CA, USA. Total annual precipitation (hydrological year, Oct. 1 to Sept. 30) in cm is shown along the y-axis. The long-term average (96 cm) is indicated with a solid line. Periods of three- to four-years of moderate drought stress (<80% of the average, dashed line) are common; periods of extreme drought stress (<60% of the average, dotted line) often were coincident with bark beetle outbreaks. Known occurrences of bark beetle outbreaks (grey triangles) were documented in annual California Pest Reports (1949 to present). (From Grulke *et al.* 2009, with permission.)

7.2.2 Wind storms

Windthrow is the uprooting of trees by the wind, and **windfall** occurs when a tree is thrown down or stems are broken off by the wind (Natural Resources Canada 1995). Windfall also describes the area on which trees have been thrown down or broken by the wind. In some areas of the world, wind is the dominant natural disturbance shaping forest stand structure (see front and back covers). In the coastal temperate rain forests of southeastern Alaska, for example, frequent small-scale wind events cause treefall gaps and patches (Figure 7.3), which are a major determinant of the structure of these forests (Deal *et al.* 1991, 2002; Nowacki and Kramer 1998). These highly frequent events result in small to moderate-sized gaps (less than 20 ha) in this forest type, but large blowdowns do sometimes occur. For example, on Prince of Wales Island in 1968, partial and complete blowdown of over 1000 patches (each 0.8 to 56 ha) merged in a single major wind event (Harris 1989). In contrast, large-scale

Figure 7.3 Uprooted white spruce following wind storm in Alaska. Photo by
J. E. Lundquist.

windthrow events that create large clearings are more frequent than treefall
gaps in tropical forests subjected to hurricane-force winds (Lugo and Scatena
1996). In Nicaraguan forests, for instance, windfall from Hurricane Joan
affected 80% of the canopy trees in an area of 500 000 ha (Boucher 1990;
Tanner and Kapos 1991), and on the island of Dominica in the Caribbean,
windfall from Hurricane David killed about 5 million trees (Lugo and Scatena
1996). In the northern hemisphere, straightline winds, or derechos, that are
associated with severe thunderstorms cause significant losses of trees in areas
not affected by hurricanes. Here, we focus the discussion on small- to moderate-
scale wind events.

   Not all forest stands are equally susceptible to wind damage. The impacts of
wind events on diameter distribution depend upon endogenous factors like
species composition and stand structure, and on exogenous factors like scale
(extent or magnitude), frequency (return time), intensity, and severity of each
disturbance (Lorimer 1977; Canham and Loucks 1984; Whitney 1986; Frelich and
Lorimer 1991; Peterson and Pickett 1991; Frelich and Reich 1995; Palik and Robl
1999). Furthermore, risk to wind damage is a scale-dependent property = tree
size and tree species are important at the stand scale, topography site and
stand factors at the landscape scale, and rainfall and wind speed at the regional
scale (Xi et al. 2008). Shorohova and his coworkers (2008) showed that damage
by severe winds often increases with increasing evenness of unharvested white
spruce stands in northern Europe and with increasing average stem diameter.

Evans *et al.* (2007) showed that stand structure, average tree age, mean elevation, range of elevations across stands, topographic position, and placement with respect to neighboring stands were significant factors predicting wind impacts in over 1000 disturbance gaps and patches following the 2003 ice storm in eastern North America (see next section). Several models have been developed to predict wind damage in forest stands (Kenderes *et al.* 2007; Kamimura and Shiraishi 2007; Zeng *et al.*, 2007; Gardiner *et al.* 2008; Xi *et al.*, 2008; Kamimura *et al.* 2009; and many others). One model developed by Ancelin *et al.* (2004) predicts that mortality is differentially distributed among sizes and species in irregular stands, but uniformly distributed in uniform stands, and that the most susceptible trees were small diameter, tall, and with small crowns. A common prediction among these models is that risk to wind damage varies in space and time across forest landscapes, and this is reflected in the spatial heterogeneity of stand structure.

Textbox 7.2 Impact and interaction of windthrow and other factors on stand structure in unharvested boreal forests

McCarthy and Weetman (2007) examined the diversity of stand structures in previously unharvested balsam fir stands in Newfoundland at various times following succession resetting infestations of spruce budworm (*Choristoneura fumiferana*) and the hemlock looper (*Lambdina fiscellaria*). They identified four different stand structures based on diameter distributions (Figure 7.4): (1) Modal distributions were composed of a uniform cohort of trees established soon after a stand-replacing event; (2) Bimodal distributions were composed of gaps in the canopy of a uniform overtopping layer of trees with established regeneration; (3) Reverse-j distributions representing trees with a range of diameters and is commonly associated with old-growth; and (4) Bi-staged distributions where widely scattered dominant individuals overtopped a dense layer of regeneration. Windthrow along with minor insect herbivory, and root and stem pathogens played a major role. According to McCarthy and Weetman (2007), stands with a bimodal distribution "are beginning to break-up from partial insect herbivory, windthrow, and butt and root rots, and show irregular tree distributions. Given time, and the absence of stand-replacing insect disturbance, these stands may develop into 'true old-growth'. Some of the old reverse-J stands and all of the irregularly structured bimodal stands are probably the product of this process transition form modal to bimodal to reverse-j distributions."

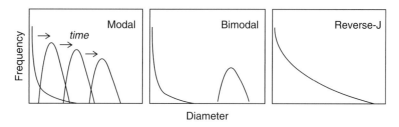

Figure 7.4 Stylized curves based on the study by McCarthy and Weetman (2007) showing chronosequence of stand structure changes following a major stand replacing event.

Light to moderate wind events commonly cause little impact on age distribution. In fact, these events may serve to speed up stand succession. Rich *et al.* (2007), for example, examined the influence of tree species, age, diameter, and intensity of wind events on wind-driven patterns of mortality in unharvested stands in the southern boreal forest in Minnesota. Rates of mortality were higher in mature stands less than 125 years old. Of the nine species examined, early successional and shade-intolerant species were most susceptible to being killed, and shade-tolerant least. The authors concluded that these patterns support the role of wind in accelerating succession, and use the term "wind-induced weeding" to describe this phenomenon.

Wind events commonly interact with other disturbance agents (Gandhi *et al.* 2007; 2009). When this happens, the impacts on age class distribution can result from the interaction in unanticipated ways. Uprooted trees cause soil disturbance, exposure of rocks, and root damage to neighboring trees. Broken trees contribute dead branches, stems, and stressed or moribund broken standing trees to the **coarse woody debris** (CWD) pool, which may increase the risk and potential impacts of wildfires. Heavy rains may amplify a wind-caused disturbance by loosening soil allowing extensive uprooting of trees (Foster 1988). Uprooting of trees during a wind event significantly alters the physical and chemical properties of the soil through mixing of soil layers (Mueller and Cline 1959; Bormann *et al.* 1995), and creation of pit-and-mound topography (Lyford and MacLean 1966). Because pits and mounds are generally preserved for a long time, they may affect tree regeneration for a correspondingly long time (Schaetzl *et al.* 1989; Oliver and Larson 1996), and thus enhance and enlarge frequency among smaller diameter classes. Many kinds of insects and pathogens sustain their populations in wood fallen during wind events, and some of these are induced to outbreak levels when windthrow levels are severe (Gandhi *et al.* 2007, 2009). Interactions of wind with other disturbance agents can be complex, leading to what has been termed "ecological surprises" (Peterson and Leach 2008), with resulting impacts on diameter distribution that are difficult to generalize.

7.2.3 *Ice damage*

Ice storm damage occurs when supercooled precipitation creates layers of ice (glaze) on leaves, twigs, branches, and boles (Lemon 1961; Irland 1998; 2000). Impact on individual trees depends on the thickness of the ice layers. The weight of ice borne by tree crowns during an ice event may increase the weight of twigs 30-fold (Hauer *et al*. 1993; Irland 1998). Oliver and Larson (1996) estimate that a 15 m-tall conifer with a mean crown width of 6 m can accumulate 5 tons of ice during a severe storm. Ice storms occur primarily in eastern North America (Lemon 1961). From 1900 to 1960, two to eight minor ice storms were recorded each decade in the eastern USA (Irland 1998). The recurrence time of 20 to 100 years for major ice storms in eastern North America makes them more frequent than all other weather-related disturbances (Irland 1998, 2000). Proulx and Greene (2001), for instance, state that ice storms caused around 50% of all mortality of canopy trees in northern forests in Quebec, and that this type of disturbance is the most frequent among all disturbances, including insect pests and tree pathogens, wildfires, and wind damage.

Tree damage is related to tree species, size and crown position, crown architecture, tree age and conditions, and site characteristics, especially slope, aspect, soil texture and depth (Rhoads *et al*. 2002). Mortality results from stem snap and root upwelling. Stem breakage depends on the weight of the ice, the arrangement of the branches, and wood strength (Lemon 1961). Broad-crowned trees with large stem diameters are more susceptible to ice storm damage than those with smaller diameters (Hauer *et al*. 1993). Most damage results from mechanical damage like twig, branch, and bole breakage, and uprooting. Ice thicknesses of 5–10 mm cause breakage of smaller branches; thicknesses of 10–25 mm cause breakage of healthy young branches and even the stems of young trees (Lemon 1961).

Textbox 7.3 Effects of the 1998 ice storm in eastern North America

A severe and widespread ice storm in January 1998 affected an area of 2000 × 400 km in South-central Canada and the northeastern USA. This major weather event and the ensuing research response marked a major increase in our knowledge of this type of disturbance on the dynamics of stand structure (Duguay, *et al*. 2001; Hooper, *et al*. 2001; Rhoads, *et al*. 2002; Hopkin, *et al*. 2003; Lafon and Kutac 2003; Shortle, *et al*. 2003; Lafon 2004; Millwood and Kraft 2004; Aril, *et al*. 2007; Takahashi, *et al*. 2007). Severity and patterns of impact varied among forest type and location. Conifers were less damaged than hardwoods (Hopkin, *et al*. 2003). Rhoads,

Textbox 7.3 (cont.)

et al. (2002) noted the inconsistency in key factors causing damage among storms and locations. Lafon (2004), however, suggested that some common damage patterns occurred, specifically, (1) loss of smaller diameter trees (Figure 7.1ii), which could create a pulse of an overdense age class, (examples presented in Chapter 1); and (2) loss of canopy in larger overstory trees (Figure 7.1i), which could facilitate late succession understory tree species or allow an increased establishment of early successional tree species (Figure 7.1iii). In a study of even-aged northern forest mixed hardwoods, Rhoads, *et al.* (2002) concluded that stands younger than 15–20 years were much less vulnerable to ice damage than older stands, and that ice damage was age-related. Takahashi, *et al.* (2007) examined an old growth beech-maple forest in eastern Canada nearly a decade after the 1998 ice storm and found that although basal area in the recovering forest was reduced by 37% and tree density decreased 61%, the species composition or diameter class distribution changed little or not at all. Aril, *et al.* (2007) found that canopy cover thinned from 93% to 83% immediately following an ice storm in beech-maple forests in eastern USA, but canopies recovered after three years, which was too soon for overstory-intolerant species to become established in *Acer-Fagus* forests.

7.3 Fire

Fire is a ubiquitous disturbance agent that operates at many spatial and temporal scales. Fire-associated mortality is a function of forest type, development stage, and fire intensity; other disturbance agents can exacerbate the effects of fire. Even large, intense fires have a role in maintaining healthy forests, despite their role in causing extensive tree mortality.

7.3.1 Fire regimes and ecosystems

Fire effects are best assessed in terms of the parameters of the **fire regime**; including fire frequency, predictability, extent, magnitude (intensity and/or severity), timing, and potential synergistic effects on future disturbances (Heinselman 1981; White and Pickett 1985; Agee 1993). A fire regime typifies the historical role of fire for a particular ecosystem, and emphasizes the complexity with which fire interacts with ecosystem patterns and processes. Heinselman developed a system of classifying fires that attempts to characterize this complexity using fire frequency and magnitude:

0. Very little natural fire
1. Infrequent ($>$ 25 years between successive fires) light surface fires
2. Frequent ($<$ 25 years between successive fires) light surface fires
3. Infrequent severe surface fires
4. Combined frequent severe surface fires and crown fires (25 to 100 years between fires)
5. Combined infrequent crown fires and severe surface fires (100 to 300 years between fires)
6. Infrequent ($>$ 300 years) crown fires and severe surface fires

Subsequent researchers (Davis *et al.* 1980; Johnson and Van Wagner 1985; Davis and Mutch 1994) have refined Heinselman's classification to better describe particular ecosystems or regions; however, Heinselman's classification has the flexibility to address fire regimes globally.

Many forest ecosystems are characterized as being adapted to fire (Pyne 1995; Jurskis 2005). Various plant species have developed the ability to survive fires by means of traits, such as thick bark or regeneration following fires by sprouting or cone serotiny (Rowe 1981). Such traits are not adaptations to fire, per se, but to a particular fire regime. The regime serves as a coarse filter that selects for certain species while eliminating others. To persist under a particular fire regime, plants require traits that enable them to complete their life cycle (Gill 1981). To persist under a fire regime characterized by lethal high-intensity fires, plants must achieve sexual maturity within the interval between successive fires or be able to regenerate vegetatively by sprouting. For example, lodgepole pines (*Pinus contorta*) produce viable seed within a decade of germination, and their cones often require the heat of a fire to release seed; oaks re-sprout after being killed back to the root collar; and many shrubs in fire-prone environments develop lignotubers or have seeds that require scarification by fire prior to germination.

Distinguishing between intensity and severity is important to characterize the effects of fire on forest ecosystems. **Intensity** is the energy output of a fire, and is a function of the energy content of the fuel, the amount of fuel consumed, and the rate of fire spread. Fire intensity is measured as the amount of energy released per unit length of the fireline. **Fire severity** is its ecological impact, and is most often measured as a percentage of overstory mortality.

7.3.2 Large-scale fire

Agee (1990, 1993) described three levels of fire severity that are useful in characterizing the extent to which a particular fire matches or deviates from the average for a particular fire regime. Low-severity fires remove less than 20% of the basal area, whereas high-severity fires kill 70% or more of the basal area. Fires of moderate severity fall between these endpoints. Differences in forest composition and structure result in fires of similar intensities having dissimilar severities (mortality).

Different fire regimes result in different spatial and temporal patterns of tree mortality at a variety of spatial scales. High-severity fires remove most of the basal area and leave few to no survivors. Very large high-intensity fires, such as those typical of boreal regions, are also high-severity fires in that mortality levels are high because trees do not have traits that allow them to survive high-intensity burns. Unburned areas within landscape-scale fires may actually increase with increasing fire size (Eberhart and Woodward 1987). Light wind-blown seeds that can travel great distances over crusted snow quickly regenerate burned-over areas to a single age cohort. Thus, fire in the boreal forests of North America and Eurasia is a landscape-scale phenomenon with periodic high mortality levels and resultant single age classes at large spatial scales.

Topography combines with fire regime to mitigate or exacerbate fire effects at smaller spatial scales (Camp *et al.* 1997). High-severity fires in topographically complex landscapes are constrained by areas that contain less abundant fuels or fuels too wet to ignite. Poulos *et al.* (2007) mapped fuels across large landscapes in western Texas and Mexico, and found topographic differences in fuel amounts that could alter patterns of fire intensity and thus tree mortality. Steep slopes accelerate fire spread and decrease the aspect duration of fire, often allowing some trees to survive. Age classes in topographically complex landscapes will mirror the complexity of burn patterns, resulting in a mosaic of age classes (Flanagan *et al.* 1998).

Use of age or size-class distributions to evaluate the health of forests in fire-prone regions must consider inherent fire regimes and their corresponding effect on forest age and structure (Ryan 2002; Wallenius 2002). Moderate-severity fire regimes have been less studied than high and low-severity regimes. Vegetation patterns in moderate-severity fire regimes are complex given the wide range of fire intensities and return intervals (but see Schellhaas *et al.* 2000; Pennanen 2002). The persistence of more species with different traits and life cycle requirements is potentially high; thus, a larger distribution of age classes would be expected, especially over longer temporal scales. Multiaged forests with age/size distributions approaching a reverse-J shape are more typical of low-severity fire regimes (Peterson and Ryan 1986; Johnson 1992). Low-severity fires proportionally damage more young and late-successional species.

When a wildfire moves through a forest stand, it can kill all of the trees if it is especially intense. But more commonly it will kill only a proportion of the trees, and leave the rest singed and scarred but able to recover, at least partially. Some survivors may be able to supply critical seed crops. Several species-specific equations have been developed to predict the probability of mortality of individual survivors (Hood *et al.* 2007). For example:

$$Pm = -(-6.8243 + 0.000568PCLC^2 + 0.6688CKR - 0.0285DBH)\frac{1}{1+e}$$

where:

    Pm = probability of survival;

    PCLC = percentage of crown length scorched;

    CKR = cambium kill rating (percentage of the cambium killed around the circumference at the base of the tree);

    DBH = diameter at breast height.

7.3.3 Changing fire regimes

Understanding inherent fire regimes is essential to properly assessing the impact of fire on forest health. Changes to historical fire regimes alter forest development patterns, including the establishment, growth, and mortality of trees. Removal of fire as a forest process may increase forest complexity, and give rise to reverse-J age/size distributions. However, forests that historically were maintained under a particular fire regime often become less healthy with removal of fire (Hessburg *et al.* 1994; Covington *et al.* 1997; Allen *et al.* 2002). In the absence of fire, forests shift in composition, leading to changes in future fire regimes and in the patterns of mortality from other disturbances, particularly disease and insect outbreaks. Fires, especially low-intensity frequent fires, maintain low forest density by killing seedlings and small trees. With fewer individuals competing for moisture and other resources, these forests are more resilient to other disturbances. Changes in fire intensity or recurrence are more likely to result in decreased forest resilience and persistence. In the western coterminous USA a complete set of statistics has been collected for every wildfire from 1970–2003. Westerling *et al.* (2006) concluded following a thorough analysis of data from all 1116 large (greater than 400 ha) wildfires that there had been a sudden and dramatic increase in the frequency and duration of large wildfires, and that the wildfire season had become extended. Wildfires were four times more frequent and extended over six times the land area for 1987–2003 compared to 1970–1986.

7.3.4 Fire suppression

Fire suppression has created forest health problems. Studies of eucalyptus decline in Australia (Jurskis 2005) and oak decline in Arkansas (Guyette *et al.* 2006) implicate fire exclusion as a contributing factor in decline. See also the textbox on fusiform rust in Chapter 4. In interior western North America, increased forest density resulting from fire exclusion has exacerbated forest health problems associated with drought (Guarin and Taylor 2005; Fule 2008), bark beetles (Klenner *et al.* 2008; Fonseca-Gonzales *et al.* 2008), herbivores (Swetnam and Lynch 1993; Veblen *et al.* 2000; Ryerson *et al.* 2003), and root disease pathogens (Thies 2001 Parker *et al.* 2006). Mortality resulting from these disturbance agents along with increased complexity in forest structure resulting from fire exclusion that increased the vertical and horizontal contiguity of fuels, predisposed stands to large, intense (and severe) fires.

Aboriginal peoples used fire to manage their environment. It is often difficult to differentiate between the effects of natural and anthropogenic fire on ecosystems. In some instances, fire-adapted ecosystems developed because anthropogenic activities favored plants with traits that conferred a competitive advantage under frequent burning. The original human inhabitants of Australia and western North America used fire extensively over millennia, giving rise to ecosystems adapted to the frequency and magnitude of their burning (Pyne 1995). More recently, fires were excluded from ecosystems previously adapted to periodic fires. Livestock grazing eliminated the grasses that carried fires across the landscape. Roads also broke up fine fuel continuity, decreasing fire size and spread. Direct fire suppression was effective when fuel levels were low, but now suppressing fires under extreme weather conditions in forests choked by decades of fuel buildups is impossible. Humans still affect fire regimes through fire use and fire suppression. In tropical forests that may have historically burned only once or twice a millennium and then only during severe ENSO (El Niño–Southern Oscillation) periods, agricultural conversion and population pressure have greatly increased fire frequency. In the Brazilian Amazon, anthropogenic burning of previously forested land to increase pasture productivity has led to fire incursion into adjacent rain forest. Together with logging, fire increases the vulnerability of tropical forests to future burning (Goldammer 1999); however, multiple fires so reduce fuel loads that in some cases this vulnerability dampens over time.

7.3.5 *Intensifying fire regimes*

Various factors influence fire frequency and severity including geographic location, forest type, elevation band, previous land-use history, and temperature and precipitation patterns. In the western USA, the factor with the greatest influence on fire frequency and severity was spring temperatures. Specifically, unusually warm spring temperatures coupled with reduced precipitation and earlier snowmelt dates caused drought conditions and more rapid and thorough drying of coarse woody debris and other forest fuels. The moisture equilibrium relationship between dead woody tissue and the ambient air is fairly clear, but the relationship between low soil moisture and tree mortality is not. It often takes three to four consecutive drought years before conifer mortality rates increase in most western forests (N. Grulke, Research Plant Pathologist, USDA Forest Service, Pacific Southwest Research Station, Riverside, California, pers. comm.). Background mortality rates have increased in recent decades in 76 unmanaged forests older than 200 years in the western USA (van Mantgem *et al.* 2009). Increases in mortality also are appearing widely across elevations, tree sizes, dominant genera, and past fire histories. Forest density and basal area declined slightly suggesting that increasing mortality was not caused by endogenous increases in competition. Because mortality increased in small trees, the overall increase in mortality rates cannot be attributed solely to aging of large trees. From the 1970s to 2006 in these 76 plots, the mean annual temperature of the Western United States increased at a rate of 0.3 to 0.4°C per decade. May this be the dominant contributor to the increases in tree mortality rates across the region?

7.3.6 *Impacts of wildfires*

From a utilitarian forest health perspective, a fire event well within inherent fire regime parameters, may still result in an "unhealthy" condition, if postfire forest structure no longer meets societal expectations (management objectives). For example, the much publicized 1988 Yellowstone fires in the western USA were well within historical parameters but the public outcry curtailed all efforts to restore the role of fire in ecosystem sustainability. Infrequent, high-intensity fires are generally considered catastrophic because the forests are unable to recover. Although many recent fires across the globe have resulted in extreme loss of property, damage to infrastructure, and even loss of human life, they are not necessarily without historical precedent (Strauss *et al.* 1989; Gill and Grant 2008; Keane *et al.* 2008).

In the Mediterranean Basin, large fires were common during the late Quaternary (Carrion *et al.* 2003). But in the current human-dominated and more frequently ignited landscape, fire may pose an ecological threat (Pausas 2008). Although coastal shrub ecosystems and oak forests are resilient to a higher incidence of fire, pine woodland ecosystems are less able to recover from frequent fire; especially problematic are the effects of fire on highly erodible soils. In some cases, vulnerability to fire in the Mediterranean Basin is a by-product of millennia of questionable land use policies (see Chapter 8).

Extreme fires in *Nothofagus* forests within historical ranges of variability for the region occurred in southern Argentina and Chile during the last two decades (Kitzberger and Veblen 1997; Veblen *et al.* 1999), underscoring the need to understand their historical antecedents and the role of fire. These fires were associated with droughts, and not just with more recent colonial land management practices. Nonetheless, the forest health consequences from current large, intense fires are exacerbated by increased fuel flammability resulting from natural forest conversion to exotic conifer plantations (Veblen *et al.* 2008). More frequent ignitions resulting from human incursion into wildlands is also increasing forest vulnerability to fire. The rain forests of Southeast Asia were thought to be immune to the effects of natural fires. The fires that did occur were a direct result of recent logging and land conversion. But more recent evidence has shown that these forests burn only during extreme ENSO events (Goldammer 1993; Hope *et al.* 2005). During the ENSO events of 1982–83 and 1997–98, continental and insular Southeast Asia experienced extreme droughts accompanied by extensive fires. In Kalimantan, the fires burned as much as 5 million ha during each event (Malingreau *et al.* 1985; Siegert *et al.* 2001). For fire to occur, even with extreme drought, there must be a source of ignition. Burning for land clearing adjacent to intact rain forest may play an important role. Small fires at the periphery of the HKK Wildlife Sanctuary in Thailand became the burning front that ignited hundreds of square kilometers of forest in January 1998 (Baker *et al.* 2008). Even where fire intensity was low, fire severity was extremely high, likely the result of rain forest trees lacking fire-adapted traits (Baker *et al.* 2008). Increased fire frequency in these non-adapted forests could lead to loss of both plant and animal biodiversity. A recent prolonged drought in Australia has led to large, high-intensity fires with loss of property and life (McLeod 2003), leading to the conclusion that burn severity was uniformly high (Bowman 2003), and that such fires were negatively impacting forest health and biodiversity (Hardy 2005). Although some areas within the fires' perimeters did experience high-severity burning, other areas were less impacted (Bradstock 2008).

7.3.7 Increased frequency of less-intense fires also impacts forest communities

A decrease in *Pinus cembra* populations in the European Alps is consistent with 20th-century increases in fire frequency. In other forest types, fire frequency is decreasing (Heyerdahl *et al.* 2007), allowing the incursion of species less adapted to frequent fires. As described above, the resulting increase in forest density greatly affects forest health, especially during dry periods.

7.4 Air pollution

The air pollutants of primary concern to forest health are acid deposition and ozone. Acid deposition increases soil acidity, affects nutrient availability, and weakens the ability of plants to withstand disturbances such as drought, winter freezing, and pest outbreaks (Shortle and Smith 1988; de Hayes *et al.* 1999; Driscoll *et al.* 2001; Schaberg *et al.* 2001). In sensitive populations and at high concentrations, acid deposition also causes direct foliar injury (Siccama *et al.* 1982; Craig and Friedland 1991; Zeng *et al.* 2005; Fischer *et al.* 2007). High levels of ozone (O_3) can be toxic to plants, causing cellular damage resulting in foliar injury and consequent growth reduction (Augustaitis and Bytnerowicz 2008).

7.4.1 *Acid deposition*

The primary ingredients of **acid desposition** are sulfur dioxide (SO_2), a by-product of burning coal, and nitrogen oxides (NOx) emitted from burning fossil fuels. Both react with oxygen and water in the atmosphere to form strong, highly water-soluble acids. These acids are readily removed from the atmosphere with precipitation, and disassociate in the soil solution as hydrogen (H^+), sulfate (SO_4^{2-}) and nitrate (NO_3^-) ions. The resulting decrease in pH causes plant nutrients, such as the bivalent cations (calcium [Ca^{2+}]) and (magnesium [Mg^{2+}]) to leach from the soil, and mobilizes toxic cations, such as aluminum (Al^{3+}) (Likens and Borman 1995; Driscoll *et al.* 2001; Puhe and Ulrich 2001).

Global critical loads of nitrogen and sulfur deposition have been modeled to identify forest areas sensitive to acid deposition (Bouwman *et al.* 2002). According to this model, areas with low temperatures, dry soil conditions, long frost periods, and low base saturation have high-sensitivity (Bouwman *et al.* 2002). Critical loads of acidity are exceeded in most of Europe, eastern North America, southeastern Brazil and the La Plata region, parts of Siberia, the southern part of West Africa, Central Africa, and South China (Tao and Feng 2000).

Acid desposition affects forests at three levels: (1) individual plant, (2) sensitive species and populations, and (3) ecosystem. Specific effects on forest health include direct foliar injury, growth reduction, nitrogen fertilization, increased susceptibility to other stressors, heavy metal toxicity, and nutrient impoverishment (deHayes *et al.* 1999; Schaberg *et al.* 2001; Bytnerowicz *et al.* 2007, among others). Nonetheless, there is little evidence of direct cause and effect between acid deposition alone and any of these factors (Driscoll *et al.* 2001). In all cases, acid deposition acts within a complex of stressors including climate change, drought, insects, diseases, and other air pollutants.

Plant-level effects. Acid deposition can cause acute, direct foliar injury and crown damage especially harmful to conifers, which cannot withstand extensive defoliation (Craig and Friedland 1991; deHayes *et al.* 1999; Schaberg *et al.* 2001; Fischer *et al.* 2007). In nitrogen-limited systems, such as most temperate forests, nitrogen deposition may act as a fertilizer; however, excess nitrogen can lead to deficiencies in other nutrients, particularly calcium (Driscoll *et al.* 2001). Acid deposition may interfere with calcium and magnesium nutrition and calcium-dependent processes, although the mechanisms are poorly understood (Schaberg *et al.* 2001; Puhe and Ulrich 2001). Nutrient deficiencies can lead to increased susceptibility to other stressors and disturbances, fine root decline (Puhe and Ulrich 2001; Park *et al.* 2008), aluminum toxicity (Puhe and Ulrich 2001), and growth reduction.

Sensitive species. Most published research about acid deposition and forest effects has been conducted in the northeastern United States and Europe, although there have been studies in Asia as well. Extensive work has been done in the United States on high-elevation red spruce (*Picea rubens*) in northern New England, which experienced high mortality in the 1980s (Siccama *et al.* 1982). Exposure to acidic mist and cloud water may have reduced the cold tolerance of red spruce by leaching membrane-associated calcium from the needles causing increased susceptibility to winter freezing (de Hayes *et al.* 1999; Driscoll *et al.* 2001).

Episodic sugar maple (*Acer saccharum*) dieback over large areas of northwestern Pennsylvania and southwestern New York has been attributed to acid deposition in combination with other stressors (Drohan *et al.* 1999; Horsley *et al.* 1999; Driscoll *et al.* 2001). It is hypothesized that dieback was caused in part by depletion of nutrient cations from marginal soils (Horsley *et al.* 1999; and Chapter 6).

Scots pine (*Pinus sylvestris*) defoliation has been attributed to acid deposition in Lithuania (Augustaitis and Bytnerowicz 2008), and high sulfate deposition is significantly related to higher defoliation in Norway spruce (*Picea abies*) and Scots pine in Europe (Puhe and Ulrich 2001).

Ecosystems. The most significant effect of acid deposition on forests is a change in soil chemistry. Increased input of H^+ from dissolved acids increases soil acidity, decreases availability of nutrient cations, and mobilizes toxic metals (Driscoll *et al.* 2001; Bailey *et al.* 2005). Addition of nitrogen in previously nitrogen-limited forest ecosystems can cause a decline in mycorrhizae populations and inhibition of nitrogen fixation (Parrent *et al.* 2006, also see Chapter 6). Cation depletion may result in a decreased productivity. However, the added nitrogen may act as a fertilizer in the short term. Increased nitrogen may improve foliage nutrition thus increasing insect herbivory (Throop and Lerdau 2004). Complex interactions between resource availability, climate change, acid deposition, ozone pollution, and other forms of disturbance will determine productivity; changes in nutrient status are just part of the equation. Some mosses, lichens, and phytopathogenic fungi are highly sensitive to SO_2. Decline in populations of these species could significantly affect productivity in boreal and alpine forest ecosystems (Harden *et al.* 1997).

Species composition may change in ecosystems where sensitive species have a higher than baseline mortality rate. There is generally a long ecosystem response time to environmental stresses such as air pollution. Studies have not yet shown widespread ecosystem changes that can be attributed to air pollution, except in areas of high deposition from point sources, such as smelters and dirty-coal-burning power plants (Munton 2002; Bernal-Salazar *et al.* 2004). Where species experience decline and higher than baseline mortality, age class distribution will shift to a younger cohort, providing that adequate advance regeneration is present. At the ecosystem level, age class distribution may or may not change depending on the extent of species decline, the change in baseline mortality of sensitive species, the mix between sensitive and non-sensitive species at the stand and landscape scales, and the mosaic of species composition and structure across the landscape.

7.4.2 Ozone

Ozone is formed in the atmosphere through the interaction of nitric oxide (NO), sunlight, and hydrocarbons, and is highest in areas with high levels of both sunlight and fossil fuel emissions. Such areas include the southwestern and eastern USA, eastern Europe, the Mediterranean, western Asia, and north-eastern China (Felzer *et al.* 2007). It is projected that 50% of the northern hemisphere forests will be affected by toxic levels of ozone by 2100 (Fowler *et al.* 1999).

Plant-level effects. Damage from current ambient ozone levels on northern hemisphere trees causes crown defoliation, and reduced leaf area, tree height, diameter growth, and root-shoot ratios, with consequent loss of photosynthetic capacity and lower biomass production (Skärby *et al.* 1998; Felzer *et al.* 2007; Augustaitis and Bytnerowicz 2008; Wittig *et al.* 2009). Ozone enters with water through stomata, causing direct cellular damage. Drought may reduce risk of O_3 injury because plants close stomata under moisture stress (Wittig *et al.* 2007). Populations are most sensitive when peak ozone concentrations coincide with the growing season and no moisture stress.

Sensitive species. Sensitive species in the United States include certain geno-types of eastern white pine (*Pinus strobus*), trembling aspen (*Populus tremuloides*), southern pines, black cherry (*Prunus serotina*) (Karnosky *et al.* 2007) and western pines (Richardson *et al.* 2007; Bytnerowicz *et al.* 2008). Ambient ozone levels have been associated with growth reduction in mature southern pines, particularly loblolly pine (*Pinus taeda*) (Felzer *et al.* 2007). In Europe, Aleppo pine (*Pinus halepensis*) in the Mediterranean Basin as well as Swiss stone pine (*Pinus cembra*) in the timberline ecotone of the European mountains have shown signs of ozone damage (Richardson *et al.* 2007). Ozone has been implicated in reduced stem growth of Scots pine in Central Europe (Augustaitis and Bytnerowicz 2008).

Several pine species in Mexico show ozone-induced damage similar to pines in the western United States (Richardson *et al.* 2007).

Ecosystems. Where species experience decline and higher mortality than baseline mortality, age-class distribution will shift to a younger cohort, so long as there is adequate advanced regeneration. If the disturbance is chronic, mortality will remain higher than baseline.

7.5 Large-scale infrequent disturbances

Disturbances are a natural part of every forest ecosystem. Some occur at more or less predictable intervals, and occur over limited areas; others (e.g., hurricanes, volcanic eruptions, floods) occur rarely, or at irregular intervals, or both, and over large areas. The latter have been termed "**large infrequent disturbances (LIDs)**". Whether LIDs qualitatively differ from small-scale disturbances, or are only quantitative extensions of the latter is a debated topic (Romme *et al.* 1998). Some well-known and well-studied LID examples are the Mount St Helens eruption in 1980, the Yellowstone wildfires in 1988, floods along the Mississippi in 1993, and the spruce beetle outbreaks on the Kenai Peninsula in the mid-1990s.

7.5.1 Tropical storms

Tropical storms are large-scale extreme wind events. Meteorologists classify them based on their scale, wind intensity, and location. Some of the more common definitions based on windspeeds are: tropical depression (winds less than 61 kph), and tropical storm (winds between 61 and 119 kph). There are several equivalent terms for storms with the higher wind velocities: hurricanes (North Atlantic Ocean, the northeast Pacific Ocean east of the dateline, or the South Pacific Ocean east of 160°E); typhoons (northwest Pacific Ocean west of the dateline); severe tropical cyclones (southwest Pacific Ocean west of 160°E or southeast Indian Ocean east of 90°E); severe cyclonic storms (Indian Ocean and tropical cyclones in the southwest Indian Ocean).

These latter storms can cause catastrophic tree mortality in both tropical and temperate forests, where the width of catastrophic damage is usually limited to the width of the eyewall (where the most damaging winds and most intense rain occur), which rarely exceeds 50 km (Foster and Boose 1994). The amount of forest area affected by catastrophic wind events at locations such as the Luquillo Mountains of Puerto Rico, for example, is actually less than background mortality of wind events when return times and frequency of events are factored in (Lugo and Scatena 1996). Other catastrophic wind events have eyewalls that approach the entire width of the Caribbean islands they impact, such as the track of Hurricane Gilbert over Jamaica in 1988 (Wunderle *et al.* 1992). In addition, the

Figure 7.5 Effect of Hurricane Georges in 1998 on forest canopy in Sabana, a valley closest to the point of landfall in El Yunque National Forest of Puerto Rico. Note the heterogeneity of damage due to embedded meteorological events and topographic exposure in the lower, post-hurricane photo. Mortality from treefalls occurred on steep unstable slopes just behind the building, whereas the larger trees behind them on the ridge that were either delimbed or topped mostly survived and recovered. Photo by D. J. Lodge.

long tracks of some hurricanes can induce catastrophic wind damage in forests in widely separated areas. Hurricane Gilbert struck both Jamaica and the Yucatan Peninsula (Whigham *et al.* 1991; Wunderle *et al.* 1992); Hurricane Hugo damaged forests in Guadeloupe (Benito-Espinal and Benito-Espinal 1991), Puerto Rico (Walker 1991; Zimmerman *et al.* 1994; Lugo and Scatena 1996) and South Carolina (Gresham *et al.* 1991); and Hurricane David devastated both Dominica and the Dominican Republic, and then spawned tornado damage in the USA from the middle-Atlantic States to New England in 1979.

Patterns of wind damage, although appearing chaotic when viewed at local scales (Figure 7.5), are controlled by a set of predictive factors (Foster and Boose 1992; Boose *et al.* 1994; Foster *et al.* 1998, 1999). At larger, regional scales (100 to

500 km), patterns of forest damage are determined by hurricane size, intensity, and storm track; weakening of storms through interactions with coastlines and mountains; and regional variation in vegetation. At smaller landscape scales of about 10 km, storm damage is controlled by interactions of gradients in wind speed and direction, embedded meteorological phenomena such as downbursts and tornadoes, topographic exposure, and differential stand susceptibility to wind (Figure 7.5). Stand susceptibility to wind is determined by factors such as site conditions (steep, unstable slopes or shallow rooting owing to waterlogged soils; Figure 7.5) (Basnet *et al.* 1992; 1993; Scatena and Lugo 1995; Everham and Brokaw 1996), and stand structure and composition, both of which are strongly influenced by previous natural and human disturbances (Zimmerman *et al.* 1994, 1995; Foster *et al.* 1998, 1999).

The effects of hurricanes on the diameter distribution of residual forest stands following a storm depend on topographic position, exposure to wind, and previous disturbances. Background tree mortality in tropical forests ranges from ca. 0.5% to 3.5%, with a mean of 1.6% per year (Lugo and Scatena 1996).

Direct mortality from hurricane winds in the Caribbean can be as high as 46%, such as the impact of Hurricane David on Dominica, which killed about 5 million trees in 10 hours (Lugo and Scatena 1996). Bole breaks plus uprooting can be as high as 80% (Tanner and Kapos 1991). Hurricane Joan broke or uprooted 80% of the trees in Nicaragua (Boucher 1990; Yih *et al.* 1991), and Hurricane Hugo caused similar damage to 25% to 55% of the trees in wet forest of Guadeloupe, depending on size class (Benito-Espinal and Benito-Espinal 1991). Generalizations regarding differential damage according to size classes are unreliable and site-specific (Tanner and Kapos 1991) because the effect of hurricane winds on diameter distributions of the residual forest varies greatly depending on wind-speed, the initial forest structure and species composition, previous disturbances, and various state factors previously noted. In tabonuco forests in the Luquillo Mountains of Puerto Rico, catastrophic tree mortality was higher on slopes than on ridges owing to the ability of the dominant trees on ridges to withstand winds (Basnet *et al.* 1993; Scatena and Lugo 1995) and the ability of most trees to resprout (Walker 1991). Stands of uniform, young, flexible trees had little mortality from Hurricane Gilbert in Jamaica (Wunderle *et al.* 1992), Hurricane Hugo in South Carolina (Gresham *et al.* 1991), or Hurricane Georges in limestone forest of the Dominican Republic (Uriarte *et al.* 2004). In contrast, young stands with large remnant trees in human-impacted coastal forests and wet limestone forests with mixtures of large and small trees in Jamaica had disproportionately higher mortality in the intermediate size classes (> 8 to 23 cm diameter) caused by branches falling from the larger trees. Greatest reduction in intermediate size classes was also observed in the Bisley Watersheds in Puerto Rico, an area with the highest impact by Hurricane Hugo in the Luquillo Mountains because they were closest to the point of landfall and faced directly into the storm winds (50% overall mortality, data of Scatena and Lugo cited in Walker 1991; Basnet *et al.* 1992; Heartsill-Scalley *et al.* 2007). Although the largest trees had the lowest proportion of stems lost of any size class from Hurricane Gilbert on Jamaica (Wunderle *et al.* 1992), Hurricane Hugo in wet forest on Guadeloupe (25% vs. 55%, Benito-Espinal and Benito-Espinal 1991), and Hurricane Hugo on the windward side of Puerto Rico. Walker (1991) found at El Verde on the leeward side of the Luquillo Mountains in Puerto Rico that large trees had proportionately more damage, and Dittus (1985) found that a cyclone that struck Sri Lanka killed disproportionately more canopy than smaller diameter subcanopy trees (46% vs. 29%).

Disturbance history greatly influences damage from hurricanes. For example, clearcutting subtropical wet forest in Puerto Rico about 60 years prior to Hurricane Hugo resulted in stands dominated by fast-growing secondary tree species (especially *Casearia arborea*) that were differentially more susceptible to direct hurricane mortality (Zimmerman *et al.* 1994; Thompson *et al.* 2002). Selective cutting can lead to stands with mixed canopy heights that result in greater mortality of the intermediate diameter classes when exposed to extreme hurricane winds. In addition, fire history can influence damage from subsequent hurricanes. Platt *et al.* (2002) compared mortality from stem breakage and delayed mortality (primarily bark beetle attack) in Everglades slash pine (*Pinus elliottii*) savannas with different fire histories during the decade preceding Hurricane Andrew (1992) in south Florida. Direct mortality from wind and delayed mortality were lowest in stands burned during the wet (lightning fire) season, intermediate in unburned stands, and highest in stands burned during the dry (anthropogenic fire) season.

Hurricane damage to forests is not restricted to wind damage. Wet hurricanes in mountainous terrain are frequently associated with landslides. There were 285 landslides associated with Hurricane Hugo in Puerto Rico, primarily in areas receiving over 200 mm of rain (Scatena and Larsen 1991). In coastal areas, salt intrusion from overwash caused by storm surge often causes longer-lasting effects on forest ecosystems than direct wind damage (Blood *et al.* 1991; Gardner *et al.* 1991; Liu *et al.* 2008). Storm surge in South Carolina from Hurricane Hugo extended several hundred kilometers inland and more than 150 m into the forest from the marsh edge, leading to persistent changes in soil chemistry and structure in addition to direct tree mortality (Blood *et al.* 1991; Gardner *et al.* 1991). Furthermore, hurricane damage to forests in the Caribbean Basin and Gulf Coast frequently predispose these areas to catastrophic fires, which have a much greater impact on subsequent forest recovery than direct damage from wind (Furley and Newey 1979; Whigham *et al.* 1991; Myers and van Lear 1998; Liu *et al.* 2008).

7.6 Geological events

Landslides, volcanic eruptions, tsunamis, and other geological events can be extraordinarily destructive because they often occur in highly populated locations. **Landslides** are gravity-driven, massive down-slope movements of the landscape. Mudflows, creep, block slide, avalanches, slumps, and other similar events are called landslides. Damage depends on the rate of movement of soil, rock, and other debris, which, in turn, depends on such factors as steepness of the slope, freeze and thaw temperature patterns, amount of water saturation, earth movements, and instabilities caused by recent construction or streambank erosion. Landslides are usually associated with very wet periods with heavy precipitation or rapidly warming times with rapid snowmelt. Impacts differ because the rate and magnitude of movement differ. Debris flow is a type of landslide commonly referred to as mudflows/slides or lahars. Areas where forest vegetation has been destroyed by wildfires are particularly susceptible to landslides following rainstorms. Debris flows can be extremely destructive when caused by volcanic activity. Landslides can cause severe, sometimes complete, loss of vegetation and concurrent extreme impacts of diameter class distribution and thus sustainability, but the spatial scales are usually limited, and have little impact on the overall diameter distribution forest-wide.

Volcanic eruptions range from explosive blasts with volcanic dust and rock (tephra) to gurgling lava spreading locally. The former, referred to as felsic volcanoes, can influence forest ecosystems for great distances by spreading tephra, which settles on the landscape surface, eventually working its way into the soil. The latter, referred to as mafic volcanoes, are associated with flowing basaltic lava that smothers and burns any and all vegetation in its path, covering existing soils to varying depth, but impacting only nearby forest ecosystems. Some volcanoes have characteristics of both the mafic and felsic types. Perhaps the most well-known and well-studied recent example is Mount St. Helens in Washington State in the western USA. Forested areas near the volcano were leveled by the blast. The diameter class distribution within these areas were changed dramatically, if only locally (Weber *et al.* 2006) – health, as defined in Chapter 1, is obviously a scale-dependent phenomenon. The vast amounts of tephra belched by this volcano stimulated a great deal of research on the impacts of this substance on forest ecosystems. Impacts ranged from restricting photosynthesis by coating leaf surfaces and reducing light to causing tree mortality.

The impacts of tephra are broadly distributed across tree diameter classes and probably have little impact on diameter distribution or basal mortality.

Coastal mangrove forests and tsunamis have a unique relationship to forest health. Tsunamis highlight the important role played by coastal forests, and the value to human health and property serviced by sustained health of these ecosystems. **Tsunamis**, or tidal waves, are created by geological events above or beneath the sea that cause a rapid displacement of water. Powerful earthquakes, underwater landslides, or other causes of mass movements of earth and water can cause exceptionally big tsunamis that can cross oceans creating waves thousands of miles away from the source. The distance between waves of a tsunami can be many miles and much longer than wavelengths of common wind-generated waves, which are usually measured by hundreds of feet. When a tsunami meets the shoreline, its height is modest but its persistence is long. The power embedded in a tsunami and the huge amount of water that it carries provide the potential for great damage. Coastal forests can mediate the effects of tsunami. The ability to reduce impacts of the tsunami is a function of stem density, stem diameter, wave period, path width, and inundation depth.

Textbox 7.4 Tsunami protection by coastal forests in Sumatra

On December 26, 2001, a tsunami washed ashore on Sumatra. By the time the ocean settled, over 300 000 people had perished. Coastal mangrove forests were less impacted than other areas along the coast (Tanaka 2009). Gaps in this forest amplified flow rates of water and debris, which damaged buildings and other physical assets and harmed and killed people. A 30% attenuation occurred in forest groves where tree density was 0.2 trees/m^2 and average diameter at breast height was 15 cm under a 30-minute wave period. The mediating effect of the forest was reduced when inundation depth was greater than 3 m, and nearly lost when it exceeded 10 m. The impact of the Sumatra tsunami on coastal forest health varied and depended on the interacting characteristics of the inundation and the forest. Stem diameters in mangrove forests were related to survival of trees (Yanagisawa, *et al.* 2009). Diameter distributions in these forests were affected because smaller diameter trees were less likely to survive than larger trees. Specifically, trees with diameters between 25 and 30 cm had a 72% chance of survival, whereas those with diameters between 15 and 20 cm had only a 19% chance of survival. With a decreased frequency of small diameter classes, mid-sized classes will be reduced in the future. The tsunami created an unhealthy condition where forests were affected.

7.7 Emergent stressors in a changing climate

Climate is the average of weather phenomena over a period of time, usually 30 years (IPCC 2007). Many believe that the climate is changing. In many regions of the world, the last several decades have shown weather patterns not inconsistent with climate change. During this time, a significant increase in mean global temperature has been reported (CIRMOUNT 2006). Many believe that this trend will continue for the foreseeable future. Although tropical forests are not immune from effects of climate change, northern boreal and sub-boreal forests are expected to be most affected (IPCC 2001; Wunderle *et al.* 2009). A changing climate would lead to novel ecosystems (Hobbs *et al.* 2006), increased frequency and intensity of disturbances (Dale *et al.* 2001; Emanuel 2005; Hoyos *et al.* 2006; Klotzbach 2006), and unanticipated impacts on stand structure (IPCC 2001). Insect pests, diseases, and other stress agents, for example, would become increasingly prevalent as vegetation readjusts itself to new climatic norms, and would facilitate and catalyze these adjustments largely by killing stressed trees and other vegetation. Descriptions of the potential effects of climate change on forest insect pests and diseases have appeared (e.g., Williams and Liebhold 1995; Ayres and Lombardero 2000; Kliejunas *et al.* 2008). Many more have been published for specific forest host-pest-disease systems.

Although climate change usually is portrayed as increasing temperature, or global warming, the phenomenon actually expresses itself in many other ways as well. Along with a changing temperature, acid rain, precipitation, UV-B radiation, metal deposition, trophospheric ozone, atmospheric carbon dioxide, and other climatic attributes are changing also (Valladares 2008). The phenomenon called climate change is a truly multivariate phenomenon.

Climatic factors are pervasive in time and space, occur on spatial scales not normally perceived by humans, and are thus outside of our day to day experience. Therefore, evidence of a changing climate effects on forest health is difficult to document. In some forests, wildfires occur earlier and more frequently, severe droughts persist longer (IPCC 2001), thaw-freeze events are more frequent and widespread, bark beetle and defoliator outbreaks are more frequent and severe, and decline diseases and other complex multiple-agent diseases are more common and widespread, and more difficult to diagnose (Jurskis 2005). Many believe that these occurrences are connected to a changing climate (Dale *et al.* 2001).

Deforestation and other changes in land use can affect local or regional climate, which in turn can affect forest health, especially at higher elevations. Conversion of forest to pasture in lowland Costa Rica was associated with changes in cloud forests. Such local or regional climate changes can interact with global climate change with loss of cumulus cloud formation during the dry season and lifting of the cloud base in adjacent mountain ranges (Lawton *et al.* 2001). Conversion of coastal forest to pasture on the island of Puerto Rico disrupted the advective flow of moisture from the Atlantic Ocean thereby reducing cloud formation at higher elevation (Scatena 1998; Schellekens *et al.* 2000; Van der Molen 2002). Such local or regional changes will likely exacerbate the effects of increased summer drying in the Caribbean and Central American region brought about by global climate change (Neelin *et al.* 2006), and result in a contraction or extirpation of cloud forests on tropical mountains. Loss of cloud forests may already be occurring in Central America (Foster 2001; Benning *et al.* 2002), and global climate change is expected to reduce the extent of cloud forests in biodiversity hotspots of the Andes (Bush *et al.* 2004) and Hawaii (Benning *et al.* 2002).

Emerging stressors in a changing climate are illustrated below by drought in the boreal forest, yellow cedar decline in coastal temperate forests of southeastern Alaska, and intensifying fire regimes in tropical forests.

7.7.1 *Boreal drought*

The boreal forest occupies an area of not less than 1.2 billion ha equivalent to approximately 17% of the Earth's land surface, and occurs between 45° and 70° N latitude (Larsen 1980). One-third of this forest is in Central and western Alaska and in Canada from the Yukon Territory to Labrador. The rest is in Eurasia from northern Europe across Siberia to the Pacific Ocean. The major trees include various species of larch (*Larix*), spruce (*Picea*), fir (*Abies*), birch (*Betula*), poplar (*Populus*), willow (*Salix*), and alder (*Alnus*). This forest biome is expected to experience the greatest impacts of climate change sooner than forest biomes southward (ICPP 2001). Temperature is a limiting factor of tree distribution in the boreal forest. Atmospheric temperatures are expected to increase significantly in the northern portion of the boreal forest (IPCC 2001). Growth rates of trees are expected to increase because photosynthesis is correlated with increasing temperature. Indeed, many studies indicate that growth and tree species distribution is increasing and expanding in the boreal zones (Myneni *et al.* 1997; Sturm *et al.* 2001). Other studies, however, indicate otherwise (Chapin *et al.* 2006a).

The relationship between tree growth and survival and global warming in the boreal region is more complicated than it appears. According to Soja *et al.* (2006), "Despite its relative simplicity, boreal forest composition results from a complex interaction between climate, solar radiation, topography, geology, nutrient availability, soil moisture, soil temperature, permafrost, depth of forest floor organic layer, ecology of species, forest fires, and infestations." Trees growing in certain locations in boreal Alaska, particularly those on north-facing slopes, actually showed a decreased growth rate with increasing summer temperatures (Barber *et al.*, 2000; Lloyd and Fastie 2002; Wilmking *et al.* 2004). The cause of this growth decline is not perfectly known, but it is assumed that evapotranspiration during the summer warm season is greater than the precipitation replenishing the water used, creating moisture stress, a condition that some have referred to as "boreal drought" (Chapin *et al.* 2006b).

Textbox 7.5 Impacts of drought on aspen stands in the prairie provinces of Canada

The northern forest is expected to migrate northward as the climate changes. It is less appreciated that the southern fringes of this forest will become a zone of increasing stress to resident trees. Some of these populations are expected to recede northward and to be eliminated from the ecotone by invading southern species and by stress-related insect pests and pathogens. Trembling Aspen has a widespread distribution across North America and is a dominant tree species in prairie woodlots in the western Canadian interior at the northern fringe of the Great Plains. A 300% increase in aspen mortality rate and 30% reduction in growth rate followed a severe drought here in 2001–02. Variation in productivity was positively correlated to site conditions, as measured by climate moisture index and mineral soil silt content, and negatively correlated to insect feeding, which included defoliation by the large aspen tortrix (*Choristoneura conflictana*) and wood boring by the poplar borer (*Saperda calcarata*), the flatheaded borers (*Agrilus liragus* and *Dicercas* spp.), and the ambrosia beetle (*Trypodendron retusum*). Mortality, in turn, was strongly correlated to drought severity (measured by minimum annual climate moisture index). Regeneration apparently does not replace the more mature aspen trees lost. In this case, aspen will eventually no longer be sustainable in this ecosystem.

7.7.2 Shifting vegetation zones

Many climate change impact forecasts are based on complex computer models, which predict existing forest vegetation will expand into new environments displacing current residents. Predicting patterns, extent, and rates of these shifting tree distributions is vital to forest managers who need to make decisions about adapting to and mitigating these impacts. Climatic envelope modeling is one method of predicting the future distributions of organisms under a changing climate (Berry *et al.* 2002). With this method, climatic factors associated with current distributions are used to project distributions under different climate change scenarios. As community members differ in their threshold response levels, phenotypic plasticity characteristics, genetic diversity, resilience to change, adaptability to new habitats, competitive abilities, and other invasive abilities, intact communities are not likely to move in concert (Bazzaz *et al.* 1995). Instead, different organisms will survive, migrate, or recover at different rates or not at all. New stresses likely will confront these organisms, especially at the moving fronts. In these ecotones, novel pathosystems will determine patterns of death for different species in different stand types.

Textbox 7.6 Yellow cedar decline in Alaska

Yellow cedar is a valuable tree species in southeast coastal Alaska that has been dying since the late 1800s. Mortality of this long-lived tree species has occurred over an area of approximately 200 000 ha. Alaska is the northern edge of its range. Southward, this species is limited to higher elevations. In affected stands, 70% or more of the trees are affected. The condition was first noticed in 1909, subsequently continuing with a noticeable increase after 1970. Dead trees remain standing for up to 100 years, creating what can be called a ghost forest. Affected trees grow at low elevations in soils that stay wet for extended periods mostly on south and west slopes. Mortality is distributed where snow accumulations are limited and winter temperatures are relatively warm. Determining the etiology of this decline required efforts over nearly 30 years by a diverse range of experts. At first, various biotic agents including pathogens and insect pests were examined. Later, the cause was found to involve a complex interaction of abiotic factors and timing and has been explained as follows. "Yellow cedar trees growing on poorly drained soils have shallow roots. Exposure on these wet sites is created from open canopy conditions that allow for solar radiation to warm soil and shallow roots. Canopy exposure also promotes rapid temperature fluctuation and more extreme cold temperatures. Premature dehardening of roots due to warmer springs and earlier melting and less abundant snow pack coincide resulting in root freezing as the primary injury mechanism (Hennon, *et al.* 2008).

7.7.3 Intensifying fire regimes in tropical forests

Periodic climate oscillations influence fire intensity and duration, especially in the tropics. The most powerful of these is the Pacific Decadal Oscillation, also known as the **El Niño Southern Oscillation (ENSO)**. During an El Niño event, a significant rise in temperature occurs over a large (approximately 15 000 000 km²) portion of the western tropical Pacific Ocean, and this condition lasts 6 to 18 months. El Niño phenomena occur approximately three to seven years apart (Drollette 2005), alternating with a condition of extreme cooling in the central and east-central Pacific, a condition known as La Niña. During an El Niño year, severe drought occurs in Australia, Indonesia, and the Philippines as high-pressure cells develop over the northern part of these land masses creating persistent hot and dry conditions. El Niño events also affect weather in western North America by raising temperatures, but its effects on wildfire in that region are unclear because rising temperatures also are accompanied by increased rainfall (Miller *et al.* 2009; Westerling *et al.* 2006). The intensity of El Niño events has been increasing in the last half century, and the severity of the droughts associated with them intensifying (Slik 2004).

Wildfires in Australia during El Niño events have become legendary for their intensity and size. The most recent of these occurred in 2009. Fortunately, a majority of the fire-adapted Australian tree species have special mechanisms that allow them to survive or reforest quickly during or following fire. For example, some of the eucalyptus species possess thick bark, white bark (which allows the reflection of heat), an ability to sprout from epicormic branches under the bark of trunks and limbs, the regrowth from lignotubers, and an ability to produce copious amounts of seed with a genetic constitution geared for rapid growth soon after germinating in the nutrient-rich natural seed-bed left in the wake of these fires (Costermans 1983). The impacts of climate change combined with El Niño years remains to be seen. Responses to massive ENSO-related forest fires in dipterocarp forests of Indonesia have been quite different, resulting in massive deforestation and lack of regeneration. A graphic example from the Island of Kalimantan is described in the case study below.

Textbox 7.7 El Niño-related fire causing deforestation on the Kalimantan Island, Indonesia

Drought associated with the ENSO is the "most significant" type of natural catastrophic disturbance" in Borneo (Harrison 2001). Wildfires precipitated by drought can significantly impact stand structure and sustainability. In late 1982 and early 1983, a major El Niño event caused extensive fires in Southeast Asia. The fires on East Kalimantan Island in Borneo were permitted to burn until rains returned the following year. Many of the fires were in old-growth dipterocarp forests that require shade for regeneration; conditions destroyed by the fires. The high intensity and

Textbox 7.7 (cont.)

large extent of these fires (up to 12 500 km^2) eliminated viable seed sources for regeneration. The grasses and mosses that colonized the burns provided neither food nor perches to potential seed dispersers such as birds and bats, limiting forest regeneration even near the forest edge. Small diameter classes were restricted, and the change in diameter distribution significantly varied from baseline mortality pattern that challenged the sustainability of the current structure in affected stands. After 10 years without forest regeneration, the Indonesian government granted forest concessions to companies that established nurseries and regenerated forest in exchange for a tax-free portion of the profits on subsequent harvest of the new timber. Although four tree nurseries were established beginning in 1991, no suitable native species were available for this task. *Pinus caribaea* was planted on one small area (50 000 ha) of acid sands. All other soils and climates required hardwoods. Among the successful species were a few eucalypts, *Gmelina arborea*, *Acacia mangium*, and *Paraserianthes (Albizia) falcataria*. The hope was that after just a few rotations of these pioneer species the original "climax," shade-requiring species could be successfully reintroduced. The strategy has worked well in some parts of the tropics (Parrotta 1993; Parrotta, *et al.* 1997).

7.8 Conclusion

The abiotic disturbance factors examined above represent only a small sampling of the many different abiotic stresses that exist in forests. Numerous studies have addressed the impacts of abiotic disturbances on some aspect of stand structure, but few examine the impact on diameter distributions across the entire range of size classes. Nonetheless, available studies clearly show that these factors can significantly influence diameter and age class distributions during the life of a forest. They also emphasize that trees growing in the forest interact simultaneously with a multitude of disturbances and other types of ecological processes, and that distribution, scale, patterns, and magnitude in time and space vary among these different processes, which often, but not always interact in complex ways. Comparing observed mortality to baseline mortality is a potentially useful way of sorting out the relative impacts of different abiotic factors on sustainability of forest ecosystems, and an operationally useful way of defining, assessing, and monitoring forest health.

Although each specific case will have its own specific cause and affect characteristics, some general principles about the impacts of abiotic disturbances on
stand structure and diameter/age distribution can be proposed:

(1)   Larger diameter trees are more exposed to exogenous mortality agents,
      like strong wind and temperature shift events.

(2)   Stands with an uneven-age/diameter composition have a lower risk of
      catastrophic damage due to abiotic disturbances.

(3)   Impact and health are scale-dependent properties. Small-scale disturb-
      ances can be catastrophic if they impact valuable management object-
      ives. Relevant scale depends on management objectives.

(4)   Severe large-scale disturbances usually leave patches of pre-existing
      vegetation, which act as biotic legacies for future stand development.

(5)   Mild or moderate and uniformly distributed disturbances can impact
      diameter distribution by enhancing conditions for regeneneration usu-
      ally by thinning overstory crown density.

(6)   Abiotic factors interact with other stresses that also can cause trees to
      die. Because there can be so many interconnected relationships among
      these factors, determining cause and effect can be complicated.

(7)   Severe storms tend to reset succession; moderate storms tend to speed
      it up.

References

Agee, J. K. 1990. The historical role of fire in Pacific Northwest forests. In: *Natural and
      Prescribed Fire in Pacific Northwest Forests*. Walstad, J. *et al.* (eds). Oregon State
      University Press, Corvallis.
Agee, J. K. 1993. *Fire Ecology of Pacific Northwest Forests*. Island Press, Washington DC, USA.
Agrios, G. N. 2005. *Plant Pathology*. 5th edition. Elsevier Academic Press, Burlington, MA.
Allen, C. D., Savage, M., and Falk, D. A. 2002. Ecological restoration of southwestern
      ponderosa pine ecosystems: a broad perspective. *Ecological Applications*
      12: 1418–1433.
Amatulli, G., Peréz-Cabello, F., and de la Riva, J. 2007. Mapping lightning/human-
      caused wildfires occurrence under ignition point location uncertainty. *Ecological
      Modelling* **200**: 321–333.
Ancelin, P., Courbaud, B., and Fourcaud, T. Y. 2004. Development of an individual tree-
      based mechanical model to predict wind damage within forest stands. *Forest
      Ecology & Management* **203**: 101–121.
Aril, K. and Lechowicz, M. J. 2007. Changes in understory light regime in a beech-maple
      forest after a severe ice storm. *Candian Journal Forest Research* **37**: 1770–1776.
Augustaitis, A. and Bytnerowicz, A. 2008. Contribution of ambient ozone to Scots pine
      defoliation and reduced growth in the Central European forests: A Lithuanian
      case study. *Environmental Pollution* **155**: 436–445.

Ayres, M. P. and Lombardero, M. J. 2000. Assessing the consequences of global change for forest disturbance from herbivores and pathogens. *The Science of the Total Environment* **262**: 263–286.

Bailey, S. W., Horsley, S. B., and Long, R. P. 2005. Thirty years of change in forest soils of the Allegheny Plateau, Pennsylvania. *Soil Science Society of America Journal* **69**: 681–690.

Baker, P. J., Bunyavejchewin, S., and Robinson A. P. 2008. The impacts of large-scale low- intensity fires on the forests of continental South-east Asia. *International Journal of Wildland Fire* **17**: 782–792.

Baker, W. L. 1992. The landscape ecology of large disturbances in the design and management of nature reserves. *Landscape Ecology* **7**: 181–194.

Bale, J. S., Masters, G. J., Hodkinson, I. D., *et al.* 2002. Herbivory in global climate change research: direct effects of rising temperature on insect herbivores. *Global Change Biology* **8**: 1–16.

Barber, V. A., Juday, G. P., and Finney, B. P. 2000. Reduced growth of Alaska white spruce in the twentieth century from temperature-induced drought stress. *Nature* **405**: 668–673.

Brasier, C. M. 1996. *Phytophthora cinnamomi* and oak decline in southern Europe. Environmental constraints including climate change. *Annales Des Sciences Forestieres* **53**: 347–358.

Basnet, K., Likens, G. E., Scatena, F. N., and Lugo, A. E. 1992. Hurricane Hugo: damage to a tropical rain forest in Puerto Rico. *Journal Tropical Ecology* **8**: 47–55.

Basnet, K., Likens, G. E., Scatena, F. N., and Lugo, A. E. 1993. Ecological consequences of root grafting in tabonuco (*Dacryodes excelsa*) trees in the Luquillo Experimental Forest, Puerto Rico. *Biotropica* **25**: 28–35.

Battles, J., Robards, T., Das, A., *et al.* 2008. Climate change growth on forest growth and tree mortality: a data-driven modeling study in mixed conifer forest of the Sierra Nevada, California. *Climatic Change* **87**(Suppl 1): S193–S213.

Bazzaz, F. A., Jasienski, M., Thomas, S. C., and Wayne, P. 1995. Microevolutionary responses in experimental populations of plants to CO_2-enriched environments: parallel results from two model systems. *Proceedings National Academy Science USA* **92**: 8161–8165.

Beatty, S. W. 1984. Influence of microtopography and canopy species on spatial patterns of forest understory plants. *Ecology*: **65**: 1406–1419.

Benito-Espinal, F. P and Benito-Espinal, E. 1991. *L'Ouragan Hugo. Genèse, Incidences, Géographiques et Ecologiques su la Guadeloupe.* Les Presses de l'Imprimerie Désormeaux à Fort-de-France, Guadeloupe.

Benning, T. L., LaPointe, D., Atkinson, C. T., and Vitousek, P. M. 2002. Interactions of climate change with biological invasions and land use in the Hawaiian Islands: modeling the fate of endemic birds using a geographic information system. *Proceedings National Academy Science USA* **99**: 14246–14249.

Bernal-Salazar, S., Terrazas, T., and Alvarado, D. 2004. Impact of air pollution on ring width and tracheid dimensions in *Abies religiosa* in the Mexico City basin. *Iawa Journal* **25**: 205–215.

Berry, P. M., Dawson, T. P., Harrison, P. A., and Pearson, R. G. 2002: Modelling potential impacts of climate change on the bioclimatic envelope of species in Britain and Ireland. *Global Ecology and Biogeography* **11**: 453–62.

Black, M. P., Mooney, S. D., and Haberle, S. G. 2007. The fire, human, and climate nexus in the Sydney Basin, eastern Australia. *The Holocene* **17**: 469–480.

Blood, E. R., Anderson, P., Smith, P. A., *et al.* 1991. Effects of Hurricane Hugo on coastal soil solution chemistry in South Carolina. *Biotropica* **23**(suppl.): 348–355.

Boose, E. R., Foster, D. R., and Fluet, M. 1994. Hurricane impacts to tropical and temperate forest landscapes. *Ecological Monographs* **64**: 369–400.

Bormann, F. H. and Likens, G. E. 1979. Catastrophic disturbance and the steady-state in northern hardwood forests. *American Scientist* **67**: 660–669.

Bormann, F. H., Spaltenstein, H., McClellan, M. H., *et al.* 1995. Rapid soil development after windthrow disturbance in pristine forests. *Journal Ecology* **83**: 747–757.

Boucher, D. H. 1990. Growing back after hurricanes; catastrophes may be critical to rain forest dynamics. *BioScience* **40**: 163–166.

Bouget, C. and Duelli, P. 2004. The effects of windthrow on insect communities: a literature review. *Biological Conservation* **118**: 281–299.

Bouwman, A. F., Van Vuuren, D. P., Derwent, R. G., and Posch, M. 2002. A global analysis of acidification and eutrophication of terrestrial ecosystems. *Water Air Soil Pollution* **141**: 349–382.

Bowman, D. M. J. S. 2003. Australian landscape burning: a continental and evolutionary perspective. In: *Fire in Ecosystems of South-West Western Australia: Impacts and Management.* Abbott, I. and Burrows N. (eds). Backhuys.

Boykoff, M. 2007. Changing patterns in climate change reporting in United States and United Kingdom media. *Presentation at Carbonundrums: Making Sense of Climate Change Reporting around the World, Reuters Institute for the Study of Journalism and Environmental Change* June 27, 2007.

Bradstock, R. A. 2008. Effects of large fires on biodiversity in south-eastern Australia: disaster or template for diversity? *International Journal of Wildland Fire* **17**: 809–822.

Bréda, N., Roland, H., Granier, A., and Dreyer, E. 2006. Temperate forest trees and stands under severe drought: a review of ecophysiological responses, adaptation processes and long-term consequences. *Annals Forest Science* **63**: 625–644.

Bush, M. B., Silman, M. R., and Urrego, D. H. 2004. 48 000 years of climate change in a biodiversity hotspot. *Science* **303**: 827–829.

Bytnerowicz, A., Arbaugh, M., Schilling, S., *et al.* 2008. Ozone distribution and phytotoxic potential in mixed conifer forests of the San Bernardino Mountains, Southern California. *Environmental Pollution* **155**: 398–408.

Bytnerowicz, A., Omasa, K., and Paoletti, E. 2007. Integrated effects of air pollution and climate change on forests: A northern hemisphere perspective. *Environmental Pollution* **147**: 438–445.

Camp, A., Oliver, C., Hessburg, P., and Everett, R. 1997. Predicting late-successional fire refugia pre-dating European settlement in the Wenatchee Mountains. *Forest Ecology & Management* **95**: 63–77.

Canham, C. D. and Loucks, O. L. 1984. Catastrophic windthrow in the presettlement forests of Wisconsin. *Ecology* **65**: 803–809.

Carrion, J. S., Sanchez-Gomez, P., Mata, J. F., *et al.* 2003. Holocene vegetation dynamics, fire, and grazing in the Sierra de Gador, southern Spain. *The Holocene* **13**: 839–849.

Chakraborty, S. 2005 Potential impact of climate change on plant–pathogen interactions. *Aust. Plant Pathol* **34**: 443–448.

Chakraborty, S., Tiedemann, A. V., and Teng, P. S. 2000. Climate change: potential impact on plant diseases. *Environmental Pollution* **108**: 317–326.

Chapin, F. S. III, Yarie, J., Van Cleve, K., and Viereck, L. A. 2006a. The conceptual basis of LTER studies in the Alaskan boreal forest. In: *Alaska's Changing Boreal Forest.* Chapin, F. S. III, Oswood, M. W., and Van Cleve, K., *et al.* (eds). Oxford University Press, New York.

Chapin, F. S. III, Oswood, M. W., Van Cleve, K., *et al.* (eds). 2006b. *Alaska's Changing Boreal Forest.* Oxford University Press, New York.

CIRMOUNT Committee. 2006. Mapping new terrain: climate change and America's West. *Report of the Consortium for Integrated Climate Research in Western Mountains (CIRMOUNT). Misc. Pub., PSW-MISC-77, Albany, CA. Pacific Southwest Research Station, USDA Forest Service.*

Coakley, S. M., Scherm, H., and Chakraborty, S. 1999. Climate change and plant disease management. *Annual Review Phytopathology* **37**: 399–426.

Coder K. D. 1999. Drought damage to trees. *University of Georgia School of Forest Resources Extension Publication FOR99-010*

Cohen, D., Dellinger, B., Klein, R., and Buchanan, B. 2007. Patterns in lightning-caused fires at Great Smoky Mountains National Park. *Fire Ecology* **3**: 68–82.

Condit, R., Hubbell, S. P., and Foster, R. B. 1995. Mortality rates of 205 neotropical tree and shrub species and the impact of a severe drought. *Ecological Monographs* **65**: 419–439.

Connell, J. H. 1978. Diversity in tropical rain forests and coral reefs. *Science* **199**: 1302–1310.

Costermans, L. 1983. *Native Trees and Shrubs of South-eastern Australia.* Weldon, Sydney, Australia.

Coulson, R. N., Hennier, P. B., Flamm, R. O., *et al.* 1983. The role of lightning in the epidemiology of the southern pine beetle. *Z. Ang. Entomol* **96**: 182–193.

Covington, W. W., Fule, P. Z., Moore, M. M., *et al.* 1997. Restoring ecosystem health in ponderosa pine forests of the southwest. *Journal Forestry* **95**: 21–29.

Craig, B. W. and Friedland, A. J. 1991. Spatial patterns in forest composition and standing dead red spruce in montane forests of the Adirondacks and Northern Appalachians. *Environmental Monitoring and Assessment* **18**: 129–143.

Dale, V. H., Joyce, L. A., McNulty, S., *et al.* 2001. Climate change and forest disturbances. *BioScience* **51**: 723–734.

Davis, K. M. and Mutch, R. W. 1994. Applying ecological principles to manage wildland fire. In: *Fire in Ecosystem Management.* National Advanced Resources Technology Center.

Davis, K. M., Clayton, B. D., and Fischer, W. C. 1980. Fire ecology of Lolo National Forest habitat types. *USDA Forest Service Gen. Tech. Rep. INT-79.*

de Hayes, D. H., Schaberg, P. G., Hawley, G. J., and Strimbeck, G. R. 1999. Acid rain impacts on calcium nutrition and forest health-alteration of membrane-associated calcium leads to membrane destabilization and foliar injury in red spruce. *BioScience* **49**: 789–800.

Deal, R. L., Oliver, C. D., and Bormann, B. T. 1991. Reconstruction of mixed hemlock-spruce stands in coastal southeast Alaska. *Canadian Journal Forest Research* **21**: 643–654.

Deal, R. L., Tappeiner, J. C., and Hennon, P. E. 2002. Developing silvicultural systems based on partial cutting in western hemlock-Sitka spruce stands of southeast Alaska. *Forestry* **75**: 425–431.

Deuber, C. G. 1940. The glaze storm of 1940. *American Forests* **46**: 210–211, 235.

Dickson, R. E. and Isebrands, J. G. 1991. Leaves as regulators of stress response. In: *Response of Plants to Multiple Stresses*. Mooney H. A., Winner, W. E., and Pell, E. J. (eds). Academic Press, New York.

Dittus, W. P. J. 1985. The influence of cyclones on the dry evergreen forest of Sri Lanka. *Biotropica* **17**: 1–14.

Doyle, T. W. 1981. The role of disturbance in the gap dynamics of a montane rain forest: an application of a tropical succession model. In: *Forest Succession Concepts and Application*. West, D. C., Shugart, H. H., and Botkin, D. B. (eds). Springer-Verlag, New York.

Driscoll, C. T., Lawrence, G. B., Bulger, A. J., *et al.* 2001. Acidic deposition in the northeastern United States: Sources and inputs, ecosystem effects, and management strategies. *BioScience* **51**: 180–198.

Drohan, P., Stout, S., and Petersen, G. 1999. Spatial relationships between sugar maple (*Acer saccharum* Marsh), sugar maple decline, slope, aspect, and atmospheric deposition in northern Pennsylvania. In: *Sugar Maple Ecology and Health: Proceedings of an International Symposium*. USDA Forest Service, Northeastern Research Station, Radnor, PA, Warren, PA, U.S.A. Horsley, S. B. and Long, R. P. (eds).

Drollette, D. 2005. Fire down under. *Natural History* **114**: 44–50.

Duguay, S. M., Arii, K., Hooper, M., and Lechowicz, M. J. 2001. Ice storm damage and early recovery in an old-growth forest. *Environmental Monitoring and Assessment* **67**: 97–108.

Eberhart, K. E. and Woodward, P. M. 1987. Distribution of residual vegetation associated with large fires in Alberta. *Canadian Journal Forest Research* **17**: 1207–1212.

Eckberg, T. B., Schmid, J. M., Mata, S. A., and Lundquist, J. E. 1994. Primary focus trees for the mountain pine beetle in the Black Hills. *USDA For. Serv. Res. Note* RM-531.

Emanuel, K. 2005. Increasing destructiveness of tropical cyclones over the past 30 years. *Nature* **436**: 686–688.

Evans, A. M., Camp, A. E., Tyrrell, M. L., and Riely, E. E. 2007. Biotic and abiotic influences on wind disturbance in forests of NW Pennsylvania, USA. *Forest Ecology & Management* **245**: 44–53.

Everham, E. M. and Brokaw, N. V. L. 1996. Forest damage and recovery from catastrophic wind. *Botanical Reviews* **62**: 113–185.

Felzer, B. S., Cronin, T., Reilly, J. M., *et al.* 2007. Impacts of ozone on trees and crops. *C. R. Geoscience* **339**: 784–798.

Fischer, R., Mues, V., Ulrich, E., *et al.* 2007. Monitoring of atmospheric deposition in European forests and an overview on its implication on forest condition. *Applied Geochemistry* **22**: 1129–1139.

Flanagan, P. T., Morgan, P., and Everett, R. L. 1998. Snag recruitment in subalpine forests. *Northwest Science* **72**: 303–309.

Fonseca Gonzalez, J., Santos Posadas, H. M. D., Llanderal Cazares, C., *et al.* 2008. Ips and woodborer insects in *Pinus montezumae* trees damaged by fire. *Madera y Bosques* **14**: 69–80. [In Spanish].

Foster, D. R. 1988. Species and stand response to catastrophic wind in central New England, USA. *Journal Ecology* **76**: 135–151.

Foster, D. R. and Boose, E. R. 1992. Patterns of forest damage resulting from catastrophic wind in central New England, USA. *Journal Ecology* **80**: 79–98.

Foster, D. R. and Boose, E. R. 1994. Hurricane disturbance regimes in temperate and tropical forest ecosystems. In: *Wind Effects on Trees, Forests and Landscapes.* Coutts, M. (ed.). Cambridge University Press, New York.

Foster, D. R., Knight, D. H., and Frankin, J. F. 1998. Landscape patterns and legacies resulting from large, infrequent forest disturbances. *Ecosystems* **1**: 497–510.

Foster, D. R., Fluet, M., and Boose, E. R. 1999. Human or natural disturbance: Landscape-scale dynamics of the tropical forests of Puerto Rico. *Ecological Applications* **9**: 555–572.

Foster, P. 2001. The potential negative impacts of global climate change on tropical montane cloud forests. *Earth-Science Reviews* **55**: 73–106.

Fowler, D., Cape, J. N., Coyle, M., *et al.* 1999. The global exposure of forests to air pollutants. *Water Air Soil Pollution* **116**: 5–32.

Frelich, L. E. and Lorimer, C. G. 1991. Natural disturbance regimes in hemlock-hardwood forests of the upper Great Lakes Region. *Ecological Monographs* **61**: 145–164.

Frelich, L. E. and Reich, P. B. 1995. Spatial patterns and succession in a Minnesota southern-boreal forest. *Ecological Monographs* **65**: 325–346.

Fule, P. Z. 2008. Does it make sense to restore wildland fire in a changing climate? *Restoration Ecology* **16**: 526–531.

Furley, P. A. and Newey, W. W. 1979. Variations in plant communities with topography over tropical limestone soils. *Journal Biogeography* **6**: 1–15.

Gandhi, K. J. K., Gilmore, D. W., Katovich, S. A., *et al.* 2007. Physical effects of weather events on the abundance and diversity of insects in North American forests. *Environmental Reviews* **15**: 113–152.

Gandhi, K. J. K., Gilmore, D. W., Haack, R. A., *et al.* 2009. Application of semiochemicals to assess the biodiversity of subcortical insects following an ecosystem disturbance in a sub-boreal forest. *Journal Chemical Ecology* **35**: 1384–1410.

Gardiner, B., Byrne, K., Hale, S., *et al.* 2008. A review of mechanistic modeling of wind damage risk to forests. *Forestry* **81**: 447–463.

Gardner, L. R., Michner, W. K., Blood, E. R., *et al.* 1991. Ecological impacts of Hurricane Hugo–salinization of a coastal forest. *Journal Coastal Research* **8**: 301–317.

Garrett, K. A., Dendy, S. P., Frank, E. E., *et al.* 2006. Climate change effects on plant disease: genomes to ecosystems. *Annual Review Phytopathology* **44**: 489–509.

Gill, A. M. 1981. Fire adaptive traits of vascular plants. In: *Fire Regimes and Ecosystem Properties.* USDA Forest Service Gen. Tech. Rep. WO26. Mooney H. A. *et al.* (eds).

Gill, A. M. and Grant, A. 2008. Large fires, fire effects and the fire-regime concept. *International Journal Wildland Fire* **17**: 688–695.

Goldammer, J. G. 1993. Historical biogeography of fire: tropical and subtropical In: *Fire in the Environment: The Ecological, Atmospheric, and Climatic Importance of Vegetation Fires.* Crutzen, P. J. and Goldammer, J. G. (eds). Wiley and Sons, New York.

Goldammer, J. G. 1999. Forests on fire. *Science* **284**: 1782–1783.

Gregory, F. A. and Sabat, A. M. 1996. The effect of hurricane disturbance on the fecundity of sierra palms (*Prestoea montana*). *Bios* **67**: 135–139.

Gresham, C. A., Williams, T. M., and Lipscomb, D. J. 1991. Hurricane Hugo wind damage to southeastern U.S. coastal forest tree species. *Biotropica* **23**: 420–426.

Grulke, N. E., Minnich, R. A., Paine, T. D., *et al.* 2009. Air pollution increases forest susceptibility to wildfires: A case study in the San Bernardino Mountains in southern California. In: *Air Pollution and Fire, Developments in Environmental Science,* Vol. **8**. Bytnerowicz, A., Arbaugh, M., Riebau, A., and Anderson, C. (eds). Elsevier, Amsterdam.

Guarin, A. and Taylor A. H. 2005. Drought-triggered tree mortality in mixed conifer forests in Yosemite National Park, California, USA. *Forest Ecology & Management* **218**: 229–244.

Guyette, R. P., Spetich, M. A., and Stambaugh, M. C. 2006. Historic fire regime dynamics and forcing factors in the Boston Mountains, Arkansas, USA. *Forest Ecology & Management* **234**: 293–304.

Harden, J. W., Trumbore, S. E., Veldhuis, H., and Stocks, B. J. 1997. Moss and soil contributions to the annual net carbon flux of a maturing boreal forest. *Journal of Geophysical Research-Atmospheres* **102**: 28805–28816.

Hardy, C. C. 2005. Wildland fire hazard and risk: problems, definitions, and context. *Forest Ecology & Management* **211**: 73–82.

Harrington R., Fleming, R. A., and Woiwod, I. P. 2001. Climate change impacts on insect management and conservation in temperate regions: can they be predicted? *Agricultural and Forest Entomology* **3**: 233–240.

Harris, A. S. 1989. Wind in the forests of southeast Alaska and guides for reducing damage. *USDA Forest Service, Pacific Northwest Research Station, Gen. Tech. Rep. PNW-GTR-244.*

Harrison, R. D. 2001. Drought and the consequences of El Nino in Borneo: a case study of figs. *Population Ecology* **43**: 63–75.

Hauer, R. J., Wang, W., and Dawson, J. O. 1993. Ice storm damage to urban trees. *Journal Arboriculture* **19**: 187–194.

Heartsill-Scalley, T., Scatena, F., Estrada, N. C., *et al.* 2007. Disturbance and long-term patterns of rainfall and throughfall nutrient fluxes in a subtropical wet forest in Puerto Rico. *Journal Hydrology* **333**: 472–485.

Heinselman, M. L. 1973. Fire in the virgin forest of the Boundary Waters Canoe Area, Minnesota. *Quaternary Research* **3**: 329–382.

Heinselman, M. L. 1981. Fire intensity and frequency as factors in the distribution and structure of northern ecosystems. In: *Fire Regimes and Ecosystem Properties: USDA Forest Service Gen. Tech. Rep. WO 26.* Mooney, H. A. *et al.* (eds).

Hennon, P. E., D'Amore, D. V., Wittwer, D. T., and Caouette, J. P. 2008. In: *Integrated Restoration of Forested Ecosystems to Achieve Multiresource Benefits: Proc. 2007 National Silviculture Workshop. Gen. Tech. Rep. PNW-GTP73.* Deal, R. L. (tech. ed.). Portland OR: USDA Forest Service Pacific Northwest Research Station.

Hessburg, P. F., Mitchell, R. G., and Filip, G. M. 1994. Historical and current roles of insects and pathogens in eastern Oregon and Washington forested landscapes. *USDA For. Serv. Gen. Tech. Rep. PNW-GTR-327.*

Heyerdahl, E. K., Lertzman, K., and Karpuk, S. 2007. Local-scale controls of a low-severity fire regime (1750–1950), southern British Columbia, Canada. *Ecoscience* **14**: 40–47.

Hildebrand, D. 2003. Lightning tracking an important tool in land management and wildland fire suppression. *Vaisala News* **162**: 32–33.

Hobbs, R. J., Arico, S., Aronson, J., *et al.* 2006. Novel ecosystems: theoretical and management aspects of the new ecological world order. *Global Ecology and Biogeography* **15**: 1–7.

Hood, S. M. 2007. Evaluation of a post-fire tree mortality model for western USA conifers. *International Journal of Wildland Fire* **16**: 679–689.

Hood, S. M., Smith, S. L., and Cluck, D. R. 2007. Delayed conifer tree mortality following fire in California. In: *Restoring Fire-adapted Ecosystems: Proceedings 2005 National Silviculture Workshop. Gen. Tech. Rep. PSW-GTR-203.* Powers, R. F. (tech. ed.). USDA Forest Service, Albany, CA: Pacific Southwest Research Station.

Hooper, M. C., Arii, K., and Lechowicz, M. J. 2001. Impact of a major ice storm on an old-growth hardwood forest. *Canadian Journal Botany* **79**: 70–75.

Hope, G., Chokkalingam, U., and Anwar, S. 2005. The stratigraphy and fire history of the Kutai Peatlands, Kalimantan, Indonesia. *Quarternary Research* **64**: 407–417.

Hopkin, A., Williams, T., Sajan, R., *et al.* 2003. Ice storm damage to eastern Ontario forests: 1998–2001. *Forestry Chronicle* **79**: 47–53.

Horsley, S. B., Long, R. P., Bailey, S. W., *et al.* 1999. Factors contributing to sugar maple decline along topographical gradients on the glaciated and unglaciated Allegheny Plateau. In: *Sugar Maple Ecology and Health: Proceedings International Symposium.* Horsley, S. B. and Long, R. P. (eds). USDA Forest Service, Northeastern Research Station, Radnor, PA.

Hoyos, C. D., Agudelo, P. A., Webster, P. J., and Curry, J. A. 2006. Deconvolution of the factors contributing to the increase in global hurricane intensity. *Science* **312**: 94–97.

IPCC (Intergovernmental Panel on Climate Change). 2001. *Climate Change 2001: the Scientific Basis. Contribution of Working Group I to the Third Assessment Report of the Intergovernmental Panel on Climate Change.* Cambridge University Press, New York.

IPCC (Intergovernmental Panel on Climate Change). 2007. *Climate Change 2007: Impacts, Adaptation and Vulnerability. Contribution of Working Group II to the Fourth Assessment Report of the Intergovernmental Panel on Climate Change.* Cambridge University Press, New York.

IPCC (Intergovernmental Panel on Climate Change). 2007. Summary for policymakers. In: *Climate Change 2007: the Physical Science Basis. Contribution of Working Group 1 to the*

Fourth Assessment Report of the Intergovernmental Panel on Climate Change. Solomon, S, Qin, D, Manning, M, *et al.* (eds). Cambridge University Press, New York.

Irland, L. C. 1998. Ice storm 1998 and the forests of the northeast. *Journal Forestry* **96**: 32–40.

Irland, L. C. 2000. Ice storms and forest impacts. *Science of the Total Environment* **262**: 231–242.

James, A. and Dupuis, J. 2005. The impacts of brush fires on the vegetation of Dominica. In: *12th Meeting of the Caribbean Foresters*. Weaver, P. L. and González, K. A. (eds). USDA Forest Service, International Institute of Tropical Forestry, Río Piedras.

Johnson, E. A. 1992. *Fire and Vegetation Dynamics: Studies from the North American Boreal Forest*. Cambridge University Press, Cambridge.

Johnson, D. W. and Curtis, P. S. 2001. Effects of forest management on soil C and N storage: meta analysis. *Forest Ecology & Management* **140**: 227–238.

Johnson, E. A. and Van Wagner, C. E. 1985. The theory and use of two fire history models. *Canadian Journal Forest Research* **15**: 214–220.

Jones, N. 2005. Wildland fires, management, and restoration in Barbados. In: *12th Meeting of the Caribbean Foresters*. Weaver, P. L. and González, K. A. (eds). USDA Forest Service, International Institute of Tropical Forestry, Río Piedras.

Jurskis, V. 2000. Vegetation changes since European settlement of Australia: an attempt to clear up some burning issues. *Australian Forestry* **63**: 166–173.

Jurskis, V. 2005. Eucalypt decline in Australia, and a general concept of tree decline and dieback. *Forest Ecology & Management* **215**: 1–20.

Kamimura, K. and Shiraishi, N. A review of strategies for wind damage assessment in Japanese forests. *Journal Forest Research* 12: 162–176.

Kamimura, K., Gardiner, B., Kato, A., *et al.* 2008. Developing a decision support approach to reduce wind damage risk – a case study on sugi (*Cryptomeria japonica* (L.f.)D.Don) forests in Japan. *Forestry* 81: 429–445.

Karnosky, D. F., Skelly, J. M., Percy, K. E., and Chappelka, A. H. 2007. Perspectives regarding 50 years of research on effects of tropospheric ozone air pollution on US forests. *Environmental Pollution* **147**: 489–506.

Katovich, S. A., McDougall, D., and Chavez, Q. 1998. Impact of forest stressors on the tree species of the Nicolet National Forest- past, present and future. *USDA Forest Service, Northeastern Area State and Private Forestry, Forest Health Protection, NA-TP-02-98*

Kayll, A. J. 1968. Heat tolerance of tree seedlings. *Proceedings Tall Timbers Fire Ecology Conference* **8**: 89–105.

Keane, R. E., Agee, J. K., Fule, P., *et al.* 2008. Ecological effects of large fires on US landscapes: benefit or catastrophe. *International Journal of Wildland Fire* **17**: 696–712.

Keane, R. E., Austin, M., Field, C., *et al.*. 2001. Tree mortality in gap models: application to climate change. *Climate Change* **51**: 509–540.

Kenderes, K., Aszalos, R., Ruff, J., *et al.* 2007. Effects of topography and tree stand characteristics on susceptibility of forests to natural disturbances (ice and wind) in Borzsony Mountains (Hungary). *Community Ecology* **8**: 209–220.

Kershaw, A. P., Clark, J. S., Gill, A. M., and D'Costa, D. M. 2002. A history of fire in Australia. In: *Flammable Australia: the Fire Regimes and Biodiversity of a Continent*. Bradstock, R. A. *et al.* (eds). Cambridge University Press, Cambridge.

Kimmins, J. P. 2003. *Forest Ecology*. 3rd edition. Benjamin Cummings Publishing Co., San Francisco, CA.

Kitzberger, T. and Veblen, T. T. 1997. The influence of humans and ENSO on fire history of *Austrocedrus chilensis* woodlands in northern Patagonia, Argentina. *Ecoscience* **4**: 508–520.

Klenner, W., Walton, R., Arsenault, A., and Kremsater, L. 2008. Dry forests in the southern interior of British Columbia: historic disturbances and implications for restoration and management. *Forest Ecology & Management* **256**: 1711–1722.

Kliejunas, J. T., Geils, B., Micales Glaeser, J., *et al.* 2008. Climate and forest diseases of western North America: A literature review. White Paper prepared for The Western Wildlands Environmental Threat Assessment Center, Prineville, OR.

Klotzbach, P. J. 2006. Trends in global tropical cyclone activity over the past twenty years (1986–2005). *Geophysical Research Letters* **33**: L10805.

Krieger, D. J. 2001. *Economic Value of Forest Ecosystem Services: A Review*. The Wilderness Society, Washington DC.

Kulakowski, D. and Veblen, T. T. 2002. Influences of fires history and topography on the pattern of a severe wind blowdown in a Colorado subalpine forest. *Journal Ecology* **90**: 806–819.

Lafon, C. W. 2004. Ice-storm disturbance and long-term forest dynamics in the Adirondack Mountains. *Journal Vegetation Science* **15**: 267–276.

Lafon, C. W. and Kutac, M. J. 2003. Effects of ice storms, southern pine beetle infestation, and fire on table mountain pine forests of southwestern Virginia. *Physical Geography* **24**: 502–519.

Larsen, J. A. 1980. The boreal ecosystem. *Physiological Ecology*. Academic Press, New York.

Larjavaara, M., Kuuluvainen, T., and Rita, H. 2005. Spatial distribution of lightning-ignited forest fires in Finland. *Forest Ecology & Management* **208**: 177–188.

Lawton, R. O., Nair, U. S., Pielke Sr., R. A., and Welch, R. M. 2001. Cimate impact of tropical lowland deforestation on nearby montane cloud forests. *Science* **294**: 584–587.

Lemon, P. C. 1961. Forest ecology of ice storms. *Bulletin Torrey Botanical club* **88**: 21–29.

Likens, G. E. and Bormann, F. H. 1995. *Biogeochemistry of a Forested Ecosystem*. 2nd edition. Springer-Verlag New York Inc.

Liu, K. B, Lu, H., and Shen, C. 2008. A 1200-year proxy record of hurricanes and fires from the Gulf of Mexico coast: testing the hypothesis of hurricane-fire interactions. *Quarternary Research* **69**: 29–41.

Lloret, F., Siscart, D., and Dalmases, C. 2004. Canopy recovery after drought dieback in holm-oak Mediterranean forests of Catalonia (NE Spain). *Global Change Biology* **10**: 2092–2099.

Lorimer, C. G. 1977. The presettlement forest and natural disturbance cycle of Northeastern Maine. *Ecology* **58**: 139–48.

Lugo, A. E. and Scatena, F. N. 1995. Ecosystem-level properties of the Luquillo Experimental Forest with emphasis on the tabonuco forest. In: *Tropical Forests:*

Management and Ecology. Lugo, A. E. and Lowe, C. (eds). Springer-Verlag, New York.

Lugo, A. E. and Scatena, F. N. 1996. Background and catastrophic tree mortality in tropical moist, wet and rain forests. *Biotropica* **28** (suppl.): 585–599.

Lundquist, J. E. and Hamelin, R. C. (eds.). *Forest Pathology – From Genes to Landscapes*. APS Press, St. Paul, MN, USA.

Lundquist, J. E. and Negron, J. F. 2000. Endemic forest disturbances and stand structure of ponderosa pine (*Pinus ponderosa*) in the Upper Pine Creek Research Natural Area, South Dakota, USA. *Natural Areas Journal* **20**: 126–132.

Lyford, W. H. and MacLean, D. W. 1966. Mound and pit relief in relation to soil disturbance and tree distribution in New Brunswick, Canada. *Harvard Forest Paper* 15.

Major, J. 1951. A functional factorial approach to plant ecology. *Ecology* **32**: 392–412.

Malingreau, J. P., Stephens, G., and Fellows, L. 1985. Remote sensing of forest fires: Kalimantan and North Borneo in 1982–83 El Niño-Southern Oscillation event. In: *Tropical Forests and the World Atmosphere. AAAS Selected Symposium 101*. Prance, G. T. (ed.). American Association for the Advancement of Science, Washington, DC.

Manion, P. D. 1991. *Tree Disease Concepts*. 2nd edition. Prentice-Hall, Englewood Cliffs, NJ.

Manion, P. D., Griffin, D. H., and Rubin, B. D. 2001. Ice damage impacts on the health of northern New York State Forest. *Forestry Chronicle* **77**: 619–625.

Mann, M. E. and Emanuel, K. A. 2006. Atlantic hurricane trends linked to climate change. *EOS* **87**: 233–244.

Martin, H. C. and Weech, P. S. 2001. Climate change in the Bahamas? Evidence in the meterological records. *Bahamas Journal of Science* **5**: 22–32.

McCarthy, J. W. and Weetman, G. 2007. Stand structure and development of an insect-mediated boreal forest landscape. *Forest Ecology & Management* **241**: 101–114.

McDowell, N., Pockman, W. T., Allen, C. D., *et al.* 2008. Mechanisms of plant survival and mortality during drought: why do some plants survive while others succumb to drought? *New Phytologist* **178**: 719–739.

McLeod, R. 2003. *The inquiry into the operational response to the January 2003 bushfires*. Australia Capital Territory Government report prepared for Chief Minister. Canberra.

Millenium Ecosystem Assessment. 2005. *Ecosystems and Human Well-Being: Synthesis*. Island Press, Washington DC, USA.

Miller, J. D., Saafford, H. D., Crimmins, M., and Thodes, A. E. 2009. Quantitative evidence for increasing forest fire severity in the Sierra Nevada and Southern Cascade Mountains, California and Nevada, USA. *Ecosystems* **12**: 16–32.

Miller, M. J. and Smolarkiewicz, P. K. 2008. Predicting weather, climate, and extreme events. *Journal of Computational Physics* **227**: 3429–3430.

Miller, R. M. and Lodge, D. J. 2007. Fungal responses to disturbance–Agriculture and Forestry In: *The Mycota, IV, Environmental and Microbial Relationships*. 2nd edition. Esser, K., Kubicek, P., and Druzhinina, I. S. (eds). Springer-Verlag, Berlin.

Millward, A. A. and Kraft, C. E. 2004. Physical influences of landscape on a large-extent ecological disturbance: The northeastern North American ice storm of 1998. *Landscape Ecology* **19**: 99–111.

Mueller, O. P. and Cline, M. G. 1959. Effects of mechanical soil barriers and soil wetness on rooting of trees and soil mixing by blow-down in central New York. *Soil Science* **88**: 107–111.

Mueller, R. C., Scudder, C. M., Porter, M. E., *et al.* 2005. Differential tree mortality in response to severe drought: evidence for long-term vegetation shifts. *Journal Ecology* **93**: 1085–1093.

Munton, D. 2002. Fumes, forests and further studies: environmental science and policy inaction in Ontario. *Journal of Canadian Studies* **37**: 130–163.

Myers, R. K. and van Lear, D. H. 1998. Hurricane–fire interactions in coastal forests of the south: a review and hypothesis. *Forest Ecology & Management* **103**: 265–276.

Myneni, R. B., Keeling, C. D., Tucker, C. J., *et al.* 1997. Increased plant growth in the northern high latitudes due to enhanced spring time warming. *Nature* **386**: 698–702.

Natural Resources Canada. 1995. Silvicultural terms in Canada. *Natural Resources Canada, Canadian Forest Service*. 2nd edition. Ottawa.

Nealis, V. and Peter, B. 2008. Risk assessment of the threat of mountain pine beetle to Canada's boreal and eastern pine forests. *Natural Resources Canada, Canadian Forest Service, Information Report BC-X-417*, Victoria, British Columbia.

Neelin, J. D., Münnich, M., Su, H., *et al.* 2006. Tropical drying trends in global warming models and observations. *Procedings National Academy Science USA* **103**: 6110–6115.

Negri, A. J., Burkardt, N., Golden, J. H., *et al.* 2005, The hurricane-flood-landslide continuum. *Bulletin American Meteorological Society* **86**: 1241–1247.

Nepstad, D. C., Tohver, I. M., Ray, D., *et al.* 2007. Mortality of large trees and lianas following experimental drought in an Amazon forest. *Ecology* **88**: 2259–2269.

Nowacki, G. J. and Kramer, M. G. 1998. The effects of wind disturbance on temperate rain forest structure and dynamics of southeast Alaska. *USDA Forest Service, Pacific Northwest Research Station, Gen. Tech. Rep. PNW-GTR-421*.

Oliver, C. D. and Larson, B. C. 1996. *Forest Stand Dynamics*. John Wiley and Sons, Inc., New York.

Palik, B. J. and Robl, J. 1999. Structural legacies of catastrophic windstorm in a mature Great Lakes aspen forest. *North Central Research Station Res. Pap. NC-337*, St. Paul, MN.

Park, B. B., Yanai, R. D., Fahey, T. J., *et al.* 2008. Fine root dynamics and forest production across a calcium gradient in northern hardwood and conifer ecosystems. *Ecosystems* **11**: 325–341.

Parker, T. J., Clancy, K. M., and Mathiasen, R. L. 2006. Interactions among fire, insects, and pathogens in coniferous forests of the interior western United States and Canada. *Agricultural and Forest Entomology* **8**: 167–189.

Parrent, J. L., Morris, W. F., and Vilgalys, R. 2006. CO_2-enrichment and nutrient availability alter ectomycorrhizal fungal communities. *Ecology* **87**: 2278–2287.

Parrotta, J. A. 1993. Secondary forest regeneration on degraded tropical lands. In: *Restoration of Tropical Forest Ecosystems*. Lieth, H. and Lohmann, M. (eds). Kluwer Academic Publishers, The Hague.

Parrotta, J. A. and Lodge, D. J. 1991. Fine root dynamics in a subtropical wet forest following hurricane disturbance. *Biotropica* **23**: 343–347.

Parrotta, J. A., Turnbull, J. W., and Jones, N. 1997. Catalyzing native forest regeneration on degraded tropical lands. *Forest Ecology & Management* **99**: 1–7.

Parsons, M., McLoughlin, C. A., Kotschy, K. A., *et al.* 2005. The effects of extreme floods on the biophysical heterogeneity of river landscapes. *Frontiers in Ecology and the Environment* **3**: 487–494.

Pausas, J. G., Llovet, J., Rodrigo, A., and Vallejo, R. 2008. Are wildfires a disaster in the Mediterranean Basin? A review. *International Journal of Wildland Fire* **17**: 713–723.

Pennanen, J. 2002. Forest age distribution under mixed-severity fire regimes: a simulation-based analysis for middle boreal Fennoscandia. *Silva Fennica* **36**: 213–231.

Peterson, C. J. 2000. Catastrophic wind damage to North American forests and the potential impact of climate change. *The Science of the Total Environment* **262**: 287–311.

Peterson, C. J. and Leach, A. D. 2008. Limited salvage logging effects on forest regeneration after moderate-severity windthrow. *Ecological Applications* **18**: 407–420.

Peterson, C. J. and Pickett, S. T. A. 1991. Treefall and resprouting following catastrophic windthrow in old-growth hemlock-hardwoods forest. *Forest Ecology & Management* **42**: 205–217.

Peterson, C. J. and Rebertus, A. J. 1997. Tornado damage and initial recovery in three adjacent, lowland temperate forests in Missouri. *Journal Vegetation Science* **8**: 559–564.

Peterson, D. L. and Ryan, K. C. 1986. Modeling post-fire conifer mortality for long-range planning. *Environmental Management* **10**: 797–808.

Phillips, J. D. 2002. Global and local factors in earth surface systems. *Ecological Modelling* **149**: 257–272.

Platt, W. J. B., Beckage, R., Doren, F., and Slater, H. H. 2002. Interactions of large-scale disturbances: prior fire regimes and hurricane mortality of Savanna pines. *Ecology* **83**: 1566–1577.

Platt, W. J. and Connell, J. H. 2003. Natural disturbances and directional replacement of species. *Ecological Monographs* **73**: 507–522.

Podur, J. J., Martell, D. L., and Csillag, F. (2003) Spatial patterns of lightning caused forest fires in Ontario, 1976–1998. *Ecological Modeling* **164**: 1–20.

Poulos, H. M, Camp, A. E., Gatewood, R. G., and Loomis, L. 2007. A hierarchical approach for scaling forest inventory and fuels data from local to landscape scales in the Davis Mountains, Texas, USA. *Forest Ecology & Management* **244**: 1–15.

Proulx, O. J. and Greene, D. F. 2001. The relationship between ice thickness and northern hardwood tree damage during ice storms. *Canadian Journal Forest Research* **31**: 1758–1767.

Puhe, J. and Ulrich, B. 2001. Implications of the deposition of acid and nitrogen. In: *Global Climate Change and Human Impacts on Forest Ecosystems*. Puhe, J. and Ulrich, B. (eds). Springer, Berlin.

Pyne S. J. 1995. *World Fire: The Culture of Fire on Earth*. Henry Holt, New York, USA.

Resh, V. H., Brown, A. V., Covich, A. P., *et al.* 1988. The role of disturbance in stream ecology. *Journal North American Benthological Society* **7**: 433–455.

Rhoads, A. G., Hamburg, S. P., Fahey, T. J., *et al.* 2002. Effects of an intense ice storm on the structure of a northern hardwood forest. *Canadian Journal Forest Research* **32**: 1763–1775.

Rich, R. L., Frelich, L. E., and Reich, P. B. 2007. Wind-throw mortality in the southern boreal forest: effects of species, diameter and stand age. *Journal Ecology* **95**: 1261–1273.

Richardson, D. M., Rundel, P. W., Jackson, S. T., *et al.* 2007. Human impacts in pine forests: past, present, and future. *Annual Review of Ecology, Evolution and Systematics* **38**: 275–297.

Romme, W. H. and Knight, D. H. 1981. Fire frequency and subalpine forest succession along a topographic gradient in Wyoming. *Ecology* **62**: 319–326.

Romme, W. H., Everham, E. H., Frelich, L. E., *et al.* 1998. Are large, infrequent disturbances qualitatively different from small, frequent disturbances? *Ecosystems* **1**: 524–534.

Rouault, G., Candau, J. N., Lieutier, F., *et al.* 2006. Effects of drought and heat on forest insect populations in relation to the 2003 drought in Western Europe. *Annals of Forest Science* **63**: 613–624.

Rowe, J. S. 1981. Concepts of fire effects on plant individuals and species. In: *The Role of Fire in Northern Circumpolar Ecosystems*. Wein, R. W. and Maclean D. A. (eds). John Wiley and Sons, New York.

Ryan, K. C. 2002. Dynamic interactions between forest structure and fire behavior in boreal ecosystems. *Silva Fennica* **36**: 13–39.

Ryerson, D. E., Swetnam, T. W., and Lynch A. M. 2003. A tree-ring reconstruction of western spruce budworm outbreaks in the San Juan Mountains, Colorado, USA. *Canadian Journal Forest Research* **33**: 1010–1028.

Sanford, R. L., Jr., Parton, W. J., Ojima, D. S., and Lodge, D. J. 1991. Hurricane effects on soil organic matter dynamics and forest production in the Luquillo Experimental Forest, Puerto Rico: Results of simulation modelling. *Biotropica* **23**: 364–372.

Sartwell, C. 1971. Thinning ponderosa pine to prevent outbreaks of Mountain Pine Beetle. In: *Proceeding Short Course on Precommerical Thinning of Coast and Intermountain Forests in the Pacific Northwest, February 3–4, 1971*, Pullman, Washington, DC.

Scatena, F. N. 1998. Climate change and the Luquillo Experimental Forest of Puerto Rico: Assessing the impacts of various climate change scenarios. *American Water Resources Association TPS-98-2*: 193–198.

Scatena, F. N. and Larsen, M. C. 1991. Physical aspects of Hurricane Hugo in Puerto Rico. *Biotropica* **23**(suppl.): 317–323.

Scatena, F. N. and Lugo, A. E. 1995. Geomorphology, disturbance, and -the soil and vegetation of two subtropical wet steepland watersheds of Puerto Rico. *Geomorphology* **13**: 199–213.

Schaberg, P. G., DeHayes, D. H., and Hawley, G. J. 2001. Anthropogenic calcium depletion: A unique threat to forest ecosystem health? *Ecosystem Health* **7**: 214–228.

Schaetzl, R. J., Johnson, D. L., Burns, S. F., and Small, T. W. 1989. Tree uprooting: a review of terminology, process, and environmental implications. *Canadian Journal Forest Research* **19**: 1–11.

Schellekens, J., Bruijnzeel L. A., Scatena F. N., *et al.* 2000. Evaporation from a tropical rain forest, Luquillo Experimental Forest, eastern Puerto Rico. *Water Resources Research* **36**: 2183–2196

Schellhaas, R., Camp, A. E., Spurbeck, D., and Keenum, D. 2000. Report to the Colville National Forest on the results of the South Deep watershed fire history research. USDA Forest Service PNW Research Station, Wenatchee Forestry Sciences Laboratory.

Shepon, A. and Gildor, H. 2007. The lightning-biotic climatic feedback. *Global Change Biology* **14**: 440–450.

Shinneman, D. J. and Baker, W. I. 1997. Nonequilibrium dynamics between catastrophic disturbances and old-growth forests in ponderosa pine landscapes of the Black Hills. *Conservation Biology* **11**: 1276–1288.

Shorohova, E., Fedorchuk, V., Kuznetsova, M., and Shvedova, O. 2008. Wind-induced successional changes in pristine boreal *Picea abies* forest stands: evidence from long-term permanent plot records. *Forestry* **81**: 335–359.

Shortle, W. C. and Smith, K. T. 1988. Aluminum-induced calcium deficiency syndrome in declining red spruce. *Science* **240**: 1017–1018.

Shortle, W. C., Smith, K. T., and Dudzik, K. R. 2003. Tree survival and growth following ice storm injury. *USDA Forest Service Northeastern Research Station, Research Paper NE-723*

Siccama, T. G., Bliss, M., and Vogelmann, H. W. 1982. Decline of red spruce in the Green Mountains of Vermont. *Bulletin Torrey Botanical Club* **109**: 162–168.

Siegert, F., Ruecker, G., Hinrichs, A., and Hoffman, A. A. 2001. Increased damage from fires in logged forests during droughts caused by El Nino. *Nature* **414**: 437–440.

Skärby, L., Ro-Poulsen, H., Wellburn, F. A. M., and Sheppard, L. J. 1998. Impacts of ozone on forests: a European perspective. *New Phytologist* **139**: 109–122.

Slik, J. W. F. 2004. El Niño droughts and their effects on tree species composition and diversity in tropical rain forests. *Oecologia* **141**: 114–120.

Soja A. J., Tchebakova, N. M., French, N. H. F., *et al.* 2006. Climate-induced boreal forest change: Predictions versus current observations. *Global and Planetary Change* **56**: 274–296.

Stark, R. W. 1987. Impacts of forest insects and diseases: significance and measurement. *CRC Critical Reviews in Plant Sciences* **5**: 161–201.

Stone, R. 2008. Natural disasters: Ecologists report huge storm losses in China's forests. *Science* **319**: 1318–1319.

Strauss, S., Bednar, L., and Mees, R. 1989. Do one percent of the forest fires cause ninety-nine percent of the damage? *Forest Science* **35**: 319–328.

Sturm, M., Racine, E., and Tape, K. 2001. Climate change: increasing shrub abundance in the Arctic. *Nature* **411**: 546–547.

Swetnam, T. W. and Lynch, A. M. 1993. Multi century, regional-scale patterns of western spruce budworm outbreaks. *Ecological Monographs* **63**: 241–246.

Takahashi, K., Aril, K. and Lechowicz, M. J. 2007. Quantitative and qualitive effects of a severe ice storm on an old-growth beech-maple forest. *Canadian Journal Forest Research* **37**: 598–606.

Tainter, F. H. and Baker, F. A. 1996. *Principles of Forest Pathology*. John Wiley & Sons, Inc., New York.

Taiz, L. and Zeiger, E. 2006. *Plant Physiology.* 4th edition. Sinauer Associates, Inc., Sunderland, MA.

Tanaka, N. 2009. Vegetation bioshields for tsunami mitigation: review of effectiveness, limitations, construction, and sustainable management. *Landscape Ecological Engineering* **5**: 71–79.

Tanner, E. J. V. and Kapos, V. 1991. Hurricane effects on forest ecosystems in the Caribbean. *Biotropica* **23**: 513–521.

Tao, F. and Feng, Z. 2000. Terrestrial ecosystem sensitivity to acid deposition in South China. *Water, Air and Soil Pollution* **118**: 231–243.

Thies, W. G. 2001. Root diseases in eastern Oregon and Washington. *Northwest Science* **75**: (Special Issue) 38–45.

Thompson, J., Brokaw, N. V. L., Zimmerman, J., *et al.* 2002. Land use history, environment, and tree composition in a tropical forest. *Ecological Applications* **12**: 1344–2002.

Throop, H. L. and Lerdau, M. T. 2004. Effects of nitrogen deposition on insect herbivory: Implications for community and ecosystem processes. *Ecosystems* **7**: 109–133.

Turner, M. G., Baker, W. L., Peterson, C. J., and Peet, R. K. 1998. Factors influencing succession: lesson from large, infrequent, natural disturbances. *Ecosystems* **1**: 511–523.

Turner, M. G. and Dale, V. H. 1998. Comparing large, infrequent disturbances: what have we learned? *Ecosystems* **1**: 493–496.

Uriarte, M., Rivera, L. W., Zimmerman, J. K., *et al.* 2004. Effects of land use history on hurricane damage and recovery in a neotropical forest. *Plant Ecology* **174**: 49–58.

Valladares, F. 2008. A mechanistic view of the capacity of forests to cope with climate change. In: *Managing Forest Ecosystems: The Challenge of Climate Change.* Bravo, F. *et al.* (eds). Kluwer Academic Press.

Van der Molen, 2002. Meteorological impacts of land use change in the maritime tropics. PhD dissertation, Vrije Universiteit, Amsterdam.

Van Dyke, O. 1999. A literature review of ice storm impact on forests in Eastern North America. *SCSS Technical Report #112.* Pembroke, Ontario: Landmark Consulting.

Van Mantgem, P. J., Stephenson, N., Byrne, J. C., *et al.* 2009. Widespread increase in tree mortality rates in the Western United States. *Science* **323**: 521–524.

Van Wagner, C. E. 1973. Height of crown scorch in forest fires. *Canadian Journal Forest Research* **3**: 373–378.

Veblen, T. T., Kitzberger, T., and Donnegan, J. 2000. Climatic and human influences on fire regimes in ponderosa pine forests in the Colorado Front Range. *Ecological Applications* **10**: 1178–1195.

Veblen, T. T., Kitzberger, T., Raffaele, E., *et al.* 2008. The historical range of variability of fires in the Andean – Patagonian *Nothofagus* forest region. *International Journal of Wildland Fire* **17**: 724–741.

Veblen, T. T., Kitzberger, T., Villalba, R., and Donnegan J. 1999. Fire history in northern Patagonia: the roles of humans and climatic variation. *Ecological Monographs* **69**: 47–67.

Vygodskaya, N. N., Schulze, E. D., Tchebakova, N. M., *et al.* 2002. Climatic control of stand thinning in unmanaged spruce forests in the southern taiga in European Russia. *Tellus Series B – Chemical and physical meteorology* **54**: 443–461.

Walker, L. R. 1991. Tree damage and recovery from Hurricane Hugo in the Luquillo Experimental Forest, Puerto Rico. *Biotropica* **23**(suppl.): 379–385.

Walker, L. R., Zimmerman, J. K., Lodge, D. J., and GuzmánGrajales, S. 1996. An elevational comparison of growth and species composition in hurricane-damaged forests in Puerto Rico. *Journal Ecology* **84**: 877–889.

Wallenius, T. 2002. Forest age distribution and traces of past fires in a natural boreal landscape dominated by *Picea abies*. *Silva Fennica* **36**: 201–211.

Wallenius, T., Kuuluvainen, T., Heikkilä, R., and Lindholm, T. 2002. Spatial tree age structure and fire history in two old-growth forests in eastern Fennoscandia. *Silva Fennica* **36**: 185–199.

Weaver, P. L. 1989. Forest changes after hurricanes in Puerto Rico's Luquillo Mountains. *Interciencia* **14**: 181–192.

Weaver, P. L. and González, K. A. 2005. Wildland fire management and restoration. In: *12th Meeting of the Caribbean Foresters*. Weaver, P. L. and González, K. A. (eds). USDA Forest Service, International Institute of Tropical Forestry, Río Piedras.

Weber, M. H., Hadley, K. S., Frenzen, P. M., and Franklin, J. F. 2006. Forest development following mudflow deposition, Mount St. Helens, Washington. *Canadian Journal Forest Research* **36**: 437–449.

Westerling, A. L., Hidalgo, H. G., Cayan, D. R., and Swetnam, T. W. 2006. Warming and earlier spring increases western U.S. forest wildlife activity. *Science* **313**: 940–943.

Whigham, D. F., Olmsted, I., Cabrera Cano, E., and Harmon, M. E. 1991. The impact of Hurricane Gilbert on trees, litterfall, and woody debris in a dry tropical forest in the northeastern Yucatan Peninsula. *Biotropica* **23**(suppl.): 434–441.

White, P. S. and Jentsch, A. 2001. The search for generality in studies of disturbance and ecosystem dynamics. *Prog. Bot* **62**: 399–450.

White, P. S. and Pickett, S. T. A. 1985. Natural disturbance and patch dynamics: An introduction. In: *The Ecology of Natural Disturbance and Patch Dynamics*. Pickett, S. T. A. and White, P. S. (eds). Academic Press, New York.

Whitney, G. G. 1986. Relation of Michigan's presettlement pine forests to substrate and disturbance history. *Ecology* **67**: 1548–1559.

Wiens, J. A. 1989. Spatial scaling in ecology. *Functional Ecology* **3**: 385–397.

Williams, D. W. and Liebhold, A. M. 1995. Herbivorous insects and global change – potential changes in the spatial-distribution of forest defoliator outbreaks. *Journal Biogeography* **22**: 665–671.

Williams, R. J. and Bradstock, R. A. 2008. Large fires and their ecological consequences: an introduction to the special issue. *International Journal Wildland Fire* **17**: 685–687.

Wilmking, M., Juday, G. P., Barber, V. A., and Zald, H. S. 2004. Recent climate warming forces contrasting growth responses of white spruce at treeline in Alaska through temperature thresholds, *Global Change Biology* **10**: 1724– 1736.

Wittig, V. E., Ainsworth, E. A., and Long, S. P. 2007. To what extent do current and projected increases in surface ozone affect photosynthesis and stomatal conductance of trees? A meta-analytic review of the last 3 decades of experiments. *Plant Cell and Environment* **30**: 1150–1162.

Wittig, V. E., Ainsworth, E. A., Naidu, S. L., *et al.* 2009. Quantifying the impact of current and future tropospheric ozone on tree biomass, growth, physiology and biochemistry: a quantitative meta-analysis. *Global Change Biology* **15**: 396–424.

Wolf, A., Kozlov, M. V., and Callaghan, T. V. 2008. Impact of non-outbreak insect damage on vegetation in northern Europe will be greater than expected during a changing climate. *Climate Change* **87**: 91–106.

Wunderle Jr., J. 2009. From the past to the globalized future of Caribbean birds. *Journal Caribbean Ornithology* **21**: 69–79.

Wunderle Jr., J. M., Lodge, D. J., and Waide, R. B. 1992. Short-term effects of Hurricane Gilbert on terrestrial bird populations on Jamaica. *Auk* **109**: 148–166.

Xi, W. N., Reet, R. K., Decoster, J. K., and Urban, D. L. 2008. Tree damage risk factors associated with large, infrequent wind disturbances of Carolina forests. *Forestry* **81**: 317–334.

Yanagisawa, H., Koshimura, S., Goto, K., *et al.* 2009. The reduction effects of mangrove forest on a tsunami based on field surveys at Pakarang Cape, Thailand and numerical analysis. *Estuarine Coastal and Shelf Science* **81**: 27–37.

Yih, K., Boucher, D. H., Vandermeer, J. H., and Zamorra, Z. 1991. Recovery of the rain forest of southestern Nicaragua after destruction by Hurricane Joan. *Biotropica* **23**: 106–113.

Zausen G. L, Kolb, T. E., Bailey, J. D., and Wagner, M. R. 2005 Long-term impacts of stand management on ponderosa pine physiology and bark beetle abundance in northern Arizona: A replicated landscape study. *Forest Ecology & Management* **218**: 291–305.

Zeng, G. M., Zhang, G., Huang, G. H., *et al.* 2005. Exchange of Ca^{2+}, Mg^{2+} and K^+ and uptake of H^+, $NH4^+$ for the subtropical forest canopies influenced by acid rain in Shaoshan forest located in Central South China. *Plant Science* **168**: 259–266.

Zeng, H. C., Talkkari, A., Peltola, H., and Kellomaki, S. 2007. A GIS-based decision support system for risk assessment of wind damage in forest management *Environmental Modelling & Software* **22**: 1240–1249.

Zimmerman, J. K., Everham, III, E. M., Waide, R. B., *et al.* 1994. Responses of tree species to hurricane winds in subtropical wet forest in Puerto Rico: implications for tropical tree life histories. *Journal Tropical Ecology* **82**: 911–922.

Zimmerman, J. K., Aide, T. M., Rosario, M., *et al.* 1995. Effects of land management and a recent hurricane on forest structure and composition in the Luquillo Experimental Forest in Puerto Rico. *Forest Ecology & Management* **77**: 65–76.

Section III   FOREST HEALTH AND THE
             HUMAN DIMENSION

8

Timber harvesting, silviculture, and forest management: an axe does not a forester make

C.A. NOWAK, R.H. GERMAIN, AND A.P. DREW

8.1 Introduction

Silviculture and **forest management** are cores of the forestry profession. They are the sustainable way to plan and to conduct activities in a forest to control natality (birth), growth and development, and mortality (death) of trees and forest ecosystems to produce desired services and values (e.g., wood products, wildlife habitat, quality water, recreational experience). Forests are more than trees, and forestry additionally attends to other related forest elements and processes – but forestry (silviculture and forest management together) focuses on managing tree communities to create forests that satisfy societal needs.

Silviculture and forest management deal directly with baseline mortality by integrating a need to change forest conditions to meet landowner objectives, while creating a forest that exists in a **normal**, fully functioning state, with the latter defined in part by baseline mortality. A community of trees (from a stand to a forest) can exist in non-normal conditions for long periods, and by the baseline mortality concept, be unhealthy. Forestry activities can be used to bring an unhealthy community of trees to a more healthy state through regeneration and **tending** activities. These activities can be guided by tools such as **stocking charts** or stand-structure diagrams, which are based in large measure on the baseline mortality concept (*Note*: silviculturists and forest managers have been guided by baseline mortality long before it was an official concept).

Forestry as a profession has existed in its general current state of development for centuries, though generally only in the temperate zone of the northern

Forest Health: An Integrated Perspective, ed. John D. Castello and Stephen A. Teale. Published by Cambridge University Press. © Cambridge University Press 2011.

hemisphere. It has become more complex as societal interests and desires have increased in complexity, and as the level of ecological knowledge has increased. Today, people still recognize the need to harvest trees, but they also are concerned about the future condition of their forests.

Humans have exploited forests for thousands of years. Often, exploitation occurs when the forest is used to meet basic life needs such as heating and cooking. Exploitative forest use is commonplace even today. Exploitation not only is associated with fulfilling basic needs, but also occurs in developed countries where decisions are made to maximize current harvests without thought to healthy forests of the future. In reality, forestry is regularly practiced only on a small fraction of the world's forests. If however, the mere presence of trees is insufficient, then landowner objectives including the overall diversity of forest systems become important components of sustainability, and a broader perspective on forest health develops.

We expand on these ideas by exploring human uses of the forest and forest resilience, development of forestry as a discipline and profession, and common forestry tools that can be connected to the baseline mortality concept. The chapter includes a set of textboxes with case studies from around the world to illustrate these concepts and ideas.

8.2.1 Historical perspective

Forests were relatively unchanged by humans for much of the existence of *Homo sapiens*. It is with the use of land to grow crops, first in small patches and shifting systems, to sedentary, persistent clearing and use of forests as agricultural lands over the past 10 000 years, that humans began to significantly alter forests around the world. As human populations grew, the use of forest products increased, as did clearing of forest land for more agriculture to provide food for more people. Wood also was the foundation upon which early societies were built. Forests were regularly exploited for a long list of structural items required to sustain households and communities. Up until the 20th century, wooden equipment and related products were critical to industry and the machinations of war. Chief among those uses was metalworking, which required large supplies of wood for smelting and other processing.

Deforestation to supply human exploitative and extractive needs has not proceeded over the centuries and millennia uninterrupted, but has unfolded in fits and starts in association with the rise and fall of civilizations. The loss of forests not only exhausted the flow of various wood products necessary to sustain communities, but the accompanying land degradation contributed to a collapse of ecological conditions across the landscape. For instance, in 400 BC, wood scarcity became such a concern in Athens that both Plato and Aristotle promoted an early ecological consciousness by encouraging the protection of wooded hillsides in order to prevent massive soil erosion and flooding. The loss of topsoil and disruption of the water cycle resulted in crop failure, famine, and disease. People often were forced to emigrate to new forested frontiers and start anew, leaving behind a degraded landscape to begin the long process of recovery, which depended on the ecology of a given region. In some cases, the changes were irreversible. For example, with much of the Italian countryside deforested during the first century AD, the Romans exploited the forests of northern Africa, present day France, Spain, Germany, and England to sustain the Empire. After a century of exploitation, the Roman "provinces" began to resemble the sparsely forested Italian countryside. The loss of wood resources contributed to the collapse of the Roman Empire (Perlin 1989). Over the centuries, the forests of Central Europe have shown incredible resilience from repeated exploitation (see Textbox 8.1 How do we determine forest health in the ancient woodlands of Germany?); however, the more fragile landscape of northern Africa could not sustain repeated deforestation. Thus, the degree of forest resiliency has played a critical role in gauging forest health across a broad temporal scale.

Textbox 8.1 How do we determine forest health in the ancient woodlands of Germany?

Beyond the ruins of the Heidelberg castle lies the 800 ha Schlierbach Wald (forest), the largest of eight districts within the 3300-ha Heidelberg communal forest. The owner, in this case the city of Heidelberg, representing its citizens, defines the goals and objectives for the communal forest. The forest is managed under a multiple-use system, offering traditional commodity and non-commodity forest values including timber and firewood production, wildlife habitat, soil and water conservation, and a long list of recreational opportunities such as hiking, biking, bird-watching and hunting.

The Schlierbach forest shares the history of most temperate forests of Central Europe. Over the centuries, there has been massive exploitation, leading to cycles of deforestation followed by reforestation. The early 19th century ushered in a formal system of silviculture and forest management, which sustained Germany's forests through the industrial revolution of the late 1800s and two World Wars during the 20th century. Today, the Schlierbach forest is host to groves of 200-year old white oaks that represent the legacy of those early forest management initiatives. More commonplace are intensively managed even-aged stands of European beech (33%), Norway spruce (25%), Scots pine (10%), red and white oak (9%), Douglas-fir (7%), sweet

Textbox 8.1 (cont.)

chestnut (3%) and other hardwoods and softwoods varying in age from 10 to greater than 120 years old. Age classes are well distributed, providing a mosaic of vertical and horizontal diversity across the forest. Mortality is controlled and monitored through intensive management of each stand. Frequent tending operations throughout the rotation of each stand provide opportunities for "sanitizing" against forest pests and pathogens such as Neonectria canker on the beech or bark beetles on the Norway spruce. The Schlierbach wald is a good example of a regulated forest with a sustainable forest structure consistent with baseline mortality that is meeting landowner objectives of multiple uses and benefits. Are there some shortcomings in terms of biodiversity? Absolutely, but overall this forest can be considered healthy.

Sixteen hundred years later, the English found themselves in the same predicament as the Romans, having deforested their own land and forced to access timber elsewhere in Europe and beyond. In particular, an expanding British Navy was in dire need of large timbers for ship masts. Eventually, they were forced to exploit the virgin forests of the American colonies in New England.

In the cases of the Roman and British Empires, there was some acknowledgment and concerted effort to ameliorate the unsustainable consumption of forest resources. For instance, to buffer against wood shortages, Italian farmers of the first century began to practice short-rotation coppice silviculture with willow. The bark of the willow was used for turning rope while the stem was used for baskets, tools, chairs, and other household items. In 17th century England, it was the British Navy commissioners who requested the Royal Society to address the scarcity of timber. The result was John Evelyn's treatise on forestry, *Sylva*. In it he stated that "the waste and destruction of our woods has been so universal, nothing less than a universal planting of all sorts of trees will supply and well encounter the defect." He went on to insist that depending on natural regeneration (**resilience**) would be too slow since success would require complete curtailment of activities related to industry (ironworks) and farming. Not only did the book provide instruction on tree planting, but it played a vital role in instructing landowners to earn "continual and present profit" by coppicing hardwoods on an equal area over a 16-year rotation. Landowners were encouraged to be patient and to grow some trees into maturity for future use as timbers (Perlin 1989). Both examples highlight attempts to grow and harvest wood at sustainable levels. Although forest health is not the explicit goal, acknowledging that forests have value and require tending is perhaps a first step in promoting forest health.

8.2.2 Forests across the world today: resilient in the face of past exploitation

Reforestation following exploitation has occurred via natural and artificial means across much of the world, with the exception of some developing countries. Improvements in agricultural technology and productivity have contributed to this positive shift in forestlands. **Secondary succession**, also termed "natural regrowth", is returning forests to disturbed areas if kept free of ongoing disturbance, which has been reflected in an increase in the coverage of forests (FAO 2005). Natural regrowth is occurring in Europe and in the northeastern United States as forests recover from widespread deforestation in the 18th and 19th centuries (FAO 2005; Birdsey *et al.* 2006). The regrowth could be viewed in terms of the innate resiliency of forests, and their ability to recover following disturbance. Sometimes an unhealthy forest is only a temporary state leading to a healthy forest. Chestnut blight removed the American chestnut from forests of North America, but over time, has produced a healthy forest as oaks and hickories have replaced the chestnuts (Chapters 3 and 5). In some situations, the regrowth to a healthy forest may be viewed as a resilient transition made possible only by landowners' broader views or objectives.

Textbox 8.2 Effects of land use change on Puerto Rico's forests

In 1828, Puerto Rico's forests occupied 66% of a total land area of 890 300 ha, which by 1931 had decreased to 9%. Further deforestation led to a minimum forest area of 57 000 ha in 1948, 6% of island area. Population growth accompanied by unemployment led many farmers into subsistence agriculture such that from the 1800s into the mid-1900s many forests were converted to pasture and cropland. The early 20th century saw the growth of coffee as a major industry where much of the interior highlands were converted from natural forests to coffee shade plantations. When coffee declined as a major crop, the bushes were removed, but the shade trees remained. These tree species today dominate many of the secondary forests of Puerto Rico (Birdsey and Weaver 1982). The mid to late 1900s saw much of the island's population migrate to San Juan and other urban areas, or emigrate to the USA removing pressure off of disturbed lands in the interior and allowing forests to regrow.

Following the 1948 nadir, forested area increased to 9% in 1960, then dramatically to 32% in 1972 and to 57% in 2003 (Brandeis, *et al.* 2007). Throughout the late 1900s coffee plantations were abandoned, but served as

Textbox 8.2 (cont.)

sites of species regeneration from nearby seed sources. Although forest coverage in Puerto Rico had declined to 6%, and has since recovered, no noticeable loss of species has occurred (Lugo and Brown 1981). This may be a consequence of the many hectares of abandoned coffee shade trees that have probably served as refugia for native species regeneration in understories beneath former coffee shade. Since the highlands of Puerto Rico are highly dissected, species also could have survived on ridgetops and in ravines during periods of heavy disturbance. Little and Wadsworth (1964) and Little, *et al.* (1974) document 547 tree species native to Puerto Rico and the Virgin Islands.

Successive island-wide forest surveys in 1980 and 1990 illustrate changes that have occurred in stocked timberland categorized as active coffee shade, abandoned coffee shade, and secondary forest. In 1990, abandoned coffee shade understories had 1556 trees in the 5 cm diameter class compared to only 573 in the same class of active coffee shade. In 1980, the same figures were 1307 and 1068, respectively, as the abandoned coffee shade forests became more nearly similar to secondary forests in terms of numbers of trees in the smaller diameter classes (Birdsey and Weaver 1982; Franco, *et al.* 1997).

The imbalanced size distribution of the abandoned coffee shade has apparently been beneficial in terms of providing a suitable habitat for many shade-tolerant species that may not have been present in large numbers in nearby remnants of natural forest. Under the objective of timber management, such an imbalanced reverse J-curve would not have been tolerated, but the management objective of these forests was coffee, not commercial timber. Over the long run, these shifts will produce a healthy forest even though there has been a temporary, non-sustainable period of what might best be termed "unhealthy forest."

As noted earlier, the degree of resiliency will fluctuate based on the eco-region. Past deforestation in many arid regions (i.e., North Africa) has resulted in irreversible changes in species composition, sometimes leading to desertification. In North Africa, roughly along the 13th parallel, there are vast, dry lands bordering the Sahara – the Sahel. Fifty million poor, disempowered people live as pastoralists, nomads, and settled peoples here. Periodic droughts cause pulsed contractions in the forest along this great desert edge; infrequent, low level rain can lead to expansion. In this area of the world, growth and mortality of trees are strongly controlled by low rainfall – only 150–600 mm per year. Regular droughts coupled with tree cutting for home heating and cooking, overgrazing, overcultivation, and erosion of soils have led to a degradation and total loss of woodlands and forests (Kerkhof 2000). While the area is generally known as semi-arid grassland, it can be forest. The low resiliency of the Sahel system causes forest degradation when the ecosystem is stressed by either or both the environment and people. The baseline mortality concept supports the notion of an unhealthy forest here. The environment and people do not allow forests to recover from heavy use and drought so as to fully occupy areas of the Sahel.

The Food and Agriculture Organization of the United Nations (FAO) has assessed global forest resources every five to ten years since 1946. The net global change for 1990–2000 was ~8.9 million ha, and between 2000 and 2005 deforestation resulted in a net loss of forest area of 7.3 million ha per year. Comparing the two periods leaves one to believe that the net rate of forest loss is slowing down (FAO 2005). But, the marked reduction in deforestation is due to new plantings as well as natural expansion of existing forests (FAO 2005). It is the latter – the expansion of existing forests – that indicates a basic resiliency in forest systems that is a basis for forest health as defined by both landowner objectives and forest function, or baseline mortality. Planting is a silvicultural and forest management activity that also is in line with forest health.

The greatest deforestation by region is occurring in South America and Africa (FAO 2005). Deforestation in South America is due primarily to conversion of rainforest in Brazil to soy production and cattle ranching, although Brazil has invested heavily in high yield, intensively managed, short rotation (5 to 15 years) fiber plantations as well. Recent falling prices for soy and beef have helped to slow down Brazil's high deforestation rate. As crude oil prices increase, palm-oil farming for bioenergy becomes increasingly attractive to farmers in the Amazon and Congo basins and provides economic justification for further clearing of rainforests. Loss of forests in Africa relates to shifting cultivation and removal of wood for fuelwood purposes. Regions of greatest forest gain include China due mainly to their large-scale afforestation programs, and Europe due to natural regrowth of forest, a decrease in total volume of wood removals, and an increase in productive forest plantations. The focus of forest management in Central Europe has shifted away from wood production towards conservation of biological diversity, protection, and multiple uses.

8.2.3 Primary forest

"Forests of native species, in which there are no clearly visible indications of human activity and ecological processes are not significantly disturbed," (FAO 2005) accounts for 36% of the global forest area. Six million

Figure 8.1 A native Dominica forest stand being exploited through selective cutting of large gommier (*Dacryodes excelsa*) (foreground; right side of photo). This tree apparently was harvested illegally with logs processed into lumber right at the site (see boards on the ground in the middle of the photo). Photo by A. P. Drew.

hectares of these forests were lost or modified each year since 1990 due in part to deforestation as well as selective logging and other human interventions. Illegal removal of trees from natural forests is practically invisible and makes accounting for disturbance difficult, if not impossible (Figure 8.1). The problem is pervasive throughout Asia, Africa, South and Central America, and the Caribbean.

Textbox 8.3 Selective harvesting in Caribbean forests

Dominica, independent from Great Britain since 1978, has maintained large acreages of intact forest. The Caribbean island, located in the Lesser Antilles, has 61% of its total land area in forests compared to 29% for countries of Central America and the Caribbean (FAO 2001). The forests of Dominica are part of the regional *Dacryodes-Sloanea* rainforest association. *Dacryodes excelsa*, known locally as gommier, constituted 22.3% of all forest species with a diameter equal to or exceeding 30 cm dbh (diameter breast height) according to a 1987 FAO forest inventory (DeMilde 1987).

Dominica's forests are relatively intact and "undisturbed" according to many sources. According to EarthTrends (2003) the original forest coverage of Dominica was 65%, not far from its present forest coverage of 61%.

Textbox 8.3 (cont.)

Commercial logging companies have not been able to operate successfully in Dominica due to the mountainous terrain and lack of good roads in the interior.

Gommier, a large evergreen tree attaining a height of 37 m with a diameter of 90 to 150 cm, is the main commercial species being used for furniture and cabinet-making, flooring and construction (see Chapter 3). The FAO survey (FAO 1989) pointed to a "slow, but definite, degradation" of the forest resource. Gommier was said to be in decline with larger trees being hollow or rotten and with a lack of regeneration along with fewer young trees in the understory (DeMilde 1987). If a high proportion of overmature trees are felled, other species may come to dominate the canopy changing the forest species composition.

Today, gommier is being harvested, as it has for some time, in areas not leased for this purpose. Throughout the island, individuals with chainsaws will cut large trees illegally from the forest whether protected or not (David Lang, personal communication). They are adept at felling a tree, cutting it into straight-edged boards at the site of felling, and carrying them directly to market without the tree having to be run through a sawmill. The logger is both harvester and seller, thus avoiding the "middleman." Over the years, much of the forests of Dominica have been selectively harvested in this manner. There apparently have been no surveys of this type of forest damage, but it is similar to the high-grading that characterized northeastern forests of the USA, although it differs in that often only a single large individual is removed. The age and size class distribution of the forest is changed over the short term, producing an unhealthy forest in which the long-term result is a different species composition of the forest. Observed mortality is low in the smaller diameter classes, well below baseline mortality, while the observed mortality (selective removal) in the larger diameter classes is higher than baseline mortality, producing an unstable age structure.

8.2.4 From forest exploitation to forestry

Forestry is the "profession embracing the science, art, and practice of conserving forests and associated resources for human benefit in a sustainable manner to meet desired goals, needs and values" (Helms 1998). Kimmins (1992; 1997) described forestry and its development along the following four-phase model.

8.2.5 The phases of forestry

Phase I: Preforestry

- Much of human existence
- Forest directly provides basic life needs (food, shelter)
- End of preforestry is associated with population growth and unregulated exploitation of forest land for other land uses (agriculture) or extraction of trees for secondary uses (war, industry)
- Exploitative and extractive uses of forests exceed natural regenerative capacity and leads to regional deforestation and shortages in wood supply
- Depletion of forest resources and shortages of wood and other forest-based values and services results in the development of forestry.

Phase II: Forestry stage 1 – administrative forestry

- Laws, rules and regulations are set to control harvesting of trees
- Administrative focus is on a regular supply of forest products, mainly for industry or military, although sometimes for wildlife and protection (e.g., feudal game lands)
- Lack of ecological foundation results in a non-sustainable system and the development of stage 2.

Phase III: Forestry stage 2 – ecologically based forestry

- Forestry practices are based on scientifically derived, ecologically based knowledge
- Forestry based on science sustains functional processes of forest ecosystems, and sustained supply of conventional forest products ("sustained yield management")
- May not lead to the sustaining of all the values desired by a wealthy, post-industrial society (e.g., biodiversity, aesthetics, spiritual renewal), leading to the final stage of forestry development – social forestry.

Phase IV: Forestry stage 3 – social forestry

- Ecologically based and biologically sustainable
- Sustains a wide variety of social and environmental values in forested landscapes
- Emphasizes stakeholder involvement in planning and accounting of forest management.

Kimmins' phases of forestry development parallel Maslow's *Hierarchy of Needs*. When people must use the forest for basic life needs of food and shelter, concerns for sustainability and forest health are very low. It is only with the removal of people from a direct life-needs connection to forests that the later phases of development can occur. This is as important today as in the past – because in many places in the world the use of the forest is still primary, where trees and forest ecosystems are necessary to meet basic life needs. Forest health concerns are low in these places.

Forestry today in many places around the world are fully in Kimmins' fourth phase where ecological, social and economic elements of management have been joined to produce a multidimensional complex representing sustainable development and management. This holistic concept has been developed over the past two decades through various conferences and conventions, including the World Commission on Environment and Development set up by the United Nations in 1983, led by Brundtland, where the following definition was provided in the *Our Common Future* report: "**Sustainable development** is development that meets the needs of the present without compromising the ability of future generations to meet their own needs" (Brundtland 1987) (as described in Burger (2000)). In 1992, the United Nations held the world "Conference on Environment and Development" in Rio de Janeiro. At this conference, sustainable development was described as a global partnership for economically viable, socially just, and environmentally sound development. The conference led to the Biodiversity Convention and the Framework Convention on Climate Change, where the importance of forests to sustainable development was framed, and a definition of sustainable forest management was developed. The criteria and indicators of forest sustainability became known as the Montreal Process. In a separate, related effort in Helsinki 1993, a joint response from Europe was made to the many forest-related decisions from Rio at the Conference on Security and Cooperation in Europe that focused on the development of criteria and indicators for the sustainable development of boreal and temperate forests. In concert with these developments was the evolution of certification as a means of marketing and expanding the implementation of sustainable forest management – this fourth stage of the development of forestry. Today, millions of hectares of forest land have been certified as being well managed and sustainable by various certification bodies. Forest health as defined in this text is central to sustainable management of forests and forest certification. The sustainable production of forest values and services are predicated on a healthy forest. Forest management focuses on creating and maintaining healthy and productive forest systems as an outcome of management, with an expectation that the outputs of benefits and services are to be sustainably available from those forest systems. In relation to the baseline mortality concept, the general approach to management is to create and to maintain – manage – forests so that they have a high degree of site occupancy at all stages of forest development – from newly regenerated to primary, old-growth – with a diversity of tree species. The core ideal here is that a sustainable system is one that can adapt to change (Holling 1978). It directly follows that the diversity of elements in a system (in our case the diversity of tree species in a forest) provides for the capacity to change. For example, if an insect or disease develops that extirpates a tree species from a forest, other species of trees in the forest can expand their presence and still produce a normal, functioning, healthy forest – that is, one that follows normal baseline mortality, and is set to meet the broad array of societal interests and needs.

8.3.1   *Silviculture as the core discipline in forestry*

Silviculture is the art and science of controlling the establishment, growth, composition, health and quality of stands to meet the diverse needs of landowners and society on a sustainable basis (Helms 1998). Silviculturists conduct forestry work along four main lines of function: control, protect, facilitate, and salvage (Nyland 2002). All four functions bear upon forest health and baseline mortality. Natality and mortality are controlled by the addition and removal of trees and other organisms (e.g., insects, deer, interfering plants) over time, and by changing site conditions (e.g., site preparation for regeneration, fertilization or liming) to create new habitats for trees. Populations of trees are protected from damage due to artificial agents, such as timber harvesting, and natural agents such as wind, ice, snow, insects, and diseases. Access to forest ecosystem services and values are facilitated by efforts to control and to protect tree communities. And, finally, if there is a breakdown in the system and trees die at rates that are in excess of landowner objectives or in amounts that are inconsistent with normal processes (such as associated with the baseline mortality concept), silviculture is set to salvage values by judicious harvest of trees so as to tend to the remaining trees; or as a means to foster the reproduction of a new forest through artificial (seeding or planting) or natural regeneration (Figure 8.2).

Stands are the central unit in silviculture for forestry practice. Stands are units of land, generally tens to hundreds of hectares in size defined by tree cover that is uniform in density, structure, and species composition to make them practically meaningful for planning, manipulation, and management. Stand uniformity is the result of uniform site conditions coupled with similar disturbance history and availability of tree propagules. Stand uniformity allows for predictable responses to change as produced by silviculture.

In contrast to silviculture, forest management occurs at the forest level. Forests are ecosystems "characterized by a more or less dense and extensive tree cover, often consisting of stands varying in characteristics such as species composition, structure, age classes, and associated processes; and commonly

Figure 8.2 Timber harvesting can be part of a healthy forest – it can work within the baseline mortality concept via the application of silviculture and forest management, and can be a featured part of meeting landowner objectives as usually associated with commodities from sawn trees, and by creating new forests that are rich in tree species as a basis for future values and services (logging operation from northern New Hampshire, northeastern United States). Photo by C. A. Nowak.

including meadows, streams, fish and wildlife" (as defined by the Society of American Foresters; see Helms 1998). Forests include "special kinds such as industrial forests, non-industrial private forests, plantations, public forests, protection forests, and urban forests, as well as parks and wilderness." In forest management, forests are collections of stands that can range from hundreds to many thousands of hectares in size. Forest management effects on tree populations are produced by the collective effects of silviculture over time, and related activities as produced at the stand-level. **Forest management** includes the organization of silvicultural activities to produce desired, forest-level effects of tree community change, based on scientifically derived information from biology and ecology, by careful renewal and tending of communities of trees and associated plants, to sustainably produce benefits and values that are desired by a landowner (Helms 1998). Efforts to affect forest health then occur one stand at a time through silviculture.

Forests are commonly used without silviculture, specifically in association with timber harvesting. Many landowners and land users are not willing or capable of making the necessary investments of capital and knowledge to conduct silviculture and forest management. In the northeastern USA, over the past few decades silviculture has occurred on only a small portion of forest land harvested for timber (Munsell and Germain 2007). In terms of Kimmins' stages of forest development, the USA, Europe, Australia, and other such developed parts of the world are purportedly in a final stage, yet much forest land is being treated as if the country is in an exploitative phase. Throughout the world, forestry is being practiced at a much lesser rate, if at all.

Harvesting of trees without silviculture or forest management can jeopardize the sustained production of some, if not most, forest values. Without careful tending and regeneration of tree communities, tree population structure, density, and species composition can become unbalanced. Extractive, exploitative uses of wood products from forests – that is, forests being used without silviculture and forest management – can lead to unsustainable populations of trees, and eventually unhealthy forest conditions. Silviculture is a tool to promote forest health by carefully managing the balance of diverse tree populations to sustainably meet societal needs over time and space.

8.3.2 Silvicultural tools and baseline mortality

Silviculture is very simply framed as the need to follow two general acts with tree communities: (1) **regeneration**, and (2) **tending**. In **even-aged systems** – where there is dominantly only one age class of trees – these acts occur separately over time. In **uneven-aged systems** – where there are dominantly three or more age classes of trees – these acts both occur in a stand at the same time. Silvicultural systems (plans and procedures for the different silvicultural interventions in time and space) have been developed over the past few centuries to produce desirable direction in the course and rate of stand development and forest succession. Changes in course and rate are developed by controlling birth (natality), growth and development, and death (mortality) of trees.

Various tools have been developed to manage even-aged and uneven-aged stands by controlling birth, growth, and death of trees in ways that are directly related to the baseline mortality concept. Two examples of these tools are presented: density management in even-aged stands, and structure management in uneven-aged stands. Both are based on an ecological foundation, including the baseline mortality concept as embodied in long-standing understanding of species survivorship patterns (Figure 8.3).

8.3.3 Density management in even-aged stands

Mortality usually occurs in even-aged stands of trees (and all plants for that matter) at constant and predictable rates as associated with density-dependent processes (mostly competition), at least until trees in a stand approach biological maturity. Competition among trees for space and limited resources (sunlight, water, and nutrients) occurs as soon as trees grow and

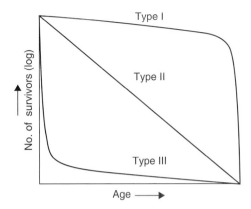

Figure 8.3 Hypothetical survivorship curves (after Deevey 1947, as cited in Barbour, *et al.* 1987, with permission). Tree populations generally follow a Type II Survivorship Curve. In relation to the baseline mortality concept, average stand diameter for an even-aged stand and average diameter for each age cohort in an uneven-aged stand can be used in place of "Age" on the x-axis. This graphical portrayal of population response over time is a key ecological underpinning of the baseline mortality principle, and for the various density and stand structure management tools used in silviculture.

interact with each other. Initiation and intensity of competition is a function of the number of trees per unit area and their size. Fewer, bigger trees may produce the same level of competition and mortality as many, smaller trees in the same area. Few, small trees in an area will have less competition than many small trees in the same area.

The relationship among the number of individuals, their size, and the degree of competition has been quantitatively studied so as to produce tools for applying silviculture. One first such tool is Reineke's Stand Density Index (SDI) model, which depicts the relationship (log-log) between numbers of trees per unit area and average diameter (Figure 8.4). The Reineke SDI model allows a practitioner to judge the current state of competition (degree of crowdedness) within a stand against the standard, normal maximum. A variety of different types of stand density management tools have been developed over the past 50 years using SDI as a foundational concept.

Silviculture is commonly used to control competition among trees in a stand with reference to the level of normal competition and mortality that is expected to occur without management or other exogenous disturbance (Smith *et al.* 1997; Nyland 2002). If a population of trees is experiencing abnormal patterns of mortality and/or inter-/intra-specific relationships with other organisms within a stand, it will not develop normally, nor will it respond to silviculture in predictable ways. A healthy stand is expected to proceed toward a normal

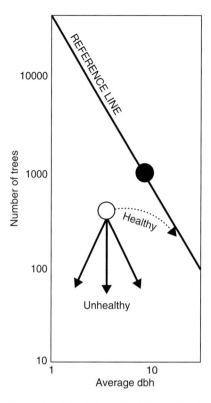

Figure 8.4 Reineke's original Stand-Density Index diagram as a model for tools used in silviculture to judge and to regulate stand density for various management objectives in even-aged stands (from Reineke 1933, as cited in Daniel, *et al.* 1979, with permission). The upper curve is the reference curve – it is the maximum number of trees per average stand diameter (where the average stand diameter is the diameter at breast height [DBH] of the tree of average basal area) (DBH is the diameter of a tree stem at 1.37 m above ground line). The curve is known as the "normal" curve = the normal number of trees for a given average stand diameter without undue influences of exogenous disturbance agents. Exogenous disturbance will move a stand (current stand; closed circle) to a position lower on the stand development surface (open circle). A healthy stand is expected to recover from outside disturbances and grow back to the reference curve (see dashed curve/ arrow – the trajectory of stand development) – if it does not (three solid arrows for three different possible directions for stand development), then we have an unhealthy stand. NOTE: The reference line curve is essentially the same as the baseline mortality curve – it represents how a stand will develop over time with normal stand development. In most areas of the world the unhealthy conditions in a stand may shift to healthy with enough time, specifically as the unhealthy species are replaced by other species.

state that is represented by the maximum expressed relationship between tree size and number of trees per unit area. If a healthy population of trees is disturbed, and the relationship between tree size and numbers changed, the stand will develop to regain a normal state. An unhealthy population is one that does not develop back to normality (Chapter 1).

8.3.4 Structure management in uneven-aged stands

Uneven-aged stands are defined by the presence of trees in three or more, somewhat balanced age classes, either mixed or in small groups (Helms 1998; Nyland 2002). Foresters use silviculture to balance age classes in uneven-aged stands by controlling stand structure. Structure in both unmanaged and managed uneven-aged stands has been persistently observed to follow characteristic reverse J-shape diameter distributions (Figure 8.5), which are essentially the same as the baseline mortality curve, but are applicable to a stand. The baseline mortality concept typically is used to describe forest or landscape patterns of tree abundances over time (where time is represented by a chronosequence of observed stand conditions).

Uneven-aged stands of trees can be viewed in three ways as a basis for management: (1) maximum age/size of tree allowed in a stand; (2) measured abundance of trees across all age and size classes; and (3) relative presence of trees by size class (Daniel *et al.* 1979), all of which are expressed in the stand structure curve, or diameter distribution diagram (Figure 8.5). The position of the curve on the abscissa is fixed by the presence of the largest diameter trees. Height of the curve is a function of the stocking level, or total number of trees and the space that they occupy. The maximum size of trees left in a stand with silviculture is controlled by the type of tree species and the site quality. Slope of the curve is determined by the distribution of trees across diameter classes, where diameter class is viewed as an index of age – smaller trees are young and larger trees are old. The slope of the curve has historically been defined by a diminution quotient (q), which is the number of trees in any diameter class related to the number of trees in the next highest diameter class. Values of q typically range from 1.3 to 2.0, when 2 inch (5 cm) diameter classes are used to describe stand structure. A low q produces a flat curve, and a high q produces a steep curve.

Management of uneven-aged stands is based on comparing the diameter distribution of a stand with the desired distribution. The desired distribution always follows a reverse-J shape, but its height and length depend on treatment cycle length (years between silvicultural interventions) and size of tree at maturity, which is defined by the land owner. Deficiencies and excesses of trees in the various diameter classes are accounted for, and decisions are made on whether a

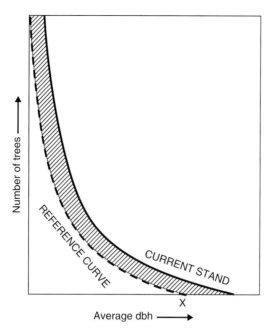

Figure 8.5 Diameter distribution of a balanced uneven-aged stand under intensive management, indicating the number of trees of different diameter classes that could be removed in a single cutting using selection system methods. (From Smith, *et al.* 1997, with permission; also see Nyland 2002.) All trees larger than diameter X, which has been set as the index of rotation age, are removed as being mature, making space in the stand for a new age class of trees. The trees smaller than X also are reduced in abundance with thinning (see hatched area between curves – all these trees would be removed through harvesting). Removing trees from across the diameter classes creates a new stand with a balanced structure causing the stand to uniformly grow back to a new, current stand curve. This system provides for continuous supply of forest products and consistent forest conditions associated with the balanced presence of trees at a stand level (uneven-aged stand). NOTE: The diameter-distribution curves can be converted to straight lines by plotting logarithms of numbers of trees over arithmetic values of diameter at breast height. This transformed curve is the same as the baseline mortality curve used in this text, but at the stand level, rather than at a forest or landscape level.

silvicultural intervention is needed. The oldest trees in the stand may be considered mature. Removing trees in the mature age class through timber harvesting is based on a predetermined maximum tree size for that stand, which is dependent on landowner desires. Harvesting mature trees is considered as the regeneration component of the uneven-aged silvicultural system. Cutting trees in the younger age classes to structure a stand and reduce stocking is considered tending. By creating regeneration each time the stand is manipulated, and by caring for the stand by improving the vigor and growth of residual trees through thinning, a broad suite of forest conditions and associated values, including wood products, can be sustainably harvested. Silviculturally treated, uneven-aged stands generally have a balance of structure and density that allows for consistent stand conditions over time, and a regular, predictable, even flow of products.

8.3.5 Regulating forests – accumulating the effects of silviculture

The regularity in production across the forest has long been a goal of landowners and forest managers. Forest regulation is an important principle in forest management that focuses on balancing age and size classes of trees across stands to control the flow of both commodity and non-commodity products and services in perpetuity. Although the focus often is on the sustained yield of timber products, landowner objectives may dictate that water, wildlife, recreation, or biodiversity among others, take precedence. Regardless of the product, forest regulation seeks to ensure regular returns of values over the long term by meticulously controlling the degree of extraction and use of the forest in question. Managers must regulate growth and stocking, and balance cutting with growth increment based on the capacity of the forest in order to maintain consistent yields at regular intervals. The primary goal is to seek a stable relationship between inventory, harvest, and growth that provides the landowner with predictable outcomes into the future. The landowner must define the desired rotation age, using both economic and biological criteria. If the objective is to maximize the sustainable timber harvest volume, then the length of the rotation generally is defined using biological rules where **mean annual increment** is at its maximum. Economic criteria take into account the various markets for goods and services. For instance, local sawmills or pulp mills may prefer a specific log diameter that would economically justify cutting before biological maturity. On the other hand, wildlife or recreation objectives linked to promoting old-growth habitat may dictate rotation ages well beyond biological maturity. Forest regulation is best achieved in simplistic management regimes that feature plantations with one or two species – more often than not, pine species (Figure 8.6). (see Textbox 8.4: loblolly pine plantations in southeast United States). Achieving forest regulation in natural forests with mixed species can be far more complicated. Tree species diversity involves balancing a complex set of variables including a wide array of rotation ages, growth characteristics, regeneration requirements, commodity markets, and non-market values (Bettinger *et al.* 2009; Davis *et al.* 2001; Nyland 2002). If properly implemented, a regulated forest provides a sustainable forest structure, including diameter distribution that meets management objectives.

Figure 8.6 A plantation in the southeastern United States dominated by a single tree species – loblolly pine (*Pinus taeda*). This stand is an example of the pine forests that cover millions of ha of forest that can be considered healthy by the baseline mortality concept, and even in meeting landowner objectives, but there is concern over the low species diversity and its effect on long-term forest health (see Chapter 9). Photo by A. P. Drew.

Textbox 8.4 Loblolly pine plantations in southeast United States.

There are more than 87 million ha of forestland throughout the thirteen-state southeast United States. The area of forest is 60% of what it was in 1630 and 91% of what was present in 1907. Since the 1970s, the total area of forestland has remained relatively stable. An estimated 93% of the forestland is classified as timberland (81 million ha). Approximately 70% of the timberland belongs to private non-industrial and 20% by forest industry owners; 6% is in national forest, and 5% in other public ownership. Approximately 40% of the South is covered with pine trees. There are 12 million ha in natural pine stands, 9 million ha in mixed pine stands, and nearly 12 million ha in pine plantation. From the 1930s to the 1970s, the number of softwood plantations increased substantially. Many were established to conserve soil on abandoned agricultural lands. More recently, declines in agriculture and a shift in softwood timber production from public to private forests have increased rates of planting on crop and graze lands and conversions of native mixed-species stands to pine plantations. The area in pine plantations is expected to increase by 67% by 2040 (Wear and Greis 2002).

Textbox 8.4 (cont.)

Loblolly pine (*Pinus taeda*) is by far the most abundant species planted. It grows more rapidly than any other southern yellow pine species. On an average site, it can reach roughly 20 m in 25 years. Loblolly pine plantation forestry places a strong emphasis on timber products such as sawlogs, pulpwood, and woody biomass. More than half of the USA wood pulp supplies come from southern pines, of which a large portion is loblolly pine. Forestland owners are primarily interested in managing their forests for profit. Timber markets allow for commercial thinnings to begin between 12 to 18 years, followed by another thinning in 10 years then a final cut at 35 years. If there are lucrative markets for larger sawtimber, landowners may extend the final harvest to 45 years.

A well-managed loblolly pine plantation will support 1700 healthy stems at 13 cm dbh trees per hectare, and more than 600 healthy stems when they reach 25 cm dbh. At these densities, not enough light can break through the upper canopy to allow herbaceous plants and shrubs to thrive. Consequently, species diversity is low. Plantations do offer, however, some non-commodity values such as carbon sequestration, wildlife habitat, hunting enterprises, recreation, solace, soil conservation, and clean water to name a few.

The intensive silviculture ensures that the trees remain relatively healthy throughout the rotation, but is the forest healthy? Consider the spatial scale. Twelve million ha of monoculture pine plantations across the Southeast USA represents 15% of the forestland area. Many landowners in the Southeast USA have achieved a sustainable forest structure through forest regulation. With a variety of age classes, they can maintain an even flow of timber products, recreational opportunities, and wildlife habitat over the long term. Although plantation forestry introduces serious issues with biodiversity, it does meet the basic definition of a healthy forest using our concept. If we incorporate the relatively small plantation area into the larger forested acreage of 81 million ha, the negative attributes of plantation forestry, represented by highly sanitized monocultures, become more palatable.

8.4.1 Silviculture, or not, in the tropics

Much of what we described in this chapter for silviculture and forestry is based on experience and research in the temperate regions of the world over the course of the last 400 years. Silviculture as practiced in the subtropics and tropics is vastly different from the art and science as practiced in North America, Europe, and other temperate regions. Restrictive conditions in the tropics make it difficult to extrapolate temperate zone silviculture to the tropics. Early attempts to manage tropical forests on a sustained-yield basis focused on one or several commercial species, or particular species with characteristics making them amenable to temperate zone silvicultural practices (Mergen and Vincent 1987). Whereas natural stand silviculture and the methods associated with it are well known for temperate zone stands, in the tropics there are a number of factors that make these methods difficult to apply.

Perhaps the most commonly encountered difficulty is that tropical stands are exceedingly diverse. It is not uncommon to find between 100 and 300 tree species in a single hectare of neotropical forest (Gentry 1986). The high species diversity has been an overriding reason for the conversion of natural stands to pine, eucalyptus, or teak plantations in the tropics; i.e., an attempt at simplification. However, a recent emphasis on the planting of native species is a positive step towards diversifying forest stands (Boley *et al.* 2009; Pedraza and Williams-Linera 2003). The cutting of natural forests to establish plantations has been discouraged for some time. Additionally, mechanisms of pollination and seed dispersal as well as the phenology of fruiting and seed dispersal vary greatly from species to species making uniform stand treatments ineffective. Seed viability and longevity of rainforest trees are restricted. Adequate dispersal by wind is problematic, and animals play a greater role in seed dispersal than they do in the temperate zone (see Chapter 9). The buried seed bank also is less reliable than in the temperate zone. Soil nutrient capital and site resilience are low following disturbance. Many species are not adapted to disturbances such as wind or fire (see Chapter 7). Vines and the many unwanted species present high levels of competition for favored species. Aside from the biological problems, knowledge of species' silvics and ecology is meager. Much more needs to be learned about tropical moist forests before silvicultural practices can translate into sustainable timber production (Wadsworth 1997). Trained technical foresters and ecologists are needed in many tropical countries, because the wealth of silvicultural experience taken for granted in the temperate zone is lacking in the tropics.

Diameter-limit cutting has been used to regenerate moist tropical forests under the assumption that mature trees cover a younger understory waiting to be released. However, immature trees may be damaged in harvesting, smaller trees may remain unthinned and growing stock remains unbalanced (Wadsworth 1997) with regard to age/size class distribution, rendering the stand unhealthy. Species composition also is affected and stand quality suffers. Natural tropical forests are all-aged (i.e., by all-aged, we mean to imply many more age classes in an area than just three). Attempts to apply silvicultural practices to them usually result in unacceptable alteration of the reverse J-shaped distribution of tree size. Alternatively, "improvement treatments" aim to remove overmature or unwanted trees, leaving "useful" stems room to grow. Overstory removal and liberation thinning are common tools for improving a stand in this way (Hutchinson 1987). Enrichment planting focuses on establishing fast-growing tree species such as mahogany or eucalyptus that grow within existing secondary forest, eventually overtopping the native trees and producing a commercial crop (Weaver 1987). Conversion of natural forests to plantations is an attractive option in light of the difficulties outlined above. Natural forests are less productive than plantations, despite silvicultural treatment; however, the potential for the former to be more productive in terms of multiple benefits, e.g., wildlife, timber, water quality, biodiversity, and aesthetics is great.

Yet, specific examples of potentially successful silvicultural regeneration of tropical forests exist, and include the use of strip clearcutting as in the Palcazu Forest Management System in the Peruvian Amazon (Stocks and Hartshorn 1993), although the sustainability of the system has recently been challenged (Rondon *et al.* 2009 and post-reduced-impact logging) silviculture has been reported for Bolivian moist tropical forests where logging and additional stand treatments increased growth rates of non-commercial and commercial tree species (by 50 %) four years later (Peña-Claros *et al.* 2008).

8.5.1 *Forest health with regard to landowner type, objectives, and scale*

The health of a particular forest is linked to the goals and objectives of the landowner (see Chapter 1). For example, a government agency may have a goal of promoting biodiversity across the national forest system. It will attempt to achieve this goal through objectives that are realistic, measurable, and time specific. A forest products company with timberland assets may have a goal of sustained yield management for high quality saw logs. Similarly, it will support that goal with specific objectives. In both cases, if those respective goals and objectives are achieved at given spatial and temporal scales, it will contribute to the owner's perception and determination of whether their forestlands are healthy. Consequently, the definition of forest health through the eyes of the owner can be subjective (see Textbox 8.5 New York City Watershed – high forest cover does not equate to healthy forests). Forest management and silviculture can play a pivotal role in this determination. The application of silviculture and forest management to meet goals and objectives provides a level of predictability, and a means to monitor success. The highly regulated pine forests of the Southeast United States and Scandinavia represent management regimes that are both predictable and sustainable in relation to landowner goals and objectives.

Textbox 8.5 New York City Watershed – high forest cover does not equate to healthy forests

The forests of the northeastern United States provide a wealth of resources and ecosystem services to the urban and rural communities of the region. Perhaps most impressive of all, both economically and in terms of global media attention, the 406 000 ha forest of the Catskill/Delaware watersheds in New York State delivers over 4 billion liters of unfiltered water every day to over 9 million residents, commuters, and tourists in New York City. The area comprising the New York City Watershed Forest has a forest cover of approximately 80%. Forest ownership is approximately 75% private in this region, but New York State and New York City have combined land holdings totaling approximately 162 000 ha, including the 118 000 ha Catskill Forest Preserve. The goals and objectives of the private forestland owners play a critical role in maintaining the supply of high quality water to New York City.

The forested watershed is threatened by parcelization and development. Repeated exploitative harvesting that is often associated with property transfers has resulted in a degraded forest condition for timber management (Germain, *et al.* 2007). Although the forests are degraded (Munsell, *et al.* 2008), collectively across the 406 000 ha they do offer a balanced distribution of age and diameter classes (Germain, *et al.* 2007; Munsell and Germain 2007), indicating a sustainable forest structure consistent with baseline mortality. As long as water quality is maintained, which is the primary management objective, then we can state that the watershed forest is healthy. If, however, parcelization and development continue below the forest canopy, the watershed forest, while still defined as such based on forest cover, will witness a decrease in water quality from non-point source contamination such as lawn chemicals and fertilizers, septic systems, sump pumps, and fecal contamination; any of which can be intensified by an increase in impervious surface area. The forested landscape can invite forest cover complacency syndrome, or a false sense that as long as forest cover is widespread and stable, the forest will continue to provide benefits. The mere presence of trees on the landscape tells us little about the condition of the forest ecosystem and the flow of benefits it provides to human communities. Beyond a certain threshold, the forest will no longer meet its intended primary goal of supplying high-quality water. Other forest values also may be compromised. Landowner goals and objectives may dictate that this forest is no longer healthy (see Chapter 1).

The scale of the ownership will strongly influence what forest uses and values are emphasized. Large ownerships, spanning many thousands, even millions, of hectares, will likely have multiple goals and associated objectives that are more likely to incorporate multiple uses and values. In contrast, smaller ownerships with perhaps hundreds of hectares (or less), will often have simple goals with fewer objectives and ultimately far fewer options. As previously stated, the principles of baseline mortality are more easily applied to large areas (landscapes) such as the New York City Watershed, and less pertinent to individual forestland owners with small woodlots.

Globally, governments own an estimated 86% of the world's forests. Private ownership constitutes just over 10%, while communal forms of ownership make up the remaining 4% (Agrawal *et al.* 2008). In a global context, forest ownership varies widely. In general, the USA has the most forests under private ownership. Private ownerships are common in western Europe, whereas almost all forests in Asia, Africa, and Latin America are in public ownership. Government-owned forests come in various forms (e.g., many public forests are managed by dedicated government agencies or departments, at the federal, provincial, state, county, or township level). Forest managers customarily seek input, either voluntarily or by mandate, from stakeholders before implementing management activities. Goals and objectives are negotiated among stakeholders leading to multiple uses of the forest. Other public forests, particularly in developing countries, are managed as common property for multiple uses by local communities and community-based organizations. When public forests are treated as common property, extractive activities linked to peoples' livelihoods commonly take precedence over other uses (see Textbox 8.6 India – forest health in the face of high population densities and utilitarian demands). Many other forests classified under public ownership are effectively governed as private timber concessions by forest products companies. In this case, the forest is managed primarily for timber production.

> **Textbox 8.6** India – forest health in the face of high population
> densities and utilitarian demands (based on research
> by C. Ghosh, PhD candidate, SUNY-ESF).
>
> The panorama of Indian forests ranges from evergreen tropical rain forests in the Andaman and Nicobar Islands, the Western Ghats, and the northeastern states, to dry alpine scrub highlands in the Himalaya to the north. Between the two extremes, the country has semi-evergreen rainforests, deciduous monsoon forests, thorn forests, subtropical pine forests in the lower montane zone, and temperate montane forests (Lal 1989).

Textbox 8.6 (cont.)

India's natural resources are under extreme pressure from a growing population of people and livestock. Although it has only 2.5% of the world's geographic area, India holds 17% of the world's population at just over 1 billion people representing a population density of 324 people per hectare. Furthermore it is home to 18% of the world's livestock population with an estimated 841 million animals (2.6 head of livestock per hectare). The combination of population and livestock densities place enormous pressure on the country's forest cover. Currently, 19.5% (64 million ha) of India's total geographic area is under forest cover (defined as 10% forest cover over 1 ha), with 38 million ha classified as well stocked (crown density above 40%). The central government has a goal of increasing forest cover to 33% by 2012 through programs promoting plantations. These reforestation efforts are countered by on-going deforestation on a scale of 15 000 km^2 annually.

An estimated 92% of India's forests are in public ownership; with 65% administered by the central government, and 27% administered by community governments. The remaining 8% is in private ownership. Nearly 600 million rural people depend on forests either for their sustenance or livelihood (Srivastava 1999), of which 275 million are directly dependent on forest resources for their survival (Paine, et al.1997). The primary use of forests comes in the form of wood for heat and cooking. People source firewood by collecting woody debris on the forest floor, pruning live trees of lower branches, and, in some cases, cutting live trees, often illegally. The leaf litter is harvested and marketed as non-wood forest products (i.e., brooms) or collected to feed cattle. Fire is commonly used to promote and improve grazing opportunities for cattle. Poor fire management and indiscriminate grazing are among the most important causes of forest degradation (Rai and Saxena 1997).

This intensive use of forestland has severe impacts on forest regeneration, ecology, and biodiversity. Generally, observed mortality in the younger age classes is well above baseline mortality leading to an unsustainable situation (Nilsson 2008). Not only are the forests unhealthy in ecological terms, but these forests are not positioned to meet their utilitarian objectives and therefore represent an unhealthy forest.

Industrial forest owners with primary wood-manufacturing facilities traditionally place the highest priority on the sustained yield production of forest-based commodities such as veneer, saw logs, pulpwood, chipwood, and firewood. The growing number of institutional investment firms that own former industrial forestland place a similar emphasis on commodity production to ensure high returns for investors. Attention to other forest values depends on the company, ownership agreement (i.e., certification programs such as the Forest Stewardship Council and Sustainable Forest Initiative) and region of the world in which they operate.

Non-industrial forest owners represent another ownership category. Collectively, this ownership group is an important player in the USA, controlling nearly 60% of the country's forestland, but generally a minor component in other parts of the world. This ownership category, often referred to as "family forests," operates on a small spatial scale (parcels < 50 ha) and a short temporal scale (land tenure < 20 years). Although timber products are generated from these ownerships, the primary reasons for owning forestland are recreation, privacy, aesthetics, and wildlife. Management activities are customarily serendipitous with little regard to forest planning.

8.6 Summary

The sciences of silviculture and forest management are centuries old. They both have a broad-based underpinning that includes, at least indirectly, a baseline mortality concept. The science for silviculture and forest management was developed primarily in the temperate regions of the world over the last two centuries, mostly in Europe and North America, which means their application has not yet been effective in the tropics – effectiveness will only come with forest-specific study of ecology and silviculture. While available for broad application, in many places in the temperate regions of the world there has been little or no use of silviculture or forest management. Yet, forests are commonly there and often at fully functioning states due to the high resiliency of temperate forest systems. To a large degree, temperate forests, and apparently even most tropical forests, function with or without humans at a level that would be considered healthy from a baseline mortality concept. We can extract values and services from forests and not jeopardize forest health due to a breakdown in baseline mortality – it appears difficult to break baseline mortality. But, of equal concern to forest health in general is judging how diverse the system is in meeting landowner objectives, or in providing a stable forest ecosystem that comes with high levels of biodiversity. It is here, then, with the need to meet landowner objectives and to fashion stands and forests to have certain diversity of species, rather than any tree species, that silviculture and forest management bring most to bear in conserving forest health.

References

Agrawal, A., Chatre, A., and Hardin, R. 2008. Changing governance of the world's forests. *Science* **320**: 1460–1462.

Barbour, M.G., Burk, J.H., and Pitts, W.D. 1987. *Terrestrial Plant Ecology*. The Benjamin/ Cummings Publishing Company, Inc., Reading, MA.

Bettinger, P., Boston, K., Sirey, J.P., and Grebner, D.L. 2009. *Forest Management and Planning*. Elsevier, New York.

Birdsey, R.A. and Weaver, P.L. 1982. The forest resources of Puerto Rico, *USDA Forest Service Resource Bulletin,* SO-85, Southern Forest Experiment Station. New Orleans, LA.

Birdsey, R., Pregitzer, K., and Lucier, A. 2006. Forest carbon management in the United States: 1600–2100. *Journal Environmental Quality (published online)* **35**: 1461–1469.

Boley, J.D., Drew, A.P., and Andrus, R.E. 2009. Effects of active pasture, teak (*Tectona grandis*) and mixed native plantations on soil chemistry in Costa Rica. *Forest Ecology & Management* **257**: 2254–2261.

Brandeis, T.J., Helmer, E.H., and Oswalt, S.N. 2007. The status of Puerto Rico's forests. *USDA Forest Service Resource Bulletin,* SRS-119, Southern Research Station. Asheville, NC.

Bruntland, G. (ed.). 1987. *Our Common Future: The World Commission on Environment and Development*. Oxford University Press, Oxford.

Burger, D. 2000. Making Rio work: The vision of sustainable development and its implementation through forest certification. In: *Sustainable Forest Management*. von Gadow, K., Pukkalo, T., and Tomé, M. (eds.) Kluwer Academic Publishers, Boston.

Daniel, T.W., Helms, J.A., and Baker, F.S. 1979. *Principles of Silviculture*. McGraw-Hill Book Company, New York.

Davis, L.S., Johnson, K.N., Bettinger, P., and Howard, T.E. 2001. *Forest Management: To Sustain Ecological, Economic and Social Value*. 4th edition. Waveland Press, Inc., Long Grove, IL.

Deevey, Jr., E.S. 1947. Life tables for natural populations of animals. *Quarterly Review Biology* **22**: 283–314.

DeMilde, R. 1987. Inventory of the exploitable forests of Dominica. *Food and Agriculture Organization of the United Nations* (FAO), Rome.

EarthTrends. 2003. *EarthTrends Country Profiles*. Forests, Grasslands, and Drylands – Dominica. http://earthtrends.wri.org

Food and Agriculture Organization of the United Nations (FAO). 1989. Assistance for the preparation of a forest inventory, Dominica. Terminal statement prepared for the Government of Dominica. Food and Agriculture Organization of the United Nations, Rome.

Food and Agriculture Organization of the United Nations (FAO). 2001. Global Forest Resources Assessment 2000 – main Report. *FAO Forestry Paper 140*. FAO, Rome.

Food and Agriculture Organization of the United Nations (FAO). 2005. Global forest resources assessment 2005, Progress towards sustainable forest management. *FAO Forestry Paper 147*. FAO, Rome.

Franco, P.A., Weaver, P.L., and Eggen-McIntosh, S. 1997. Forest resources of Puerto Rico, 1990. *US Department of Agriculture Forest Service, Resource Bulletin, SRS-22.* Southern Research Station. Asheville, NC.

Gentry, A.H. 1986. An overview of neotropical phytogeographic patterns with an emphasis on Amazonia. *Proceedings 1st Symposium on Humid Tropics, Belem, Brazil, 12–17 Nov. 1984,* Vol. **2**: 21–35.

Germain, R.H., Anderson, N., and Bevilacqua, E. 2007. The effects of forestland parcelization and ownership transfers on non-industrial private forestland forest stocking in New York. *Journal Forestry* **105**: 403–408.

Helms, J.A. (ed.). 1998. *The Dictionary of Forestry.* The Society of American Foresters, Bethesda, MD.

Holling, C.S. 1978. *Adaptive Environmental Assessment and Management.* International Institute for Applied Systems Analysis, Wiley, Chichester.

Hutchinson, I.D. 1987. The management of humid tropical forests to produce wood. In: *Management of the forests of Tropical America: Prospects and Technologies. Proceedings Conference held in San Juan, Puerto Rico, September 22–27, 1986.* Figueroa, J.C., Wadsworth, F.H., and Branham, S. (eds). Institute of Tropical Forestry, Southern Forest Experiment Station, USDA Forest Service in cooperation with University of Puerto Rico, Rio Piedras.

Kerkhof, P. 2000. *Local Forest Management in the Sahel: Towards a New Social Contract.* SOS Sahel International UK, London.

Kimmins, J.P. 1992. *Balancing Act: Environmental Issues in Forestry.* University of British Columbia Press, Vancouver, BC.

Kimmins, J.P. 1997. *Forest Ecology: A Foundation for Sustainable Management.* 2nd edition. Prentice-Hall, Inc., Upper Saddle River, NJ.

Lal, J.B. 1989. *India's Forests: Myth and Reality.* Natraj Publishers, New Delhi, India.

Little, Jr., E.L. and Wadsworth, F.H. 1964. *Common Trees of Puerto Rico and the Virgin Islands. Agriculture Handbook No. 249.* USDA Forest Service, Washington, DC.

Little, Jr. E.L., Woodbury, R.O., and Wadsworth, F.H. 1974. *Trees of Puerto Rico and the Virgin Islands, Vol II. Agriculture Handbook No. 449.* USDA, Forest Service, Washington, DC.

Lugo, A.E. and Brown, S. 1981. Tropical lands: Popular misconceptions. *Mazingira* **5**: 10–19.

Mergen, F. and Vincent, J.R. (eds). 1987. Natural management of tropical moist forests: Silvicultural and management prospects of sustained utilization. *Yale University School of Forestry and Environmental Studies,* New Haven, CT.

Munsell, J.F. and Germain, R.H. 2007. Woody biomass energy: an opportunity for silviculture on nonindustrial private forestlands in New York. *Journal Forestry* **105**: 398–402.

Munsell, J.F., Germain, R.H., and Bevilacqua, E. 2008. A tale of two forests: case study comparisons of sustained yield management on Mississippi and New York nonindustrial private forestland. *Journal Forestry* **106**: 431–439.

Nilsson, S. 2008. The Indian forestry system at a crossroads: A outsider's view. *International Forestry Review* **10**: 414–421.

Nyland, R.D. 2002. *Silviculture Concepts and Applications.* 2nd edition. McGraw-Hill, New York.

Paine, J., Byron, N., and Poffenberger, M. 1997. Asia-Pacific Forestry Sector Outlook Study: Status, trends and future scenarios for forest conservation including protected areas in the Asia-Pacific Region. *FAO Working Paper No: APFSOS/WP/04.* www.fao.org/docrep/003/W5475E/W5475E06.htm [Accessed November 2010].

Pedraza, R.A. and Williams-Linera, G. 2003. Evaluation of native tree species for the rehabilitation of deforested areas in the Mexican cloud forest. *New Forests* **26**: 83–99.

Peña-Claros, M., Fredericksen, T.S., Alarcón, A., *et al.* 2008. Beyond reduced-impact logging: Silvicultural treatments to increase growth rates of tropical trees. *Forest Ecology & Management* **256**: 1458–1467.

Perlin, J. 1989. *A Forest Journey: The Role of Wood in the Development of Civilization.* W.W. Norton & Co., New York.

Rai, S.N. and Saxena, A. 1997. The extent of forest fires, grazing and regeneration status in inventoried forest areas of India. *Indian Forester* **123**: 698–702.

Reineke, L.H. 1933. Perfecting a stand-density index for even-aged stands. *Journal Agricultural Research* **46**: 627–638.

Rondon, X.J., Gorchov, D.L., and Cornejo, F. 2009. Tree species richness and composition 15 years after strip clearcutting in the Peruvian Amazon. *Plant Ecology* **201**: 23–27.

Smith, D.M., Larson, B.C., Kelty, M.J., and Ashton, P.M.S. 1997. *The Practice of Silviculture: Applied Forest Ecology.* 9th edition. John Wiley & Sons, Inc., New York.

Srivastava, R. 1999. Controlling forest fire incidences by generating awareness. A case study from Nilgiri Biosphere Reserve, Coimbatore, India. *International Forest Fire News* No. **20**: 10–15.

Stocks, A. and Hartshorn, G. 1993. The Palcazu Project: Forest management and native Yanesha communities. *Journal Sustainable Forestry* **1**: 111–135.

Wadsworth, F.H. 1997. *Forest Production for Tropical America. USDA Forest Service, Agriculture Handbook* **710**.

Wear, D.N. and Greis, J.G. (eds). 2002. *Southern Forest Resource Assessment. Gen. Tech. Rep. SRS-53.* Asheville, NC: USDA, Forest Service, Southern Research Station.

Weaver, P.L. 1987. Enrichment plantings in tropical America. In: *Management of the forests of Tropical America: Prospects and technologies. Proceedings Conference held in San Juan, Puerto Rico, September 22–27, 1986.* Figueroa, J.C., Wadsworth, F.H., and Branham, S. (eds). Institute of Tropical Forestry, Southern Forest Experiment Station, US Department of Agriculture, Forest Service in cooperation with University of Puerto Rico, Rio Piedras.

9

Biodiversity, conservation, and sustainable timber harvest: can we have it all?

S.P. CAMPBELL, D.A. PATRICK AND J.P. GIBBS

9.1 What is biodiversity?

Biodiversity is the variety of life at all levels of its organization, including genes, species, ecosystems, and their interactions. The description of every component of biodiversity yields a hierarchical structure (Figure 9.1). At the finest level of resolution are genes and their different forms (i.e., **alleles**) found by the thousands to millions within the nucleus of each and every cell of every individual organism. Scaling up we would see morphological variation among individuals of the same species, which is the physical expression of each individual's underlying genetic constitution. Groups of individuals are distinguished by shared genetic traits distinct from those shared by other such groups. These groups, typically called **evolutionary significant units** or ESUs, are less likely to breed with members of other such groups usually because of some kind of barrier, such as a mountain range (Ryder 1986). ESUs often are the precursors to new **species**, which are groups of individuals that are incapable of successfully interbreeding due to physical or behavioral incompatibilities (Mayr 1963). Species assemble into **communities**, which are groups of species that predictably occur together, and are linked to one another through energy/nutrient transfer, competition, mutualisms, predation, and other interactions. These linkages can be extremely tight (e.g., mutualisms) or very diffuse (e.g., species that simply occur at the same place and time but do not effectively interact). Finally, a **biome** encompasses all communities found within a larger region, and represents the highest level of the biodiversity hierarchy. Such collections

Forest Health: An Integrated Perspective, ed. John D. Castello and Stephen A. Teale. Published by Cambridge University Press. © Cambridge University Press 2011.

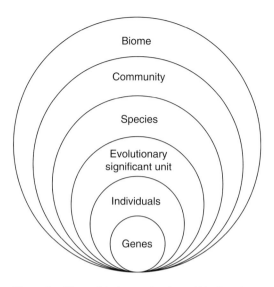

Figure 9.1 Hierarchical organization of biodiversity.

of communities are usually typical of a given biome, but different from those of another biome. Compare, for example, the many coniferous forest types characteristic of the boreal forest biome of higher latitudes with the many deciduous forest types that predominate in the temperate forest biome of mid-latitudes. The themes of relative similarity and divergence provide structure to biodiversity at all levels, from populations (more or less genetic similarity) to communities (more or less species overlap) and biomes (contrasts and similarities of communities).

Biodiversity is much easier to conceptualize and to define than it is to measure. Even a relatively straightforward measure of biodiversity such as species richness is nearly impossible to measure accurately. It has been attempted only once in a small forest (i.e., Monk's Woods) near Cambridge, England (Steele and Welch 1973). A team of scientists working for many years came up with a list of 3682 species, but even this list was incomplete for several groups and completely omitted microorganisms. It is even harder to characterize all the genetic variation present in an area, although scientists are trying, for example, by extracting all of the DNA that is present from organisms in forest soils or sea water, sequencing it, and using computer algorithms to sort out how many species might be present (O'Brien *et al.* 2005). Because of these practical difficulties, the diversity of species of some well-known indicator groups (e.g., birds) is most often used as a proxy for biodiversity and assumes, rightly or wrongly, that the number of species in the indicator group in an area reflects the numbers of species of other types of organisms in the same area.

Diversity generally refers to the number of species weighted by their relative abundances and is compiled at different spatial scales termed: alpha, beta, and gamma (Whittaker 1960). **Alpha diversity** or "within-habitat diversity" represents the species within a particular homogeneous habitat (e.g., a forest stand). **Beta diversity** or "among-habitats diversity" represents the turnover in species among different habitats (e.g., total number of species unique to either coniferous, mixed, or deciduous stands found in the forests of the Adirondack Mountains). **Gamma diversity** or "regional diversity" is a measure of overall diversity at a "geographic" scale, for example the total diversity of amphibian species in temperate deciduous forests.

Concepts of species diversity have important conservation implications. For example, maximizing diversity was historically a goal of wildlife scientists. However, simply saying more diverse areas are better can be misleading for two reasons. First, diversity does not necessarily correlate positively with species richness. For example, the bird community of a Malaysian forest exhibited a 10% increase in diversity following logging, but a 20–37% decrease in species richness (Grieser Johns 1997). Second, measures of diversity neglect the identity of the species involved (Noss 1983). If, for example, we count the number of species of birds found in open habitats, forest edges, and interiors of mature forest stands (i.e., alpha diversity), we typically find more species in the former two areas than the latter. But, when we look at differences between the kinds of birds in the three habitats (i.e., beta diversity), many of the species in the open and edge habitats are the same, and many of the species found in the forest interior are not found in edge or open habitats. Thus, increasing open and edge habitats will boost alpha diversity but at the expense of forest interior habitat, which ultimately reduces the diversity of birds in the entire landscape (i.e., gamma diversity).

9.2 Biodiversity and conservation biology

In the second half of the 20th century, the increasing attention directed towards understanding biodiversity and concern over its status gave rise to **conservation biology**, which is the study of phenomena that affect the maintenance of genes, species, communities, and ecosystems that comprise the biosphere. Conservation biology is a multidisciplinary discipline that draws on its roots in ecology, evolution, and systematics, as well as ethics, philosophy, economics, political science, and sociology (Hunter and Gibbs 2007). Not surprisingly then, this mixture of professional disciplines results in a diversity of views among conservation biologists on issues ranging from those as complex as the relative contributions of different processes to the distribution and loss of biodiversity to seemingly basic issues such as exactly what is meant by biodiversity. For example, many consider biodiversity simply as the plethora of species on earth, while others view it as the vast repository of genetic diversity that underlies all expression of biological diversity, and is therefore biodiversity in its most elemental form. Regardless of these differences, conservation biologists recognize that many components of the natural world are imperiled due to human activities, and they seek ways to understand and to mitigate the effects of these activities. In terms of forest biodiversity, conservation biologists are concerned with understanding the factors that control the distribution of biodiversity at global and local scales, the causes and effects of threats to forests and their biodiversity, and how to extract forest resources while maintaining forest biodiversity and forest health.

9.3 How does biodiversity relate to forest health?

Forest health means different things to different people, but for most people it occurs somewhere on the continuum between a utilitarian perspective (e.g., a healthy forest is one that meets the landowner's management objectives) and an ecosystem perspective (e.g., a fully functioning community of plants and animals and their physical environment) (Kolb *et al.* 1994). In an attempt to justify biodiversity conservation in utilitarian terms, research has been conducted to determine if forest ecosystems provide valuable economic services (e.g., watershed protection, carbon sequestration, wildlife habitat), and whether conserving biodiversity helps to maintain ecosystem functions (Simberloff 1999). The general conclusion is that biodiversity is key to ecosystem functioning, and it should always be a routine part of forest management policies (Hooper *et al.* 2005, Balvanera *et al.* 2006). Thus, healthy forests should be viewed as integrated biotic systems that yield a variety of services and values, which include but are not limited to products for human consumption.

The central premise of this textbook is the concept that the health of any forest can be assessed or monitored via its ability to (1) maintain a sustainable and stable diameter distribution (size structure resulting from a balanced relationship among regeneration, growth, and mortality; Manion and Griffin 2001, and Chapter 1 this volume), while (2) simultaneously meeting the landowner's management objectives. Defining forest health based on such a quantitative, ecologically based, and easy to measure metric is attractive, but how does the conservation of biodiversity fit into this concept of forest health?

Biodiversity conservation is implicitly included in this concept to the extent that it is compatible with a sustainable diameter distribution (size structure) (See Textbox 9.1). Conserving the highest levels of biodiversity, however, while

Textbox 9.1 Biodiversity and sustainable size structure

The maintenance of a stable and sustainable size structure may include elements of forest structure that are beneficial to biodiversity in many ways. First, a sustainable forest with a heterogeneous size structure and multiple layers of vegetation should provide habitats for more plant and animal species compared to a forest where the diameter distribution is more homogeneous (Tews *et al.* 2004; Bauhus 2009). Second, by retaining part of the forest as old growth with its associated structural legacies and horizontal and vertical heterogeneity, species dependent on these conditions will be able to exist (Carey 1989; Norse 1990; Ruggiero *et al.* 1991). Third, a diversity of tree size-classes with its attendant effects on the plant and animal communities is likely to increase overall stability, in terms of both **resistance** (ability of a forest to maintain itself against stresses) and **resilience** (ability to return to prior conditions after a disturbance). For example, the higher diversity of predacious arthropods and other insectivores in natural forests appear to help forests resist pest outbreaks. Furthermore, a diversity of plants, microbes, and other organisms helps to maintain positive feedback links between plants and soils that may facilitate adjustment to climate change and other unpredictable stresses, such as invasive species (Perry *et al.* 1989; 1990; Hooper *et al.* 2005). Fourth, if the sustainable size structure is within the range of size structures created by the natural disturbance regime, then the suite of native biota adapted to the size and frequencies of the natural disturbances will be able to sustain their populations. Finally, if the forest is not sustainable, then any management objective, whatever it might be, becomes irrelevant (see Chapter 1 this volume).

maintaining the current diameter distribution may not always be compatible. For example, the baseline mortality needed to sustain the current diameter distribution of the northern hardwood forests of western New York State was approximately 22%. Kraus (2003) then compared the biodiversity of forest stands in western NY with observed mortalities < 15% or > 25% (i.e., unhealthy) with those with a baseline mortality between 15 and 24% (i.e., healthy). Healthy stands did not necessarily have higher tree or understory plant species richness or diversity compared to those stands characterized as unhealthy (Kraus 2003). In fact, there tended to be higher species richness or diversity in stands with higher tree mortality than that expected in a "healthy" stand. Kraus concluded that the relationship between forest health and plant diversity is complex, and that a healthy and diverse forest landscape will most likely need to include a mosaic of all health levels. Indeed, if biodiversity is an important management objective at the stand level, it may need to be managed for separately.

9.4 Distribution of biodiversity in the world's forests

Forested ecosystems cover about 4 billion ha or 30% of the world's land area (Dixon *et al.* 1994; FAO 2006). Although the largest areas of forest (~42%) occur at higher, northern latitudes, the diversity of forest-dwelling species is far higher at lower latitudes. For example, tropical rainforests contain more than half of the world's species, yet cover only ~6% of the earth's surface. Conversely, the boreal forest (including taiga) of Canada and Russia represents the world's largest biome, yet contains vastly fewer species. Even within broadly defined forest types (e.g., tropical rainforest and temperate deciduous forest), there is a great deal of geographical variation in species diversity (Olson and Dinerstein 1998). Areas with unusually high numbers of **endemic species** (species restricted to a particular locale), termed **hot spots**, are often the focus of conservation efforts (Myers *et al.* 2000). Conversely, other areas are known as **cold spots** due to their comparative lack of species, particularly endemic species.

The factors that explain these geographical patterns of species diversity are complex, and the subject of ongoing debate (Gaston 2000; Willig *et al.* 2003). Geophysical properties, and history of the region (e.g., age, geology, size, and climate) and broad-scale evolutionary processes (e.g., species migration, speciation, and regional extinction) are recognized as key factors that control the regional pool of species, which in turn structures local species assemblages (Gaston 2000). To illustrate how these factors can interact, let us compare two forested regions with high and low levels of endemism: montane and sub-montane rainforests of Tanzania and lowland broad-leaved forests of the eastern USA, respectively (see Textbox 9.2). The Eastern Arc Mountains of Tanzania have been isolated since their formation (Lovett and Wasser 1993). Many of the mountain plateaus are separated by tens of miles of dry savannah, with little or no forest cover through which forest species can disperse. Thus, a population found on one mountain plateau is likely to diverge from other populations through time. The high solar radiation near the equator also drives higher rates of primary productivity and creates relatively constant conditions that allow for greater specialization due to less need for adaptability to a changing environment. In contrast, the broad-leaved forests in the eastern

---

Textbox 9.2 Comparison of species diversity and endemism in Tanzanian montane rainforests and broad-leaved forests of the eastern USA

The Eastern Arc Mountains of East Africa extend from southern Kenya through Tanzania to Zambia. The mountains, originally formed by volcanic activity, are actually elevated plateaus that are isolated from the surrounding dry tropical savannah. These plateaus are covered in lush montane rainforest that receive 2000 mm of rain per year and are bathed in the constant warmth of the equatorial sun. Many species are found only on a single mountain plateau of a few square kilometers (Figure 9.2). Species also tend to demonstrate an astonishing range of adaptations to their environment; for example, there are ant species that live only on a single species of host plant, a toad that occurs only at the base of a single isolated waterfall, and many plants whose seeds are reliant on elephants for successful dispersal.

The broad-leaved forests of the eastern USA receive an average of 900–1500 mm of precipitation, spread relatively equally throughout the year and experience a strong annual temperature cycle resulting in warm summers and cold winters marked by a prolonged period of freezing temperatures during which the deciduous trees shed their leaves and most of the fauna either migrate or hibernate. Compared to forests of the Eastern Arc Mountains, there are relatively few endemic animal species found in broad-leaved forests of the eastern USA. Most species tend to be highly generalized in their habitat associations and interactions with other species. For example, common species of the broad-leaved forests such as the white-tailed deer (*Odocoileus virginianus*), black bear (*Ursus americanus*), eastern chipmunk (*Tamias striatus*), eastern wild turkey (*Meleagris gallopavo*), neotropical migrant songbirds, and the eastern box turtle (*Terrapene carolina*) occur over much of the wide geographic range of the broad-leaved forests of the eastern USA, as well as in a variety of other forest types (Figure 9.3).

USA cover enormous expanses; this continuity facilitates the dispersal of the forest fauna and flora throughout the region thus hindering evolutionary divergence. Additionally, the climate in temperate North America fluctuates seasonally leading to alternating periods of high and low resource abundance. Such climatic variation tends to favor generalist species that can deal with these changing conditions, and highly mobile species that can migrate when conditions become unsuitable.

(a)   (b)   (c)   (d)

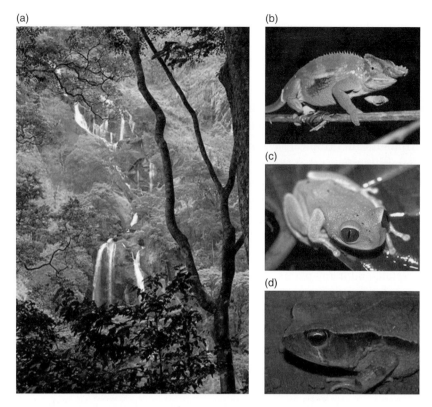

Figure 9.2 The montane rainforests of the Eastern Arc Mountains of Kenya–Tanzania (a) have high levels of endemism and species diversity. The Usambara two-horned chameleon (*Kinyongia multituberculata*) (b) is only found on a single mountain plateau and, in aggregate, amphibians, such as this tree frog (*Leptopelis uluguruensis*) and toad (*Bufo brauni*) (c and d, respectively), show globally significant high levels of diversity. Photo credits: (a) J. Gibbs, (b–d) E. Harper.

9.5 Threats to forest biodiversity

The primary threat to forest biodiversity is the conversion of forest into other land-use types (i.e., habitat loss). Rates of forest loss are variable among nations. For example, in poorer nations where the populace depends heavily on forests to meet their basic needs (e.g., Haiti), forest cover is almost gone, and what remains is rapidly disappearing (Allen and Barnes 1985, also see Chapter 8). Much of the rapid loss is occurring in tropical forests, which has particularly negative effects on global levels of biodiversity because these are among the most biologically rich ecosystems on the planet (Gaston 2000). In contrast, forests in affluent nations (e.g., USA, UK, Italy, and Japan) are actually increasing in extent (Kauppi *et al.* 2006).

The loss of forest extent usually results in the fragmentation of the remaining forest into many small and isolated patches. As forest patches decrease in size

(a)

(b)

(c)

(d)

Figure 9.3 Examples of widespread species found in the deciduous broad-leaved forests of the eastern United States (a) include the Eastern Box Turtle (*Terrapene carolina carolina*), Tufted Titmouse (*Baeolophus bicolor*), and Eastern Chipmunk (*Tamias striatus*) (b, c, and d, respectively). Photo credits: (a) E. Harper, (b) D. Tibbetts, (c) N. Child, (d) W. Butler.

and increase in isolation, local populations within them become more vulnerable to extirpation than would be expected from habitat loss per se, because fragmentation often is accompanied by a reduction in the quality of the remaining forested habitat. In particular, smaller patches of forest have an increase in **edge effects** that result from altered conditions along the forest border because of its juxtaposition with a different habitat (Matlack and Litvaitis 1999). These effects can result from abiotic factors such as light infiltration along the border of a forest patch, which deteriorates the conditions favored by forest-dependent species, or increased likelihood of wind damage due to increased exposure of edge trees. Edge effects also can result from biotic sources. Many habitat edges are invaded by either non-native species from adjacent disturbed areas that out-compete native species, or are infiltrated by predators from adjoining habitats. For example, small patches of forest surrounded by agricultural or suburban areas can have particularly deleterious effects on bird populations, due to increased rates of nest predation along forest edges (Paton 1994; Batáry and Báldi 2004).

As with most environmental problems, threats to forests usually result from the interaction of three socio-economic variables: human population size, affluence (per capita consumption), and the impact of resource-extraction technologies (Ehrlich and Ehrlich 1990). This interaction explains how rich nations with relatively small populations can have such a large environmental impact through their high affluence and use of highly destructive technology, and how poorer countries, despite their lower affluence and less destructive technology, can have a large impact because of their large populations. Wealth also correlates with the level of forest protection. For example, poorer nations have fewer resources to devote to conservation, so the destruction and degradation of the forest, although illegal, often is unchecked. Land-use policies play an additional role; those that favor short-term exploitation versus sustainable use can have dramatic implications as seen by the contrast between forestlands on the borders between the provinces of Quebec and Ontario in Canada, or between Haiti and the Dominican Republic in the Caribbean (Figure 9.4).

9.6 Why should we be concerned about forest biodiversity?

Forest biodiversity can provide a wealth of goods and services beyond the economic benefits of the trees themselves (Figure 9.5). Many indigenous peoples are heavily reliant on forest animals for food, otherwise known as bushmeat. Forests also provide sources of fuel, fodder for cattle, and crops (e.g., Brazil nuts [*Bertholletia excelsa*] and cardamom [*Elettaria* spp. and *Amomum* spp.]). Other non-timber products are valuable to industrial markets as shown by the explosion of **bioprospecting**, the search for new products in wild environments such as the rainforest. For example, the rosy periwinkle (*Catharanthus roseus*), a small flower with cancer-curing properties found in Madagascar, provides potentially important pharmaceuticals for human health. Forests also produce revenue from tourism, (e.g., Costa Rica, where tourism is the largest component of the economy, or the giant sequoia [*Sequoiadendron giganteum*] forests of California, where millions flock annually to witness their grandeur).

Arguments for conserving forest biodiversity based solely on utilitarian values are limited because most forest species have no known current economic value. Arguments based on moral and ethical stances in support of nature for its own sake (i.e., intrinsic values) also have been proposed. For example, many persons view all life forms as having an innate right to existence, regardless of their economic value, and believe that humans have a responsibility for the

(a)

(b)

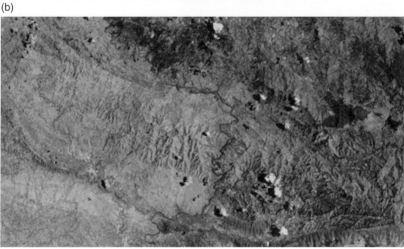

Figure 9.4 The effects of differences in forest policy. (a) Aerial view of forests on either side of Lake Abitibi on the Quebec/Ontario border in Canada. The differences in forest cover indicate the effect of land-use policies independent of human population pressure. The border is the gray dashed line running down the center of the image, with Quebec to the east and Ontario to the west. Policies in Quebec favor short-term exploitation whereas those in Ontario favor more long-term extraction of forest products. (b) Aerial view of forests in Haiti to the west of the river in the image, and the Dominican Republic to the east. The Dominican Republic has a much more stringent forest conservation policy. Photo credits: (a) © 2010 Google – Imagery © 2010 TerraMetrics, Map data © 2010 Google Tele Atlas, (b) NASA/Goddard Space Flight Center Scientific Visualization Studio/courtesy of nasaimages.org.

Figure 9.5 Forests have many important economic values to humans, for example, (a) indigenous people harvest forest animals, such as these tortoises in the Brazilian Amazon, for food; (b) the timber industry plays a major social and economic role in many countries; (c) sugar maple (*Acer saccharum*) trees are a major source of sap for the maple syrup industry in northeastern North America; (d) and species such as this chameleon from East Africa (*Kinyongia matschiei*) generate valuable sources of revenue from ecotourism and from collection for the international pet trade. Photo credits: (a and b) J. Gibbs, (c) A. Larkin, (d) P. Shirk.

stewardship of all life. Without moral considerations such as these, the justification for protecting biodiversity on its utility alone are likely to be inadequate (Noss and Cooperrider 1994).

9.7 Factors that control the distribution of forest biodiversity

9.7.1 *Abiotic limiting factors*

The distributions of plant and animal populations are heavily influenced by climate, topography, soil, substrate, and water (Gaston 2000). These abiotic factors influence organisms both directly (e.g., ability of a species to

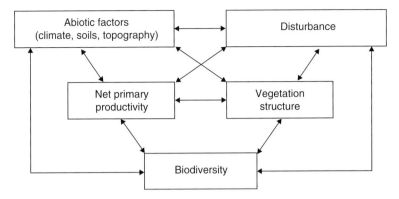

Figure 9.6 Conceptual model of the interactions between abiotic factors, ecological processes, and biodiversity. (Adapted from Hansen and Rotella 1999, with permission.)

withstand maximum and minimum annual temperatures) and indirectly (e.g., modification of ecological processes like disturbance rates that make the environment more or less suitable) (Hansen and Rotella 1999). Plants respond particularly strongly to gradients in climate and soils via changes in photosynthesis and growth rates (i.e., net primary productivity). For example, as one moves from a valley bottom to a mountain top, mean annual temperature decreases, precipitation increases, and depth, organic content, and water retention capacity of the soil decreases. Accordingly, the distributions of plant species change along this elevational gradient depending on their ability to deal with the different ambient conditions. An extreme case of this can be seen at the tree-line of tall mountains; above this line, frigid temperatures, water stress, and storm damage prevent tree growth altogether and forests are replaced by low growing cold-adapted herbs and shrubs.

Animals, although more mobile than plants, are still constrained by abiotic factors (Hansen and Rotella 1999). "Poikilotherms" or so-called "cold-blooded" creatures such as invertebrates, amphibians, and reptiles are unable to regulate body temperature via metabolism, and are therefore limited by ambient temperatures to lower elevations and latitudes. Even "homeothermic" or "warm-blooded" taxa such as mammals are rare in very cold climates. Abiotic factors also interact with primary productivity, vegetation structure, and disturbance to influence patterns of animal species richness, abundance, and demography by causing spatial variation in habitat suitability across landscapes (Figure 9.6).

9.7.2 Disturbance and successional processes

All forest ecosystems are disturbed. The effects of disturbance vary dramatically depending on the type, size, frequency, and intensity of the perturbation. Individual trees or large areas of forest may die due to windthrow, insect damage, disease, drought, and wildfires (see Chapters 4, 5, and 7). The characteristics of the natural disturbance regime depend largely on climate. For example, the longleaf pine (*Pinus palustris*) forests of the southeastern United States are characterized by frequent fire events because of the warm dry summer conditions. Fires burn every 1–10 years, and the frequent fire disturbances interact with other less frequent disturbances (e.g., hurricanes) to structure these ecosystems. These burns are rarely devastating to the community; in fact they are essential to maintain the conditions that perpetuate the ecosystem and support high levels of biodiversity (Textbox 9.3). Under the natural disturbance regime, the longleaf pine woodlands are variable in age, with even aged-cohorts regenerating in larger openings (Mitchell and Duncan 2009). In contrast to these fire-dependent ecosystems, the Acadian forests of the northeastern United States are largely fire resistant. The natural disturbance regime of these forests is dominated by small-scale (< 0.2 ha) disturbance events resulting from the death or windthrow of individual or small groups of trees (Seymour *et al.* 2002). The resulting canopy openings create small patches of early-successional vegetation within a matrix of mature, closed-canopy forests, but these openings close relatively quickly either by the lateral expansion of the surrounding canopy or regeneration of the forest within the opening.

Natural disturbances are rarely uniform in their effects (see Chapter 7). Even large disturbances diversify a landscape because of the uneven impacts across the landscape (Noss and Cooperrider 1994). For example, in fire-disturbed ecosystems some areas are unburned, others are burned to the bare ground, while others are in between these two extremes (see Chapter 7). Riparian zones and other such protected sites rarely burn while those on dry exposed south- and west-facing slopes are more apt to burn. Thus, natural disturbances do not remove all stands, nor do they selectively destroy older stands. Consequently, forests are a mosaic of different-sized patches in various stages of succession (Spies and Turner 1999).

9.7.3 Vegetation-animal relationships

Trees comprise the vast bulk of forest biomass, define forest structure, and create the habitat within which most forest-dwelling animals live. But, there are important feedbacks from animals to plants. For example, some tropical tree species rely on ants to carry their seeds underground, or on birds to pass their seeds through their gut for successful germination. Many tropical trees also rely on a chain of dispersal events, for example using birds as long-distance dispersers, followed by small mammals moving the recently defecated or

Textbox **9.3** The role of fire in the regeneration of longleaf pine ecosystems

Longleaf pine (*Pinus palustris*) ecosystems once occupied nearly 60 million acres in the southeastern USA, but they have been intensely exploited since colonial times with little regard to their regeneration (see also Chapter 4) such that by 1995 as little as 2.95 million acres remained (Outcalt and Sheffield 1996). Fire suppression activities for much of the 20th century has further endangered the sustainability of this fire-dependent ecosystem (Glitzenstein *et al.* 1995). Without fire, the nearly 200 vascular plants and several vertebrate species (most notably the endangered red-cockaded woodpecker [*Picoides borealis*]) accustomed to the open understory of longleaf pine forests virtually disappear. Thus, management activities geared towards restoring the forest and improving the conservation of biodiversity must first and foremost reintroduce fire (i.e., prescribed burning) into these ecosystems because fire plays an essential role in various stages of longleaf pine regeneration.

Longleaf pine develops very little above the ground for the first two to nine years as the root system develops. During this time the seedling exists as a bunch of needles at the soil surface that resembles a clump of grass. These "grass stage" seedlings are vulnerable to competition by brush and seedlings of other pine species for light, soil nutrients, and moisture, smothering by dead grass and litter, and brown-spot needle blight disease that prolongs the grass stage (Haywood 2007). Prescribed burning reduces these stresses and improves seedling survival because the grass-stage seedlings tolerate low-intensity fires. After the root system becomes established and the seedlings initiate height growth, competing brush still can outgrow the seedlings. Individual prescribed fires will reduce the competition with brush, but the benefits are only temporary. Disturbance-sensitive species invade rapidly, close the canopy, and exclude the biologically rich understory. Thus, the employment of prescribed fires over several decades with a sufficiently short fire-return interval may be required to restore longleaf pine-grassland communities (Haywood 2007; Mitchell and Duncan 2009).

regurgitated seeds to suitable places for growth and survival of the future tree (Levey 2001). If a rainforest is disturbed through the loss, fragmentation, and/or degradation of habitat, key dispersers may be extirpated and dispersal chains can break down (Cordeiro and Howe 2003), which can lead to further extinctions via cascading effects throughout the ecosystem. For example, many insect species that depend on a particular animal-dispersed tree as a primary host will be lost if their host does not successfully reproduce.

Human alteration of habitat does not always negatively affect vegetation-animal relationships. Many species, including some of conservation concern, thrive in altered landscapes. A prime example is provided by the Canada lynx (*Lynx canadensis*), a felid in the far northern USA and Canada that specializes on snowshoe hares (*Lepus americanus*). In the eastern United States, only Maine has significant populations of lynx largely because of a high abundance of snowshoe hares in regenerating clearcuts, which provide hares with both browse and cover from predators (Hoving *et al.* 2004) (Figure 9.7). The current number of lynx in Maine (estimated at 500) may be the highest in recorded history because clearcutting has created an abundance of early successional conditions that historically have been extremely rare.

9.7.4 What are key "habitat" components of forests for biodiversity?

Different organisms have different life-history requirements. For example, microorganisms require specific microhabitats in forest soils, beetle larvae may require wood of a certain tree species at a specific stage of decay, and some birds may require large tracts of mature, closed-canopy forests. These requirements must be present within the range of movement of sufficient numbers of individuals for populations of these species to persist.

How can forest managers help to ensure that these requirements are met for the large array of species that coexist in a forest? A good starting point is to identify the key components of forests needed to maximize biodiversity. One way to do this is to compare the attributes of forests without human alteration to those of forests that have been heavily modified by human activity. Plantation forests are some of the most intensively managed forests, and thus provide a strong contrast to the conditions of natural forests. Plantations tend to have a disturbance regime that is very different from the natural state (e.g., fewer small disturbances due to treefall, but more frequent large disturbances due to timber harvest), minimal heterogeneity in forest structure and species composition, less standing and fallen dead wood, and altered soil structure and chemistry (Hansen *et al.* 1991; Moore and Allen 1999). These missing or altered components fulfill a vital role for aggregate biodiversity (Moore and Allen 1999, and Table 9.1). For example, rare understory plants, interior forest birds, insects, and mammals all exhibited reduced abundance or richness in plantation forests relative to the native forests that they replaced (see references in Hansen *et al.* 1991 and Palik and Engstrom 1999). Indeed, the local loss of biodiversity from the conversion of natural forest to plantations can rival that

(a)

(c)

(b)

Figure 9.7 (a) Canada lynx (*Lynx canadensis*) are abundant in the early successional (b) forests created by regenerating clearcuts in Maine (c) due to the presence of their prey, snowshoe hares (*Lepus americanus*), in these areas. Photo credits: A. Fuller.

from the conversion of forest to cropland, pasture, or urban development (Noss and Cooperrider 1994). We briefly discuss the role of each of these components below.

Natural disturbance is integral to forest ecosystem health, and strongly influences other components important for the maintenance of biodiversity (Spies and Turner 1999). Natural disturbances may devastate a community at small

Table 9.1. *Important forest components for biodiversity maintenance, and management approaches to conserve them*

Component	Desired state	Value to biodiversity	Management approaches
Standing dead wood (snags)	Retain standing dead trees of different sizes & species	Food, shelter, and nest sites	Allow some stands to reach maturity, variable return intervals, avoid removal of snags
Fallen dead wood (logs)	Retain dead/down trees of different sizes, species, and decay states	Food, shelter, germination sites; microtopographic variation by creating pits and mounds	Allow some stands to reach maturity, variable return intervals; retain fallen wood
Horizontal heterogeneity	Stands of different ages and species composition consistent with natural disturbance patterns	Provide abundance of different niches for many species	Variable return intervals
Vertical heterogeneity	Forests with multiple strata	Provide abundance of different niches for many species	Variable return intervals
Soil structure and composition	Uncompacted soil with a chemistry appropriate to the location	Provide conditions suitable for native biodiversity (soil flora and fauna, plant growth etc.)	Minimize disturbance when harvesting; avoid monotypic stands of non-natives (conifers produce acidic soils) and intensive site preparation
Natural disturbance processes	Maintenance of natural disturbance regime (wind, fire etc.)	Ecosystems and constituent species are adapted to them, and may rely on them to persist	Reduce/remove fire suppression or prescribed burning, harvesting regimes that mimic natural age-class and spatial distribution

spatial and temporal scales by causing the death of plants and animals, but these same events often are essential to rejuvenate biodiversity by re-establishing earlier successional stages in the landscape and thereby maintaining biodiversity at broad spatial and temporal scales (Noss and Cooperrider 1994). Altered disturbance regimes likely will result in changes in biodiversity. For example, if disturbances are suppressed, only species associated with mature, late-successional forest will dominate in the landscape. Conversely, if disturbances are too frequent or intense, only species that can tolerate such extremes will be favored. In managed forests, the influence of natural disturbances is largely replaced by harvesting. Unless the harvesting regime closely mimics the natural disturbance regime, aggregate biodiversity may decrease.

Habitat heterogeneity links forest structure to species diversity. Thus, **vertical and horizontal heterogeneity** are key habitat components. Both result from vegetative response to disturbances and environmental gradients, and are thus interrelated. For example, the vertical heterogeneity created by forest stands in different stages of regeneration following disturbances will create horizontal heterogeneity. Similarly, the degree of horizontal heterogeneity varies depending on the vertical position in the stand. Regardless of how these two sources of heterogeneity interact, increases in vertical and/or horizontal heterogeneity create a wider variety of niches for species to occupy, leading to an overall increase in diversity. This has been well demonstrated for birds. The number of bird species at both stand and landscape scales has been linked to vegetation structure, plant species composition, and horizontal patchiness (MacArthur and MacArthur 1961; Holmes and Robinson 1981; Freemark and Merriam 1986; Deppe and Rotenberry 2008).

Dead wood is another critical habitat component (Hunter 1990). Traditionally, it has been considered a waste of wood fiber and a fire hazard, but recently managers have come to realize the myriad contributions dead wood makes to forest ecosystems (e.g., dying, dead, and down trees provide habitat for a wide array of vertebrates and invertebrates, nursery sites for germination and subsequent growth of plants, and stored nutrients to be recycled through the ecosystem) (McComb and Lindenmayer 1999). Even dead wood below the soil surface provides a nursery area for many small forest animals. Natural disturbances usually produce abundant dead wood that can, in turn, enhance biodiversity. In contrast, modern silvicultural methods often create forests that are devoid of dead wood because living trees are extracted from the system before they can die and join the dead wood reservoir. Additionally, the trees within a harvest rotation tend to be smaller and more uniform in age and size, so those that do fall create logs in a narrower range of size classes and decomposition stages. But, if managed forests are allowed to regenerate naturally for long periods, they will gradually regain dead wood as trees die, self-prune, create snags, and contribute logs to the forest floor. If the interval between harvests is too short for these to develop naturally, forest managers can compensate for these losses by leaving or creating snags and downed woody debris (Burton *et al.* 1999; Bauhus *et al.* 2009).

Soils are another essential habitat component (see Chapter 6 this volume). Soils are obviously important for the forest vegetation on which so many other organisms rely, and they are important components of biodiversity in and of themselves. Soils support as yet unknown numbers of microorganisms (i.e., bacteria, fungi, protists, and viruses), invertebrates, and other burrowing animals (Amaranthus *et al.* 1989). Plants maintain the integrity of the soil because their presence reduces erosion. If plants are removed temporarily, and the surface debris and organic layer remain intact, the effects of erosion are likely to be minimal. However, intensive forms of site preparation used in some management regimes (e.g., plantations) remove competing vegetation and logging residues and alter the soil for the planting of new trees. If not properly managed these practices can lead to increased erosion, reduced productivity through the loss of soil nutrients and mycorrhizal fungal associations, complex changes in soil biology, and changes in soil structure (e.g., compaction), all of which threaten the long-term sustainability of the soil biota and soil conditions. Foresters nowadays make concerted efforts to minimize these problems. The use of low pressure tires, reduced skidding, and less use of scarification help to maintain the function of soil communities (Thompson and Angelstam 1999). In plantation forestry, tillage may be used to improve soil aeration, reduce soil strength, and incorporate organic matter, while fertilization may be used to address nutrient limitations (Moore and Allen 1999). In the tropics, the use of reduced-impact logging results in proportionally smaller areas of disturbed soil and skid trails, less incidental damage and death of unharvested trees, greater above-ground forest biomass, and little effect on coarse root biomass compared to conventional logging practices (Pinard and Putz 1996; Putz *et al.* 2008). The environmental benefits of these practices include soil and nutrient conservation, water retention, and maintenance of forest structure and existing biodiversity (Pinard and Putz 1996).

Species relate to these different habitat components at different spatial scales. Suitable habitat, therefore, must be evaluated from the perspective of the species of interest (Spies and Turner 1999). For example, compared to amphibians, forest birds are able to move over large distances to select forest sites that best meet their needs. Indeed, many neotropical migrant bird species spend their summers nesting in the forests of Maine, Vermont, and New Hampshire; and their winter months in the southern USA, Mexico, and Central America. These birds choose a particular forested landscape in which to settle from an enormous area. At this scale, species respond more to the heterogeneity of forest and non-forest communities in the surrounding landscape than to local habitat structure, making it necessary to account for landscape context along with site-specific attributes when considering species abundance and distribution (Spies and Turner 1999). In contrast, amphibians relate to their habitat at a much finer scale (Patrick *et al.* 2008). Overland movement for amphibians is stressful; their permeable skin and small size makes them susceptible to water-loss and they are preyed upon by a wide variety of birds, reptiles, and mammals. Although some amphibian species may move long-distances during migration and juvenile dispersal, many species spend a large proportion of their time in the same few meters of space. Consequently, amphibians are much more sensitive than birds to perturbations at small scales.

9.8 Biodiversity and forest management

Biodiversity conservation always should be explicitly incorporated as a management objective. In addition to its intrinsic value, biodiversity is important for sustaining the ecological functioning of the forest (Hooper *et al.* 2005; Balvanera *et al.* 2006). While undoubtedly conflicts will arise between biodiversity conservation and other management objectives, the trade-offs should be addressed without simply dismissing biodiversity conservation because it may complicate management. For example, even plantations whose purpose is to maximize fiber yield can incorporate biodiversity concerns with little to no loss of productivity (Hartley 2002). In fact, changes in composition and diversity of associated species can potentially have positive consequences for forest production via supporting ecosystem services (e.g., improved soil fertility, pest control, pollination, provision of wildlife habitat) (Pimentel *et al.* 1992; Nabhan and Buchmann 1997; Naylor and Ehrlich 1997).

9.8.1 Biodiversity in primary natural forests, secondary natural forests, and plantations

Although individual forest types vary greatly, we can draw some broad generalizations about the effects on biodiversity caused by the conversion of primary natural (so-called "virgin") forests to secondary natural (second growth) forests (i.e., forests regenerating naturally on sites cleared by human activity) and plantations (i.e., cultivated stands of a limited number of pre-selected tree species). Primary natural forests represent a standard baseline from which to compare the effects of forest management on biodiversity (Angermeier 2000; Wesolowski 2005). So, we begin with a summary of the conditions of this forest type (Table 9.2, Figure 9.8).

Table 9.2 *Characteristics of primary natural (virgin) forests, secondary natural (second growth) forests, and plantations. Adapted from Noss and Cooperrider (1994)*

Characteristic	Forest type		
	Primary	Secondary	Plantation
Origin	post-natural disturbance	post-human disturbance	Usually same as secondary forests but also preexisting vegetation too
Regeneration	Natural reseeding, from seed bank, or vegetative propagation	Same as primary	Artificial regeneration
Within-stand diversity	High in many forest types, abundant dead wood in various size classes, and high vertical complexity	Initially low, but increasing with stand age and gap formation	Usually low unless unusually long rotations, in which case diversity increases as stand ages, and disturbance, mortality, injury, and self-pruning occur
Within-stand horizontal patchiness	Usually high, heterogeneity in physical conditions, canopy gap dynamics and horizontal variation in disturbance	Variable but initially lower, gradually increasing with age and formation of gaps	Usually low, except with long rotations, patchiness that increases over time with disturbance and mortality
Landscape diversity	Variable but generally high	Intermediate between primary forests and plantations; increasing with time since abandonment of human activities	High if variety of age classes present, but low if stands are structurally similar and monotonous in pattern
Functional diversity	High diversity of natural disturbances, diverse food webs and energy/nutrient pathways, and diverse biotic interactions	Low initially, but converging on primary condition with recovery from human activity	Usually low due to simplified structure and low species richness in monocultural, chemically manipulated stands

Table 9.2 (*cont.*)

Characteristic	Forest type		
	Primary	Secondary	Plantation
Species diversity	Varies but generally maximum for a region, especially in early/late seral stages	High in early stages with influx of weedy colonists; often low in mid succession, high in old growth	High in early stages due to weeds; lower thereafter unless long rotation permits colonization by more species as stand ages and thins
Animal population density	Variable, but probably higher than in plantations for most species	Intermediate, converging on primary condition with stand age	Episodically high for some species (e.g., herbivorous insects); otherwise generally lower than in natural forests
Stability (resistance and resilience)	Variable, but probably max for region	Intermediate, converging on primary condition with stand age	Low, often requiring continual inputs of energy and chemicals to maintain
Conservation value	Extremely high because rare in most regions	Moderate to high; increased in some regions (e.g., northeastern USA, over last century	Low or marginal value except in highly altered landscapes, where these may be the only forest available

Primary natural forests, and especially stands of old-growth forest, have higher rates of gap formation and larger gaps than younger stands (Runkle 1982; Lorimer 1989). An important consequence of these gap dynamics is the creation of horizontal and vertical heterogeneity as discussed above. Within stands of primary forests there tends to be greater vertical diversity than in stands of second growth forest as a result of multiple vegetation layers (e.g., canopy, sub canopy, shrub layer, ground cover). Further, the snags, downed logs, and pits and mounds created by the death and fall of old and large trees provide many different microhabitats for plants and animals (Meslow *et al.* 1981; Noss and Cooperrider 1994). This collection of heterogeneity helps to explain why primary natural forests are often more biologically diverse than managed forests (Textbox 9.4), and why they play an important role in harboring biodiversity (Lindenmayer and Franklin, 2002).

Figure 9.8 (a) Comparison of a plantation, (b) a forest managed for timber production, (c) and a natural forest. Plantations tend to have much less habitat heterogeneity than do less intensively managed and natural forests, resulting in less biodiversity. Photo credits: D. Patrick.

Textbox 9.4 Biodiversity in managed and unmanaged forests
in Europe

Paillet *et al.* (2010) examined the changes in biodiversity caused by forest management (i.e., anthropogenic changes related to direct forest resource use) by conducting a meta-analysis of 49 studies containing 120 comparisons between unmanaged and managed forests throughout Europe. Specifically, they examined the change in species richness of different taxonomic groups, and the variability in their response with respect to time since abandonment and intensity of forest management (Table 9.3).

In general, species richness was higher in unmanaged than in managed forests, but the response varied among taxonomic groups (Table 9.3). For example, species richness of saproxylic beetles, bryophytes, fungi, and lichens were significantly higher in unmanaged forests. These taxa are substrate dependent and are thus susceptible to reductions in microhabitat availability and diversity (e.g., presence of large logs and snags in different decay stages and establishment of pits, mounds, and root plates) in managed forests. There also were significantly more species of carabid beetles in unmanaged forests, but these were more likely to be influenced by landscape features than substrate features (Niemelä *et al.* 2007). In contrast, vascular plants and non-saproxylic beetles showed higher species richness in managed forests. Frequent disturbances in managed forests (e.g., canopy openings, litter removal, and soil disturbance) all strongly favor understory vascular plants, especially shade intolerant, ruderal, and competitive species.

In the first 20 years following abandonment, species richness of all taxa combined was higher in managed than unmanaged forests, but after 20 years, species richness was higher in unmanaged forests. Only three taxonomic groups showed significant differences in species richness with regard to time since abandonment (Table 9.3). Species richness of carabids and fungi became higher in unmanaged forests around 20 and 40 years after management abandonment, respectively. Species richness of saproxylic beetles was higher in unmanaged forests regardless of the time since abandonment.

Large and intense disturbances (i.e., clearcuts) followed by a change in tree species composition had the greatest negative effect on total species richness (Table 9.3). However, there was no clear trend among the rest of the levels of management intensity (i.e., clearcutting with no change in tree species composition, selective cutting, and selective cutting with "close-to-nature" management). Selective cutting and "close-to-nature"

Textbox 9.4 (cont.)

selective cutting significantly decreased the species richness of bryophytes, and selective cutting caused significant decreases in lichen species richness.

Several mechanisms were proposed to explain the effect of management on forest biodiversity including: changes in tree age structure, vertical stratification, and tree species composition; all of which affect light, temperature, moisture, litter, and topsoil conditions; availability of microhabitats; forest cover continuity; and legacies of extensive management in the past. The different response among the taxonomic groups likely depended on which of the above mechanisms, individually or in combination, most strongly affected that group. The generally lower species richness in the managed compared to the unmanaged forests argues for the conservation of unmanaged forests, and the creation of forest reserves on a broad scale. Further, management policies for biodiversity conservation need to be assessed with a long-term perspective because the time needed for species richness to recover from management ranged from 0 to > 40 years.

Plantation forests provide a counter-example of the role of habitat heterogeneity in increasing biodiversity (Table 9.2). The principal objective of intensive plantation management is to maximize the usable wood fiber production per unit area per unit time while simultaneously minimizing the per unit production cost (Moore and Allen 1999). To accomplish this goal, plantation forest stands are managed for homogeneity in species composition, age, and structure (Figure 9.8). Thus, they have a much more restricted range of microhabitats for different species to occupy, which can negatively affect biodiversity at a local level. Nevertheless, plantation forestry can benefit biodiversity by reducing the total amount of land needed to meet the demands for wood products (Hunter and Calhoun 1996; also see Chapter 8 Textbox 8.4 on loblolly pine plantations in the southern USA).

Second growth forests that result from timber harvesting typically are intermediate between old growth and plantation forests in terms of structural and compositional diversity (Table 9.2, Figure 9.8). They are characterized by frequent disturbances with low variability in disturbance size, more homogeneous tree species composition, age structure, and vertical structure, and a lack of senescent successional phases (Kuuluvainen *et al.* 1996, Commarmot *et al.* 2005). The extent to which a logged forest differs from an unlogged forest depends on the degree of disturbance caused by the logging operation, the elapsed time since the last logging event, and the duration of time that logging has altered the natural disturbance regime. Management employed at the appropriate spatial

Table 9.3. *Effects of forest management on species richness of all taxa combined and of different taxonomic groups in European forests, and the response of each group with respect to time since abandonment (TSA) and management intensity.*

Taxa	Species richness	TSA	Clearcut w/ tree species change	Clearcut w/o tree species change	Selective felling	"Close-to-nature" selective felling
						Management intensity[b]
All	−*a	−*	−*	+	−*	−
Vascular plants	+*	−	+*	+	+	+*
Bryophytes	−*	+		+	−*	−*
Lichens	−*	−		−	−*	
Birds	−	+			−	−*
All arthropods	+					
Acari oribatids	−					
Carabids	−*	−*				
Saproxylic beetles	−*	−*		−	−*	−*
Nonsaproxylic beetles	+	−				
Fungi	−*	−*			−	−*

[a] +/− indicates positive/negative effect of forest management and * indicates marginal significance and significance of the effect.

[b] Levels of management intensity include clearcut forest with tree species change, clearcut forests without a change in tree species (i.e., natural or artificial regeneration), selective cut forests without reference to "close-to-nature" management, and selective-cut forests with reference to "close-to-nature" management.

and temporal scales can produce horizontal and vertical structural diversity that mimics the natural disturbance regime (Franklin *et al.* 2002). For example, second growth forests can be managed to accelerate the development of old growth characteristics: structural components that are related to tree size can be manipulated efficiently through density management (e.g., thinning around large trees to enhance their growth (Textbox 9.5)), non-crop tree species or other low value trees (forked trees or trees with cavities or diseased or damaged tops) can be retained to increase diversity and structure, and felling trees and leaving slash can provide coarse woody debris (Bauhus *et al.* 2009). The provision of these components is an important management practice from the point of view of biodiversity conservation because they prevent stand homogenization and help sensitive species to persist in the managed landscape (Law and Dickman 1998; Lindenmayer and Franklin 2002, Table 9.2).

Textbox 9.5 Small mammal response to stand structure in intensively managed and natural forests

Pre-commercial thinning (PCT) and fertilization are designed to increase fiber production while maintaining or reducing production costs. If these practices can accelerate stand development, and possibly create old-growth structural features in intensively managed stands, then wildlife species associated with mature forest stages may respond to these features in intensively managed and young even-aged stands. Sullivan *et al.* (2009) tested the hypotheses that PCT and repeated fertilization of young (20–25 years) even-aged lodgepole pine (*Pinus contorta*) stands would enhance stand structure, abundance, and diversity of understory vegetation (i.e., herb and shrub layers), and abundance and diversity of forest-floor small mammals to levels similar to those of mature and old-growth forests. They compared these metrics among six stand types: young plantations, thinned stands, thinned-fertilized stands, unthinned stands, mature forests, and old-growth forests. The smaller tree sizes in the young lodgepole pine stands did not support the hypothesis that tree size would equal levels found in mature and old-growth forests. However, the densities of overstory trees and conifers, and the species and structural diversity of conifers, were similar among stand treatments. PCT and repeated fertilization of young lodgepole pine stands enhanced the abundance and species diversity of herbs and shrubs to levels found in mature and old-growth forests, suggesting that these practices may approximate the light and nutrient conditions of older unmanaged stands. But, the total abundance of mosses and lichens was lower in the young managed stands, suggesting that the young stands may need several decades to develop the diversity of microhabitats necessary to support bryophyte diversity. Ten species of small mammals were captured. Mean species richness and diversity were not significantly different among stands. Mean total abundance of small mammals was significantly different among stands with young plantations and old-growth stands having the highest numbers and thinned stands the lowest. Mean abundances of the generalist species *Peromyscus maniculatus* and *Tamias amoenus* were similar among stands, while the old forest specialist *Myodes gapperi* was largely absent from all but the mature and old-growth stands, presumably because decomposition of woody material in the younger stands had not yet reached the levels found in older closed canopy forests. Further habitat development was required before *M. gapperi* abundance levels in intensively managed stands comparable to those in older natural forests (e.g., *M. gapperi* populations in older [30–40 years] PCT stands were at levels comparable to

Textbox 9.5 (cont.)

old-growth). The insectivores, *Sorex monticolus* and *Sorex cinereus*, had as high or higher abundances in the managed stands as compared to the older unmanaged forests. *Microtus pennsylvanicus*, *Microtus longicaudus*, and *Phenacomys intermedius* prefer early successional vegetation and so were all more abundant in the four young stand types where the volume of herbaceous vegetation was the greatest.

9.8.2. Relationship between forest management, age and size distribution of trees, and biodiversity

In forested landscapes, the interaction between stand age and community composition determine suitable habitat. Timber harvesting is the primary way for forest managers to manipulate the species composition and availability of different-aged stands. As a general rule, the conservation of biological diversity in forested landscapes is promoted by maintaining a broad range of age classes over a range of spatial scales. Thus, when developing forest management plans that are compatible with conserving biodiversity, the main concern is not necessarily what harvest method will be used or how many trees will be removed, but what tree species, and age and size classes of trees will remain on a given site, and how those sites will be distributed on the landscape. For example, much of the harvested forest in the southeastern United States is managed as large even-aged plantations with very little diversity in age and size of trees within stands, and thus very little horizontal (spatial heterogeneity) and vertical (structural) diversity (Lindenmayer and Franklin 2002). Under this type of management regime, sustainable size structure and diversity exists only at very large spatial scales where multiple plantations are staggered in age across the landscape. The spatial arrangement of the plantations also is important because the distances between these different-aged stands may be prohibitive for organisms of limited mobility. By comparison, managed forests of the northeastern USA have a much greater diversity of stand ages. The transition from large-scale clearcutting to uneven-aged management practices has lead to greater age and size diversity within and between stands. In these forest types, structural diversity and a sustainable size structure is maintained at a smaller scale. Nevertheless, these silvicultural treatments disperse harvesting, and must be applied to a larger area to obtain the same volume of timber as clearcutting, which may lead to greater amounts of edge habitat and a greater loss of forest interior habitat.

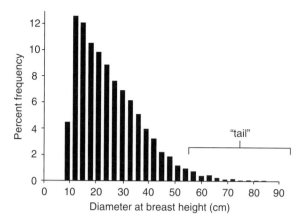

Figure 9.9 Size distribution of white pine (*Pinus strobus*) in a pine-oak forest in the mid-coastal region of Maine, USA. The distribution illustrates the presence of a "tail" (i.e., the part of the distribution that extends into the larger size [older age] classes) that is typical of forests under natural conditions.

Forest management focused on wood production commonly results in 25–150-year production cycles, whereas natural successional cycles may span several hundred to a thousand years between stand-replacing disturbances (Seymour and Hunter 1999). Consequently, managed forests typically represent only 10–40% of the potential stand development period, leading to age-class distributions skewed toward younger forests with decreased diversity of forest structure at stand and landscape scales, and the absence or underdevelopment of many natural structural attributes of old forests (e.g., high stand biomass, large number of dead standing trees, multiple canopy layers, high variation in tree sizes, and variation in size and spatial distribution of gaps) (Bauhus *et al.* 2009). Although the quantity of forest cover in a landscape may not change, species and processes sensitive to the quality of forest habitat may be negatively affected (Spies and Turner 1999; Haeussler *et al.* 2002). For example, in managed forests the "tail" of the age-class distribution often is lacking (Figure 9.9). The "tail" is the largest diameter- or oldest age-classes in the distribution that result when stands remain undisturbed for long periods of time. The loss of the tail represents a loss of old stands and old structures important for many species that require them. Consequently, managed forests tend to host fewer forest-specialist species and lower abundances of many common forest species than do unmanaged old-growth forests. (e.g., carabid beetles, bryophytes, epiphytic lichens, and mycetophilid flies, Niemelä *et al.* 2007) (Textbox 9.6). Thus, if a landowner's objective were to maintain diversity of forest-specialist species, the best management approach may be to harvest on very long production cycles, or to set aside suitable forest stands that remain undisturbed for long periods.

Textbox 9.6 Carabid beetles in managed and unmanaged boreal forests

Historical approaches to managing boreal forests (i.e., clearcutting) have homogenized species composition and tree age structure, decreased forest age, and fragmented boreal forest landscapes, all of which have impacted the boreal forest biota. Carabid beetles are among the best-studied taxa with regard to these changes. Niemelä *et al.* (2007) reviewed the effects of forestry on carabid beetle species and communities in the boreal region, and proposed ways to ameliorate the adverse effects of forestry on forest-dwelling carabids.

Forest fragmentation and fragment size were not crucial for survival of the majority of forest carabids because they could not tolerate a range of successional stages. In many cases, smaller forest fragments had greater species richness than larger fragments, primarily due to the influx of generalist and open-habitat carabid species. In contrast, forest-dwelling carabids that require certain structural elements and conditions of mature forests (i.e., abundant large-sized dead wood, patches of mesic vegetation, or micro-site characteristics under a closed canopy) were negatively affected by forest fragmentation. Similarly, edge effects were of particular concern for forest-dependent species that required interior habitat. These species were extirpated when fragments became too small and dominated by edge habitat. In fact, very small forest patches within clearcuts supported a similar carabid fauna to clearcuts, suggesting that such patches are not suitable for interior forest-dwelling species. If the patches were large enough, however, the edge functioned as an efficient barrier and prevented open-habitat species from invading the interior, thereby allowing the carabid communities of the interior to remain intact.

Carabid species richness usually increased following clearcutting because there were more open-habitat species that colonized the open, dry, and warm clearcuts than there were forest species that disappeared due to the loss of dark and cool conditions of closed-canopy spruce forests. The carabid assemblages gradually changed as the succession of vegetation proceeded, and any relict populations of forest species disappeared. About 20–30 years post clearcutting, the canopy closed and open-habitat species were replaced by species that require mature forest.

To help avert the risk to forest-dependent species in a managed landscape, harvesting practices in the boreal forests of Fennoscandia and Canada have changed in recent years to include more live and dead wood in the forest.

Textbox 9.6 (cont.)

Specifically, single-tree thinning and gap felling, which mimics windthrow, have been used as alternatives to clearcutting. In the short-term this has resulted in moderate changes to the forest carabid assemblage relative to the changes caused by clearcutting and retention cutting, because the retained trees provided enough canopy cover for the more sensitive forest species. Longer-term studies show almost no difference in total abundance and species richness between stands that were thinned or managed with single-tree cutting 15 years earlier, and un-logged mature stands, suggesting few long-term effects on the carabid biota after the first harvest rotation. At the landscape level, a range of forest types and age classes is required to maintain ground-dwelling beetle diversity. For strict old-growth species reasonable amounts of old-growth stands should be retained to act as both refugia and sources of colonists, and the spatial configuration of these stands should account for species with limited dispersal ability. At the local level, the retained old forest stands should be large enough to minimize the adverse effects of edges on forest-interior specialists; retain enough trees to shelter the ground from direct sunlight and help to maintain a constant microclimate; and include specific structural features such as woody debris, *Sphagnum*-covered patches and sensitive sites, such as spruce mires. In contrast, at the landscape and local levels few accommodations will have to be made for open-habitat carabid and forest-habitat generalists because of the widespread availability of clearcuts and their subsequent successional stages.

Forest management can have positive, negative, or neutral effects on different components of biodiversity. In the boreal forests of Canada total species richness of vascular plants and forest floor bryophytes was 30 to 35% higher in areas five to eight years following clearcutting than in mature or unmanaged boreal forest (Haeussler *et al.* 2002). Group-selection timber harvesting, a form of uneven-aged management that removes trees as small groups, benefits bird species that use the small patches of early successional vegetation created in the canopy gaps, while having little effect on the abundances of mature closed-canopy bird species (Annand and Thompson 1997; Robinson and Robinson 1999; Gram *et al.* 2003; Campbell *et al.* 2007) (Textbox 9.7). In contrast, clearcutting displaced mature-forest bird species while favoring species that require large areas of early successional vegetation (Thompson *et al.* 1992;

Textbox 9.7 Long-term response of a bird community to a group-selection timber harvest

Campbell *et al.* (2007, unpublished data) investigated the long-term effects of a group-selection timber harvest on the bird community of a pine-oak forest in Arrowsic, Maine, USA. In one half of the study area, the harvest created canopy gaps of various sizes that approximated the natural disturbance regime of the area (i.e., senescence and windthrow of individual or small groups of trees). The other half of the study area was an unmanaged control. Twenty years of bird territory mapping data (5 years of pre-harvest and 15-years of post-harvest data) was used to describe the direction, strength, and duration of the numerical and spatial responses of the birds. The numerical response was examined in each half of the study area, and the spatial redistribution of birds in response to the harvest was examined over the entire study area. At the community level, the group-selection timber harvest had neither large positive nor negative effects on the bird community,. The managed half of the study area supported slightly more species than the control half following the harvest, but the combined abundances of all species remained constant over the 20-year period. At the species level, there were two general types of response. Bird species dependent on early successional habitats (e.g. white-throated sparrows) exhibited increases in abundance, and a positive spatial response to the gaps (Figure 9.10a). In contrast, mature forest birds (e.g. ovenbird) showed little change in abundance but relatively strong distributional shifts away from the disturbed areas and their edges (Figure 9.10). Regardless of whether the effects were positive or negative, the duration of the responses were generally short-lived. By 15 years post harvest, abundance levels of nearly all species and their use of the disturbed areas had approached pre-harvest levels.

Rudnicky and Hunter 1993; Hagan *et al.* 1997). Similarly, single-tree and group-selection harvesting moderately changed the forest carabid beetle assemblage, but clearcutting and retention harvesting caused a decrease in species restricted to mature forests while favoring open-habitat species and generalists (Koivula 2002a, 2002b; Koivula and Niemelä 2002). As these few examples illustrate, it is possible to alter size class structure to benefit targeted components of biodiversity. Thus, by implementing wise management practices with clear management goals, it should be possible to maintain a sustainable size class structure while meeting biodiversity conservation goals.

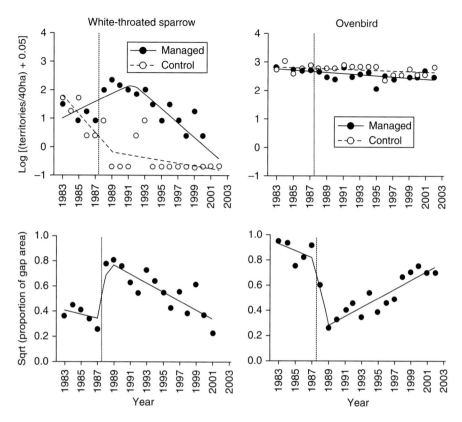

Figure 9.10 Pre and post group-selection timber harvest trends of the number of territories in the managed and control halves of the study area and of the proportion of harvest-created gap area that was within the area of the forest occupied by the bird species at the Holt Research Forest. Vertical dotted line indicates time of timber harvest. The harvest-created gaps did not exist prior to 1988, so the "gap area" during this time represents the same areas of the forest before the harvest to show their comparative use. Territory numbers and proportion of gap area were transformed to meet statistical assumptions.

The effects of timber harvesting on forest structure, and the corresponding changes in the animal communities tend to be temporary. For example, abundances of early and late-successional bird species returned to pre-harvest levels by 5–8 years after a group-selection timber harvest, and their spatial distribution returned to pre-harvest conditions after 15 years (Campbell *et al.* 2007 and unpublished data) (Textbox 9.7). Carabid beetle assemblages in selectively logged forest reverted to those observed in mature stands after 15–20 years (Vance and Nol 2003). Heyborne *et al.* (2003) documented parallel changes in beetle assemblages and plant communities from young herb-stage regrowth to mature forest. But some effects can be longer lasting. Mature-forest carabid assemblages did not recover even 27 years post-harvesting in western Canada (Niemelä et al. 1993a), but in 60-year old stands in Finland the carabid assemblage closely resembled those of mature forests (Niemelä et al. 1993b).

The variability in response to logging is in part related to how biodiversity is measured (Grieser Johns 1997). The responses of species assemblages to logging are typically expressed in terms of species richness, diversity, or similarity between logged and unlogged areas. Such measurements are insensitive to changes in species composition, so there can be general agreement in patterns of richness and diversity across managed and unmanaged sites, or among sites managed in different ways. For example, an equal or higher diversity or richness in a clearcut area can occur despite the decline or absence of mature forest specialists. In contrast, the responses of individual species often are more informative. Nevertheless, these measures reflect site-specific differences (e.g., local differences in initial population densities and specific effects of logging operations). For example, the comparison of two nearby ($<$ 1 km) areas in the same harvested compartment of Malaysian forest yielded very low congruence among the responses of individual bird species (Lambert 1992; Grieser Johns 1996). Thus, care must be used when interpreting results from a small number of sites or a limited area.

9.9 Natural disturbance regimes as a guide to maintaining a sustainable size structure at appropriate spatial and temporal scales

Baseline mortality determines the number of trees that must die as a forest ages to maintain a sustainable size structure. The concept, however, does not explicitly address the spatial pattern of mortality. The spatial configuration of the trees in the different size classes is of great importance to many forest organisms. Some species require large-tracts of continuous mature forest to settle in an area. Other species dependent on early successional vegetation stages also have minimum area requirements. Although the size distribution of trees may be consistent with sustainability, and the area of early-, mid-, and late-successional forest collectively large enough to support species dependent on these stages; if they are not in a favorable spatial configuration then the forest will not support viable populations of these species. To produce patches of favorable habitat, trees must be cut at the appropriate temporal and spatial scales.

Natural disturbance regimes offer a benchmark to forest managers who seek to extract timber from an area while simultaneously providing a range of habitat conditions at temporal and spatial scales to which various organisms are adapted (Attiwill 1994; Seymour and Hunter 1999; Seymour et al. 2002). For example, in the northeastern USA, the natural disturbance regime is dominated by the death or windthrow of individual or small groups of trees that create a mosaic characterized by small-scale gap-phase dynamics (Seymour *et al.* 2002; Lorimer and White 2003). Gaps range from <25–1000 m^2 and form at an average rate of 0.5 to 2.0% of total land area per year, yielding natural return intervals (average time between disturbances for a given site) of 50–200 years (Runkle 1982; 1985). This disturbance regime can be mimicked using group-selection timber harvesting, which creates small patches of early successional habitat similar in size to the small openings created most frequently by natural disturbance. Large-scale, stand-replacing disturbances brought on by fire or extensive windthrow also occur in this region, but their return interval is 500–1000 years (Seymour *et al.* 2002; Lorimer and White 2003). To mimic these large natural disturbances, silvicultural practices such as clearcutting would be needed. Nevertheless, given the infrequency of large-scale natural disturbances in this region, large clearcuts would be rare and so too would species dependent on large tracts of early successional forest.

9.10 Managing tree age structure and spatial distribution for biodiversity conservation

An important concern for biodiversity conservation is the similarity between the size or age and spatial distributions of trees resulting from forest management and those of a primary natural landscape (Seymour and Hunter 1999). Imagine a forest with a 1% annual stand-replacing disturbance regime (i.e., 100-year return interval). Simply setting the forest rotation equal to the 100-year disturbance interval will not accurately emulate the natural disturbance regime. Under this type of sustained yield management, 10% of the area is harvested every 10 years, no stands escape harvest, no stands age more than 100 years, and stands younger than 100 years are never harvested. Such a harvesting scheme clearly deviates from the age structure created by natural disturbance (Figure 9.11a). Specifically, natural disturbances will result in some stands being disturbed repeatedly on short cycles while others remain undisturbed for long periods. The "tail" of the distribution created by old growth stands that have escaped disturbance does not exist with this harvesting scheme. Allocating different portions of the forest to successively longer rotations (e.g., 50-year rotations for early- to mid-successional species, and up to 300-year rotations for late-successional species) more closely mimics the natural age structure (Seymour and Hunter 1999). This natural distribution can be emulated by harvesting 10% of the forest at age 300, 15% at age 200, 20% at age 150, 35% at age 100 and 20% at age 50 (Figure 9.11b). About 10% of the forest is still harvested every 10

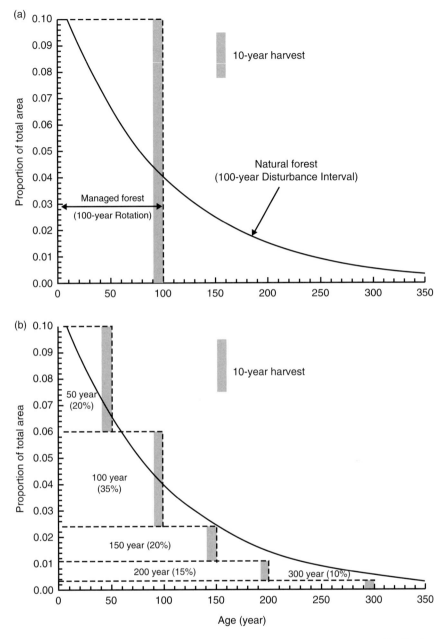

Figure 9.11 (a) Comparison of natural forest age distributions and age distributions created by a single rotation of 100 years and (b) the management of different portions of the forest on rotations of varying duration. (Redrawn from Seymour and Hunter 1999, with permission.)

years, but it is distributed among the different age classes. This management scheme, by simultaneously maintaining the full range of the natural age structure is the best way to prevent losses of forest biodiversity, while still producing a sustainable supply of timber (Seymour and Hunter 1999).

9.11 Conclusion

Numerous abiotic and biotic factors operating at multiple spatial and temporal scales control the distribution of forest biodiversity. Forest management alters these factors to varying degrees, leading to complex effects on biodiversity. The responses to forest management differ depending on the method of harvesting, the spatial and temporal patterns in tree size structure resulting from the harvest, and the taxonomic group being examined. Thus, any given management regime will benefit some components of biodiversity, negatively affect others, and leave others unaffected. Whether or not these changes are acceptable depends on landowner objectives. Thus, conserving biodiversity in forests must first begin with a clear definition of the management goal. If we wish to retain species tied to large areas of mature forest, for example the northern spotted owl (*Strix occidentalis caurina*); we may decide not to allow any timber removal at all. If we wish to increase the presence of early successional species in a forest landscape, large clearcuts may represent the best approach. These objectives, however, must be realized within the framework of sustainability (see Chapter 1).

The baseline mortality concept that is the focus of this book represents one approach to forest management. Its underlying principle of a sustainable size structure will help to retain many components of biodiversity by providing a range of tree sizes. Additional consideration, however, will need to be given to species with specific requirements. Many species are sensitive to the spatial patterns of the different-sized trees. To accommodate such species we suggest using the natural disturbance regime as a guideline to distribute the sustainable size structure at spatial and temporal scales to which particular organisms are adapted. Similarly, species that rely on structural legacies such as snags and coarse woody debris will require management regimes that provide these resources.

Biodiversity conservation should be an integral part of forest health given the importance of biodiversity to ecosystem function. Incorporating biodiversity conservation as a management objective, within the framework of the forest health concept presented in this book, provides a mechanism to account for components not covered solely by maintenance of a sustainable size structure. Thus, when used in conjunction with management that mimics the natural disturbance regime, and other measures that address the needs of organisms with specific requirements, the use of baseline mortality and sustainable size structure is a viable approach to simultaneously maintain forest health and sustain biodiversity.

References

Allen, J. C. and Barnes, D. F. 1985. The causes of deforestation in developing countries. *Annals of the Association of American Geographers* **75**: 163–184.

Amaranthus, M. P., Trappe, J. M., and Molina, R. J. 1989 Long-term forest productivity and the living soil. In: *Maintaining Long-term Productivity of Pacific Northwest Forest Ecosystems*. Perry, D. A., Meurisse, R., Thomas, B., *et al.* (Eds). Timber Press, Portland, OR.

Angermeier, P. L. 2000. The natural imperative for biological conservation. *Conservation Biology* **14**: 373–381.

Annand, E. M. and Thompson, III, F. R. 1997. Forest bird response to regeneration practices in central hardwood forests. *Journal Wildlife Management* **61**: 159–171.

Attiwill, P. M. 1994. The disturbance of forest ecosystems: the ecological basis for conservative management. *Forest Ecology & Management* **63**: 247–300.

Balvanera, P., Pfisterer, A. B., Buchmann, N., *et al.* 2006. Quantifying the evidence for biodiversity effects on ecosystem functioning and services. *Ecology Letters* **9**: 1146–1156.

Batáry, P. and Báldi, A. 2004. Evidence of an edge effect on avian nest success. *Conservation Biology* **18**: 389–400.

Bauhus, J., Puettmann, K., and C. Messier, C. 2009. Silviculture for old-growth attributes. *Forest Ecology & Management* **258**: 525–537.

Burton, P. J., Kneeshaw, D. D., and Coates, K. D. 1999. Managing forest harvesting to maintain old growth in boreal and sub-boreal forests. *Forestry Chronicle* **75**: 623–631.

Campbell, S. P., Witham, J. W., and Hunter Jr, M. L. 2007. Long-term effects of group-selection timber harvesting on abundance of forest birds. *Conservation Biology* **21**: 1218–1229.

Carey, A. B. 1989. Wildlife associated with old-growth forests in the Pacific Northwest. *Natural Areas Journal* **9**: 151–162.

Commarmot, B., Bachofen, H., Bundziak, Y., *et al.* 2005. Structures of virgin and managed beech forests in Uholka (Ukraine) and Sihlwald (Switzerland): a comparative study. *Forest Snow and Landscape Research* **79**: 45–56.

Cordeiro, N. J. and Howe, H. F. 2003. Forest fragmentation severs mutualism between seed dispersers and an endemic African tree. *Proceedings National Academy Science* **100**: 14052–14056.

Deppe, J. L. and Rotenberry, J. T. 2008. Scale-dependent habitat use by fall migratory birds: vegetation structure, floristics, and geography. *Ecological Monographs* **78**: 461–487.

Dixon, R. K., Solomon, A. M., Brown, S., *et al.* 1994. Carbon pools and flux of global forest ecosystems. *Science* **263**: 185–190.

Ehrlich, P. R. and Ehrlich, A. H. 1990. *The Population Explosion*. Simon and Schuster, New York.

Food and Agriculture Organization of the United Nations (FAO). 2006. Global Forest
Resources Assessment 2005: progress towards sustainable forest management.
Food and Agriculture Organization of the United Nations Forestry Paper No. 147.

Franklin, J. F., Spies, T. A., Van Pelt, R. V., *et al.* 2002. Disturbances and structural
development of natural forest ecosystems with silvicultural implications, using
Douglas-fir as an example. *Forest Ecology & Management* **155**: 399–423.

Freemark, K. E. and Merriam, H. G. 1986. Importance of area and habitat heterogeneity to
bird assemblages in temperate forest fragments. *Biological Conservation* **36**: 115–141.

Gaston, K. G. 2000. Global patterns in biodiversity. *Nature* **405**: 220–227.

Glitzenstein, J. S., Platt, W. J., and Streng, D. R. 1995. Effects of fire regime and habitat
on tree dynamics in north Florida longleaf pine savannas. *Ecological Monographs* **65**:
441–476.

Gram, W. K., Porneluzi, P. A., Clawson, R. L., *et al.* 2003. Effects of experimental forest
management on density and nesting success of bird species in Missouri Ozark
forests. *Conservation Biology* **17**: 1324–1337.

Grieser Johns, A. 1996. Bird population persistence in Sabahan logging concessions.
Biological Conservation **75**: 3–10.

Grieser Johns, A. 1997. *Timber Production and Biodiversity Conservation in Tropical Rain
Forests.* Cambridge University Press, Cambridge.

Haeussler, S., Bedford, L., Leduc, A., *et al.* 2002. Silvicultural disturbance severity and plant
communities of the southern Canadian boreal forest. *Silva Fennica* **36**: 307–327.

Hagan, J. M., McKinley, P. S., Meehan, A. L., and Grove, S. L. 1997. Diversity and
abundance of landbirds in a Northeastern industrial forest. *Journal Wildlife
Management* **61**: 718–735.

Hansen, A. and Rotella, J. 1999. Abiotic factors. In: *Maintaining Biodiversity in Forest
Ecosystems.* Hunter, Jr., M. L. (ed.). Cambridge University Press, Cambridge.

Hansen, A. J., Spies, T. A., Swanson, F. J., and Ohmann, J. L. 1991. Conserving
biodiversity in managed forests. *BioScience* **41**: 382–392.

Hartley, M. J. 2002. Rationale and methods for conserving biodiversity in plantation
forests. *Forest Ecology & Management* **155**: 81–95.

Haywood, J. D. 2007. Influence of herbicides and felling, fertilization, and prescribed
fire on longleaf pine establishment and growth through six growing seasons. *New
Forests* **33**: 257–279.

Heyborne, W. H., Miller, J. C., and Parsons, G. L. 2003. Ground dwelling beetles and
forest vegetation change over a 17-year-period, in western Oregon USA. *Forest
Ecology & Management* **179**: 123–134.

Holmes, R. T. and Robinson, S. K. 1981. Tree species preferences of foraging
insectivorous birds in a northern hardwoods forest. *Oecologia* **48**: 31–35.

Hooper, D. U., Chapin, F. S., III, Ewel, J. J. *et al.* 2005. Effects of biodiversity on
ecosystem functioning: a consensus of current knowledge. *Ecological Monographs*
75: 3–35.

Hoving, C. L., Harrison, D. J., Krohn, W. B., *et al.* 2004. Canada lynx *Lynx candensis*
habitat and forest succession in northern Maine USA. *Wildlife Biology* **10**:
285–294.

Hunter, M. L. 1990. *Wildlife, Forests, and Forestry*. Prentice Hall, Englewood Cliffs, NJ.

Hunter, M. L. and Gibbs., J. P. 2007. *Fundamentals of Conservation Biology*. Blackwell Publishing, Malden, MA.

Hunter, M. L. and Calhoun, A. 1996. A triad approach to land-use allocation. In: *Biodiversity in Managed Landscapes*. Szaro, R. C. and Johnston, D. W. (eds). Oxford University Press, New York.

Kauppi, P. E., Ausubel, J. H., Fang, J., *et al*. 2006. Returning forests analyzed with the forest identity. *Proceedings National Academy Science* **103**: 17574–17579.

Koivula, M. 2002a. Alternative harvesting methods and boreal carabid beetles (Coleoptera, Carabidae). *Forest Ecology & Management* **167**: 103–121.

Koivula, M. 2002b. Boreal carabid-beetle (Coleoptera, Carabidae) assemblages in thinned uneven-aged and clear-cut spruce stands. *Annales Zoologici Fennici* **39**: 131–149.

Koivula, M. and Niemelä, J. 2002. Boreal carabid beetles (Coleoptera, Carabidae) in managed spruce forests – a summary of Finnish case studies. *Silva Fennica* **36**: 423–436.

Kolb, T. E., Wagner, M. R., and Covington, W. W. 1994. Utilitarian and ecosystem perspectives: concepts of forest health. *Journal Forestry* **92**: 10–15.

Kraus, N. E. 2003. Relationships between forest health and plant diversity in western New York state forest lands. *MS Thesis*. SUNY College of Environmental Science and Forestry, Syracuse, NY.

Kuuluvainen, T., Penttinen, A., Leinonen, K., and Nygren, M. 1996. Statistical opportunities for comparing stand structural heterogeneity in managed and primeval forests: an example from boreal spruce forest in southern Finland. *Silva Fennica* **30**: 315–328.

Lambert, F. R. 1992. The consequences of selective logging for Bornean lowland forest birds. In: *Tropical Rain Forest: Disturbance and Recovery*. Marshall, A. G. and Swaine, M. D. (eds). Royal Society, London.

Law, B. S. and Dickman, C. R. 1998. The use of habitat mosaics by terrestrial vertebrate fauna: implications for conservation and management. *Biodiversity and Conservation* **7**: 323–333.

Levey, D. J., Silva, W. R., and Galetti, M. 2001. *Seed Dispersal and Frugivory: Ecology, Evolution, and Conservation*. CABI Publishing. Wallingford.

Lindenmayer, D. B. and Franklin, J. F. 2002. *Conserving Forest Biodiversity: a Comprehensive Multiscaled Approach*. Island Press, Washington, DC.

Lorimer, C. G. 1989. Relative effects of small and large disturbances on temperate hardwood forest structure. *Ecology* **70**: 565–567.

Lorimer, C. G. and White, A. S. 2003. Scale and frequency of natural disturbances in the northeastern U.S.: implications for early successional forest habitats and regional age distributions. *Forest Ecology & Management* **185**: 41–64.

Lovett, J. C. and Wasser, S. K. 1993. *Biogeography and Ecology of the Rain Forests of Eastern Africa*. Cambridge University Press, Cambridge.

MacArthur, R. H. and MacArthur, J. W. 1961. On bird species diversity. *Ecology* **42**: 594–598.

Manion, P. D. and Griffin, D. H. 2001. Large landscape scale analysis of tree death in the Adirondack Park, New York. *Forest Science* **41**: 524–529.

Matlack, G. R. and Litvaitis, J. A. 1999. Forest edges. In: *Maintaining Biodiversity in Forest Ecosystems*. Hunter, M. L. (ed.). Cambridge University Press, Cambridge.

Mayr, E. 1963. *Populations, Species, and Evolution*. Harvard University Press, Cambridge, MA.

McComb, W. and Lindenmayer, D. 1999. Dying, dead, and down trees. In: *Maintaining Biodiversity in Forest Ecosystems*. Hunter, M. L. (ed.). Cambridge University Press, Cambridge.

Meslow, E. C., Maser, C., and Verner, J. 1981. Old-growth forests as wildlife habitat. *Trans. North American Wildlife and Natural Resources Conf.* **46**: 329–335.

Mitchell, R. J. and Duncan, S. L. 2009. Range of variability in southern coastal plain forests: its historical, contemporary, and future role in sustaining biodiversity. *Ecology and Society* **14**: 17.

Moore, S. E. and Allen, H. L. 1999. Plantation forestry. In: *Maintaining Biodiversity in Forest Ecosystems*. Hunter, M. L. (ed.). Cambridge University Press, Cambridge, UK.

Myers, N., Mittermeier, R. A., Mittermeier, C. G., *et al.* 2000. Biodiversity hotspots for conservation priorities. *Nature* **403**: 853–808.

Nabhan, G. P. and Buchmann, S. L. 1997. Services provided by pollinators. In: *Nature's Services: Societal Dependence on Natural Ecosystems*. Daily, G. (ed.). Island Press, Washington, DC.

Naylor, R. L. and Ehrlich, P. R. 1997. Natural pest control services and agriculture. In: *Nature's Services: Societal Dependence on Natural Ecosystems*. Daily, G. (ed.). Island Press, Washington, DC.

Niemelä J., Langor, D., and Spence, J. R. 1993a. Effects of clear-cut harvesting on boreal ground beetle assemblages (Coleoptera: Carabidae) in western Canada. *Conservation Biology* **7**: 551–561.

Niemelä J., Spence, J. R., Langor, D., *et al.* 1993b. Logging and boreal ground-beetle assemblages on two continents: implications for conservation. In: *Perspectives on Insect Conservation*. Gaston, K. J., New, T. R. and Samways M. J. (eds.). Intercept Ltd, Andover, Hampshire.

Niemelä, J., Koivula, and Kotze, D. J. 2007. The effects of forestry on carabid beetles (Coleoptera: Carabidae) in boreal forests. *Journal Insect Conservation* **11**: 5–18.

Norse, E. A. 1990. *Ancient Forests of the Pacific Northwest*. The Wilderness Society and Island Press, Washington, DC.

Noss, R. F. 1983. A regional landscape approach to maintain diversity. *BioScience* **33**: 700–706.

Noss, R. F. and Cooperrider, A. Y. 1994. *Saving Nature's Legacy: Protecting and Restoring Biodiversity*. Island Press, Washington, DC.

O'Brien, H. E., Parrent, J. L., Jackson, J. A., *et al.* 2005. Fungal community analysis by large-scale sequencing of environmental samples. *Applied Environmental Microbiology* **71**: 5544–5550.

Olson, D. M. and Dinerstein, E. 1998. The global 200: a representative approach to conserving the earth's most biologically valuable ecoregions. *Conservation Biology* **12**: 502–515.

Outcalt K. W. and Sheffield, R. M. 1996. The longleaf pine forest: trends and current conditions. *USDA Forest Service, Southern Research Station, Asheville, North Carolina. Res. Bull. SRS-9.*

Paillet, Y., Bergès, L., Hjältèn, J., *et al.* 2010. Biodiversity differences between managed and unmanaged forests: meta-analysis of species richness in Europe. *Conservation Biology* **24**: 101–112.

Palik, B. and Engstrom, R. T. 1999. Species composition. In: *Maintaining Biodiversity in Forest Ecosystems.* Hunter, M. L. (ed.). Cambridge University Press, Cambridge, UK.

Paton, P. W. C. 1994. The effect of edge on avian nest success: how strong is the evidence? *Conservation Biology* **8**: 17–26.

Patrick, D. A., Harper, E. B., Hunter Jr., M. L., and Calhoun, A. J. K. 2008. Terrestrial habitat selection and strong density-dependent mortality in recently metamorphosed amphibians. *Ecology* **89**: 2563–2574.

Perry, D. A., Borchers, J. G., Borchers, S. L., and Amaranthus, M. P. 1990. Species migrations and ecosystem stability during climate change: the below ground connection. *Conservation Biology* **4**: 266–274.

Perry, D. A., Meurisse, R., Thomas, B., *et al.* (eds). 1989. *Maintaining Long-term Productivity of Pacific Northwest Forest Ecosystems.* Timber Press, Portland, OR, USA.

Pimentel, D., Stachow, U., Takacs, D. A., *et al.* 1992. Conserving biological diversity in agricultural/forestry systems. *BioScience* **42**: 354–362.

Pinard, M. A. and Putz, F. E. 1996. Retaining forest biomass by reducing logging damage. *Biotropica* **28**: 278–295.

Putz, F. E., Sist, P., Fredericksen, T., and Dykstra, D. 2008. Reduced-impact logging: challenges and opportunities. *Forest Ecology & Management* **256**: 1427–1433.

Robinson, W. D. and Robinson, S. K. 1999. Effects of selective logging on forest bird populations in a fragmented landscape. *Conservation Biology* **13**: 58–66.

Rudnicky, T. C. and Hunter Jr., M. L. 1993. Reversing the fragmentation perspective: effects of clearcut size on bird species richness in Maine. *Ecological Applications* **3**: 357–366.

Ruggiero, L. F., Aubry, K. B., Carey, A. B., and Huff, M. H. (tech coordinators). 1991. Wildlife and vegetation of unmanaged douglas-fir Forests. USDA Forest Service, Pacific Northwest Research Station, Portland, OR.

Runkle, J. R. 1982. Patterns of disturbance in some old-growth mesic forests of eastern North America. *Ecology* **63**: 1533–1546.

Runkle, J. R. 1985. Disturbance regimes in temperate forests. In: *The Ecology of Natural Disturbance and Patch Dynamics.* Pickett, S. T. A., and White, P. S. (eds). Academic Press, Orlando, FL.

Ryder, O. A. 1986. Species conservation and systematics: the dilemma of subspecies. *Trends in Ecology and Evolution* **1**: 9–10.

Seymour, R. and Hunter Jr., M. L. 1999. Principles of ecological forestry. In: *Maintaining Biodiversity in Forest Ecosystems.* Hunter, M. L (ed.). Cambridge University Press, Cambridge.

Seymour, R. S., White, A. S., and deMaynadier, P. G. 2002. Natural disturbance regimes in northeastern North America–evaluating silvicultural systems using natural scales and frequencies. *Forest Ecology & Management* **155**: 357–367.

Simberloff, D. 1999. The role of science in the preservation of forest biodiversity. *Forest Ecology & Management* **115**: 101–111.

Spies, T. and Turner, M. 1999. Dynamic forest mosaics. In: *Maintaining Biodiversity in Forest Ecosystems*. Hunter, M. L (ed.). Cambridge University Press, Cambridge.

Steele, R. C. and Welch, R.C. (eds). 1973. *Monk Woods. A Nature Reserve Record*. The Nature Conservancy/Natural Environment Research Council, Huntingdon.

Sullivan, T. P., Sullivan, D. S., Lindgren, P. M. F., and Ransome, D. B. 2009. Stand structure and the abundance and diversity of plants and small mammals in natural and intensively managed forests. *Forest Ecology & Management* **258**S: S127–S141.

Tews, J., Brose, U., Grimm, V., *et al.* 2004. Animal species diversity driven by habitat heterogeneity/diversity: the importance of keystone structures. *Journal Biogeography* **31**: 79–92.

Thompson, F. R., III, Dijak, W. D., Kulowiec, T. G., and Hamilton, D. A. 1992. Breeding bird populations in Missouri Ozark forests with and without clearcutting. *Journal Wildlife Management* **56**: 23–30.

Thompson, I. and Angelstam, P. 1999. Special species. In: *Maintaining Biodiversity in Forest Ecosystems*. Hunter, M. L (ed.). Cambridge University Press, Cambridge.

Vance, C. C and Nol, E. 2003 Temporal effects of selection logging on ground beetle communities in northern hardwood forests of eastern Canada. *EcoScience* **10**: 49–56.

Wesolowski, T. 2005. Virtual conservation: how the European Union is turning a blind eye to its vanishing primeval forests. *Conservation Biology* **19**: 1349–1358.

Whittaker, R. H. 1960. Vegetation of the Siskiyou Mountains, Oregon and California. *Ecological Monographs* **30**: 279–338.

Willig, M. R., Kaufman, D. M., and Steven, R. D. 2003. Latitudinal gradients of biodiversity: pattern, process, scale, and synthesis. *Annual Review of Ecology, Evolution and Systematics* **34**: 273–309.

10

Seeing the forest for the trees: forest health monitoring

M. FIERKE, D. NOWAK AND R. HOFSTETTER

10.1 Introduction

A recent definition of forest health states that it is dependent on sustainability, productivity, and pest management (Raffa *et al.* 2009), which is similar to the central premise of this text (see Chapter 1). We suggest that one way to assess sustainability, as the first component of a healthy forest, is to determine if observed landscape-level tree mortality corresponds to baseline mortality (i.e., a stable size structure is maintained so that the number of trees dying within a size class does not exceed the number necessary to replace those in the next larger size class). Meanwhile, productivity, the second component of a healthy forest, involves meeting the management objectives of the landowner.

An understanding of the evolutionary history of the forest and all associated forest processes and components; e.g., fire, climate, insects, disease, etc., is critical when considering the spatial scale at which forest health is being assessed. For example, in the western USA and in Canadian lodgepole pine forests, the baseline mortality concept would need to be applied at the level of tens of thousands or hundreds of thousands of square kilometers. These forests experience repeated long-term cycles whereby forests become susceptible to the mountain pine beetle, die as a cohort, and burn so that seeds may germinate and the forest grow again (Peterman 1978; Berryman 1986). The conflagration that follows a mortality event occurs at large spatial scales and though forests can experience up to 100% mortality of all vegetation layers, they would still be considered "healthy" as this would be an essential renewal stage.

Forest Health: An Integrated Perspective, ed. John D. Castello and Stephen A. Teale. Published by Cambridge University Press. © Cambridge University Press 2011.

Indicators of forest health, as with other indicators of ecosystem health, should be easily measured, sensitive to stressors, respond in a predictable manner to stress, and have a low variability in their response to stress (Dale and Beyeler 2001). Ecological indicators are used to assess the condition of ecosystems, provide early warnings of changes away from reference conditions, and facilitate identification of causes of deviations from reference conditions. Many processes and factors impact forest health, as identified in this text. Some of the most important of these factors, or those that best represent multiple facets have been selected as indicators of health, and a means to assess them established. Indicators commonly used in forest health monitoring include tree mortality, tree crown condition, growth of trees (as shown by basal area, height or volume changes through time), plant diversity, dominance of native species, soil morphology and chemistry, abundance of lichen communities, etc. Once forest health "indicators" are selected, they should be measured over time using designed experimentation or long-term monitoring programs to quantify trends and changes.

In addition to selecting indicators from a large number of possibilities, reference conditions (or standards) for each must be determined and agreed upon. The forest can be considered healthy when indicator values fall within a predetermined set of reference conditions. If one or more indicators do not fall within the standards, the forest is considered unhealthy. While this concept seems straight forward, it is not because it requires judgments and choices regarding the reference conditions against which to evaluate health and the spatial scales at which to apply them.

"Historical" or "natural" forest conditions often are preferred reference conditions. Unfortunately, numerous factors may have altered forest conditions in the recent past (e.g., climate change, air pollution, pest introductions, forest management), which makes identification of reference conditions difficult and oftentimes controversial. Long-term monitoring can provide data that contributes knowledge to an enhanced ecological synthesis thereby aiding refinement of reference conditions, as well as revealing deviations from reference conditions.

The spatial scale at which forest health is considered is critical. For example, a particular stand may not fall within the parameters of "health"; however, the stand is part of a larger whole; and if most of the trees/stands within a forest are healthy, then the forest as a whole is considered healthy. See Chapters 1 and 8 for a more in depth discussion of spatial scales within forested ecosystems. Inconsistencies in how forest health is viewed arise when scientists, land owners, and land managers apply their own concepts of health at different spatial scales. Seldom do landowners/managers consider how management of their forested properties fits into the larger forest ecosystem.

There are many other important considerations when monitoring forest health besides identifying indicators and reference conditions,. First, data collection must be standardized, and field crews well-trained to ensure comparable data are collected regionwide and during each measurement period. Furthermore, quality assurance protocols must be in place to ensure reliable and accurate data are collected. Documentation of data quality is essential for valid interpretation of forest health information. Forest health monitoring also should be conducted on permanent reference plots that are not destructively sampled so that re-measurements can be conducted to monitor changes in health within a time frame that allows changes to be detected. Monitoring plots should be explicitly located, either randomly or systematically, with an adequate number of plots to provide statistically reliable estimates for the forest of interest.

The terms "forest health" and "forest condition" frequently are used interchangeably (Percy and Ferretti 2004); however, these two visions of forest status will produce different monitoring systems. Forest health often denotes the degree to which normal tree processes have been disrupted (Percy 2002), while **forest condition** has been used in relation to the descriptive indicators used in routine forest assessments. Adopting a forest health or a forest condition viewpoint should not be undertaken lightly as selection of one or the other will ultimately drive the operational steps of the monitoring program (Ferretti 1997). For example, if one considers forest health to be defined only by the crown condition of trees, one will proceed to assess spatial and temporal variation of defoliation and foliar symptoms. On the other hand, if the ecosystem as a whole is considered, many different components and indicators will be taken into account, e.g., soil nutrients, soil biota, ecosystem productivity (Innes and Karnosky 2001).

10.1.2 The Montreal Process

The impetus behind many early forest health monitoring programs was the establishment of the **Montréal Process Working Group** and the subsequent development of a dynamic set of criteria and indicators for conservation and sustainable management of forests (Anon. 1995, Montreal Process Working Group 2009). This process was initiated in 1992, and in 1995 the Santiago Declaration was signed by 12 countries: Argentina, Australia, Canada, Chile, China, Japan, Republic of Korea, Mexico, New Zealand, Russian Federation, United States of America, and Uruguay. These countries account for ~ 90% of the world's temperate and boreal forests. Within the Declaration, seven criteria were adopted:

1. Conservation of biological diversity
2. Maintenance of productive capacity of forest ecosystems

3.   Maintenance of forest ecosystem health and vitality
4.   Conservation and maintenance of soil and water resources
5.   Maintenance of forest contribution to global carbon cycles
6.   Maintenance and enhancement of long-term multiple socioeconomic benefits to meet societal needs
7.   Legal, institutional and economic framework for forest conservation and sustainable management

To assess trends in monitored forests, 67 associated indicators are used. Indicators are essentially repeated observations of natural or social phenomena that provide quantitative measures of systems (Montreal Process Working Group 2009). Indicators must be timely, reliable, and relevant to established criteria or management goals. Indicators specific to criterion no. 3, Maintenance of forest ecosystem health and vitality, are:

(a)   Area and percent of forest affected by biotic processes and agents (e.g., disease, insects, invasive species) beyond reference conditions.
(b)   Area and percent of forest affected by abiotic agents (e.g., fire, storm, land clearance) beyond reference conditions.

Forest health monitoring methods have been developed, and are used in many countries around the world. The remainder of this chapter provides details on how forest health monitoring evolved as a concept, and how forest health is being monitored and assessed in various countries.

10.2 Forest health monitoring

10.2.1 USA

Forest health monitoring is conducted on an annual basis by the US Department of Agriculture Forest Service, Forest Health Monitoring Program (FHM); with the plot component led by the US Forest Service Forest Inventory and Analysis (FIA) Program. This national program was initiated in 1990, and is designed to determine the status, changes, and trends in indicators of forest condition. The FHM Program uses data from ground plots, field surveys, aerial surveys, and other sources of biotic and abiotic data to develop analytical approaches to address forest health issues that affect the sustainability of forest ecosystems (US Forest Service FHM 2009a). FHM covers all forested lands through a partnership involving the USDA Forest Service, state foresters, other state and federal agencies, and academic institutions.

The FIA defines forest lands as being at least 10% stocked with forest trees of any size, including land that formerly had such tree cover and is being naturally or artificially regenerated (see Chapter 8 for definition of forest). Forest lands include transition zones, such as areas between heavily forested and non-forested lands that are at least 10% stocked with forest trees and forest areas adjacent to urban and suburban lands. Also included are pinyon-juniper and chaparral areas in the West and afforested areas. Minimum area for classification of forest land is 1 acre (0.404 ha). Roadside, streamside, and shelterbelt strips of trees must have a crown width of at least 120 feet (36.5 m) to qualify as forest land. Unimproved roads and trails, streams, and clearings in forest areas are classified as forest if less than 120 feet wide (Smith *et al.* 2004).

Within the FHM program, there are five major activities (US Forest Service FHM 2009b):

1. Detection monitoring – annual monitoring that uses nationally standardized aerial and ground surveys to evaluate status and change in condition of forest ecosystems.
2. Evaluation monitoring – projects that determine extent, severity, and causes of undesirable changes in forest health identified through Detection Monitoring.
3. Intensive Site Monitoring – enhances understanding of cause-effect relationships by linking detection monitoring to ecosystem process studies and assessing specific issues at multiple spatial scales, e.g., calcium depletion, carbon sequestration.
4. Research on monitoring techniques – develops or improves indicators, monitoring systems, and analytical techniques. Examples include urban and riparian forest health monitoring, early detection of invasive species, multivariate analyses of forest health indicators, and spatial scan statistics (see Chapters 2 and 5).
5. Analysis and Reporting – synthesis of information from various data sources within and external to the Forest Service to produce issue-driven reports on status and change in forest health at national, regional, and state levels.

Of these five activities, detection monitoring provides core long-term field plot measurements for monitoring forest health. In addition to permanent field plots, other sources of data include Forest Service' Forest Health Protection (FHP) aerial survey data, National Oceanic and Atmospheric Administration–Palmer Drought Severity Index, Moderate Resolution Imaging Spectroradiometer (MODIS) fire data, and National Interagency Coordination Center data on forest area burned (e.g., Ambrose and Conkling 2007).

10.2.2 FHM detection monitoring design

A major data source for forest health monitoring is the FIA national field plot network, which is based on the Environmental Protection Agency's (EPA) Environmental Monitoring and Assessment Program (EMAP) hexagon grid (US EPA 2009; Moser 2008) (Figure 10.1). As a result of the 1998 "Farm Bill", the detection plot component of FHM has been integrated into the FIA Program plot network. (For detailed descriptions of the FIA program, see Bechtold and Patterson 2005).

FIA uses a three-phase systematic sampling approach for all US forested lands. In Phase 1 (P1), aerial photography and/or remote sensing are used to characterize size and locations of forest and non-forest land using interpreted "photo points" for every ~ 240 acres. In Phase 2 (P2), field crews visit accessible sample locations on forest land to collect data on forest type, land ownership, tree species, tree size, tree condition, and site attributes (e.g., land use, disturbance, slope). Plot density for P2 samples is approximately one plot per 6000 acres of forested land (or ~ 125 000 samples, nationally) (Burkman 2003; 2005). States can choose to increase the number of sample locations by contributing state funds.

Traditional forest inventory measures are collected annually on P2 sample locations with a fixed inventory-cycle length. Legislation mandates a 5-year inventory cycle in the eastern USA, and a 10-year cycle in the West. In states with a 5-year inventory cycle, 20% of the sample locations are measured each year. In states with a 10-year cycle, 10% of the samples are measured each year. Each set of annual samples are referred to as a "panel" (Burkman 2005). Sample locations are selected from a five- or ten-panel grid in a systematic manner with each sampling location assigned to a panel such that the overall design is that each panel represents an independent annual sample of forest conditions. Re-measurement consists of repeating the measurements starting with the first panel and proceeding through the remaining panels each year.

Phase 3 (P3) plots are established on a subset of P2 plots. A broader suite of forest health attributes related to ecosystem function, condition, and health is measured on every 16th P2 plot (one plot per 96 000 acres ~ 8000 forested P3 plots in the USA). P3 data generally are collected during June, July, and August when deciduous trees and other vegetation have leaves and are easily identified (Burkman 2003).

10.2.3 Sample location layout

FIA plot design consists of a cluster of four circular 1/24 acre (subplots spaced out in a fixed pattern (Figure 10.2). Three subplot centers are established 120 feet (36.5 m) from the center subplot at directions of 120°, 240° and 360°. Annual plots (1/4 acre) are established around each subplot center for tree

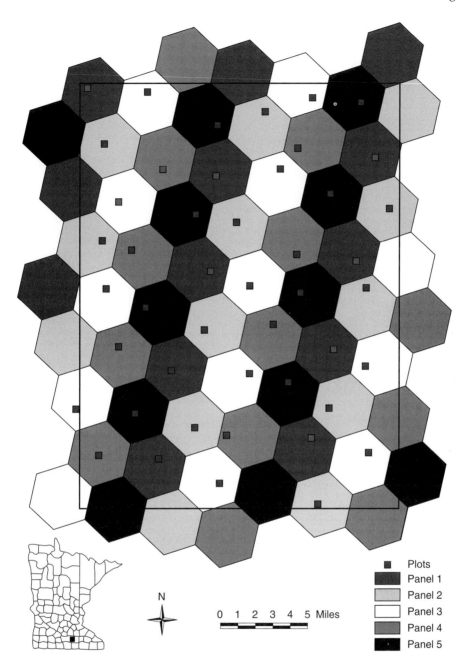

Figure 10.1 Five-panel grid showing Phase 2 hexagons from Waseca Co. Minnesota. Squares within each panel indicate sampling locations being evaluated every five years. (From Burkman 2005, with permission.)

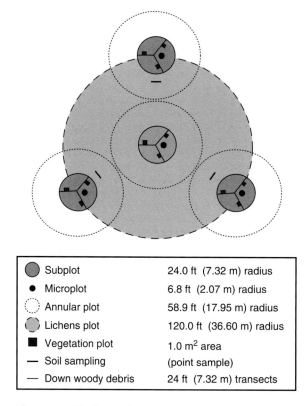

⬤ Subplot	24.0 ft (7.32 m) radius
● Microplot	6.8 ft (2.07 m) radius
○ Annular plot	58.9 ft (17.95 m) radius
◐ Lichens plot	120.0 ft (36.60 m) radius
■ Vegetation plot	1.0 m² area
— Soil sampling	(point sample)
— Down woody debris	24 ft (7.32 m) transects

Figure 10.2 Plot layout for P2/P3 FIA sampling locations. (From Burkman 2005, with permission.)

measurements that require collecting a physical sample. Within each subplot, one 1/300 acre microplot is established 12 feet (3.6 m) 90° from subplot center. Most tree measurements occur within the subplot.

Measurements of seedlings, saplings, and other vegetation are measured on microplots (Burkman 2005). This plot design provides the basis for both the P2 and P3 samples. Additional P3 variables are collected within an approximately 1 acre (2.5 ha) plot established around the center subplot (lichens), on transects that run through each subplot (down woody material), and on three 1 m² quadrats established within each subplot (vascular plants) (US Forest Service FIA 2009).

10.2.4 Forest health monitoring variables

Phase 2 variables measured include (Burkman 2003):

- Tree diameter, length, damage, amount of rotten/missing wood, and tree quality
- Tree regeneration
- Site quality information

- Stocking
- General land use
- General stand characteristics, e.g., forest type, stand age, and disturbance
- Changes in land use and general stand characteristics
- Estimates of growth, mortality, and removals.

At each P3 plot, the following additional forest health measurements are made (Burkman 2003; US Forest Service FIA 2009):

- Crown condition – including foliage transparency, uncompacted live crown ratio, crown light exposure, crown position, crown vigor class, crown density, and crown dieback. Generally, it is assumed that trees with good crown condition are vigorous and healthy while trees with poor crown condition are typically under stress.
- Soil condition – soil erosion and compaction are measured, along with forest floor and litter layer thickness, and soil texture. Soil samples are collected for analysis of physical and chemical properties including estimates of site fertility and estimates of soil carbon in the litter and upper mineral soil layers.
- Lichen communities – lichen species richness and abundance are measured on the larger 1 acre (0.4 ha) P3 plot. Presence or absence of certain lichen species are indicators of air quality, climatic changes, and ecosystem biodiversity.
- Vegetation diversity and structure – vegetation composition, ground cover distribution, species abundance, and spatial arrangement of canopy layers in forested subplots are measured. In addition, presence/absence data are collected for vascular plants in the 1 m^2 quadrats. These data are used to assess vegetation diversity, presence and abundance of introduced plant species, fuel loading, wildlife habitat suitability, and carbon cycling.
- Down woody material – measurements of the amount of coarse and fine woody material, duff, litter and fuelbed depth, and fuel loading are used to estimate carbon storage, soil erosion potential, fire fuel loading and, combined with vegetation structure data, wildlife habitat.
- Ozone bioindicator data – on a separate grid, ozone-sensitive species (e.g., *Prunus serotina*, *Pinus ponderosa*) are evaluated for the presence of foliar ozone injury during the late summer.

Many of these forest health indicators, and other forest inventory measurements, serve to meet the Santiago Declaration and accompanying criteria and indicators (Anon. 1995; Montreal Process Working Group 2009) that were adopted by the Forest Service. National forest health monitoring reports address topics such as forest fragmentation, drought occurrence, fire occurrence, ozone damage to plants, insect and disease activity, down woody materials as an indicator of wildlife habitat, fuels and carbon stocks, and physical and chemical properties of soils (e.g., Ambrose and Conkling 2007).

In addition to using the plots and other data to link to these criteria and indicators and to conduct evaluation and intensive site monitoring, the FHM program works with FIA, FHP and state and Federal Agencies to monitor forest health conditions, including providing information on invasive species and forest insect and disease conditions in the USA (e.g., US Forest Service FHP 2007).

10.2.5 Non-forest health monitoring

As FHM currently focuses on forest areas, non-forest areas are not included in the national monitoring effort; however, a significant number of trees may be present in non-forest areas. In urban areas of the USA, which includes some forest stands, there are an estimated 3.8 billion trees (Nowak et al. 2001). To help address this issue, the Forest Health Monitoring Strategic Plan (US Forest Service 2003) calls for new monitoring approaches for under-represented forest ecosystems, e.g., urban and riparian forests.

Various researchers have investigated implementation of a riparian monitoring program (US Forest Service 2009). In addition, pilot-testing of baseline monitoring of trees in urban areas has been accomplished in Indiana (Nowak et al. 2007), Wisconsin (Cumming et al. 2007), and New Jersey (Cumming et al. 2008). More recently, urban plots have been established using the basic FIA P2 plot design and grid (5-year panel) in Tennessee and Colorado, with plots measured during the in-leaf season, and some P3 crown parameters to assess tree condition (Cumming et al. 2008). To date, though urban plots have been established, no repeat measurements of plots have been made to monitor changes in forests and trees through time.

The US Forest Service is an international leader in forest health monitoring with extensive amounts of data gathered to date. A yearly technical report is compiled to summarize trends across the landscape to highlight abiotic and biotic factors affecting forest conditions (e.g., Ambrose and Conkling 2007). The FHM Program provides important established baseline information for long-term monitoring along with repeated measures to monitor change. In addition, FIA reports include information regarding forest health and forest condition at the National (e.g., Smith et al. 2009), regional (e.g., Oswalt and Turner 2009), state (e.g., Conner et al. 2004), and sub-state (e.g., Oswalt 2005) levels. Standardized data collection protocols, including field crew training and quality assurance procedures, provide for quality long-term data. Annual plot data on a fixed national grid along with supplemental information from numerous sources provide the basis for annual forest health monitoring and detection of various forest issues essential for maintaining forest health at local, regional, and national scales. Other nations are implementing forest health monitoring based on FHM protocols (Hofstetter 2007). For example, Tanzania has established plots in the Eastern Arc Mountains taking data on crown condition, tree damage, and mensuration data (species density, diameters, heights, crown position). Indonesia has established plots to monitor sustainability and biodiversity of tropical rain forests using the FHM sampling design, and several eastern European countries (e.g., Belarus, Ukraine, Lithuania, Latvia, and Estonia) are using modified FHM plots.

10.3 Canada

Almost 40% of Canada is forested, ~400 million ha (NRC 2001), which comprises ~10% of the world's forests (CCFM 2003). Natural Resources Canada recently implemented a National Forest Inventory that will provide information on the current state of forests and how they are changing through time (Gillis *et al.* 2005). This inventory and monitoring system is a plot-based system (Figure 10.3) (Canadian Forest Service 2008) using a national grid to cover the entire landmass (Gillis *et al.* 2005). There are ~1150 ground plots established in forested areas. Plots are grouped into 10-unit panels with one panel measured annually (i.e., a 10-year measurement cycle). Data measurements include:

- Two 30-m line transects for small and coarse woody debris and surface substrate
- Four 1-m^2 microplots for shrub, herb, grasses, mosses, lichen biomass, and fine woody debris
- One soil pit for soil classification, coarse fragments, organic and bulk density soil samples
- Two ecology plots for recording a list of all species and percent cover
- 50 m^2 small tree plot for small tree data and stumps
- 400 m^2 large tree plot for tree data (age, height, dbh) and plot parameters (successional stage, disturbance, plot origin, management treatments, defect or pathological indicators).

Canada is a world leader in **third-party certification standards** for sustainable forestry management (CCFM 2007). The Forest Stewardship Council (FSC) was established in 1993 (*www.fsccanada.org*), and is one of three voluntary systems in place to achieve third-party certified status. The Canadian Standards Association's Forest Management Standard (CSA) is another means of certification as well as the Sustainable Forestry Initiative (SFI), both of which are

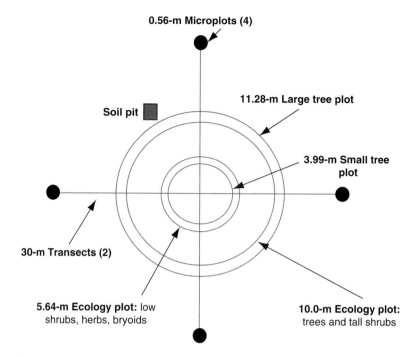

Figure 10.3 Natural Forest Inventory of Canada ground plot design. (Canadian Forest Service 2008.) Circular plot measurements are radii, e.g., the Large Tree Plot has a radius of 11.28 m.

endorsed by the Programme for the Endorsement of Forest Certification (PEFC). A goal of these systems is to maintain and enhance long-term health of forest ecosystems in Canada, while providing ecological, economic, cultural, and social opportunities. All three certification systems ensure conservation of biological diversity, wildlife habitat, soil and water resources, and sustainable timber harvest, and all require annual monitoring and public disclosure of findings (see Chapter 8 for discussion of forest certification).

10.4 Europe

Monitoring of forest conditions was initiated in the early 1980s in response to a suspected occurrence of a widespread forest decline event (Vanguelova *et al.* 2007; IWF 2008). A coordinated effort across Europe was initiated in 1985 by the United Nations Economic Commission for Europe, and implemented by the International Co-operative Programme on Assessment and Monitoring of Air Pollution Effects on Forests (ICP Forests) to improve under-standing of factors affecting forest ecosystems (UNEC-ICP 2006). Intensive forest health monitoring is implemented at two levels: Level I and Level II (EFMP).

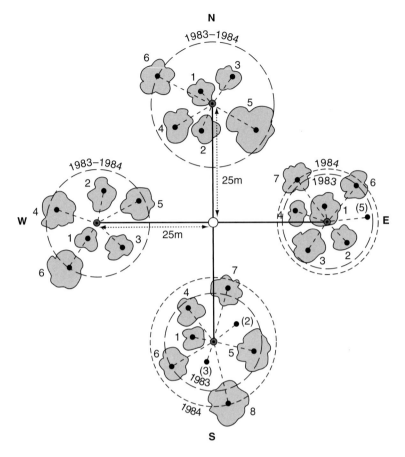

Figure 10.4 Four-point cross cluster plot for selection of trees to monitor in Level I European ICP forest sample plots. (Source: http://www.icp-forests.org/pdf/ Chapt2_compl06.pdf.)

Approximately 6200 Level I plots have been established across Europe in 33 countries on a 16 × 16 km grid. Data taken in Level I plots include annual crown defoliation and discoloration estimates, and damage visible on a total of 10–24 trees. Sample plots and trees are selected using a statistically sound procedure, an example of which is the four-point cross cluster with six trees measured in each of four subplots (Figure 10.4).

Approximately 800 Level II plots are located in managed forests representing the most important forest ecosystems (Figure 10.5). Plots are 0.25 ha, and data collected in these plots represent both stressor and response indicators including: crown condition, foliar chemistry, tree growth, ground vegetation composition, stand structure (including deadwood), epiphytic lichens, soil chemistry, soil solution chemistry, atmospheric deposition, ambient air quality, meteorology, phenology, litterfall, and remote-sensing data (Figure 10.6) (IWF 2008).

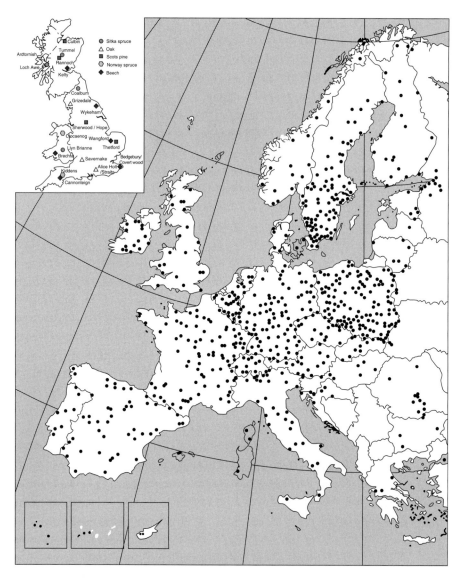

Figure 10.5 European Level II monitoring plots. (Source: http://www.forestresearch. gov.uk/images/imfe.gif/$file/imfe.gif.)

Results from Level I and Level II forest surveys are summarized annually in ICP Forest technical reports (e.g., Lorenz *et al.* 2008).

10.5 Australia

The Australian Department of Agriculture, Fisheries and Forestry have issued criteria and indicators that closely follow those outlined by the Montreal Process. Indicators specific to monitoring forest ecosystem health are

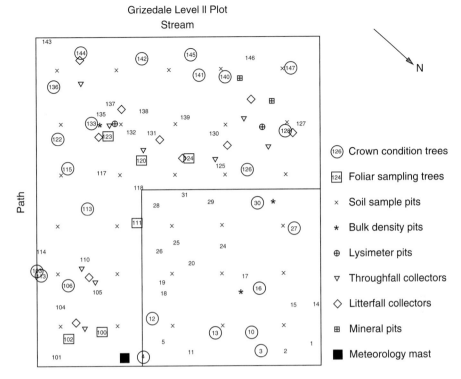

Figure 10.6 A typical Level II plot used in European forest monitoring plots. (Source: http://www.forestresearch.gov.uk/images/level2plotgrize.gif/$FILE/ level2plotgrize.gif; http://www.forestresearch.gov.uk/images/level2plotgrize.gif/$FILE/ level2plotgrize.gif.)

to quantify scale and impact of agents and processes affecting forest health and vitality as well as fire data (Australian Government 2008). Australia consists of eight states, and each has developed specific monitoring protocols established through Ecologically Sustainable Forest Management (ESFM) plans. The state governments will facilitate research and long-term monitoring to detect adverse impacts and develop practice and management plans to ameliorate identified adverse impacts in keeping with the "precautionary principle" (Commonwealth of Australia 1995). In general, objectives for ESFM plans are to maintain ecosystem health and vitality, and to control outbreaks of disease, pests or other agents affecting ecosystem health and vitality, through cooperative planning and management (Commonwealth of Australia 1995). Data requirements and monitoring methodology include identifying and quantifying factors (processes and agents) that may change ecosystem functioning. Factors may include interactions between natural events and management

actions in the following areas: fire, climatic events, river regulation, salinization, grazing, introduction of exotic biota, logging, clearing, roading, bell-miner
dieback, insects, and diseases. Relevant factors are identified and monitored on
a regional basis.

Four main health surveillance and monitoring activities are implemented
by forest managers: (1) Forest health surveillance focused on detecting and
quantifying damage; (2) Health/condition monitoring that is tree/forest-
focused and optimized to describe condition of trees and detect change;
(3) Pest population monitoring optimized to measure populations of target
pests; and (4) ad hoc detection that is damage-focused on specific pests and
disease issues (Australian Government 2008). Most states use aerial surveillance, drive-through surveys, and ground inspections in plantations with
very little monitoring occurring in native forests. Two states, however, have
established plot-based monitoring systems (Wardlaw et al. 2007; Carnegie
2008). Victoria has established surveillance methodology based on the US
FHM plot system and western Australia monitors forest health using intensive measurements in permanent "Forestcheck" sites where plant species and
cover are documented in four 1000-m plots and twenty 1-m plots) within
different forest types.

The need for coordination and compatibility of assessment and reporting
systems at the state-level is recognized in order to link these efforts at the
national level (Stone et al. 2001; Stone and Coops 2004). Unfortunately, diver-
gent management priorities for forests and plantations have resulted in
differing interpretations of what is meant by forest health, as well as how
it is assessed and monitored at the state level. Individual state priorities
and available resources and funding are limitations that greatly influence
these processes.

10.6 Indonesia

The Indonesian Forest Health Monitoring (INDO FHM) program is
charged with delineating current conditions of Indonesian tropical rain forests
with respect to sustainability and biodiversity (Soekotjo et al. 1997). The program is a collaborative research effort with the US FHM Program, and is
supported by the International Tropical Timber Organization (ITTO). INDO
FHM is initiating a plot system and using indicators similar to those of the
US FHM program. Data from these efforts will provide an assessment of forest
conditions as to the proportions of forests in poor, sub-nominal, nominal, and
optimal condition. Long-term monitoring will subsequently quantify changes
and trends through time.

10.7 China

Recognizing that forest resources are a critical issue, the Chinese Academy of Forestry, and the Chinese Ecosystem Research Network established the Chinese Forest Ecosystem Research Network (CFERN) (Wang *et al.* 2003). CFERN is comprised of 15 stations that conduct research in forested areas throughout the country where water quality, pest abundances, tree conditions, and composition are continuously monitored. These stations also collect data on forest fires, disease/pest outbreaks, and forest resources that can be used in evaluations of forest health (Xiao *et al.* 2004).

10.8 Food and Agriculture Organization (FAO) of the United Nations

Fifty-nine countries, representing 75% of the world's tropical forests and 90% of the global tropical timber trade, operate under the guidelines of the International Tropical Timber Organization (ITTO 2005). ITTO encourages member countries to strive for export of timber products from sustainably managed sources. To facilitate sustainability, ITTO provides criteria for management of tropical forests as well as tools for monitoring, assessing, and reporting changes and trends in forest conditions and management. ITTO considers seven criteria essential to sustainable forest management. Of these, the first three are relevant to forest health, and the last four concern various goods and services provided by forests (Forest production, Biological diversity, Soil and water protection, and Economic, social, and cultural aspects). Criterion 1 (Enabling conditions for sustainable forest management) outlines general legal, economic, and institutional frameworks that facilitate success of the other criteria. Criteria 2 (Extent and condition of forests) and 3 (Forest ecosystem health) are concerned with quantity, security, and quality of forest resources.

Many other countries operate under the umbrella of the FAO (Castaneda 2000). Nine countries participate under the Asian Dry Forests Process. Seven countries operate under the Leparterique Process of Central America, 13 participate under the African Timber Organization, 30 under the Near East Process, and 30 under the Dry-zone Africa Process. Forest health under the last criterion include such factors as area modified by humans, fire, storms, insects, diseases, animals, drought, invasives, percent of forest without regeneration, changes in nutrient balance and soil acidity, percent of population employed in farming, bush encroachment, and trends in crop yields. The Tarapoto process is part of the Amazon Cooperation Treaty; which includes eight countries representing a substantial proportion of tropical forests. This process includes 8 criteria and 15 indicators including: existence of policies and legal framework for land-use planning, rate of conversion of forests to other uses, and prevention measures to protect water courses from forest extraction activities.

10.9 Other countries

Many countries not specifically addressed above have forest health monitoring programs, or are in the process of establishing programs. Some focus efforts on plant pests and diseases, others on conservation, and still others on environmental services provided by forest ecosystems. Adaptations often are necessary in order to use existing indicators from temperate regions of the world. The list of indicators used within each country should necessarily be adapted to the specific forest type, and the social and economic needs of citizens of that country.

10.10 Conclusions

As indicated in Chapter 1, forest health monitoring began some time ago, but there remain questions to be addressed. Some of the most pressing include assessing if all monitoring approaches are statistically valid. If so, are they comparable? Would a healthy forest under one system be deemed unhealthy under another? Do the indicators currently being used provide the data necessary to assess forest health in a meaningful manner? Has this been rigorously evaluated for the different monitoring programs? Are there other indicators that we could monitor or calculate (e.g., baseline mortality) that would be better? Answering these questions and moving toward implementation of a global forest health monitoring network is ideal, but would need to have a common definition of "health", as well as a common system of monitoring that is statistically sound at known spatial scales across all forest ecosystems.

The most widely used indicator of biophysical forest health is probably visual estimations of crown condition of trees (Alexander and Palmer 1997). Use of this indicator is predicated on the assumption that if a majority of trees are exhibiting crown dieback, then the forest is experiencing some deleterious process, and so, is unhealthy. US forest conditions are primarily summarized based on crown condition using a combination of measurements for crown dieback and crown transparency. Observer bias and objectivity often is a problem in assessing this variable (Innes 1988). A similar variable estimating crown condition in European forest health monitoring plots has been questioned and criticized (Ferretti 1997; Ferretti and Chiarucci 2003; Seidling 2004). Crown dieback may be a good indicator of tree stress, but measuring it accurately requires extensive training of field personnel. Estimates still can vary considerably, especially if measurements are taken during different months (Seidling 2004). In addition, crown dieback often is reversible, i.e., not all trees that show crown dieback are necessarily unhealthy (see Chapter 4). Trees under stress often exhibit dieback that is reversed when the stress abates. Use of crown discoloration and assignment of causal agents is apparently even more variable (Ferretti 1998, Ferretti and Chiarucci 2002).

Calculations of baseline mortality (stable age and size class discussed in Chapters 1 through 3) from mortality data already being collected may be a strong candidate to incorporate into forest health monitoring programs considering its simplicity, and in recognition of the limitations of measuring crown condition. Information derived from it also may facilitate establishment or refinement of reference conditions critical to monitoring indicators of forest ecosystem health and vitality.

References

Alexander, S.A. and Palmer, C.J. 1997. Forest health monitoring in the United States: first four years. *Environmental Monitoring Assessment* **55**: 267–277.

Ambrose, M.J. and Conkling, B.L. 2007. Forest Health Monitoring 2005 *National Technical Report US Forest Service Southern Research Station, Gen. Tech. Rep. SRS-104*. Asheville, NC.

Anon. 1995. Sustaining the world's forests: the Santiago agreement. *Journal Forestry* **93**: 18–21.

Australian Government. 2008. Australia's Sustainable Forest Management Framework of Criteria and Indicators. Department of Agriculture, Fisheries and Forestry. Canberra, Australia. http://adl.brs.gov.au/forestsaustralia/_pubs/ciframework.pdf; http://adl.brs.gov.au/forestsaustralia/_pubs/criterion3.pdf [Accessed November 2010].

Bechtold, W.A. and Patterson, P.L. (eds). 2005. The enhanced forest inventory and analysis program – national sampling design and estimation procedures. *US Forest Service Southern Research Station, Gen. Tech. Rep. SRS-80*. Asheville, NC. http://www.srs.fs.usda.gov/pubs/20371 [Accessed November 2010].

Berryman, A.A. 1986. *Forest Insects, Principles and Practice of Population Management*. Plenum Press, New York, USA.

Burkman, B. 2003. Forest Inventory and Analysis Phase 2 and Phase 3: Ground Measurements. FIA Fact Sheet Series. http://www.ncrs.fs.fed.us/4801/local-resources/pdfs/Phase2_3.pdf [Accessed November 2010].

Burkman, B. 2005. Forest Inventory and Analysis Sampling and Plot Design. FIA Fact Sheet Series. http://fia.fs.fed.us/library/fact-sheets/data-collections/Sampling%20and%20Plot%20Design.pdf [Accessed November 2010].

Canadian Forest Service. 2008. Canada's National Forest Inventory: Ground Sampling Guidelines (V5.0). 2008. https://nfi.nfis.org/documentation/ground_plot/Gp_guidelines_v5.0.pdf [Accessed November 2010].

Canadian Council of Forest Ministers (CCFM). 2003. Defining Sustainable Forest Management in Canada, Criteria and Indicators.

Canadian Council of Forest Ministers (CCFM). 2007. Canada: A world leader in third-party certification. Factsheet. Sustainable Forest Management Canada. http://www.sfmcanada.org/english/pdf/Cert_FactSheet_E_revB4.pdf [Accessed November 2010].

Carnegie, A. 2008. A decade of forest health surveillance in Australia: an overview. *Australian Forestry*. Sept. 2008.

Castaneda, F. 2000. Criteria and indicators for sustainable forest management: international processes, current status and the way ahead. *Unasylva* **203**: 34–40.

Commonwealth of Australia. 1995. National Forest Policy Statement: A new focus for Australia's forests. http://www.daff.gov.au/__data/assets/pdf_file/0019/37612/nat_nfps.pdf [Accessed December 2010].

Conner, R.C., Adams, T., Butler, B.J., *et al.* 2004. The state of South Carolina's forests, 2001. *US Forest Service Southern Research Station, Res. Bull. SRS-096*. Asheville, NC. http://www.srs.fs.usda.gov/pubs/7507 [Accessed November 2010].

Cumming, A.B., Nowak, D.J., Twardus, D.B., *et al.* 2007. Urban Forests of Wisconsin 2002: Pilot Monitoring Project 2002. *USDA Forest Service, Northeastern Area State and Private Forestry Report, NA-FR-05–07*.

Cumming, A.B., Twardus, D.B., and Nowak, D.J. 2008. Urban forest health monitoring: large scale assessments in the United States. *Arboriculture Urban Forestry* **34**: 341–346.

Dale, V.H. and Beyeler S.C. 2001. Challenges in the development and use of ecological indicators. *Ecological Indicators* **1**: 3–10.

European Forest Monitoring Programme (EFMP). http://www.aisf.it/biodv/PPT/EFMP-0503071.pdf [Accessed November 2010].

Ferretti, M. 1997. Forest health assessment and monitoring – issues for consideration. *Environmental Monitoring Assessment* **48**: 45–72.

Ferretti, M. and Chiarucci, A. 2003. Design concepts adopted in long-term forest monitoring programs in Europe – problems for the future. *Science Total Environment* **310**: 171–178.

Gillis, M.D., Omule, A.Y., and Brierley, T. 2005. Monitoring Canada's forests: The National Forest Inventory. *Forestry Chronicle* **81**: 214–221.

Hofstetter, R. 2007. Forest Health Monitoring. Presentation at the International Seminar on Forest Administration and Management. October 2007. http://www.for.nau.edu/files/InternationalForestry/Isfam/2007/presentations/HofstetterForestHealthMonitoring.ppt [Accessed November 2010].

Innes, J.L. 1988. Forest health surveys: problems in assessing observer objectivity. *Canadian Journal Forest Research* **18**: 560–565.

Innes, J.L. and Karnosky, D.F. 2001. Impacts of environmental stress on forest health: the need for more accurate indicators. In: *Criteria and Indicators for Sustainable Forest Management*. Raison, R.J., Brown, A.G., and Flinn, D.W. (eds). CAB International, Wallingford.

Institute for World Forestry (IWF). 2008. *The condition of forests in Europe: 2008 Executive Report*. http://www.icp-forests.org/pdf/ER2008.pdf [Accessed November 2010].

International Tropical Timber Organization (ITTO). 2005. Revised ITTO Criteria and
Indicators for the Sustainable Management of Tropical Forests Including
Reporting Format. ITTO Policy Development Series No 15. Hakushudo
Printing Inc.

Lorenz, M., Fischer, R., Becher, G., *et al*. 2008. Forest Condition in Europe: 2008
technical report of ICP Forests. Institute for World Forestry, Hamburg, Annexes.
http://www.icp-forests.org/pdf/TR2008.pdf [Accessed November 2010].

Montreal Process Working Group. 2009. *What is the Montreal Process?* http://www.rinya.
maff.go.jp/mpci/criteria_e.html [Accessed November 2010].

Moser, W.K. 2008. Invasive plant data collection by NRS Forest Inventory and Analysis.
Presentation at Midwest Invasive Plant Network Symposium, December 10–11,
2008. http://www.mipn.org/Data%20Collection%20and%20Management%
20Workshop%20Jan%202008/Monitoring/Moser_FIA.pdf [Accessed
November 2010].

Gillis, MD, Power, K., and Gray, S. 2001. Canada's Forest Inventory 2001. Overview –
Inventory of Canada's forests. Natural Resources Canada, Canadian Forest Service,
Pacific Forestry Center, Victoria.

Nowak, D.J., Noble, M.H., Sisinni, S.M., and Dwyer, J.F. 2001. Assessing the U.S. urban
forest resource. *Journal Forestry* **99**: 37–42.

Nowak, D.J., Twardus, D., Hoehn, R., *et al*. 2007. National Forest Health Monitoring
Program, Monitoring Urban Forests in Indiana: Pilot Study 2002, Part 2: Statewide
Estimates Using the UFORE Model. *Northeastern Area Report*. NA-FR-01-07.

Oswalt, S.N. 2005. Forest resources of South Carolina's national forests, 2001. *US Forest
Service Southern Research Station, Res. Bull. SRS-098. Asheville, NC*. http://www.srs.fs.
usda.gov/pubs/5425 [Accessed Novmber 2010].

Oswalt, C.M. and Turner, J.A. 2009. Status of hardwood forest resources in the
Appalachian region including estimates of growth and removals. *US Forest Service
Southern Research Station, Res. Bull. SRS-142*. Asheville, NC, USA. http://www.srs.fs.
usda.gov/pubs/32058 [Accessed Novmber 2010].

Percy, K.E. 2002. Is air pollution an important factor in international forest
health? In: *Effects of Air Pollution on Forest Health and Biodiversity in Forests of the
Carpathian Mountains*. Szaro, R.C., Bytnerowicz, A., and Oszlany, J. (eds). IOS
Press, Amsterdam.

Percy, K.E. and Ferretti, M. 2004. Air pollution and forest health: toward new
monitoring concepts. *Environmental Pollution* **130**: 113–126.

Peterman, R.M. 1978. The ecological role of mountain pine beetle in lodgepole pine
forests. In: *Theory and Practice of Mountain Pine Beetle Management in Lodgepole Pine
Forests. Forest*. Berryman, A., Amman, D., Stark, R., and Kibbee, D. (eds). Wildlife and
Range Experiment Station, University of Idaho, Moscow.

Raffa, K.F., Aukema, B., Bentz, B.J., *et al*. 2009. A literal use of "forest health" safeguards
against misuse and misapplication. *Journal Forestry* **107**: 276–277.

Seidling, W. 2004. Crown condition within integrated evaluations of Level II
monitoring data at the German level. *Europan Journal Forest Research* **123**:
63–74.

Smith, B.W., Miles, P.D., Vissage, J.S., and Pugh, S.A. 2004. Forest Resources of the United States, 2002. *US Forest Service North Central Research Station, Gen. Tech. Rep. NC 241*. St. Paul, MN.

Smith, B.W., Miles, P.D., Perry, C.H., and Pugh, S.A. [Coords.]. 2009. Forest Resources of the United States, 2007. *US Department of Agriculture, Forest Service Washington Office, Gen. Tech. Rep. WO-78. Washington, DC.* http://www.treesearch.fs.fed.us/pubs/17334 [Accessed November 2010].

Soekotjo, S. and Sastrosoemarto, B. Sarbini. 1997. Forest health monitoring to monitor sustainability of Indonesian tropical rain forests. *XI World Forestry Congress. Antalya, Turkey. Vol. 2, Topic 7.*

Stone, C., Kile, G., Old, K., and Coops, N.C. 2001. Forest Health Monitoring in Australia, National and Regional Commitments and Operational Realities. *Ecosystem Health* **7**: 48–58.

Stone, C. and Coops, N.C. 2004. Assessment and monitoring of damage from insects in Australian eucalypt forests and commercial plantations. *Australian Journal Entomology* **43**: 283–292.

US Environmental Protection Agency (EPA). 2009. Environmental Monitoring & -Assessment Program. *http://www.epa.gov/emap/*

US Forest Service 2003. Forest Health Monitoring, A National Strategic Plan. http://fhm.fs.fed.us/annc/strategic_plan03.pdf [Accessed November 2010].

US Forest Service 2009. *FHM Riparian Project.* http://www.fs.fed.us/institute/fhm_riparian

US Forest Service. FHM 2009a. Forest Health Monitoring Purpose and Outcomes. *Fact Sheet Series.* http://fhm.fs.fed.us/fact/pdf_files/fhm_purpose_2009.pdf [Accessed December 2010].

US Forest Service. FHM 2009b. Forest Health Monitoring Detection Monitoring. *Fact Sheet Series.* http://fhm.fs.fed.us/fact/pdf_files/fhm_dm_2009.pdf [Accessed December 2010].

US Forest Service FHP. 2007. Forest Insect and Disease Conditions in the United States 2006. U.S. Forest Service, Forest Health Protection, Washington, DC. http://www.fs.fed.us/foresthealth/publications/ConditionsReport_06_final.pdf [Accessed November 2010].

US Forest Service FIA. 2009. Forest Inventory and Analysis Program FIA Library. FIA Field Methods for Phase 3 Measurements. Version 4.0. http://fia.fs.fed.us/library/field-guides-methods-proc/ [Accessed November 2010].

United Nations Economic Commission for Europe International Co-operative Programme on Assessment and Monitoring of Air Pollution Effects on Forests (UNEC-ICP). 2006. Manual on methods and criteria for harmonized sampling, assessment, monitoring and analysis of the effects of air pollution on forests: Part I. http://www.icp-forests.org/pdf/Chapt1_compl2006.pdf [November 2010].

Vanguelova, E., Barsoum, N., Broadmeadow, M., *et al.* 2007. Ten years of intensive environmental monitoring in British forests. Forestry Commission.

Wang, B., Jin, F., Yang, F., and Cui, X. 2003. *The Chinese Forest Ecosystem Research Network (CFERN) and its development. XII World Forestry Congress. Quebec City,*

Canada. http://www.fao.org/DOCREP/ARTICLE/WFC/XII/0048-B4.HTM [Accessed November 2010].

Wardlaw, T., Carnegie, A., and Lawson, S. 2007. The scorecard of a decade of forest health surveillance in Australia. *23rd Biennial Institute of Foresters of Australia Conference, Coffs Harbour, New South Wales.*

Xiao, F., Ouyang, H., Zhang, Q., Fu, B., and Zhang, Z. 2004. Forest ecosystem health assessment and analysis in China. *Journal Geographical Science* **14**: 18–24.

What did we learn, and where does it leave us? Concluding thoughts

J.D. CASTELLO AND S.A. TEALE

11.1 Summary of the salient points of the book (what did we learn?)

In this chapter we summarize the most important concepts of the text, first by identifying the problems faced by forest health professionals as we have struggled to define a healthy forest and the best way to assess and to monitor it, then we summarize our approach to address these problems followed by the rationale for our approach, and finally we discuss the role of forestry practices to maintain healthy forests. We end the book by looking to the challenges that future forest health professionals will need to meet to maintain the health of the world's forests.

11.1.1 Prior definitions of forest health

There have been many definitions of forest health proposed during the past 30 years. Edmonds, Agee, and Gara discuss some of these in their textbook on forest health (Edmonds *et al.*, 2000). These definitions range from entirely utilitarian to ecological in the extremes (Kolb *et al.*, 1994). Many of them are not quantifiable, are subjective, or attempt to encompass so many complex and interacting ecological processes that they become unworkable. In apparent frustration, Raffa *et al.* (2009) proposed that the term "forest health" be used "only when describing the extent to which ecosystem processes are functioning within natural historical variability."

A concise and objective definition of a healthy forest is essential if we are to assess trends in forest condition over time and across continents. The term is

Forest Health: An Integrated Perspective, ed. John D. Castello and Stephen A. Teale. Published by Cambridge University Press. © Cambridge University Press 2011.

widely used in government mandates regarding forest management goals. Although long-term health monitoring and assessment programs began about 20 years ago, and the data collected have been used to assess trends in forest condition, this is not equivalent to an assessment of forest health. Forest health often has denoted the degree to which normal tree processes have been disrupted (Percy 2002), while forest condition has been used in relation to the descriptive indicators used in routine forest assessments. If one considers forest health as equivalent to the crown condition of trees (i.e., forest condition approach), one will proceed to assess spatial and temporal variation of defoliation and foliar symptoms as an indication of trends in health. On the other hand, if the ecosystem as a whole is considered, many different living and non-living components including, but not limited to, trees will be used as indicators. (Innes and Karnosky, 2001). But in either case, there still is no framework upon which to quantitatively relate crown condition or the aggregate of multiple disparate indicators to forest health in a manner that is spatially and temporally consistent and comparable.

The beginning of true forest health assessment was the establishment of the Montréal Process Working Group, and the 1995 Santiago Declaration that followed it, from which seven criteria for the promotion of sustainable forests were adopted, of which the third was the maintenance of forest ecosystem health and vitality. To assess trends in health and vitality, 67 associated indicators were proposed and are used. So, in essence, trends in the condition of various indicators are used to assess ecosystem health even though health, per se, has not been defined or monitored. Thus, forest conditions often are monitored as a proxy because there has been no concise definition of forest health.

We discussed in Chapter 1 that healthy forests are those that are: (1) sustainable, and (2) meet the management objectives of the landowner. This definition alleviates the frustrations that forest health practitioners, educators, forest landowners, and those charged with monitoring forest health have experienced. This two-part definition overcomes the problems of either strictly utilitarian or ecological approaches to forest health.

11.1.2 The sustainability component of a healthy forest

Sustainability is key to a healthy forest. A problem, however, is that sustainability previously has not been formulated in an objective and quantifiable manner. The sustainability of populations of organisms often is assessed using life tables and transition matrix models (Caswell 1989), which enable the estimation of future population structure (i.e., stability) based on the reproduction and survival of specific age classes (Harcombe 1987). A stable diameter distribution is a demographically based measure of sustainability that describes the relationship of the density of stems in a forest to their diameter (see Chapters 1, 2, and 8). Simply put, as a cohort of trees grows, it naturally progresses from many small stems to fewer larger stems (see the Phoenix Helix discussion in Chapter 4). For many, if not most, forests this is represented by a negative exponential relationship, which when plotted on log-linear axes, becomes a linear relationship.

This concept of sustainability is based on the view of trees as the foundation species (Dayton 1972; Ellison *et al.*, 2005) of forested ecosystems. If the population structure of the foundation species is stable, then populations of other species in that ecosystem are likely to be stable, and to interact with each other in a manner typical of that community. Conversely, if populations of the foundation species are not sustainable, then neither will be the populations of other species in the ecosystem.

11.1.3 Mortality is the key to sustainability

In stable populations of organisms, the capacity for reproduction always is much greater than that which the limited resources of the environment can support. Thus, stable and presumably "healthy" populations of trees (i.e., a forest) will have dead and dying trees in it. The fundamental questions then are (1) How much mortality is needed to maintain a sustainable diameter distribution? And (2), is it possible to determine desirable levels of mortality? Fortunately, the answer to both these questions is yes. In addition, dead trees are both easy to recognize and to measure, and require no special training for field crews.

11.1.4 Baseline mortality is the reference condition by which sustainability can be assessed

The baseline mortality concept of forest health as first developed by Manion and Griffin (2001), and which we wish to promulgate as the basis for a new understanding of forest health, is based on a demographic model (the negative exponential function, see Chapters 2 and 3), which is predicated on size-class structure. Observed mortality above or below baseline in any diameter classes creates instability in the system such that the forest structure will change. The baseline mortality approach gives us an ecologically based framework and corresponding methodology with which to assess the sustainability of any forest by determining if the mortality caused by any agent of disturbance is causing instability in the system. But, a change in the current diameter distribution (i.e., size structure) of the forest may or may not be consistent with the management objectives for that forest. So sustainability of the current diameter distribution, by itself, is not equivalent to health.

The matrix that we constructed in Chapter 1 (Table 1.1) provides the framework by which a forest can be considered healthy or not. We define as healthy only a forest that is both sustainable and productive (meets management objectives). So our concept of forest health is both ecologically based, and utilitarian in its approach.

11.1.5 Management objectives

While the term "management objectives" tends to conjure up images of resource extraction and commodity production, no forest manager would argue that creating and maintaining opportunities for recreation or supporting and protecting wildlife populations are not important management objectives. In fact, they are often more important than those associated with resource extraction. However, management objectives include a much wider array of ecosystem products and services ranging from water purification and carbon sequestration to the conservation of biological diversity (see Chapters 8 and 9). Although these are essential components of forest ecosystems regardless of the objectives of people to manage them, they all are dependent on the stability of the trees in the forest for their existence. A forest with reduced biodiversity may be sustainable, though not desirable, but an unsustainable forest with high biodiversity will not maintain its biodiversity for long. This is why it is essential to separate management objectives from sustainability in the assessment of forest health.

In no way does this suggest that ecological management objectives (biodiversity and various ecosystem services) are less important than the economic management objectives or the sustainability of the forest. Most of the world's terrestrial biodiversity occurs in forested ecosystems, and the protection of biological diversity is a responsibility of all forest managers. The term "productivity" in this context is not limited to the production of commodities, but rather it refers to the ability of the forest to meet all ecological and economic objectives that have been explicitly set by the landowner. It has become apparent in recent decades that biodiversity is critical to a properly functioning ecosystem and that a properly functioning ecosystem is necessary to maintain biodiversity. For example, we have learned that undesirable impacts of insects and diseases increase with decreasing biodiversity. The integration of biodiversity conservation concerns into all forest landowner management objectives is a challenge that must be met by future forest health professionals and forest landowners.

Management objectives will necessarily vary from place to place so this aspect of forest health may not be directly comparable where management objectives vary substantially. This is another reason why it is so important to separate management objectives from sustainability as distinct components of forest health. The assessment of sustainability by the baseline mortality method is globally applicable and comparable. The development of similarly uniform means of assessing biodiversity and other complex ecological variables would enable global comparisons of them as well.

11.1.6. Benefits of the sustainability-productivity approach to forest health

The baseline mortality concept provides not only the foundation upon which a healthy forest can be defined, but the framework upon which the health of any forest can be monitored, assessed, and compared to itself or to any other forest anywhere, or at anytime (at least when and where the necessary data are available). Second, the impacts of any stresses can be evaluated in terms of their effects on the sustainability of the current diameter distribution. Third, mortality events that alter the current diameter distribution in a forest may be predictable, and silvicultural treatments can be implemented to proactively correct those changes if desired by the landowner. This, in our opinion, is perhaps the greatest advantage of the baseline mortality approach. The following sections provide some examples discussed in the text, plus some additional datasets that may provide additional examples of the utility of the method.

11.1.7 Mortality agents

Most natural biotic and abiotic agents of mortality in a forest (e.g., insects, diseases, wind, drought, etc.) provide the baseline mortality needed to maintain a sustainable diameter distribution in that forest. From the perspective of baseline mortality, the causal agent of mortality is irrelevant. But the specific agents of mortality may be important from a management perspective. For example, it may be useful to know if a particular insect pest or disease problem is causing sufficient mortality to warrant intervention (see Chapter 3, Alaska white spruce case study). Similarly, it may be important to know if one or more tree species is experiencing unusually high mortality (e.g., Chapter 3, yellow birch case study) that may require research into the cause. Has an invasive pest or pathogen impacted sustainability or productivity (e.g., Chapter 3, beech bark disease case study), or have past management practices (e.g., logging) altered sustainability (see Chapter 3, northern New York forest case study)? The baseline mortality approach can be used to address such questions.

Native insects and diseases are essential components of an ecosystem because they provide the mortality that is essential to maintain stable forest structure. Nonetheless, when native biotic agents interfere with management objectives, they are considered pests that require control or management. In reality, many instances of insect or disease outbreaks often result from an accumulation of insufficient mortality that has produced an unstable forest structure, or from anthropogenic disturbances that created unusual conditions e.g., radical changes in species composition or population densities (e.g., textbox on fusiform rust in Chapter 4, or the discussion of chestnut blight in Chapter 5).

11.1.8 Many factors interact to affect forest health

Many factors impact the diameter distribution of the tree species in a forest. In this textbook we have discussed many such factors, but certainly not all of them. These factors can and often do interact in innumerable ways to affect the health of the forest.

Every forest has been disturbed by natural processes and human activities in some way, even the seemingly most pristine forests. Some examples of anthropogenic disturbance include exploitative timber harvesting practices (see the discussion of exploitative forestry practices in ancient Greece and Rome, as well as the textboxes on forests in India and the Sahel in Chapter 8), poor site conditions (textbox on maple decline in Chapter 6), fire suppression (textbox on fusiform rust in Chapter 4), air pollution (see the discussion of mycorrhizae in Chapter 6), invasive species (Chapter 5), and finally climate change (Chapter 7 and the boreal forest). Often, it is these interacting factors and events that can trigger mortality levels in excess (or below – e.g., fire suppression) of baseline, to create unhealthy forest conditions.

There are additional datasets that may be amenable to baseline mortality analysis to evaluate the impact of global climate change on forest health, as well as the utility of the method to evaluate the health of tropical forests (e.g., Pasoh or Kalimantan). Alaska yellow cedar decline (see textbox in Chapter 7) has been attributed to climate change (Hennon *et al.* 2008). USDA Forest Service Forest Inventory and Analysis data may provide the mortality data by diameter class that is needed to assess and to compare the sustainability of forests in southeastern Alaska where Alaska yellow cedar decline occurs and where it does not. Similarly, van Mantgem *et al.* (2009) have attributed recent increased levels of conifer mortality in the southern Sierra Nevada of California to global climate change. But are these levels of mortality problematic, above or below baseline levels, or predictable? Their dataset contains mortality data by diameter class for multiple conifer species on elevational gradients. Such a dataset is ideal for baseline mortality analysis to determine the impact of global climate change on the sustainability of several conifer species in this region. Condit *et al.* (1995) conducted an analysis of the effect of drought on the mortality rates of 205 neotropical tree and shrub species on a 50-ha plot on Barro Colorado Island in Panama. This dataset may prove amenable to baseline mortality analysis to determine if the method is more broadly applicable to intensively sampled tropical forest plots.

11.1.9 Forestry

Forestry (i.e., silviculture and forest management) provides the tools that can be used to meet the challenges that will confront our forests and future generations of forest and resource managers. Baseline mortality is not a new concept to a forester. The silvicultural systems employed by foresters for over 100 years have been designed to produce sustainable forests (Chapter 8). A community of trees (from a stand to a forest) can exist in non-normal (i.e., unhealthy) condition for a long time. Forestry activities can return an unhealthy community of trees to a more healthy state through regeneration and tending activities guided by various tools based in large measure on the baseline mortality concept.

True forestry is practiced on only a small percentage of the world's forests. Most forestry is conducted in the temperate forests of the world, where the discipline was developed. Silviculture as practiced in the subtropics and tropics is vastly different from the art and science as practiced in temperate regions because it has proven difficult to extrapolate temperate zone silviculture to the tropics. Thus, there is a need to develop the methods, and then to train foresters with expertise in tropical forestry.

11.2 The future of global forest health (where do we go from here?)

The greatest threats to forest health worldwide are development (i.e., land use change, including both urban and agricultural expansion), invasive species, unsustainable timber harvesting, fire, and climate change. These threats have been present for centuries, have increased in recent decades and are likely to continue to increase into the foreseeable future. This leads to the inevitable questions: Is the situation hopeless? Are the world's forests doomed? What can be done to protect forests? Not long ago, the answers to these questions, in part, would have included the words pesticides and fire suppression. We now know that these approaches often (but not always) create more problems than they solve. We now have a greater understanding of the complexity of ecosystems and, more to the point, how human activities frequently have unintended ecological consequences. Thus, international trade has exacerbated problems with non-indigenous invasive species; growing human populations in developing nations have accelerated the encroachment of urban infrastructure and agricultural land use into previously forested areas; and the burning of fossil fuels, forest fires, and land use conversion have created legitimate concerns over increasing levels of atmospheric CO_2 and climate change. The magnitude of these problems is truly gargantuan and there are no easy fixes. Solutions will come gradually, if at all, and will entail increased awareness of the problems and their causes and consequences, technological and scientific advances, and policy changes and enforcement. In the remainder of this chapter, we discuss these problems, how they interact, and how the concepts covered earlier in this book can be brought to bear.

11.2.1 Interacting global threats

Threats to the world's forests can be categorized as land use change or degradation, although the distinction is not always clear. Land use change may be reversible or permanent and may be caused by clear cutting followed by agriculture (e.g., slash and burn), urban sprawl, wildfire, dam construction, and volcanic eruptions, among others. When lands are permanently cleared of forests, forest health is no longer an issue, but when previously deforested land is reforested, numerous forest health issues may arise. For instance, tree species composition and site quality may change substantially from the original forest as often happens when agricultural or mined lands are returned to forests. Nutrient depletion, loss of organic matter, destruction of soil horizons and susceptibility to invasion by indigenous species resulting from agricultural use may make a site unsuitable for the tree species that originally grew there. Consequently, colonizing trees poorly matched to the site may experience poor growth, reduced pest and pathogen resistance, and excessive levels of mortality. Concomitantly, ecosystem products and services may fall short of management objectives. Thus, both ecological and utilitarian aspects of forest health may suffer.

On a broader scale, climate change, deforestation, fire, and interactions among them are expected to play important roles in the world's forests in coming decades. Furthermore, each of these contributes to the others in an escalating cycle. While there has been no truly global trend in the area or intensity of forest burned, evidence suggests that in the latter half of the 20th century, there was a considerable increase in both intensity and area burned in South America and Southeast Asia and a slight increase in boreal forests (Flannigan et al. 2009). The cumulative impact of burning forest biomass on this scale is substantial. Of all anthropogenic sources of greenhouse gases, the forestry sector is responsible for an estimated 17.4% (IPPC 2007) which represents a little more than half to two-thirds of the carbon (mainly as CO_2, CO, CH_4) released globally by wildland fire (roughly 80% of fire worldwide is in grasslands and savannas). Not only does this add to greenhouse gases that are produced by the combustion of fossil fuels, but deforested lands that are not reforested are less effective carbon sinks than forests. Where forests are fire-adapted and the fire regime does not change, the long-term carbon balance of the system will be stable. Although there is considerable regional variation in wildland fire trends, on balance there has been an increase since the middle of the 20th century with a corresponding increase in the release of greenhouse gases, which climate models associate with increasing average temperatures.

Increasing temperatures similarly have positive effects on fire. Because air holds more moisture at higher temperatures, evapotranspiration of living plants will increase, which lowers water tables, and increased evaporation will desiccate fuel wood. Warmer temperatures are also associated with increased lightning, so if temperatures increase as climate models predict, there should be more frequent sources of ignition. Fire seasons also may become longer in many regions as the summers become longer (Flannigan *et al.* 2009). Thus, increasing fire contributes significantly to atmospheric CO_2 which, in turn, promotes more fire.

We saw in Textbox 7.1 (bark beetles in western North America) that aberrations in normal climatic conditions, especially precipitation patterns, can disrupt normal insect-tree interactions resulting in extensive tree mortality that is unquestionably well above the baseline mortality level. The extent to which such precipitation and temperature anomalies are temporal or regional phenomena as opposed to global will be difficult to determine. However, the number of hectares of forest that are impacted by insects and pathogens is several times greater than that killed by fire (Dale *et al.* 2001). The net effect of trees killed by insects and pathogens on atmospheric accumulations of greenhouse gases is less severe than that due to fire because the affected forests typically recover and act as carbon sinks and because the carbon is released slowly through decomposition compared to rapidly by fire. So, although climate change has certainly increased insect and pathogen-induced losses in forests, the inverse does not appear to hold.

Interactions between fire and biotic agents of tree mortality run in both directions and each may have positive or negative effects on the other. Bark beetles, various pyrophilous insects and even defoliators often exploit fire-stressed trees adding to the total tree mortality associated with wildfire. However, the shift in forest species composition toward late successional species and altered age structure that is often associated with fire suppression in fire-adapted ecosystems promotes a variety of forest insects and pathogens (Keane *et al.* 2002), as well as an increase in susceptibility of the forest to wildfire. Thus, fire suppression may have consequences that are ultimately worse than fire itself, at least natural levels of fire. With the observed increase in the incidence of wildland fires, and negative effects of fire suppression, it seems that the options for forest managers are limited, to say the least.

The degradation of forests by the introduction and establishment of non-indigenous invasive species also has increased in recent decades as discussed in Chapter 5. Attempts to predict which species are at greatest risk for introduction into a given country or region are worthwhile because they may help prevent some invasions, but new invasions will inevitably occur because so many invasives are innocuous non-problems in their home ranges and are overlooked or not considered likely to become invasive in risk assessments. In a world in which considerable effort is expended assessing the risk of accidental introductions and in evaluating the "invadability" of disturbed ecosystems, the only certainty is that the probability of future invasions is 100%. This is unlikely to change in the face of increasing international travel and trade. It is interesting that the broad base of support for global trade is based in large part upon economic models that show shared economic benefits – at least as long as environmental costs, including those associated with invasive species, are largely omitted. Modeling the real economic costs of invasive species impacts is a daunting task (Simpson 2010), but one that is of the utmost importance if we are to make sound policy to reduce the risk associated with international travel and trade.

The problems facing the world's forests are immense and they will not be solved any time soon. However if forest health professionals, scientists and policy makers cannot come to a consensus on what a healthy forest is, then there is little hope that the processes that reduce and degrade forests can be objectively assessed. Without objective assessment, the allocation of appropriate levels of resources and regulation that are needed to address a problem are impossible. The concept of forest health that has been the common thread throughout this book provides the needed objectivity as well as the flexibility to include economic and environmental values from timber extraction and recreation to important ecosystem products and services including biodiversity, water purification, and carbon sequestration. Central to meeting these challenges is a clear and concise concept of forest health, an objective method by which it can be assessed that is applicable to all forests worldwide, and by which the health of forests can be compared in time and in space. The challenge to forest landowners and forest health professionals then is to create and to maintain biologically diverse and sustainable forests that meet the varied and multiple uses of forests (i.e., healthy forests). The next generation of forest health professionals will need to meet these challenges, and the concepts and methods presented in this text can provide the framework by which these challenges can be met.

References

Caswell, H. 1989. *Matrix Population Models: Construction, Analysis and Interpretation.* Sinauer Associates, Sunderland, MA.

Condit, R., Hubbell, SP., and Foster, RB. 1995. Mortality rates of 205 neotropical tree and shrub species and the impact of a severe drought. *Ecological Monographs* **65**: 419–439.

Dale, VH., Joyce, LA., McNulty, S. *et al.* 2001. Climate change and forest disturbances. *BioScience* **51**: 723–734.

Dayton, PK. 1972. Toward an understanding of community resilience and the potential effects of enrichments to the benthos at McMurdo Sound, Antarctica. In: *Proceedings of the Colloquium on Conservation Problems in Antarctica.* Parker, BC. (ed.). Allen Press, Lawrence, KS.

De Liocourt, F. 1898. De l'amenagement des sapinieres. *Bull. Triemestriel Societe Forestiere de Franche-Comte et Belfort, Besancon*: 396–409.

Edmonds, RL., Agee, JK., and Gara, RI. 2000. The concept of forest health, In: *Forest Health and Protection.* McGraw-Hill, Boston, MA.

Ellison, AM., Bank, MS., Clinton, BD. *et al.* 2005. Loss of foundation species: consequences for the structure and dynamics of forested ecosystems. *Frontiers in Ecology and Environment* **3**: 479–486.

Flannigan, MD., Krawchuk, MA., de Groot, WJ. *et al.* 2009. Implications of changing climate for global wildland fire. *International Journal Wildland Fire* **18**: 483–507.

Harcombe, PA. 1987. Tree life tables: Simple birth, growth and death data encapsulate life histories and ecological roles. *BioScience* **37**: 557–568.

Hennon, P.E., D'Amore, DV., Wittwer, DT., and Caouette, JP. 2008. pp. 233–245. In: *Integrated Restoration of Forested Ecosystems to Achieve Multiresource Benefits: Proc. 2007 National Silviculture Workshop. Gen. Tech. Rep. PNW-GTP73.* Deal, RL. (tech. ed.). Portland OR: USDA Forest Service Pacific Northwest Research Station.

Innes, JL. and Karnosky, DF. 2001. Impacts of environmental stress on forest health: the need for more accurate indicators. In: *Criteria and Indicators for Sustainable Forest Management.* Raison, RJ., Brown, AG., and Flinn, DW. (eds). CAB International, Wallingford.

Intergovernmental Panel on Climate Change. 2007. Climate change 2007: synthesis report. IPCC fourth assessment report. Geneva, Switzerland.

Keane, RE., Ryan, KC., Veblen, TT. *et al.* 2002. The cascading effects of fire exclusion in Rocky Mountain ecosystems. In: *Rocky Mountain Futures: An Ecological Perspective.* Barton, JS. (ed.). Island Press, Washington, DC, USA.

Kolb, TE., Wagner, MR., and Covington, WW. 1994. Concepts of forest health. *Journal Forestry* **92**: 10–15.

Malthus, TR. 1798. *An Essay on the Principle of Population.* J. Johnson. London.

Manion, PD. and Griffin, DH. 2001. Large landscape scale analysis of tree death in the Adirondack Park, New York. *Forest Science* **47**: 542–549.

More, TA. 1996. Forestry's fuzzy concepts: An examination of ecosystem management. *Journal Forestry* **94**: 19–23.

Percy, KE. 2002. Is air pollution an important factor in international forest health? In: *Effects of Air Pollution on Forest Health and Biodiversity in Forests of the Carpathian*

Mountains. Szaro, RC., Bytnerowicz, A., and Oszlany, J. (eds). IOS Press, Amsterdam.

Raffa, K., Aukema, B., Bentz, BJ. *et al.* 2009. A literal use of "forest health" safeguards against misuse and misapplication. *Journal Forestry* **107**: 276–277.

Simpson, DR. 2010. If invasive species are "pollutants", should polluters pay? In: *Bioinvasions and Globalization: Ecology, Economics, Management and Policy.* Perrings, C., Mooney, H., and Williamson, M. (eds). Oxford University Press, Oxford.

USDA Forest Service. 1993a. Healthy forests for America's future: A strategic plan. *USDA Forest Service MP-1513.*

USDA Forest Service. 1993b. *National Center of Forest Health Management strategic plan. USDA Forest Service.* Morgantown, WV.

USDA Forest Service. 2003. Strategic Plan for Forest Health Protection: 2003–2007. *USDA Forest Service MP-1590.*

Van Mantgem, PJ., Stephenson, N., Byrne, JC. *et al.* 2009. Widespread increase in tree mortality rates in the Western United States. *Science* **23**: 521–524.

Appendix A

Instructions for fitting the negative exponential function using Microsoft® Excel® 2007 for the dataset from Puerto Rican forests presented in Chapter 2

A real data set is used to demonstrate how to fit the negative exponential function (eq. [2.10]) step by step using Microsoft® Excel® (Office 2007). These sample data were collected from Puerto Rico in 2000 combining four tree species (see the PR dataset.xls file in the Chapter 2 folder on the website). All tree observations were grouped by a 2-cm diameter class interval. The dataset (contains the following columns labeled: **D** (i.e., diameter class), **N** (i.e., number of live trees), **M** (i.e., number of dead trees), and **TN** (i.e., total number of trees = N + M).

1. **Data preparation for model fitting**. Download the Excel file named PR dataset.xls from the folder named Chapter 2 on the website. It is always a good idea to make a copy of the Excel sheet of the raw data (name the copied data sheet **PR 2000 Data (2)** in the datasheet tab). Follow the steps below:

   1) Add name labels to the next three columns in the following order: **OM** (i.e., observed mortality rate), **BM** (i.e., baseline mortality), and **ln(N)** (i.e., natural log of N).
   2) On the first cell underneath the column **OM**, type =C3/D3 and press **ENTER**. A number will show up (0.346153852). **Autofill** the column **OM** by double left clicking on the cross hairs at the bottom right corner of the first cell.
   3) On the first cell underneath the column **ln(N)**, type =ln(B3) and press **ENTER**. A number will show up (8.13153071). **Autofill** the column **ln(N)** by double left clicking on the cross hairs at the bottom right corner of the first cell (**Note**: if it is not working,

hold the left button on cross hairs at the bottom right corner of the first cell and drag the mouse until the row 26).

At this time, leave the **BM** column blank. The value of **BM** will be obtained once we fit eq. [10] to the data later and will add the **BM** value to this column. However, the order of the columns **OM**, **BM** and **ln(N)** is important to keep in order to draw the graphics. Now the modified data is ready for drawing graphics and fitting the model.

2. **Draw a diameter histogram and the relationship of ln(N)-D.** It is important to know how much the diameter distribution of the available data deviates from the reverse-J shape and how close the relationship between ln(N) and D is to linear. Follow the steps below:
    1) In the data sheet **2000 Data (2)**, **highlight** all seven columns until the bottom cell.
    2) Click on **CHART WIZARD** in the **Excel Toolbars**, choose **CUSTOM TYPES**, scroll down the chart type list and choose **LINE–COLUMN ON 2 AXES**. Click **NEXT**.
    3) In the **Chart Source Data** window, click on **SERIES** tab. In the series list highlight and click the **REMOVE** button to delete D, M, TN, OM, BM one by one. Leave N and ln(N) in the series list.
    4) Click on the blank window of **Category (X) axis labels** and see the blinking cursor in the window. Move the cursor to the first cell underneath the column **D** in the data sheet and hold the left button of the mouse to highlight all numbers in the column **D** and release the button, the ='2000 data (2)'!$A$3:$A$26 should show up in the blank window. At this step, the diameter class **D** is used as the X axis (not showing in the series list), the number of trees **N** is used as the first Y axis, and the log-transformation **ln(N)** is used as the second Y axis. Click **NEXT**.
3. **Modify the graphic output to better display the diameter histogram and the relationship of ln(N)-D.** Follow the steps below:
    1) In the window of **Chart Wizard – Step 3 of 4**, click on **Titles** tab, and type **Diameter Class (cm)** in the window of **Category (X) axis**, type **Number of Trees** in the window of **Value (Y) axis**, type **ln(N)** in the window of **Second value (Y) axis**. Click **NEXT**.
    2) Save the chart **As new sheet** and name it **N-D-lnN**. Click **FINISH**.
    3) In this newly created chart, double click on **Plot Area** and change the background from gray to white. Drag the legend to the top-right corner of the chart. Double click on each name of the 3 axes and change the font and alignment (as you wish).

Double click on the 3 axes and change the pattern, scale, and font of the tick marks (as you wish).

4) Double click on the histogram bars and the window of **Format Data Series** shows up. Click on the **Patterns** tab, change the **Border** color of the bar and choose **None** for **Area**. Click on the **Options** tab, change the **Gap width** from 150 to 0. Click **OK**.

5) Double click on the ln(N)-D relationship and the window of **Format Data Series** shows up. Click on the **Patterns** tab, change the **Line's** type, color, and width (if do not want to link the observations, choose **None** for **Line**), and change the **Marker's** style, color and size (as you wish). Finally, the graphic of diameter histogram and relationship of ln(N) vs. D is created (Figure 2.3a). In this example, the Line's type was set to None, the Marker's style was set to Dot, both foreground and background color were changed to black, and the size of the marker was changed to 8 pts.

4. **Fit eq. [10] to the sample data to estimate the two regression coefficients**. Go to the data sheet **2000 Data (2)**. Follow the steps below:

1) Click on the **TOOLS** pull-down menu in the **Excel Toolbars** and choose **DATA ANALYSIS** (if **DATA ANALYSIS** is not in the menu, refer to end of these instructions for statistical ToolPak activation instructions).

2) In the **DATA ANALYSIS** window, scroll down the function list and highlight **REGRESSION**. Click **OK**.

3) In the **REGRESSION** window, click on the blank window of **Input Y Range**, and go to the data sheet to highlight the name and numbers of the **ln(N)** column. Click on the blank window of **Input X Range**, and go to the data sheet to highlight the name and numbers of the **D** column. Because you included the names of the two columns, click on **Labels** to indicate the first cell is just a name and is not used for computation.

4) Click **OK** and the model fitting results are output to a new sheet. Rename the datasheet tab of the output sheet as **Model**.

Now, the Excel Regression function has fitted the eq. [10] to the example data using **ln(N)** as the Y variable and **D** as the X variable. The output is similar to Table 1 below.

The regression results showed: (1) the "best-fit" linear regression model was $\ln(N) = b_0 + b_1 \cdot D = 7.4217 - 0.0927 \cdot D$, and (2) the baseline mortality can be calculated as four tree species combined.

Table 1. *Excel output for fitting eq. [10] to the sample data*

SUMMARY OUTPUT

Regression Statistics	
Multiple R	0.97932816
R Square	0.95908364
Adjusted R Square	0.9572238
Standard Error	0.27686701
Observations	24

ANOVA

	df	SS	MS	F	Significance F
Regression	1	39.52979541	39.5297954	515.682204	9.225E-17
Residual	22	1.686417511	0.07665534		
Total	23	41.21621293			

	Coefficients	Standard error	t Stat	P-value	Lower 95%	Upper 95%
Intercept D	7.42167935	0.116658049	63.6190935	1.944E-26	7.17974537	7.6636133
	−0.0927008	0.004082181	−22.708637	9.225E-17	−0.1011667	−0.0842348

5. **Draw the mortality chart.** Go back to the data sheet **2000 Data (2)**. Follow the steps below:

   1) On the first cell underneath the column **BM**, type the number 0.1692. **Autofill** the column **BM** by double left clicking on the cross hairs at the bottom right corner of the first cell.

   2) **Highlight** all seven columns until the bottom cell, click on **CHART WIZARD** in the **Excel Toolbars**, choose **CUSTOM TYPES**, scroll down the chart type list and choose **LINES ON 2 AXES**. Click **NEXT**.

   3) In the **Chart Source Data** window, click on **SERIES** tab. In the series list highlight and click on the **REMOVE** button to delete D, N, M, TN one by one. Leave OM, BM, and ln(N) in the series list.

   4) Click on the small window of **Category (X) axis labels** and input the data of the column **D** in the data sheet. For this graph, the diameter class **D** is used as the X axis (not showing in the series list), the observed mortality rate **OM** is used as the first Y axis

(the baseline mortality BM shares the first Y axis), and the **ln(N)** is used as the second Y axis. Click **NEXT**.

5) In the window of **Chart Wizard – Step 3 of 4**, click on **Titles** tab, and type **Diameter Class (cm)** in the window of **Category (X) axis**, type **Mortality Rate** in the window of **Value (Y) axis**, type **ln(N)** in the window of **Second value (Y) axis**. Click **NEXT**.

6) Save the chart **As new sheet** and name it **Mortality Chart**. Click **FINISH**.

7) In this newly created chart, double click on **Plot Area** and change the background from gray to white. Drag the legend inside the chart. Change the name and tick mark of the 3 axes for color, font, pattern, scale, etc. (as you wish).

8) Double click on the **OM** line and the window of **Format Data Series** shows up. Click on the **Patterns** tab, change the **Line**'s type, color, and width, and change the **Marker's** style, color and size (as you wish). In this example, the OM Line's color was set to green, the Marker's color was set to green, style was set to square, and size was set to 8 pts.

9) Modify the **BM** line similarly. In this example, the BM Line's color was set to red, and the Marker's style was set to **None**.

10) Double click on the ln(N)-D relationship and the window of **Format Data Series** shows up. Click on the **Patterns** tab, choose **None** for **Line** and change the **Marker's** style to dot, both foreground and background color to black, and size to 8 pts. Point the cursor to any black **dot** and click the right button of the mouse and a small window shows up. Choose **Add Trendline** in the pop-up window. Click **OK**. Finally, the mortality chart is created (Figure 2.3b).

Activation of the Data Analysis ToolPak in Microsoft® Excel®

The Data Analysis ToolPak is an add-in included with Microsoft® Excel®. If you have not loaded the Data Analysis ToolPak, you will have to install it from your original Excel installation disks, following the instructions in your Excel User's Guide.

1. **How to access the Statistics ToolPak in Microsoft Office 2003 and earlier versions:**
   (1) Open Excel.
   (2) Click Tools in the Excel's menu bar and you will see a pull-down menu.

(3) Click Add-Ins and you will see the Add-Ins window.

(4) Click the checkboxes for both Analysis ToolPak and Analysis ToolPak-VBA.

(5) Click OK.

The Data Analysis ToolPak does not add a new menu item to the Excel's menu bar; instead it adds a new command at the bottom of the Tools pull-down menu.

2. **How to access the Statistics ToolPak in Excel 2007:**

(1) Open Excel 2007.

(2) Click the Office Button on the top-left corner of the screen and you will see a pull-down menu.

(3) At the bottom of the pull-down menu, click on Excel Options.

(4) Click the Add-ins in the left panel of the Excel Options menu.

(5) At the bottom, you will see Manage with "Excel add-ins" in a small window. Click on Go.

(6) You will see another window with the available add-ins items. Check both Analysis ToolPak and Analysis ToolPak – VBA and click on OK.

(7) Excel may ask you to install the add-ins and you should go ahead to let Excel to install them.

(8) After the installation, Data Analysis should show up (at the right end of the tool bar) if you click on the Data on the top of the Excel screen. The operation of Data Analysis is the same as Excel 2003.

Appendix B

Instructions for baseline mortality analysis of New York dataset using Microsoft® Excel® 2007

1) Copy the main northern New York dataset (The worksheet named "Combined Dataset" in the file named "NNY & AFP Datasets.xls") from the website and paste it into two worksheets in a new Excel file.

    i) Label one of the new worksheets "ref" and the other one "dataset" by right clicking at the worksheet tab at the bottom of the page (right click on the tab, select rename, type new name).

    ii) Copy all the data in the Combined Datasetworksheet into the newly created worksheet by first clicking on the triangle in the top left corner of the original then copying (Ctrl+C). Then select the first cell in the new worksheet (cell A1) and paste (Ctrl+V) in the copied data. Do the same for the data in the ref worksheet.

2) Because these data originate from prism plots, it is necessary to convert the data from trees/prism plot to trees/acre. This requires calculation of an expansion factor. So, on the ref worksheet, we must calculate an expansion factor to convert trees/sample plot (prism plot) to trees/acre.

    Expansion factor $= 43560/[(\text{tree dbh}^*2.75)^2 \ \pi]$ or in Excel $(43560/(((\text{dbh}^*2.75)\wedge 2)^*3.1416))$. To get^2 press shift 6, then 2.

    $43560 = \text{ft}^2$ /acre. Radius of the tree plot= tree dbh*2.75, where 2.75 is a constant that adjusts for the conversion from inches to feet, etc.

    Area of the tree plot $= (\text{tree dbh}^*2.75)^2 \ ^* \ \pi \ (=3.1416)$.

    The expansion factor for stems less than or equal to 3.5 inches dbh, however, is calculated from the following formula: 43560/

[(5.8²)3π]. This is necessary because saplings were sampled within three smaller radial plots, not over the entire overstory sampling area.

In the ref worksheet label column B "expfactor".

    ii)   Go to the cell directly below the heading (B2) and type: =(43560/((5.8^2)*3*3.1416)) Enter. Copy this formula down to cell B31.

    iii) In cell B32 type =(43560/(((A32*2.75)^2)*3.1416)) Go to the bottom right-hand corner of that cell until you see a black cross hair "+", then double click. Entire column should autofill. If not, click the bottom right corner and drag down until all cells are filled.

3)   **Use the insert name procedure and the V lookup function to first establish a name for the expansion factor that you created on the ref worksheet, and to fill a new column in the main dataset labeled trees/ac (trees/acre).**

    i)   In the ref worksheet, highlight dbh through expansion factor (columns A and B) all the way down to the last row of numbers.

    ii)   Go to the Formulas tab and click Define Name. Type "expfactor" into name field, OK.

    iii) In the dataset worksheet, insert a column next to the dbh column (right click on column to the right of the dbh column, then click on the letter at the top of that column, insert, column). Label the new column trees/ac.

    iv) If f(x) is not an icon on your toolbar, then go to VIEW, toolbars, click off formatting or other options (all you need is standard).

    v)   Go to f(x), category: all, function name: Vlookup, OK (move box down so you can see column headings) lookup_value:C2 (dbh). Table_array:expfactor. Col__index__num: 2. Range lookup: False (it means it has to be the exact value. True will give closest value.

    vi) Go to first cell under tr/ac heading in datasheet (D2), right click on bottom right corner. You should get a crosshair, double left click. Make sure it autofilled all the way to the bottom of the page.

4)   **Use the round function to fill a new column in the main datasheet labeled dclass (diameter class).**

    i)   Insert new column to the right of dbh and name it dclass.

    ii)   Click on cell below dclass heading, go to f(x) all, round number: C2 (dbh). # digits: 0 (no decimals).

    iii) Save!

5) Use the PIVOT TABLE function to generate a worksheet that summarizes trees/acre living, dead, and total for each diameter class. The pivot table will use dclass for Row, alive for Column, and tr/ac for Data.

    i) Highlight entire dataset worksheet by double clicking in the triangle at the upper left of the worksheet. Then, go to the INSERT tab, PivotTable, (make sure entire range is highlighted, if it is it will have blinking dashes around entire worksheet). Make sure the option to place the report into a new worksheet is selected. Click OK.

    ii) Left click on dclass and drag to the Row field.

    iii) Left click on alive and drag to Column field.

    iv) Left click on trees/ac and put it in the Data field.

    v) In the Values box of the Pivot Table Field List click on Count tr/ac, select Value Field Settings, then click SUM.

    vi) Rename sheet "Pivot Table."

6) Using number of trees/acre as the Y variable and diameter class as the X variable from the pivot table output above, use the REGRESSION function to generate the parameters for the best-fit regression line for the density distribution across diameter classes.

    i) Pick an empty column next to the pivot table output. Label cell G4'observed trees/acre'. In cell G5 type =B5/462 (the number of sampling plots). Left double click on bottom right corner to autofill.

    ii) Label next column Ln (observed trees/acre). On the first cell underneath column heading type = ln(cell under heading observed trees/acre). Autofill by double left clicking on the cross in the bottom right corner of the cell.

    v) Go to the DATA tab, data analysis, regression, OK

    *) If data analysis is not present, click the circular Microsoft Office button in the top left corner of the Excel window. Click on Excel Options in the bottom right corner of the menu, select Add-Ins. Below the Inactive Application Add-ins header click Analysis ToolPak, then Go. Check the box next to Analysis Toolpak, then OK. Excel will now install the selected add-ins.

    vi) Input Y range: click on icon at the corner of the blank, highlight the column labeled Ln observed trees/acre (do not include the total at the bottom).

    vii) Input X range: click on icon next to blank, highlight the column labeled d class.

viii)   If you have highlighted the column headings, then click on LABELS.

ix)   Click on residuals and residual plots, then OK. (if your computer crashes, try the regression again, but this time click on residuals but NOT residual plots).

x)   Write down the slope from the regression output. In the output table this value is the coefficient of the x variable.

xi)   Rename the datasheet tab as Regression.

7)   **From the regression output calculate expected density or predicted trees/acre.**

i)   On the regression datasheet label a column "predicted trees/acre" (D24, next to the residuals column at the bottom of the page). In D25 type =exp (click on cell under column heading predicted, B25). B25 must be in parentheses. Autofill.

ii)   Highlight and copy the columns predicted trees/acre.

iii)   PASTE VALUES, into pivot table worksheet. SAVE!!!

8)   **From the regression output, calculate the baseline % mortality (percent mortality per diameter inch to maintain stability within the population).**

i)   In the Regression worksheet, INSERT another column to right of predicted trees/acre and label it baseline % mortality. This is the baseline mortality calculated from the regression equation using the formula (1−2.7^(slope of regression line multiplied by the diameter class size, 1 inch in this case)*100.

ii)   Copy this column and paste the values into the PivotTable worksheet to the right of Predicted trees/ac

iii)   Back in the Regression worksheet, label the column next to baseline % mortality, predicted baseline mortality. =((D25-D26)/D25)*100. Autofill. Baseline mortality calculated by both methods should be equivalent. I just wanted you to see that for yourselves.

9)   **Calculate actual mortality or Observed % mortality.**

i)   In the pivot table worksheet, label a column "observed % mortality" next to the "predicted trees/acre" and "baseline % mortality" columns that you just copied and pasted from the regression output.

ii)   In the first cell underneath the column heading type = (C5/E5) *100. Autofill.

10)   **Arrange the four columns labeled: "observed trees/acre," "predicted trees/ acre," "baseline % mortality," and "observed % mortality," in the pivot**

table worksheet so that they are together by moving the "Ln observed trees/acre" column. Now we will generate a chart to display these data.

    i) Before moving the columns: copy, PASTE VALUES.

    ii) In the INSERT tab click Line Chart, then Line with Markers from the menu.

    iii) A blank graph window will appear. Right click within this and click Select Data. Click on Add in Legend Entries (Series). Type Observed trees/acre in the Series Name field. Next, click the button at the right end of the Series Values field and highlight the data range, cells G5-G38 in this example. Hit enter and click OK in the Edit Series window.

    iv) To add additional data to the chart, again, click Add in Legend Entries (Series). Follow the instructions detailed above, but this time for Predicted trees/acre. Now do the same for Baseline % Mortality and Observed % Mortality. Make sure the data ranges selected span the same range of cell rows. Otherwise your plot lines will be out of sync.

    v) Next we will add horizontal axis values. Do this by clicking Edit in the Horizontal (Category) Axis Labels box, highlight the range of diameter classes you want to use, cells A5–A38 in this example. Click OK.

    vi) Click OK in the Select Data Series window. This will generate a chart, albeit a fairly messy one.

    vii) Relocate chart to its own worksheet by clicking the DESIGN tab and selecting Move Chart. Click New Sheet and type NNY Chart in the neighboring field.

11)   Format chart to clearly display data series, label axes, and create a title.

    i) The two trees/acre data are based on logarithmic data; therefore we must reformat the y-axis. Right click on this axis, select Format Axis and check the box left of Logarithmic Scale. Also, in the Horizontal Axis Crosses section, click Axis Value and type 0.01 in the field box. Click Close. The Predicted trees/acre line should now appear linear, while the Observed trees/acre line will be roughly so.

    ii) Right click on the Baseline % Mortality line and select Format Data Series. Within Series Options: Plot Series on, click Secondary axis. Click close. Do this also for the Observed % Mortality line.

    iii) Set the right y-axis range from 0–100 by right clicking on the axis and selecting Format Axis. In Axis Options, switch Maximum from Auto to Fixed and type 100 in the field box. Click close.

iv) To label the axes, click the LAYOUT tab then Axis Titles. In the menu place your cursor over an axis type and select the label type you want (i.e., vertical or horizontal) and type the name into the formula bar. Enter. Do this for all three axes. The first y-axis should be labeled Log of living trees, the second y-axis as Percent mortality, and the x-axis as Diameter class.

v) To create a title for this chart, click on Chart title in the LAYOUT tab, select a placement option from the menu and type the title into the formula bar.

12) **Statistical comparison of observed mortality and baseline mortality for each diameter class using Chi-square analysis.**

i) Label the two rightmost empty columns as X2 and Significance.

ii) The X2 column will contain chi-square values for each corresponding diameter class. These values are calculated from the following formula: (observed % mortality – baseline % mortality)^2/baseline % mortality. In the first blank cell type =([click first observed % mortality value]-[click first baseline % mortality value])^2/ [click first baseline % mortality value]. Hit Enter and Autofill this column.

iii) Because we will be performing multiple statistical comparisons (one for each diameter class) we need to adjust the alpha value associated with our critical chi-square value first. This is done to correct for alpha inflation, an increase in the chance of a type one error (false rejection of the null hypothesis) occurring while making multiple comparisons. This is done by dividing the alpha value (0.05) by the number of comparisons to be made.

iv) Using the adjusted alpha value and 1 degree of freedom, a critical chi-square value can be obtained from a chi-square table.

v) Compare the calculated values in the X2 column against the critical value obtained in the above step. If the calculated value is greater than the critical value, the observed % mortality of that diameter class is significantly different from baseline % mortality. In the Significance column type Y for each significant diameter class and a N for each nonsignificant class.

Instructions for baseline mortality analysis of 1983 NZ mt. beech dataset using Microsoft® Excel® 2007

1) Copy the main mountain beech dataset (The worksheet named "All Plots" in the file named "Harper_Datasets.xls") from the website and

paste it into a worksheet in a new Excel file. Label this worksheet "Combined."

  i) Open "Harper_Datasets.xls." Copy all of the data in the "Combined" worksheet and paste it into a blank worksheet in the newly created excel file. Copy and paste the "Damaged" and "Undamaged" data, in the same manner.

2) **Unlike the northern New York State dataset, these data were collected using fixed area plots so we need not calculate an expansion factor as we had done previously. We will now conduct a linear regression using the natural log of the number of living trees in each diameter class.**

  i) Open the Combined worksheet and Type ln(live) into cell E1. In this column we will calculate the natural log of the living tree count, to be used in the regression. In cell E2 type =ln(C2). Enter. Click back on cell E2 and move your cursor to the bottom right corner of the cell until your cursor becomes a black cross, double click. This should autofill the formula down to cell E18.

  ii) Notice that a value of zero was returned in cell E15. We will not use this or the values after this in the regression analysis

  iii) Go to the DATA tab, data analysis, regression, OK

  iv) If data analysis is not present, click the circular Microsoft Office button in the top left corner of the Excel window. Click on Excel Options in the bottom right corner of the menu, select Add-Ins. Below the Inactive Application Add-ins header click Analysis ToolPak, then Go. Check the box next to Analysis Toolpak, then OK. Excel will now install the selected add-ins.

  v) Input Y range: click on icon at the corner of the blank, highlight cells E1–E14 in the column labeled "ln (live)," column E.

  vi) Input X range: click on icon next to blank, highlight cells A1-A14 in the column labeled "Diameter Class," column A.

  vii) Since we have highlighted the column headers, we need to let Excel know; click on LABELS check box.

  viii) Click on residuals and residual plots, then OK. (if your computer crashes, try the regression again, but this time click on residuals but NOT residual plots).

  ix) Write down the slope from the regression output. In the output table this value is the coefficient of the x variable.

  x) Rename the datasheet tab as Regression.

3) **With the slope of the regression on hand we can now calculate baseline percent mortality and, using the number of dead and total trees, observed percent mortality for each diameter class.**

i)   Back in the Combined worksheet, type "Baseline % Mortality" into cell F1 and "Observed % Mortality" into cell G1.

ii) We will now calculate baseline % mortality using the formula (1–2.7^(slope of regression line multiplied by the diameter class size, 5 cm in this case)*100. In cell F2 type =(1–2.7^([type slope of regression]*5)*100. Enter. Copy this formula down to cell F14.

iii) Observed percent mortality is calculated using the equation ((number of dead trees in a diameter class)/(total number of trees in that diameter class))*100. In cell G2 type =(B2/D2)*100. Enter. Copy this formula down to cell G14.

4) **Next, we can generate a figure displaying the data calculated thus far.**

i)   In the INSERT tab click Line Chart, then Line with Markers from the menu.

ii) A blank graph window will appear. Right click within this and click Select Data. Click on Add in Legend Entries (Series). Type "ln of living" in the Series Name field. Next, click the button at the right end of the Series Values field and highlight the data range, cells E2-E21 in this example. Hit enter and click OK in the Edit Series window.

iii) To add additional data to the chart, again, click Add in Legend Entries (Series). Follow the instructions detailed above, but this time for Baseline % Mortality and Observed % Mortality. Make sure the data ranges selected span the same range of cell rows; otherwise your plot lines will be out of sync.

iv) Next we will add horizontal axis values. Do this by clicking Edit in the Horizontal (Category) Axis Labels box, highlight the range of diameter classes you want to use, cells A2-A14 in this example. Click OK.

v)   Click OK in the Select Data Series window. This will generate a chart, albeit a fairly messy one.

vi) Relocate chart to its own worksheet by clicking the DESIGN tab and selecting Move Chart. Click New Sheet and type "Combined Chart" in the neighboring field.

5) **Format chart to clearly display data series, label axes, and create a title.**

i)   Right click on the Baseline % Mortality line and select Format Data Series. Within Series Options: Plot Series on, click Secondary axis. Click close. Do this also for the Observed % Mortality line.

ii) Set the right y-axis range from 0–100 by right clicking on the axis and selecting Format Axis. In Axis Options, switch

Maximum from Auto to Fixed and type 100 in the field box. Click close.

iii)   To label the axes, click the LAYOUT tab then Axis Titles. In the menu place your cursor over an axis type and select the label type you want (i.e., vertical or horizontal) and type the name into the formula bar. Enter. Do this for all three axes. The first y-axis should be labeled Log of living trees, the second y-axis as Percent mortality, and the x-axis as Diameter class.

iv)   To create a title for this chart, click on Chart title in the LAYOUT tab, select a placement option from the menu and type a title into the formula bar.

6)   **Statistical comparison of observed mortality and baseline mortality for each diameter class using Chi-square analysis.**

i)   In cells H1 and I1 type "X2" and "Significance," respectively.

ii)   The X2 column will contain chi-square values for each corresponding diameter class. These values are calculated from the following formula: (observed % mortality − baseline % mortality)^2/baseline % mortality. In the cell H2 type =((G2-F2)^2)/F2. Enter. Autofill this column.

iii)   Because we will be performing multiple statistical comparisons (one for each diameter class) we need to adjust the alpha value associated with our critical chi-square value before continuing. This is done to correct for alpha inflation, an increase in the chance of a type one error (false rejection of the null hypothesis) occurring while making multiple comparisons. This is done by dividing the alpha value (0.05) by the number of comparisons to be made, thirteen in this example. In cell K2 type =0.05/13.

iv)   Using the adjusted alpha value of 0.003 and 1 degree of freedom, a critical chi-square value can be obtained from a chi-square table. For this exercise our critical value is 8.38.

v)   Compare the calculated values in the X2 column against the critical value obtained in the above step. If the calculated value is greater than the critical value, the observed % mortality of that diameter class is significantly different from baseline % mortality. In the Significance column type Y for each significant diameter class and a N for each nonsignificant class.

7)   **Use the instructions presented in sections 1–5 above to calculate baseline and observed percent mortality for 1993 and 1999 data and add these values to the figure previously generated. Once these data are added to the figure, you will have something similar to Figure 3.7.**

i) Using the Damaged and Undamaged data you copied in Section 1.1, calculate baseline and observed percent mortality and generate figures displaying these values using the steps described above. Additionally, calculate chi-squared values, as detailed in section 6, and test for statistically significant difference between observed and baseline mortality.

Glossary of terms

Acid deposition consists of sulfur dioxide (SO_2), a by-product of burning coal, and nitrogen oxides (NOx) emitted from burning fossil fuels that react with oxygen and water in the atmosphere to form strong, highly water-soluble acids. These acids are readily removed from the atmosphere with precipitation, and disassociate in the soil solution as hydrogen (H^+), sulfate (SO_4^{2-}) and nitrate (NO_3^-) ions.

Alleles are variations in the DNA sequence of a particular gene.

Alpha diversity is the diversity within a particular area or ecosystem; see also beta and gamma diversity.

Baseline mortality Is the number of stems of a given size class that must die in order for the population to maintain a stable size structure.

Beta diversity is a measure of diversity used to examine the change in species diversity between areas or ecosystems; it is based on the total number of species that are unique to each of the areas or ecosystems being compared; see also alpha and gamma diversity.

Biodiversity is the variety within and among living organisms at all levels of organization from genes to species to broad-scale ecosystems.

Biome is a large geographic area of distinctive plant and animal communities that are adapted to the environment of that particular area.

Bioprospecting is the searching, collecting, and developing of useful organic compounds or genetic material from samples of biodiversity for commercialized pharmaceutical, agricultural, industrial, or chemical end products.

Classical biological control is a method of pest control whereby a non-native natural enemy is brought from elsewhere and released with the expectation that it will become established and attack the target pest, which also is usually non-native.

Climate is the average of weather phenomena over a period of time, usually 30 years.

Coarse woody debris consists of dead, decomposing trees on the forest floor that provide important microhabitats for many kinds of organisms, and help to conserve biodiversity in the forest ecosystem.

Cold spots are areas with relatively low biodiversity that may be important to conserve if it represents a threatened ecosystem, or is the only location where a rare species is found.

Communities are groups of actually or potentially interacting species that are living in some defined area.

Conservation biology is the scientific study of the distribution and status of earth's biodiversity with the aim of protecting it from extinction.

Conservation biological control involves manipulation of the environment in a manner that favors natural enemies of a pest.

Damage is a measurable loss associated with injury.

Declines are a third category of tree diseases that affect populations of mature trees, and are caused by an interacting but specifically ordered set of causal agents grouped into predisposing, inciting, and contributing factors; which will vary from one specific decline disease to another. Declines cause tree mortality.

Delimitation surveys are surveys used to determine the exact geographic distribution of the invasive organism in its new environment.

Detection monitoring is annual monitoring conducted by the USDA Forest Service, Forest Health Monitoring Program that uses nationally standardized aerial and ground surveys to evaluate status and change in condition of forest ecosystems.

Diameter distributions are graphs or mathematical functions that describe the density of trees per unit area as a function of tree diameter.

Dieback is the death of the branches in the crown of a tree (i.e., crown dieback). Dieback often is one symptom of decline, but it is not synonymous with it.

Diseases are chronic irritations that prevent the affected host from reaching its maximum genetic potential.

Disease development cycle The following seven steps in the development of biotic plant diseases that involve an interaction between the pathogen and host life cycles: inoculation, penetration, infection, incubation, invasion, reproduction, and dissemination.

Disease triangle A concept which states that biotic disease only results when the interaction of the host, the pathogen, and the environment are favorable in time and space. In other words, the host must be susceptible to the particular pathogen present, the pathogen must be virulent on that particular host, the environmental factors must be favorable for disease development, and all of these factors must come together in the correct temporal and spatial dimensions for biotic disease to occur.

Disturbances are any natural or anthropogenic perturbation to an ecosystem that increases the availability of limiting resources such as space, light, or nutrients, or alters trophic interactions (from Von Holle and Simberloff 2005). (E.g., logging, fire, windthrow, drought, insect outbreak, or climate change.)

Drought is an extended period (months or years) of water supply deficiency. Generally, this occurs when a region receives consistently below average precipitation, although land use practices (overfarming, excessive irrigation, massive water diversion, deforestation, or erosion) can trigger a drought.

Edge effect is the change in habitat conditions along the boundary between juxtaposed habitats resulting from the mutual influence of each habitat.

El Niño Southern Oscillation (ENSO) is a significant rise in water temperature that occurs over a large (approximately 15 000 000 km^2) portion of the western tropical Pacific Ocean, which can last from 6 to 18 months and occur approximately 3 to 7 years apart. El Nino events affect weather patterns as far away as Australia, Southeast Asia, and western North America.

Endemic species are those whose distributions are naturally restricted to a limited area.

Epidemiology is the study of how diseases spread in populations.

Epiphytotic is an increase in plant disease in time.

Evaluation Monitoring is conducted by the USDA Forest Service, Forest Health Monitoring Program that determine extent, severity, and causes of undesirable changes in forest health identified through Detection Monitoring.

Even-aged systems are a planned sequence of silvicultural treatments designed to maintain and to regenerate a stand with one age class.

Evolutionary significant unit is a population or group of populations that is substantially reproductively isolated from other conspecific populations and that is considered genetically distinct for purposes of conservation.

Fire intensity is the energy output of a fire, and is a function of the energy content of the fuel, the amount of fuel consumed, and the rate of fire spread. Fire intensity is measured as the amount of energy released per unit length of the fireline.

Fire regime typifies the historical role of fire for a particular ecosystem, and emphasizes the complexity with which fire interacts with ecosystem patterns and processes including fire frequency, predictability, extent, magnitude (intensity and/ or severity), timing, and potential synergistic effects on future disturbances.

Fire severity is the ecological impact of a fire, and is most often measured as a percentage of overstory mortality.

Forest condition relates to the descriptive indicators used in routine forest assessments (e.g., the crown conditions of the trees in a given forest).

Forest entomology is the study of forest insect pests. The applied science that deals with solving practical forest management problems related to tree pests.

Forest insect pests are insects that have a negative effect on trees and forests. The term pest itself has no biological meaning, but refers to organisms that interfere with human objectives. Thus, insects that reduce the amount of food, fiber, or other resources available for human use are labeled as pests.

Forest management is the practical application of biological, physical, quantitative, managerial, economic, social, and policy principles to the regeneration, management, utilization, and conservation of forests, to meet specified goals and objectives while maintaining the productivity of the forest – note forest management includes management for aesthetics, fish, recreation, urban values, water, wilderness, wildlife, wood products, and other forest resource values.

Forest pathology is the study of tree diseases. The applied science that deals with solving practical forest management problems related to tree diseases.

Forestry is the profession embracing the science, art, and practice of creating, managing, using and conserving forests and associated resources for human benefit and in a sustainable manner to meet desired goals, needs and values.

Foundation species the primary producers that dominate an ecosystem in both abundance and influence.

Functional response is the increase in the number of prey killed per predator per unit time as the prey population density increases.

Gamma diversity is the overall diversity for all the different areas or ecosystems within a region; see also alpha and beta diversity.

Healthy forest a forest that is both productive and sustainable according to this text.

Horizontal heterogeneity is the variability or degree of patchiness in plant structure or species composition across multiple locations; see also vertical heterogeneity.

Hot spots are areas with exceptional levels of endemism that are experiencing high rates of habitat loss.

Induced secondary metabolites are defensive chemicals produced in plants in response to herbivory.

Injury is an acute or short-term irritation.

Inoculum the agent of pathogen dispersal (e.g., a fungal spore or a bacterial cell).

Integrated Pest Management (IPM) is a pest control strategy that uses an array of management activities including habitat manipulation, biological control, chemical control, and others, that balances expenses with the value of the resource, while also minimizing adverse environmental effects.

Inundative biological control involves the release of large numbers of laboratory-reared natural enemies to control native pests.

Invasive species are non-indigenous species whose introduction was directly or indirectly facilitated by anthropogenic forces and causes or is likely to cause significant ecological or economic harm in natural and managed ecosystems.

Koch's Postulates the set of four rules that must be followed to prove that a suspected organism is the causal agent of a particular biotic disease syndrome.

> First, there must be a constant (100%) association of the suspect pathogen and the specific disease syndrome.
> Second, the suspect pathogen must be isolated from the diseased host and grown in pure culture.

Third, when inoculated into healthy plants, the suspect pathogen must induce the disease symptoms.

Fourth, re-isolation from the inoculated host must yield the same pathogen. These postulates apply to all biotic diseases whether the host is a human, pig, plant, or microorganism.

Landscape pathology is the science that integrates the disciplines of landscape ecology and plant pathology, and is concerned with how ecological and pathological factors vary in space, how this variability influences biotic and abiotic interactions within the ecosystem, and how these interactions can be managed to achieve specific objectives.

Landslides are gravity-driven massive down-slope movements of the landscape. Mudflows, creep, block slide, avalanches, slumps, and lahars are types of landslides.

Large infrequent disturbances (LIDs) are those disturbances that occur rarely, or at irregular intervals, or both, and over large areas (e.g., hurricanes, volcanic eruptions, floods).

Law of de Liocourt mathematically describes the relationship of the density of stems in a forest to their diameter. As a cohort of trees grows, it naturally progresses from many small stems to fewer larger stems. For many, if not most, forests this is represented by a negative exponential ("reverse J") relationship.

Mean annual increment is the total increment of a stand (standing trees plus wood removed in thinning) up to a given age, divided by that age.

Montréal Process Working Group was initiated in 1992, and developed a dynamic set of criteria and indicators for conservation and sustainable management of the world's temperate and boreal forests. This process, and in 1995 the Santiago Declaration, was signed by 12 countries: Argentina, Australia, Canada, Chile, China, Japan, Republic of Korea, Mexico, New Zealand, Russian Federation, United States of America, and Uruguay. These countries account for ~90% of the world's temperate and boreal forests. Within the Declaration, seven criteria were adopted:

1. Conservation of biological diversity
2. Maintenance of productive capacity of forest ecosystems
3. Maintenance of forest ecosystem health and vitality
4. Conservation and maintenance of soil and water resources
5. Maintenance of forest contribution to global carbon cycles

6. Maintenance and enhancement of long term multiple socioeconomic benefits to meet societal needs

7. Legal, institutional and economic framework for forest conservation and sustainable management

Mycorrhizae are mutualistic symbioses between plant roots and certain fungi. This word is constructed of two Greek roots, myc=mushroom and rhiz=root. The singular form is mycorrhiza and the plural form is variously given with a Latin (mycorrhizae) or English ending (mycorrhizas).

Negative density-dependent feedback is the increase in mortality or decrease in birth rate that is associated with over consumption of the food supply (e.g., an increase in pest population density causes the pest abundance to decrease).

Negative exponential function describes the reverse-J relationship between tree density and diameter when it is plotted on log-linear axes to become a linear relationship. Therefore, the slope of this linear regression line defines the number of trees in a given diameter class that must die in order for the forest stand to maintain a stable diameter structure. An important characteristic of this function is the constant rate of reduction in the number of trees from one diameter class to the next larger.

Neoclassical biological control is the use of non-native natural enemies to control native pests, and is occasionally used in agriculture but less often in forests.

Net primary production (NPP) is equivalent to gross primary production or respiration, and is the ultimate measure of productivity because it is an expression of carbon assimilation.

Normal forest as defined by Helms as with "normal forest" and "normal stand" is as follows: a forest that has a normal age-class distribution, i.e., a complete series of age classes that permits equal volume (normal) yields from annual or periodic harvesting of trees under the given rotation and silvicultural system; a normal stand is assumed to have average maximum competition or the average density of a fully stocked stand.

Numerical response is the increase in the natural enemy population density in response to an increase in the prey population.

Outbreak threshold is the population density of pests that display positive density-dependent feedback above which the birth rate is greater than the death rate, and the population increases toward outbreak levels. Below the threshold, the birth rate is lower than the death rate and the population declines toward extinction.

Ozone often is formed in the atmosphere through the interaction of nitric oxide (NO), sunlight, and hydrocarbons, and is highest in areas with high levels of both sunlight and fossil fuel emissions.

Parasitoids are parasites that kill their hosts as larvae, but are free living as adults, and thus affect their host population numbers more like predators than true parasites.

Pathogens are biotic causal agents of disease. Examples include fungi, bacteria, viruses, dwarf mistletoes, etc.

Pathways are the routes on which invasive species travel.

Pedogenesis is the process of soil formation.

Phoenix helix a concept which states that a forest, like the mythical bird, derives life from death. The forest forms an upwardly spiraling population of increasingly larger, but fewer trees where diameter growth, tree density, and time interact to form an upward and inwardly directed helix. Thus, a healthy (balanced growth and mortality) forest evolves from a continuous dynamic process involving multiple cohorts with a predictable relative mortality across diameter classes to produce a forest with a stable age and size-class structure.

Podzolization is the process of organic matter decomposition to generate organic acids, which dissolve and move downward with percolating water in those regions where precipitation exceeds evapotranspiration. These acids strip organic matter and mineral coatings from the soil particles, leaving quartz and feldspar mineral particles, giving a visually striking morphology to the E horizon.

Positive density-dependent feedback is when an increase in the pest population results in a further increase in the pest population density.

Primary forest is an original forest, usually containing large trees, that has not been significantly disturbed or influenced by human activity.

Prism plots are used to conduct a type of forest sampling called "point sampling," whereby trees are selected by their size rather than by their frequency of occurrence.

Productive forest a forest that is meeting the landowners' management objectives.

Propagule pressure incorporates estimates of the absolute number of individuals involved in any given release event (propagule size) and the number of discrete release events (propagule number) as relates to the spread of an invasive species.

q **ratio**. For a diameter distribution based on equal-width diameter classes, *q* is defined as the ratio of the density of trees per hectare in one diameter class divided by the density of trees in the next larger diameter class. The expected surviving fraction of trees (as trees grow from one diameter class to the next) then is $1/q$ (or the ratio of the density of trees in a diameter class divided by the density in the next smaller class).

Regeneration is the act of renewing tree cover by establishing young trees naturally or artificially.

Resilience is the capacity of a stand or forest (plant community) to maintain or regain normal function and development following disturbance.

Resistance is the ability of a community to maintain itself against stresses such as invading species.

Rotated-sigmoid function is an alternative model where the slope of the diameter distribution is steeper (i.e., higher mortality rates) for small- and large-sized trees than for mid-sized (co-dominant) trees in the diameter distribution.

Secondary succession is the gradual supplanting of one plant community by another over time after the primary forest has been removed.

Signs are visible evidence of the causal agent of disease on or in the host (e.g., fungal fruiting bodies on a symptomatic leaf).

Silviculture is the art and science of controlling the establishment, growth, composition, health, and quality of forest stands to meet the diverse needs of landowners and society on a sustainable basis.

Simple linear regression describes a straight-line relationship between two quantities: one dependent or response variable *Y*, and one independent or predictor variable *X*.

Site quality is the capacity for vegetative production on a given site for a specific purpose.

Soil quality is "the capacity of a soil to function within ecosystem boundaries, to sustain biological productivity, to maintain or enhance water and air quality, and to support human health and habitation."

Soil structure is the aggregation of sand, silt, and clay-sized particles into secondary units, which modifies the effects of texture. Soil structure is promoted by organic matter.

Soil texture is defined as the relative proportion of sand (2–0.05 mm), silt (0.05 − 0.002 mm) and clay (< 0.002 mm) particles in a given soil.

Space-time permutation scan statistic (STPSS) defines areas with similar diameter distributions that differ from the region as a whole.

Spatial scan statistic (SSS) is designed to identify one or more spatial areas where disease or mortality rates are statistically different from the corresponding level elsewhere.

Species is a set of actually or potentially interbreeding natural populations.

Stability is the ability of an ecosystem to resist change.

Stands are the central unit in silviculture for forestry practice; units of land, generally tens to hundreds of ha in size defined by tree cover that is uniform in density, structure, and species composition to make them practically meaningful for planning, manipulation, and management; uniformity is the result of uniform site conditions coupled with similar disturbance history and availability of tree propagules; uniformity allows for predictable responses to change as produced by silviculture.

Stand profiling is a methodology designed to determine how much disease is optimal for different management objectives. The method involves ordination to classify stands according to important variables for different management objectives.

Stocking chart is a diagram that shows growing space occupancy relative to a pre-established standard, usually presented as the total abundance of trees that a site can support in the absence of abnormal disturbance (e.g., a catastrophic wind event) – note common indices of stocking are based on percent occupancy using measures of basal area.

Sustainable development meets the needs of the present without compromising the ability of future generations to meet their own needs.

Sustainable forest is one that maintains a stable diameter distribution or structure, and a balanced relationship between growth and mortality. A forest in which observed mortality is not significantly above or below baseline mortality.

Sustained-gradient outbreak dynamics are the result of forest insects responding to favorable environmental conditions over an extended period of time.

Symptoms are the response of the host to a causal agent of disease (e.g., leaf spots).

Tending is any silvicultural treatment designed to enhance growth, quality, vigor, and composition of a stand after establishment or regeneration, and prior to final harvest.

Third-party certification standards attempt to maintain and enhance long-term health of forest ecosystems in Canada; while providing ecological, economic, cultural, social opportunities, ensure conservation of biological diversity, wildlife habitat, soil and water resources, and sustainable timber harvest. Such standards require annual monitoring and public disclosure of findings.

Tropical storms are large-scale extreme wind events. Meteorologists classify them based on their scale, wind intensity, and location.

Tsunamis, or tidal waves, are created by geological events above or beneath the sea that cause a rapid displacement of water that can cause immense coastal damage.

Uneven-aged systems are a planned sequence of silvicultural treatments designed to maintain and to regenerate a stand with three or more age classes.

Vectors are insects and other animals that transmit pathogens from one host to another.

Vertical heterogeneity is the variability in the heights of plants at a single location; see also horizontal heterogeneity.

Weather is the set of all phenomena occurring in a given atmosphere at a given time. Weather phenomena include wind, clouds, rain, snow, fog, dust storms, ice storms, hurricanes, tornadoes, and others.

Windfall occurs when a tree is thrown down or stems are broken off by the wind. Windfall also describes the area on which trees have been thrown down or broken by the wind.

Windthrow is the uprooting of trees by the wind.

Index

DATE DUE